Inflation Rate
(GDP Deflator)

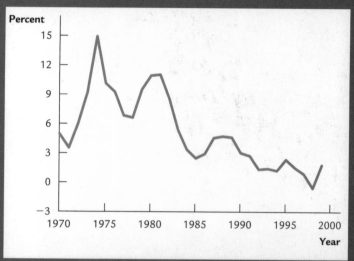

Nominal Interest Rate
(Three-Month Treasury Bills)

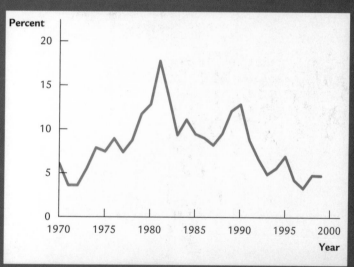

macroeconomics

Black Inset Wall Piece, 4 Blue Lines With Blue, Interior   1992
Acrylic altered cement and powdered pigment; 17″ × 17″ × 3 7/8″

Jackie Winsor was born in St. John's, Newfoundland. She holds degrees in Fine
Arts from the Massachusetts College of Art, Boston, and from Rutgers University, New Brunswick, New Jersey. This Canadian artist is the recipient of many
awards and her work is in the permanent collections of the Whitney and
Guggenheim Museums and the Museum of Modern Art in New York and the
Stedelijk Museum in Amsterdam. In addition, her work has appeared in over
twenty one-person shows and more than one hundred and fifty group shows
world-wide. Many of her pieces, like this cast wall relief, reflect the simplicity
and silence of her childhood home in northeastern Canada.

macroeconomics

Canadian edition

SECOND EDITION

N. GREGORY MANKIW
Harvard University

WILLIAM SCARTH
McMaster University

Worth Publishers

Macroeconomics, Second Canadian Edition

Copyright © 2001, 1995 by Worth Publishers

Manufactured in the United States of America

Library of Congress Catalog Card Number: 00 133088
ISBN: 1-57259-973-1
Printing: 1 2 3 4 5 04 03 02 01 00

Acquisition Editor: Alan McClare
Development Editor: Jane Tufts
Art Director/Cover Design: Barbara Reingold
Interior Design: Lissi Sigillo
Production Editor: Margaret Comaskey
Production Manager: Barbara Anne Seixas
Composition and Separations: Progressive Information Technologies
Printing and Binding: Von Hoffmann Press, Inc.
Photo Credit: p. vi. © Ingrid Kannel, Wellesley, MA
Front and Back Cover Art: Jackie Winsor

Worth Publishers
41 Madison Avenue
New York, NY 10010
http://www.worthpublishers.com

TO DEBORAH AND KATHY

about the authors

N. Gregory Mankiw is Professor of Economics at Harvard University. He began his study of economics at Princeton University, where he received an A.B. *summa cum laude* in 1980. After earning a Ph.D. in economics from MIT, he began teaching at Harvard in 1985 and was promoted to full professor in 1987. Today, he regularly teaches both undergraduate and graduate courses in macroeconomics.

Professor Mankiw is a prolific writer and a regular participant in academic and policy debates. His research ranges across many fields within economics and includes work on price adjustment, consumer behavior, financial markets, monetary and fiscal policy, and economic growth. In addition to his duties at Harvard, he has served as Director of the Monetary Economics Program of the National Bureau of Economic Research, as an adviser to the Federal Reserve Bank of Boston and the Congressional Budget Office, and as a columnist for *Fortune* magazine. He is also author of the popular introductory textbook, *Principles of Economics*.

Professor Mankiw lives in Wellesley, Massachusetts, with his wife, Deborah, and their children, Catherine, Nicholas, and Peter.

William M. Scarth is Professor of Economics at McMaster University. His introduction to the subject came at Queen's University, where he obtained the Gold Medal in economics upon graduating with his B.A. After receiving M.A. and Ph.D. degrees at the universities of Essex and Toronto, he began teaching at McMaster. He has held a number of visiting positions at other universities in Canada, Australia, and England.

Professor Scarth has published many articles in academic journals, often writing on such topics as the stabilization policy problems faced by small open economies and the challenges posed by the desire to generate—and share fairly—rising living standards. He is also the author of other textbooks—one that introduces graduate students to advanced methods in macroeconomics, and two introductory books. In addition to research and teaching at McMaster, he is a Research Fellow at the C. D. Howe Institute, Canada's leading nonprofit policy institute.

Professor Scarth lives in Ancaster, Ontario, with his wife, Kathy. They enjoy the frequent visits of their grown sons, Brian and David.

brief contents

contents

part TWO
The Economy in the Long Run   43

part FOUR
Macroeconomic Policy Debates — **409**

Those branches of politics, or of the laws of social life, on which there exists a collection of facts sufficiently sifted and methodized to form the beginning of a science should be taught *ex professo*. Among the chief of these is Political Economy, the sources and conditions of wealth and material prosperity for aggregate bodies of human beings. . . .

The same persons who cry down Logic will generally warn you against Political Economy. It is unfeeling, they will tell you. It recognises unpleasant facts. For my part, the most unfeeling thing I know of is the law of gravitation: it breaks the neck of the best and most amiable person without scruple, if he forgets for a single moment to give heed to it. The winds and waves too are very unfeeling. Would you advise those who go to sea to deny the winds and waves—or to make use of them, and find the means of guarding against their dangers? My advice to you is to study the great writers on Political Economy, and hold firmly by whatever in them you find true; and depend upon it that if you are not selfish or hard-hearted already, Political Economy will not make you so.

—*John Stuart Mill*
1867

An economist must be "mathematician, historian, statesman, philosopher, in some degree. . . . as aloof and incorruptible as an artist, yet sometimes as near the earth as a politician." So remarked John Maynard Keynes, the great British economist who, as much as anyone, could be called the father of macroeconomics. No single statement summarizes better what it means to be an economist.

As Keynes's assessment suggests, students who aim to learn economics need to draw on many disparate talents. The job of helping students find and develop these talents falls to instructors and textbook authors. When writing this textbook for intermediate-level courses in macroeconomics, our goal was to make macroeconomics understandable, relevant, and (believe it or not) fun. Those of us who have chosen to be professional macroeconomists have done so because we are fascinated by the field. More important, we believe that the study of macroeconomics can illuminate much about the world and that the lessons learned, if properly applied, can make the world a better place. We hope this book conveys not only our profession's accumulated wisdom but also its enthusiasm and sense of purpose.

This Book's Approach

Although macroeconomists share a common body of knowledge, they do not all have the same perspective on how that knowledge is best taught. Let us begin this new edition by recapping four of our objectives, which together define this book's approach to the field.

First, we try to offer a balance between short-run and long-run issues in macroeconomics. All economists agree that public policies and other events influence the economy over different time horizons. We live in our own short run, but we also live in the long run that our parents bequeathed us. As a result, courses in macroeconomics need to cover both short-run topics, such as the business cycle and stabilization policy, and long-run topics, such as economic growth, the natural rate of unemployment, persistent inflation, and the effects of government debt. Neither time horizon trumps the other.

Second, we integrate the insights of Keynesian and classical theories. Although Keynes's *General Theory* provides the foundation for much of our current understanding of economic fluctuations, it is important to remember that classical economics provides the right answers to many fundamental questions. In this book we incorporate many of the contributions of the classical economists before Keynes and the new classical economists of the past two decades. Substantial coverage is given, for example, to the loanable-funds theory of the interest rate, the quantity theory of money, and the problem of time inconsistency. At the same time, however, we recognize that many of the ideas of Keynes and the new Keynesians are necessary for understanding economic fluctuations. Substantial coverage is given also to the *IS–LM* model of aggregate demand, the short-run tradeoff between inflation and unemployment, and modern theories of wage and price rigidity.

Third, we present macroeconomics using a variety of simple models. Instead of pretending that there is one model that is complete enough to explain all facets of the economy, we encourage students to learn how to use and compare a set of prominent models. This approach has the pedagogical value that each model can be kept relatively simple and presented within one or two chapters. More important, this approach asks students to think like economists, who always keep various models in mind when analyzing economic events or public policies.

Fourth, we emphasize that macroeconomics is an empirical discipline, motivated and guided by a wide array of experience. This book contains numerous case studies that use macroeconomic theory to shed light on real-world data or events. To highlight the broad applicability of the basic theory, we have drawn the case studies both from current issues facing the world's economies and from dramatic historical episodes. The case studies analyze the policies of Paul Martin and Gordon Thiessen, many former Canadian politicians and central bankers, government initiatives in other countries, and even the policies of Henry Ford. They teach the reader how to apply economic principles to issues from fourteenth-century Europe, the island of Yap, the land of Oz, and today's newspaper.

What's New in the Second Edition?

We have improved this book in its second edition in several ways. Most obviously, the book has been updated to incorporate new events, data, and ideas. Since the first edition was written, the federal budget deficit has been eliminated, the unemployment rate has fallen by 5 percentage points, Japan experienced a deep recession, Europe adopted a common currency, and capital flight forced several Asian currencies to collapse. As always, new research has refined our understanding of economic growth and fluctuations. Although the basics of macroeconomic theory are much the same as they were 5 years ago, enough has changed in the details and practice of macroeconomics to warrant publishing a new edition.

In addition, the book's coverage, pedagogy, and organization have been further refined. Here are some of the most notable changes:

➤ The analysis of economic growth, now in two chapters (4 and 5), includes a more extensive discussion of the new theories of endogenous growth.

➤ The connection between saving, investment, the current account, and long-term living standards is covered in more detail. Foreign debt accumulation is formally linked to the current account, making possible an evaluation of "trickle-down" economics in Chapter 8.

➤ Expanded coverage of unemployment theory in Chapter 6 permits detailed analysis of several important issues: the connection between high taxes and unemployment, rising income inequality, and "percolate-up" economics.

➤ Several extensions to the Mundell–Fleming model (supply-side effects of the exchange rate, flexible prices, and exchange-rate expectation) are now covered in Chapter 12, making possible a detailed discussion of the pros and cons of alternative exchange-rate policies, and whether a flexible exchange rate acts as a "shock absorber."

➤ The detailed explanation of the explosion in government debt during the 1970s and 1980s—and why this trend was reversed in the 1990s—is expanded in Chapter 15. There is now full coverage of the "fiscal dividend," including a simulation of the next few years that allows students to evaluate budget policy.

The chapter on recent developments in the theory of economic fluctuations, Chapter 19, which discusses real business cycle theory and new Keynesian economics, has been moved to the end of the book, although instructors who wish to cover this material earlier can continue to do so. Throughout the book, new case studies have been added, and some old ones have been omitted or revised. Together with various editors and students, we have scrutinized each sentence of the book to see whether it can be made clearer.

Finally, all the changes that we made, and the many others that we considered, were evaluated keeping in mind the benefits of brevity. From our own experience as students, we know that long books are less likely to be read. Our goal in this book is to offer the clearest, most up-to-date, most accessible course in macroeconomics in the fewest words possible.

The Canadian Perspective

Maintaining brevity was not our only concern as we added the new material in this edition. We were determined to strengthen the other feature of the first edition that was most appreciated by users—that the book truly integrates theory and policy. Thus, the new formal material is used directly in our discussion of Canadian productivity growth performance, trends in the unemployment rate, debt reduction, and the fiscal dividend, alternatives for raising living standards, the debate on currency union, and the implications of the Bank of Canada's inflation-targeting policy. Sometimes this material is contained in the case studies that form an integral part of the flow of each chapter, and sometimes it is simply part of the text.

All the important policy issues are covered in detail. To mention just a few:

➤ the role of tax incentives and disinflation in stimulating saving and investment,

➤ the importance of credibility and time-consistency,

➤ how the Bank of Canada uses its Monetary Conditions Index,

➤ how the Bank's inflation target affects the economy's built-in stability properties,

> ➤ how the benefits of lower interest rates and lower debt can be measured,

> ➤ the spillover effects of provincial fiscal policy,

> ➤ the implications of the aging baby-boom generation,

> ➤ calculation of the "sacrifice ratio,"

> ➤ challenges to the natural-rate hypothesis, and

> ➤ the different implications of unanticipated and anticipated fiscal policies.

Systematically relating macro theory to the "big" issues in Canadian policy debates is one of the ways we hope to transfer our excitement about our discipline to as many readers as possible.

Finally, there are two important things concerning the new Canadian edition that are not in the book itself. With this edition, two of the many supplements are available in Canadian editions. Students will value the *Student Guide and Workbook,* and instructors will be grateful for the *Test Bank.*

The Arrangement of Topics

This new edition maintains the strategy of first examining the long run when prices are flexible and then examining the short run when prices are sticky. That is, it begins with classical models of the economy and explains fully the long-run equilibrium before discussing deviations from that equilibrium. This strategy has several advantages:

> ➤ Because the classical dichotomy permits the separation of real and monetary issues, the long-run material is easier for students to understand.

> ➤ When students begin studying short-run fluctuations, they understand fully the long-run equilibrium around which the economy is fluctuating.

> ➤ Beginning with market-clearing models makes clearer the link between macroeconomics and microeconomics.

> ➤ Students learn first the material that is less controversial among macroeconomists.

When this organizational strategy was proposed in the first U.S. edition, some instructors greeted it with skepticism. But this skepticism has faded with time and experience. Many instructors have reported to us that this organization greatly simplifies the teaching of macroeconomics.

We move now from strategy to tactics. What follows is a whirlwind tour of the book.

Part One: Introduction

The introductory material in Part One is brief so that students can get to the core topics quickly. Chapter 1 discusses the broad questions that macroeconomists address and the economist's approach of building models to explain the world. Chapter 2 introduces the key data of macroeconomics, emphasizing gross domestic product, the consumer price index, and the unemployment rate.

Part Two: The Economy in the Long Run

Part Two examines the long run over which prices are flexible. Chapter 3 presents the basic classical model of national income. In this model, the factors of production and the production technology determine the level of income, and the marginal products of the factors determine its distribution to households. In addition, the model shows how fiscal policy influences the allocation of the economy's resources among consumption, investment, and government purchases, and it highlights how the real interest rate equilibrates the supply and demand for goods and services.

Chapters 4 and 5 make the classical analysis of the economy dynamic by using the Solow growth model to examine the evolution of the economy over time. The Solow model provides the basis for discussing why the standard of living varies so widely across countries and how public policies influence the level and growth of the standard of living. Chapter 5 also introduces the student to the modern theories of endogenous growth.

Chapter 6 relaxes the assumption of full employment by discussing the dynamics of the labour market and the natural rate of unemployment. It examines various causes of unemployment, including job search, minimum-wage laws, union power, and efficiency wages. It also presents some important facts about patterns of unemployment and policy options concerning less-skilled workers.

Money and the price level are introduced in Chapter 7. Because prices are assumed to be fully flexible, the chapter presents the prominent ideas of classical monetary theory: the quantity theory of money, the inflation tax, the Fisher effect, the social costs of inflation, and the causes and costs of hyperinflation.

The study of open-economy macroeconomics begins in Chapter 8. Maintaining the assumption of full employment, this chapter presents models to explain the trade balance and the exchange rate. Various policy issues are addressed: the relationship between the budget deficit and the trade deficit, the macroeconomic impact of protectionist trade policies, the effect of monetary policy on the value of a currency in the market for foreign exchange, and the effects of government debt reduction and tax reform on standards of living.

Part Three: The Economy in the Short Run

Part Three examines the short run when prices are sticky. It begins in Chapter 9 by introducing the model of aggregate supply and aggregate demand as well as the role of stabilization policy. Subsequent chapters refine the ideas introduced here.

Chapters 10 and 11 look more closely at aggregate demand. Chapter 10 presents the Keynesian cross and the theory of liquidity preference and uses these models as building blocks for developing the *IS–LM* model. Chapter 11 uses the *IS–LM* model to explain economic fluctuations and the aggregate demand curve. It concludes with an extended case study of the Great Depression.

The study of short-run fluctuations continues in Chapter 12, which focuses on aggregate demand in an open economy. This chapter presents the Mundell–Fleming model and shows how monetary and fiscal policies affect the economy under floating and fixed exchange-rate systems. It also discusses the debate over whether exchange rates should be floating or fixed. Several extensions to the basic model are covered in the appendix.

Chapter 13 looks more closely at aggregate supply. It examines various approaches to explaining the short-run aggregate supply curve and discusses the short-run tradeoff between inflation and unemployment and challenges to the natural-rate hypothesis.

Part Four: Macroeconomic Policy Debates

Once the student has command of standard long-run and short-run models of the economy, the book uses these models as the foundation for discussing some of the key debates over economic policy. Chapter 14 considers the debate over how policymakers should respond to short-run economic fluctuations. It emphasizes two broad questions. Should monetary and fiscal policy be active or passive? Should policy be conducted by rule or by discretion? The chapter presents arguments on both sides of these questions.

Chapter 15 focuses on the various debates over government debt and budget deficits. It gives some sense of the magnitude of government indebtedness, discusses why measuring budget deficits is not always straightforward, recaps the traditional view of the effects of government debt, presents Ricardian equivalence as an alternative view, and discusses various other perspectives on government debt. As in the previous chapter, students are not handed conclusions but are given the tools to evaluate the alternative viewpoints on their own, and to evaluate the debate on the "fiscal dividend."

Part Five: More on the Microeconomics Behind Macroeconomics

After developing theories to explain the economy in the long run and in the short run and then applying those theories to macroeconomic policy debates, the book turns to several topics that refine our understanding of the economy. The last four chapters analyze more fully the microeconomics behind macroeconomics. These chapters can be presented at the end of a course, or they can be covered earlier, depending on an instructor's preferences.

Chapter 16 presents the various theories of consumer behaviour, including the Keynesian consumption function, Fisher's model of intertemporal choice, Modigliani's life-cycle hypothesis, and Friedman's permanent-income hypothesis. Chapter 17 examines the theory behind the investment function. Chapter 18 provides additional material on the money market, including the role of the banking system in determining the money supply, monetary policy indicators, and the Baumol-Tobin model of money demand. Chapter 19 discusses advances in the theory of economic fluctuations, including the theory of real business cycles and new Keynesian theories of sticky prices; these recent theories apply microeconomic analysis in an attempt to better understand short-run economic fluctuations.

Epilogue

The book ends with a brief epilogue that reviews the broad lessons about which most macroeconomists agree and discusses some of the most important open questions. Regardless of which chapters an instructor chooses to cover, this capstone chapter can be used to remind students how the many models and themes of macroeconomics relate to one another. Here and throughout the book we emphasize that, despite the disagreements among macroeconomists, there is much that we know about how the economy works.

Alternative Syllabus

Instructors differ in the emphasis they place on various topics and in the sequence of topics they prefer. We have, therefore, tried to make this book as flexible as possible. Many of the chapters are self-contained. Instructors can change the emphases of their courses by rearranging chapters or by omitting some chapters entirely.

One example of an alternative syllabus is presented here. This syllabus maintains the strategy of first examining the economy in the long run when prices are flexible, but it introduces sticky prices and short-run fluctuations earlier in the course. It does this by deferring all open-economy macroeconomics until after the study of fluctuations and deferring the study of economic growth until the end of the course. It omits altogether the chapters on microfoundations and, therefore, allows the instructor to spend more time on the other topics.

Introduction
1. The Science of Macroeconomics
2. The Data of Macroeconomics

Income, Unemployment, and Inflation in the Long Run
3. National Income: Where It Comes From and Where It Goes
6. Unemployment
7. Money and Inflation

Short-Run Economic Fluctuations
9. Introduction to Economic Fluctuations
10. Aggregate Demand I
11. Aggregate Demand II
13. Aggregate Supply

Macroeconomic Policy
14. Stabilization Policy
15. Government Debt and Budget Deficits

Open-Economy Macroeconomics
8. The Open Economy
12. Aggregate Demand in the Open Economy

Economic Growth

4. Economic Growth I

5. Economic Growth II

Epilogue

Learning Tools

We are pleased that students have found the previous edition of this book user friendly. We have tried to make this second edition even more so.

Case Studies

Economics comes to life when it is applied to understanding actual events. Therefore, the numerous case studies (many new or revised in this edition) are an important learning tool. The frequency with which these case studies occur ensures that a student does not have to grapple with an overdose of theory before seeing the theory applied. Students report that the case studies are their favorite part of the book.

FYI Boxes

These boxes present ancillary material "for your information." We use these boxes to clarify difficult concepts, to provide additional information about the tools of economics, and to show how economics relates to our daily lives. Several are new or revised in this edition. A particularly useful FYI box appears on the opposite page.

Graphs

Understanding graphical analysis is a key part of learning macroeconomics, and we have worked hard to make the figures easy to follow. New to this edition, we use four colours and comment boxes within figures that describe briefly and draw attention to the important points that the figures illustrate. Both innovations should help students both learn and review the material.

Mathematical Notes

We use occasional mathematical footnotes to keep more difficult material out of the body of the text. These notes make an argument more rigourous or present a proof of a mathematical result. They can easily be skipped by those students who have not been introduced to the necessary mathematical tools.

Chapter Summaries

Every chapter ends with a brief, nontechnical summary of its major lessons. Students can use the summaries to place the material in perspective and to review for exams.

f y i

MACROECONOMIC DATA FOR CANADA

While the text contains many graphs and tables containing data pertaining to the Canadian economy (see, in particular, the convenient graphs on the inside front and bank covers of the book), readers of both the text and the study guide will want to have convenient access to the latest observations that emerge after these books have been published. We indicate the most straightforward options here.

First, individuals can visit the government documents section of their university or college library. The *Canadian Economic Observer* (published monthly by Statistics Canada) and the *Bank of Canada Review* (published quarterly) contain almost everything that will be needed.

The second and third options involve the internet. The most recent observations on many major series are available on Statistics Canada's Website:

http://www.statcan.ca

Click on *Canadian Statistics* to access the data that relate to macroeconomic issues. While convenient, this free-access site provides only the most recent observations. Entire historical time series are available from the Computing in the Humanities and Social Sciences (CHASS) facility at the University of Toronto. Most Canadian universities are subscribers to the services provided by this facility. To verify that your university is a subscriber (which gives you free access), check the list of schools at:

http://datacenter2.chass.utoronto.ca/
subscribers.html

To access all the data you could ever want on Canadian macroeconomics, visit the Canadian Socio-economic and Information and Management Database (CANSIM) at:

http://datacenter2.chass.utoronto.ca/cansim/

Click on *Search and Retrieve CANSIM*, and then on *Retrieve a single CANSIM series by label*. The first item that you are asked for is the CANSIM label for the series that you want. You get this label from the source listed in the graphs and tables that are provided in the text. For example, the unemployment rate is graphed on page 139 in the text. The source lists the unemployment rate series as CANSIM D984954. Enter this label and click on *Retrieve*. If you do not want separate observations for each month, select "annual" for *frequency*, and "average" for *conversion method*. The two options that are most convenient for *output format* are "plain" and "spreadsheet." "Plain" allows you to read the series and detailed description. "Spreadsheet" allows you to save the series, so that you can open it as a spreadsheet file for further analysis or graphing. If you opt for "spreadsheet," save the series as a text file. When opening the text file in your spreadsheet, choose "fixed width" (not "delimited") for the original data type, and choose general for the column data format. Once you have the series in your spreadsheet, you can analyze it, perhaps by graphing it along with other series.

Other useful Web sites are:

http://www.fin.gc.ca

The Federal Department of Finance site has a "Frequently Asked Questions" section, as well as the annual *Budget* documents (each spring) and the annual *Fiscal Update* (each fall).

http://www.bank-banque-canada.ca

The Bank of Canada site has useful "Backgrounders" and the semi-annual *Monetary Report*.

http://www.cabe.ca

The Canadian Association of Business Economists site gives links to many interesting sources of information, including the macroeconomic analyses provided by the economics departments of Canada's major chartered banks.

Key Concepts

Learning the language of a field is a major part of any course. Within the chapter, each key concept is in **boldface** when it is introduced. At the end of the chapter, the key concepts are listed for review.

Questions for Review

After studying a chapter, students can immediately test their understanding of its basic lessons by answering the Questions for Review.

Problems and Applications

Every chapter includes Problems and Applications designed for homework assignments. Some of these are numerical applications of the theory in the chapter. Others encourage the student to go beyond the material in the chapter by addressing new issues that are closely related to the chapter topics.

Chapter Appendixes

Several chapters include appendixes that offer additional material, sometimes at a higher level of mathematical sophistication. These are designed so that professors can cover certain topics in greater depth if they wish. The appendixes can be skipped altogether without loss of continuity.

Glossary

To help students become familiar with the language of macroeconomics, a glossary of more than 250 terms is provided at the back of the book.

Supplements for Students

There are two supplements for students that instructors can use in their courses.

Student Guide and Workbook

The study guide, by Roger Kaufman (Smith College) and William Scarth, offers various ways for students to learn the material in the text and assess their understanding.

- *Fill-In Questions* give students the opportunity to review and check their knowledge of the key terms and concepts in the chapter.
- *Multiple-Choice Questions* allow students to test themselves on the chapter material.
- *Exercises* guide students step by step through the various models using graphs and numerical examples.
- *Problems* ask students to apply the models on their own.
- *Questions to Think About* require critical thinking as well as economic analysis.
- *Data Questions* ask students to obtain and learn about readily available economic data.

Macroeconomics Companion Website

The *Macroeconomics Companion Website* offers a wealth of resources, including interactive flash cards, online quizzing (with results stored for the instructor), "Economics in the News" essays, example test questions with outlined answers, and links to other writings.

The *Macroeconomics* Website can be found on the internet at http://www.worthpublishers.com/mankiw. Be sure to click on the Canadian edition icon to access the links to Canadian data and policy documents.

Two items available on the Website pertain to the U.S. economy. Nevertheless, since much of the book covers items which are not specific to the small open economy case, Canadian students may find these items instructive. The innovative software package for students prepared by David Weil (Brown University) is available over the internet. *MacroBytes* provides a range of activities to aid and motivate the student throughout the course.

> ➤ *Data Plotter*. Students can explore macroeconomic data with time-series graphs and scatterplots.

> ➤ *Macro Models*. These modules provide simulations of the models presented in the book. Students can change the exogenous variables and see the outcomes in terms of shifting curves and recalculated numerical values of the endogenous variables. Each module contains exercises that instructors can assign as homework.

> ➤ *2001: A Game for Macroeconomists*. The game allows students to become President of the United States in the year 2001 and to make macroeconomic policy decisions based on news events, economic statistics, and approval ratings. It gives students a sense of the complex interconnections that influence the economy. It is also fun to play.

Supplement for Instructors

An additional supplement is available from Worth Publishers to help instructors enhance their courses.

Test Bank

Nancy Jianakoplos (Colorado State University) and William Scarth have produced a *Test Bank* that includes over 1000 multiple-choice questions to accompany the Canadian edition. Several short numerical problems are also provided for each chapter.

Acknowledgments

We benefited from the input of many reviewers, colleagues, and government agencies. Several Canadian economists were particularly helpful in the preparation of either the first or second Canadian edition. Norm Cameron (University of Manitoba), Bryan Campbell (Concordia University), Miquel Faig (University of Toronto), George Georgopoulos (University of Toronto),

Ron Kneebone (University of Calgary), Tony Myatt (University of New Brunswick), and Leon Sydor (University of Windsor) all made many useful suggestions. In addition, we wish to acknowledge the discussions we have had with colleagues at our own universities and the input given by a number of economists teaching in the United States (whose helpful comments found their way into this Canadian edition). This latter group is listed in the fourth U.S. edition of the book.

The people at Worth Publishers have continued to be congenial and dedicated. I am grateful to Alan McClare (Editor), Chris Narozny (Project Director), Margaret Comaskey (Project Editor), Barbara Anne Seixas (Production Manager), John Schmerein (Editorial Assistant), Stacey Alexander (Supplements Manager), and Lissi Sigillo (Designer).

Many other people in publishing made valuable contributions as well. Most important, Jane Tufts, freelance developmental editor, worked her magic on this book for the first time in this edition, and her improvements show on almost every page. Alexandra Nickerson once again did a great job preparing the index. I must also thank Paul Shensa, whose contributions to the first three editions are still very evident in this one.

Finally, we would like to thank our families for being so understanding, supportive, and inspirational.

N. Gregory Mankiw

Cambridge, Massachusetts
April 2000

William Scarth

Hamilton, Ontario
April 2000

macroeconomics

part ONE

Introduction

Part One introduces you to the study of macroeconomics. Chapter 1 discusses why macroeconomics is an exciting and important subject, explains the tools that economists use to analyze the economy, and outlines the plan of this book. Chapter 2 discusses the types of data that economists and policymakers use to keep track of what's happening in the economy.

1

The Science of Macroeconomics

The whole of science is nothing more than the refinement of everyday thinking.

—*Albert Einstein*

1-1 What Macroeconomists Study

Why have some countries experienced rapid growth in incomes over the past century while others stay mired in poverty? Why do some countries have high rates of inflation while others maintain stable prices? Why do all countries experience recessions and depressions—recurrent periods of falling incomes and rising unemployment—and how can government policy reduce the frequency and severity of these episodes? **Macroeconomics,** the study of the economy as a whole, attempts to answer these and many related questions.

To appreciate the importance of macroeconomics, you need only read the newspaper or listen to the news. Every day you can see headlines such as GDP GROWTH SLOWS, THE BANK OF CANADA MOVES TO COMBAT INFLATION, THE FISCAL DIVIDEND GROWS, or STOCKS FALL AMID RECESSION FEARS. Although these macroeconomic events may seem abstract, they touch all of our lives. Business executives forecasting the demand for their products must guess how fast consumers' incomes will grow. Senior citizens living on fixed incomes wonder how fast prices will rise. Recent graduates looking for jobs hope that the economy will boom and that firms will be hiring.

Because the state of the economy affects everyone, macroeconomic issues play a central role in political debate. Voters are keenly aware of how the economy is doing, and they know that government policy can affect the economy in powerful ways. As a result, the popularity of the government rises when the economy is doing well and falls when it is doing poorly. During the federal election of 1993, for example, Liberal strategists kept the former government on the defensive by keeping the campaign focused on the economy. Every speech included the refrain "jobs, jobs, jobs."

Macroeconomic issues are also at the center of world politics. In recent years, Europe has moved toward a common currency, many Asian countries have experienced financial turmoil and capital flight, and, in Canada, after rising foreign debts and a falling currency, serious debate on North American currency union surfaced in 1999.

Although the job of making economic policy falls to world leaders, the job of explaining how the economy as a whole works falls to macroeconomists. Toward this end, macroeconomists collect data on incomes, prices, unemployment, and many other variables from different time periods and different countries. They then attempt to formulate general theories that help to explain these data. Like astronomers studying the evolution of stars or biologists studying the evolution of species, macroeconomists cannot conduct controlled experiments. Instead, they must make use of the data that history gives them. Macroeconomists observe that economies differ from one another and that they change over time. These observations provide both the motivation for developing macroeconomic theories and the data for testing them.

To be sure, macroeconomics is a young and imperfect science. The macroeconomist's ability to predict the future course of economic events is no better than the meteorologist's ability to predict next month's weather. But, as you will see, macroeconomists do know quite a lot about how the economy works. This knowledge is useful both for explaining economic events and for formulating economic policy.

Every era has its own economic problems. In the 1970s, the Liberal government of Pierre Trudeau wrestled in vain with a rising rate of inflation. In the 1980s, inflation subsided, but the Conservative government of Brian Mulroney presided over large federal budget deficits. In the 1990s, as the Liberals formed the government once again, the budget deficit shrank and even turned into a small budget surplus, but federal taxes as a share of national income reached a historic high. Although the basic principles of macroeconomics do not change from decade to decade, the macroeconomist must apply these principles with flexibility and creativity to meet changing circumstances.

CASE STUDY

The Historical Performance of the Canadian Economy

Economists use many types of data to measure the performance of an economy. Three macroeconomic variables are particularly important: real gross domestic product (GDP), the inflation rate, and the unemployment rate. **Real GDP** measures the total income of everyone in the economy (adjusted for the level of prices). The **inflation rate** measures how quickly prices are rising. The **unemployment rate** measures the fraction of the labour force that is out of work. Macroeconomists study how these variables are determined, why they change over time, and how they interact with one another.

Figure 1-1 shows real GDP per person for the Canadian economy—widely regarded as a measure of our standard of living. Two aspects of this figure are noteworthy. First, real GDP grows over time. Real GDP per person today is

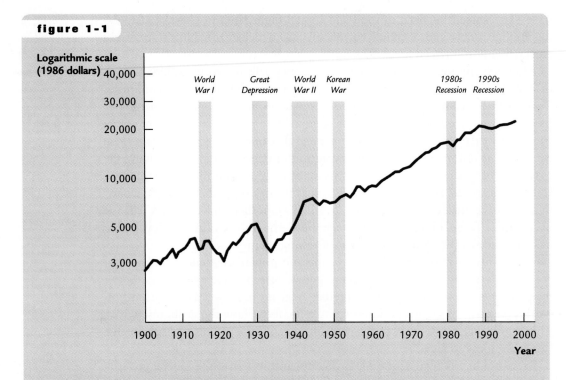

figure 1-1

Logarithmic scale (1986 dollars)

World War I   Great Depression   World War II   Korean War   1980s Recession   1990s Recession

Real GDP per Person in the Canadian Economy Real GDP measures the total output of the economy. Real GDP per person measures the income of the typical person in the economy.

Note: Real GDP is plotted here on a logarithmic scale. On such a scale, equal distances on the vertical axis represent equal *percentage* changes. Thus, the distance between $5,000 and $10,000 is the same as the distance between $10,000 and $20,000.

Source: Reproduced and adapted by authority of the Minister of Industry, 1994. Statistics Canada, CANSIM Series D14872 and D1; also *Canadian Economic Observer Catalogue 11-210,* (Historical Statistical Supplement 1991/92): 7, 98 and *Catalogue 11-010* (Statistical Summary, March 1994): 4, 12; Morris Altman, "Revised Real GNP Estimates and Canadian Economic Growth, 1870-1926," *Review of Income and Wealth,* Series 38, No. 4 (December 1992): 458-59; and *Canada 1930: A Handbook of Present Conditions and Recent Progress in the Dominion Bureau of Statistics* (Ottawa: Dominion Bureau of Statistics): 40.

about eight times its level in 1900. Second, the growth in real GDP is not steady. There are repeated periods during which real GDP is falling, a dramatic example being the 1930s. Such periods are called **recessions** if they are mild and **depressions** if they are more severe.

Figure 1-2 shows the Canadian inflation rate. You can see that inflation varies substantially. Before 1945, the inflation rate averaged about zero. Periods of falling prices, called **deflation,** were almost as common as periods of rising prices. In more recent history, inflation has been the norm. The inflation problem became most severe during the mid-1970s, when prices rose persistently at a rate of almost 10 percent per year. Inflation returned to near zero in the 1990s.

Figure 1-3 shows the Canadian unemployment rate since 1921, the first year for which data exist. This figure shows that there is always some unemployment and that the amount varies from year to year. Recessions and depressions

figure 1-2

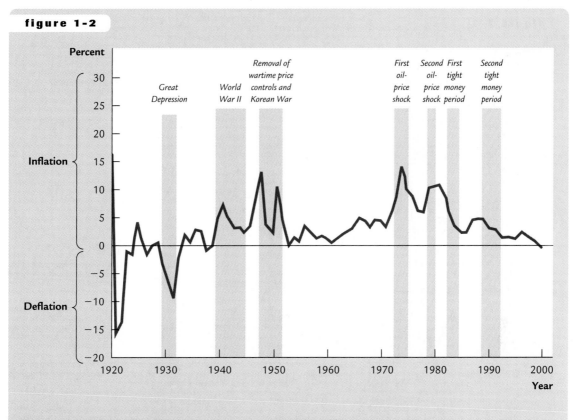

The Inflation Rate in the Canadian Economy The inflation rate measures the percentage change in the average level of prices from the year before. A negative inflation rate indicates that prices are falling.

Note: The inflation rate is measured here using the GDP deflator.

Source: Reproduced and adapted by authority of the Minister of Industry, 1994, Statistics Canada, CANSIM Series D15612; also *Canadian Economic Observer* (Historical Statistical Supplement, 1991/92): 27 and (Statistical Summary, March 1994): 22; Morris Altman, "Revised Real GNP Estimates and Canadian Economic Growth, 1870–1926," *Review of Income and Wealth*, Series 38, No. 4.

are associated with unusually high unemployment. The highest rates of unemployment were reached during the Great Depression of the 1930s. As the figure shows, since World War II, there has been a gradual upward trend in unemployment. We will discuss the likely causes of this troubling fact in Chapter 6. Evidence for the 1990s suggests that this disturbing trend may be starting to reverse itself.

These three figures offer a glimpse at the history of the Canadian economy. They show that unemployment falls and inflation rises when total spending is high (such as during World War II and the early 1960s), and that unemployment rises when inflation is reduced by government policy that decreases total spending (such as during the early 1980s and 1990s).

In the chapters that follow, we first discuss how these variables are measured and then explain how they behave—both in the long run and in the short run.

figure 1-3

The Unemployment Rate in the Canadian Economy The unemployment rate measures the fraction of the labour that does not have a job.

Source: Reproduced and adapted by authority of the Minister of Industry, 1994, Statistics Canada, CANSIM Series D984954; also *Canadian Economic Observer* (Historical Statistical Supplement, 1991/92): 38 and (Statistical Summary, March 1994): 16; Frank Leacy (Ed.), "Statistics Canada," *Historical Statistics of Canada, 2e, Catalogue 11-516*, Series D223, D132 (1983).

We are then in a position to evaluate the government's fiscal policy (its changes in government spending and taxing) and its monetary policy (changes in the growth of the nation's money supply).

1-2 | How Economists Think

Although economists often study politically charged issues, they try to address these issues with a scientist's objectivity. Like any science, economics has its own set of tools—terminology, data, and a way of thinking—that can seem foreign and arcane to the layman. The best way to become familiar with these tools is to practice using them, and this book will afford you ample opportunity to do so. To make these tools less forbidding, however, let's discuss a few of them here.

pizza market does a good job of addressing that issue. Yet if our goal is to explain why towns with three pizzerias have lower pizza prices than towns with one pizzeria, the simple model is less useful.

The art in economics is in judging when an assumption is clarifying and when it is misleading. Any model constructed to be completely realistic would be too complicated for anyone to understand. Simplification is a necessary part of building a useful model. Yet models lead to incorrect conclusions if they assume away features of the economy that are crucial to the issue at hand. Economic modeling therefore requires care and common sense.

A Multitude of Models

Macroeconomists study many facets of the economy. For example, they examine the influence of fiscal policy on economic growth, the impact of employment insurance on the unemployment rate, and the effect of inflation on interest rates. Macroeconomics is as diverse as the economy.

Although economists use models to address all these issues, no single model can answer all questions. Just as carpenters use different tools for different tasks, economists uses different models to explain different economic phenomena. Students of macroeconomics, therefore, must keep in mind that there is no single "correct" model useful for all purposes. Instead, there are many models, each of which is useful for shedding light on a different facet of the economy. The field of macroeconomics is like a Swiss army knife—a set of complementary but distinct tools that can be applied in different ways in different circumstances.

This book therefore presents many different models that address different questions and that make different assumptions. Remember that a model is only as good as its assumptions and that an assumption that is useful for some purposes may be misleading for others. When using a model to address a question, the economist must keep in mind the underlying assumptions and judge whether these are reasonable for the matter at hand.

Prices: Flexible Versus Sticky

Throughout this book, one group of assumptions will prove especially important—those concerning the speed with which wages and prices adjust. Economists normally presume that the price of a good or a service moves quickly to bring quantity supplied and quantity demanded into balance. In other words, they assume that a market goes to the equilibrium of supply and demand. This assumption is called **market clearing** and is central to the model of the pizza market discussed earlier. For answering most questions, economists use market-clearing models.

Yet the assumption of *continuous* market clearing is not entirely realistic. For markets to clear continuously, prices must adjust instantly to changes in supply and demand. In fact, however, many wages and prices adjust slowly. Labour contracts often set wages for up to three years. Many firms leave their product prices the same for long periods of time—for example, magazine publishers typically change their newsstand prices only every three or four years. Although market-clearing models assume that all wages and prices are **flexible,** in the real world some wages and prices are **sticky.**

The apparent stickiness of prices does not necessarily make market-clearing models useless. After all, prices are not stuck forever; eventually, they do adjust to changes in supply and demand. Market-clearing models might not describe the economy at every instant, but they do describe the equilibrium toward which the economy slowly gravitates. Therefore, most macroeconomists believe that price flexibility is a good assumption for studying long-run issues, such as the growth in real GDP that we observe from decade to decade.

For studying short-run issues, such as year-to-year fluctuations in real GDP and unemployment, the assumption of price flexibility is less plausible. Over short periods, many prices are fixed at predetermined levels. Therefore, most macroeconomists believe that price stickiness is a better assumption for studying the behaviour of the economy in the short run.

Microeconomic Thinking and Macroeconomic Models

Microeconomics is the study of how households and firms make decisions and how these decisionmakers interact in the marketplace. A central principle of microeconomics is that households and firms *optimize*—they do the best they can for themselves given their objectives and the constraints they face. In microeconomic models, households choose their purchases to maximize their level of satisfaction, which economists call *utility,* and firms make production decisions to maximize their profits.

Because economy-wide events arise from the interaction of many households and many firms, macroeconomics and microeconomics are inextricably linked. When we study the economy as a whole, we must consider the decisions of individual economic actors. For example, to understand what determines total consumer spending, we must think about a family deciding how much to spend today and how much to save for the future. To understand what determines total investment spending, we must think about a firm deciding whether to build a new factory. Because aggregate variables are simply the sum of the variables describing many individual decisions, macroeconomic theory inevitably rests on a microeconomic foundation.

Although microeconomic decisions always underlie economic models, in many models the optimizing behaviour of households and firms is implicit rather than explicit. The model of the pizza market we discussed earlier is an example. Households' decisions about how much pizza to buy underlie the demand for pizza, and pizzerias' decisions about how much pizza to produce underlie the supply of pizza. Presumably, households make their decisions to maximize utility, and pizzerias make their decisions to maximize profit. Yet the model did not focus on these microeconomic decisions; it left them in the background. Similarly, in much of macroeconomics, the optimizing behaviour of households and firms is left implicit.

1-3 | How This Book Proceeds

This book has five parts. This chapter and the next make up Part One, the Introduction. Chapter 2 discusses how economists measure economic variables, such as aggregate income, the inflation rate, and the unemployment rate.

Part Two, The Economy in the Long Run, presents the classical model of the economy. The key assumption of the classical model is that prices are flexible. That is, with only a few exceptions, the classical model assumes market clearing. For the reasons we have discussed, this assumption is best viewed as describing the economy in the long run.

Part Three, The Economy in the Short Run, examines the behaviour of the economy when prices are sticky. The non-market-clearing model developed here is designed to analyze short-run issues, such as the reasons for economic fluctuations and the influence of government policy on those fluctuations.

Part Four, Macroeconomic Policy Debates, builds on the previous analysis to consider what role the government should take in the economy. It considers how, if at all, the government should respond to short-run fluctuations in real GDP and unemployment. It also examines the various views on the effects of government debt.

Part Five, More on the Microeconomics Behind Macroeconomics, presents some of the microeconomic models that are useful for analyzing macroeconomic issues. For example, it examines the household's decisions regarding how much to consume and how much money to hold and the firm's decision regarding how much to invest. These individual decisions together form the larger macroeconomic picture. The goal of studying these microeconomic decisions in detail is to refine our understanding of the aggregate economy.

Summary

1. Macroeconomics is the study of the economy as a whole—including growth in incomes, changes in prices, and the rate of unemployment. Macroeconomists attempt both to explain economic events and to devise policies to improve economic performance.

2. To understand the economy, economists use models—theories that simplify reality in order to reveal how exogenous variables influence endogenous variables. The art in the science of economics is in judging whether a model usefully captures the important economic relationships for the matter

at hand. Because no single model can answer all questions, macroeconomists use different models to look at different issues.

3. A key feature of a macroeconomic model is whether it assumes that prices are flexible or sticky. According to most macroeconomists, models with flexible prices describe the economy in the long run, whereas models with sticky prices offer a better description of the economy in the short run.

4. Microeconomics is the study of how firms and individuals make decisions and how these decisionmakers interact. Because macroeconomic events arise from many microeconomic interactions, macroeconomists use many of the tools of microeconomics.

KEY CONCEPTS

Macroeconomics

Real GDP

Inflation rate

Unemployment rate

Recession

Depression

Deflation

Models

Endogenous variables

Exogenous variables

Market clearing

Flexible and sticky prices

Microeconomics

QUESTIONS FOR REVIEW

1. Explain the difference between macroeconomics and microeconomics. How are these two fields related?

2. Why do economists build models?

3. What is a market-clearing model? When is the assumption of market clearing appropriate?

PROBLEMS AND APPLICATIONS

1. What macroeconomic issues have been in the news lately?

2. What do you think are the defining characteristics of a science? Does the study of the economy have these characteristics? Do you think macroeconomics should be called a science? Why or why not?

3. Use the model of supply and demand to explain how a fall in the price of frozen yogurt would affect the price of ice cream and the quantity of ice cream sold. In your explanation, identify the exogenous and endogenous variables.

4. How often does the price you pay for a haircut change? What does your answer imply about the usefulness of market-clearing models for analyzing the market for haircuts?

The Data of Macroeconomics

*It is a capital mistake to theorize before one has data. Insensibly one be-
gins to twist facts to suit theories, instead of theories to fit facts.*

— Sherlock Holmes

Scientists, economists, and detectives have much in common: they all want to
figure out what's going on in the world around them. To do this, they rely on
a combination of theory and observation. They build theories in an attempt to
make sense of what they see happening. Having developed these theories, they
turn to more systematic observation to evaluate the theories' validity. Only
when theory and data come into line do they feel they understand the situation.

This chapter discusses the types of data used to create and test macroeconomic theories. The most obvious source of information about the economy is
casual observation. When you go shopping, you see how fast prices are rising.
When you look for a job, you learn whether firms are hiring. Because we are
all participants in the economy, we get some sense of economic conditions as
we go about our lives. These casual observations provide the first clues about
how the economy works.

Economic statistics are a more systematic and objective source of information. The government regularly surveys households and firms to learn about
their economic activity—how much they are earning, what they are buying,
what prices they are charging, and so on. From these surveys, various statistics
are computed that summarize the state of the economy. These statistics are used
by economists to study the economy and by policymakers to monitor economic developments and formulate appropriate policies.

This chapter focuses on the three economic statistics that economists and
policymakers use most often. **Gross domestic product,** or **GDP,** tells us the
nation's total income and the total expenditure on its output of goods and services. The **consumer price index,** or **CPI,** measures the level of prices. The
unemployment rate tells us the fraction of workers who are unemployed. In
the following pages, we see how these statistics are computed and what they
tell us about the economy.

2-1 | Measuring the Value of Economic Activity: Gross Domestic Product

Gross domestic product is often considered the best measure of how well the economy is performing. This measure, which Statistics Canada computes every three months, attempts to summarize in a single number the dollar value of economic activity. More precisely, GDP equals the total value of all final goods and services produced within Canada during a particular year or quarter. *If* it were the case that (1) no Canadian worker had a job in another country, (2) no foreigner had a job in Canada, and (3) all machines and factories used both here and elsewhere were owned by domestic residents, then this total value of goods produced would also measure the total value of Canadians' incomes. But, since some income *is* received from individuals owning capital equipment in other countries, GDP is not a perfect measure of total Canadian income. Thus, statisticians also compute **gross national product (GNP).**

GDP Versus GNP

Here is the distinction between GDP and GNP:

> ➤ *GDP* is total income earned *domestically*. It includes income earned domestically by foreigners, but it does not include income earned by domestic residents on foreign ground.

> ➤ *GNP* is total income earned by *nationals* (that is, by residents of a nation). It includes the income that nationals earn abroad, but it does not include the income earned within a country by foreigners.

As noted, these two measures of income differ because a person can earn income and reside in different countries.

To further understand the difference between GDP and GNP, consider several examples. Suppose a resident of Hong Kong comes temporarily to Vancouver to work. The income he earns in Canada is part of Canadian GDP because it is earned domestically and it represents economic activity that takes place here. But the income is not part of Canadian GNP because the worker is not a Canadian national.

As another example, suppose a Japanese resident owns a factory in Ontario. The profit she earns is part of Canadian GDP because this income is earned domestically. But the profit is not part of Canadian GNP, because the Japanese owner is not a Canadian.

For the purpose of stabilizing employment, we are interested in a broad measure of job-creating activity within Canada. GDP is that measure. For evaluating trends in the standard of living of Canadians, GNP is more appropriate. In 1998, GNP was 3.3 percent less than GDP, primarily because (1) foreigners owned some capital equipment operating within Canada and (2) Canadians were in debt to foreigners. This gap meant that only 96.7 percent of the economic activity taking place within Canada actually generated income for Canadians. Despite this gap, we simplify by ignoring the difference between GDP and GNP (and focus only on GDP) for many discussions within this book. This is partly because it is GDP that is reported in the media, and partly because the cyclical swings in GDP and GNP are almost identical, so this simplification does not limit the applicability of our analysis.

Thus, throughout much but not all of this book, we abstract from the phenomenon of foreign-owned factors of production, and we assume that GDP simultaneously measures all three of the following concepts:

➤ The total output of goods and services

➤ The total income of all individuals

➤ The total expenditure of all individuals.

To see how GDP can measure all these things at once, we must discuss **national accounting,** the accounting system used to measure GDP and many related statistics.

Income, Expenditure, and the Circular Flow

Imagine an economy that produces a single good, bread, from a single input, labour. Figure 2-1 illustrates all the economic transactions that occur between households and firms in this economy.

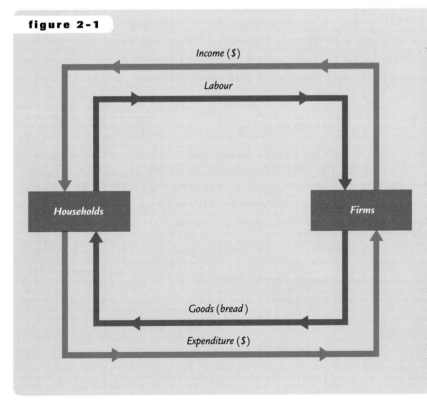

figure 2-1

Income ($)

Labour

Households

Firms

Goods (bread)

Expenditure ($)

The Circular Flow This figure illustrates the flows between firms and households in an economy that produces one good, bread, from one input, labour. The inner loop represents the flows of labour and bread: households sell their labour to firms, and the firms sell the bread they produce to households. The outer loop represents the corresponding flows of dollars: households pay the firms for the bread, and the firms pay wages and profit to the households. In this economy, GDP is both the total expenditure on bread and the total income from the production of bread.

The inner loop in Figure 2-1 represents the flows of bread and labour. The households sell their labour to the firms. The firms use the labour of their workers to produce bread, which the firms in turn sell to the households. Hence, labour flows from households to firms, and bread flows from firms to households.

The outer loop in Figure 2-1 represents the corresponding flow of dollars. The households buy bread from the firms. The firms use some of the revenue from these sales to pay the wages of their workers, and the remainder is the profit belonging to the owners of the firms (who themselves are part of the household sector). Hence, expenditure on bread flows from households to firms, and income in the form of wages and profit flows from firms to households.

GDP measures the flow of dollars in this economy. We can compute it in two ways. GDP is the total income from the production of bread, which equals the sum of wages and profit—the top half of the circular flow of dollars. GDP is also the total expenditure on purchases of bread—the bottom half of the circular flow of dollars. To compute GDP, we can look at either the flow of dollars from firms to households or the flow of dollars from households to firms.

These two ways of computing GDP must be equal because the expenditure of buyers on products is, by the rules of accounting, income to the sellers of those products. Every transaction that affects expenditure must affect income, and every transaction that affects income must affect expenditure. For example, suppose that a firm produces and sells one more loaf of bread to a household. Clearly this transaction raises total expenditure on bread, but it also has an equal effect on total income. If the firm produces the extra loaf without hiring any more labour (such as by making the production process more efficient), then profit increases. If the firm produces the extra loaf by hiring more labour, then wages increase. In both cases, expenditure and income increase equally.

Some Rules for Computing GDP

In the hypothetical economy that produces only bread, we can compute GDP simply by adding up the total expenditure on bread. A nation's economy, however, includes the production and sale of a vast number of diverse goods and services. To interpret correctly what GDP measures, we must understand some of the rules that economists follow in constructing this statistic.

Adding Apples and Oranges The Canadian economy produces many different goods and services—hamburgers, haircuts, cars, computers, and so on. GDP combines the value of these goods and services into a single measure. The diversity of products in the economy complicates the calculation of GDP because different products have different values.

Suppose, for example, that the economy produces four apples and three oranges. How do we compute GDP? We could simply add apples and oranges and conclude that GDP equals seven pieces of fruit. But this makes sense only if we thought apples and oranges had equal value, which is generally not true.

f y i

STOCKS AND FLOWS

Many economic variables measure a quantity of something—a quantity of money, a quantity of goods, and so on. Economists distinguish between two types of quantity variables: stocks and flows. A **stock** is a quantity measured at a given point in time, whereas a **flow** is a quantity measured per unit of time.

The bathtub, shown in Figure 2-2, is the classic example used to illustrate stocks and flows. The amount of water in the tub is a stock: it is the quantity of water in the tub at a given point in time. The amount of water coming out of the faucet is a flow: it is the quantity of water being added to the tub per unit of time. Note that we measure stocks and flows in different units. We say that the bathtub contains 50 *litres* of water, but that water is coming out of the faucet at 5 *litres per minute*.

GDP is probably the most important flow variable in economics: it tells us how many dollars are flowing around the economy's circular flow per unit of time. When you hear someone say that the Canadian GDP is $900 billion, you should un-

derstand that this means that it is $900 billion *per year*. (Equivalently, we could say that Canadian GDP is $2.5 billion per day.)

Stocks and flows are often related. In the bathtub example, these relationships are clear. The stock of water in the tub represents the accumulation of the flow out of the faucet, and the flow of water represents the change in the stock. When building theories to explain economic variables, it is often useful to determine whether the variables are stocks or flows and whether any relationships link them.

Here are some examples of related stocks and flows that we study in future chapters:

➤ A person's wealth is a stock; his income and expenditure are flows.

➤ The number of unemployed people is a stock; the number of people losing their jobs is a flow.

➤ The amount of capital in the economy is a stock; the amount of investment is a flow.

➤ The government debt is a stock; the government budget deficit is a flow.

figure 2-2

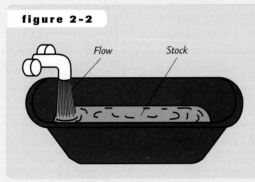

Flow   Stock

Stocks and Flows The amount of water in a bathtub is a stock: it is a quantity measured at a given moment in time. The amount of water coming out of the faucet is a flow: it is a quantity measured per unit of time.

(This would be even clearer if the economy had produced four watermelons and three grapes.)

To compute the total value of different goods and services, the national accounts use market prices because these prices reflect how much people are willing to pay for a good or service. Thus, if apples cost $0.50 each and oranges cost $1.00 each, GDP would be

$$
\begin{aligned}
\text{GDP} &= (\text{Price of Apples} \times \text{Quantity of Apples}) \\
&\quad + (\text{Price of Oranges} \times \text{Quantity of Oranges}) \\
&= (\$0.50 \times 4) + (\$1.00 \times 3) \\
&= \$5.00.
\end{aligned}
$$

GDP equals $5.00—the value of all the apples, $2.00, plus the value of all the oranges, $3.00.

Used Goods   When a sporting goods company makes a package of hockey cards and sells it for 50 cents, that 50 cents is added to the nation's GDP. But what about when a collector sells a rare Rochet Richard card to another collector for $500? That $500 is not part of GDP. GDP measures the value of currently produced goods and services. The sale of the Rochet Richard card reflects the transfer of an asset, not an addition to the economy's income. Thus, the sale of used goods is not included as part of GDP.

The Treatment of Inventories   Imagine that a bakery hires workers to produce more bread, pays their wages, and then fails to sell the additional bread. How does this transaction affect GDP?

The answer depends on what happens to the unsold bread. Let's first suppose that the bread spoils. In this case, the firm has paid more in wages but has not received any additional revenue, so the firm's profit is reduced by the amount that wages are increased. Total expenditure in the economy hasn't changed because no one buys the bread. Total income hasn't changed either— although more is distributed as wages and less as profit. Because the transaction affects neither expenditure nor income, it does not alter GDP.

Now suppose, instead, that the bread is put into inventory to be sold later. In this case, the transaction is treated differently. The owners of the firm are assumed to have "purchased" the bread for the firm's inventory, and the firm's profit is not reduced by the additional wages it has paid. Because the higher wages raise total income, and greater spending on inventory raises total expenditure, the economy's GDP rises.

What happens later when the firm sells the bread out of inventory? This case is much like the sale of a used good. There is spending by bread consumers, but there is inventory disinvestment by the firm. This negative spending by the firm offsets the positive spending by consumers, so the sale out of inventory does not affect GDP.

The general rule is that when a firm increases its inventory of goods, this investment in inventory is counted as expenditure by the firm owners. Thus, production for inventory increases GDP just as much as production for final sale. A sale out of inventory, however, is a combination of positive spending (the purchase) and negative spending (inventory disinvestment), so it does not influence GDP. This treatment of inventories ensures that GDP reflects the economy's current production of goods and services.

Intermediate Goods and Value Added   Many goods are produced in stages: raw materials are processed into intermediate goods by one firm and then sold to another firm for final processing. How should we treat such products when computing GDP? For example, suppose a cattle rancher sells one-quarter pound of meat to McDonald's for $0.50, and then McDonald's sells you a hamburger for $1.50. Should GDP include both the meat and the hamburger (a total of $2.00), or just the hamburger ($1.50)?

The answer is that GDP includes only the value of final goods. Thus, the hamburger is included in GDP but the meat is not: GDP increases by $1.50, not by $2.00. The reason is that the value of intermediate goods is already included as part of the market price of the final goods in which they are used. To add the intermediate goods to the final goods would be double counting—that is, the meat would be counted twice. Hence, GDP is the total value of final goods and services produced.

One way to compute the value of all final goods and services is to sum the value added at each stage of production. The **value added** of a firm equals the value of the firm's output less the value of the intermediate goods that the firm purchases. In the case of the hamburger, the value added of the rancher is $0.50 (assuming that the rancher bought no intermediate goods), and the value added of McDonald's is $1.50 − $0.50, or $1.00. Total value added is $0.50 + $1.00, which equals $1.50. For the economy as a whole, the sum of all value added must equal the value of all final goods and services. Hence, GDP is also the total value added of all firms in the economy.

Housing Services and Other Imputations   Although most goods and services are valued at their market prices when computing GDP, some are not sold in the marketplace and therefore do not have market prices. If GDP is to include the value of these goods and services, we must use an estimate of their value. Such an estimate is called an **imputed value.**

Imputations are especially important for determining the value of housing. A person who rents a house is buying housing services and providing income for the landlord; the rent is part of GDP, both as expenditure by the renter and as income for the landlord. Many people, however, live in their own homes. Although they do not pay rent to a landlord, they are enjoying housing services similar to those that renters purchase. To take account of the housing services enjoyed by homeowners, GDP includes the "rent" that these homeowners "pay" to themselves. Of course, homeowners do not in fact pay themselves this rent. Statistics Canada estimates what the market rent for a house would be if it were rented and includes that imputed rent as part of GDP. This imputed rent is included both in the homeowner's expenditure and in the homeowner's income.

Imputations also arise in valuing government services. For example, police officers, fire fighters, and legislators provide services to the public. Giving a value to these services is difficult because they are not sold in a marketplace and therefore do not have a market price. The national accounts include these services in GDP by valuing them at their cost. That is, the wages of these public servants are used as a measure of the value of their output.

In many cases, an imputation is called for in principle but, to keep things simple, is not made in practice. Because GDP includes the imputed rent on owner-occupied houses, one might expect it also to include the imputed rent on cars, lawn mowers, jewelry, and other durable goods owned by households. Yet the value of these rental services is left out of GDP. In addition, some of the output of the economy is produced and consumed at home and never enters the marketplace. For example, meals cooked at home are similar to meals cooked at a restaurant, yet the value added in meals at home is left out of GDP. Statistics Canada does not try to estimate the value of "household production" like this on any regular basis. Just to give some idea of the magnitude involved, however, the agency published an estimate for 1991. According to this study, household production in Canada is equal to about one-third of the measured GDP.

Finally, no imputation is made for the value of goods and services sold in the *underground economy*. The underground economy is the part of the economy that people hide from the government either because they wish to evade taxation or because the activity is illegal. Home construction, repairs, and cleaning services paid "under the table" are examples of the underground economy. The illegal drug trade is another.

Because the imputations necessary for computing GDP are only approximate, and because the value of many goods and services is left out altogether, GDP is an imperfect measure of economic activity. These imperfections are most problematic when comparing standards of living across countries. The size of the underground economy, for instance, varies from country to country. Yet as long as the magnitude of these imperfections remains fairly constant over time, GDP is useful for comparing economic activity from year to year.

Real GDP Versus Nominal GDP

Economists use the rules just described to compute GDP, which values the economy's total output of goods and services. But is GDP a good measure of economic well-being? Consider once again the economy that produces only apples and oranges. In this economy GDP is the sum of the value of all the apples produced and the value of all the oranges produced. That is,

$$\text{GDP} = (\text{Price of Apples} \times \text{Quantity of Apples})$$
$$+ (\text{Price of Oranges} \times \text{Quantity of Oranges}).$$

Notice that GDP can increase either because prices rise or because quantities rise.

It is easy to see that GDP computed this way is not a good gauge of economic well-being. That is, this measure does not accurately reflect how well the economy can satisfy the demands of households, firms, and the government. If all prices doubled without any change in quantities, GDP would double. Yet it would be misleading to say that the economy's ability to satisfy demands has doubled, because the quantity of every good produced remains the same. Economists call the value of goods and services measured at current prices **nominal GDP.**

A better measure of economic well-being would tally the economy's output of goods and services and would not be influenced by changes in prices. For this purpose, economists use **real GDP,** which is the value of goods and services measured using a constant set of prices. That is, real GDP shows what would have happened to expenditure on output if quantities had changed but prices had not.

To see how real GDP is computed, imagine we wanted to compare output in 1999 and output in 2000 in our apple-and-orange economy. We could begin by choosing a set of prices, called *base-year prices,* such as the prices that prevailed in 1999. Goods and services are then added up using these base-year prices to value the different goods in both years. Real GDP for 1999 would be

Real GDP = (1999 Price of Apples × 1999 Quantity of Apples)
+ (1999 Price of Oranges × 1999 Quantity of Oranges).

Similarly, real GDP in 2000 would be

Real GDP = (1999 Price of Apples × 2000 Quantity of Apples)
+ (1999 Price of Oranges × 2000 Quantity of Oranges).

And real GDP in 2001 would be

Real GDP = (1999 Price of Apples × 2001 Quantity of Apples)
+ (1999 Price of Oranges × 2001 Quantity of Oranges).

Notice that 1999 prices are used to compute real GDP for all three years. Because the prices are held constant, real GDP varies from year to year only if the quantities produced vary. Because a society's ability to provide economic satisfaction for its members ultimately depends on the quantities of goods and services produced, real GDP provides a better measure of economic well-being than nominal GDP.

The GDP Deflator

From nominal GDP and real GDP we can compute a third statistic: the GDP deflator. The **GDP deflator,** also called the implicit price deflator for GDP, is defined as the ratio of nominal GDP to real GDP:

$$\text{GDP Deflator} = \frac{\text{Nominal GDP}}{\text{Real GDP}}.$$

The GDP deflator reflects what's happening to the overall level of prices in the economy.

To understand this better, consider again an economy with only one good, bread. If P is the price of bread and Q is the quantity sold, then nominal GDP is the total number of dollars spent on bread in that year, $P \times Q$. Real GDP is the number of loaves of bread produced in that year times the price of bread in some base year, $P_{base} \times Q$. The GDP deflator is the price of bread in that year relative to the price of bread in the base year, P/P_{base}.

The definition of the GDP deflator allows us to separate nominal GDP into two parts: one part measures quantities (real GDP) and the other measures prices (the GDP deflator). That is,

$$\text{Nominal GDP} = \text{Real GDP} \times \text{GDP Deflator}.$$

Nominal GDP measures the current dollar value of the output of the economy. Real GDP measures output valued at constant prices. The GDP deflator measures the price of output relative to its price in the base year.

Chain-Weighted Measures of Real GDP

We have been discussing real GDP as if the prices used to compute this measure never change from their base-year values. If this were truly the case, over time the prices would become more and more dated. For instance, the price of computers has fallen substantially in recent years, while the price of a year at university has risen. When valuing the production of computers and education, it would be misleading to use the prices that prevailed ten or twenty years ago.

To solve this problem, the traditional approach involves Statistics Canada updating periodically the prices used to compute real GDP. About every five years, a new base year is chosen. The prices are then held fixed and used to measure year-to-year changes in the production of goods and services until the base year is updated once again.

Statistics Canada now has a new policy for dealing with changes in the base year. In particular, it now calculates *chain-weighted* measures of real GDP. With these new measures, the base year changes continuously over time. In essence, average prices in 1998 and 1999 are used to measure real growth from 1998 to 1999; average prices in 1999 and 2000 are used to measure real growth from 1999 to 2000; and so on. These various year-to-year growth rates are then put together to form a "chain" that can be used to compare the output of goods and services between any two dates.

This new chain-weighted measure of real GDP is better than the more traditional measure because it ensures that the prices used to compute real GDP are never far out of date. For most purposes, however, the differences are not important. It turns out that the two measures of real GDP are highly correlated with each other. The reason for this close association is that most relative prices change slowly over time. Thus, both measures of real GDP reflect the same thing: economy-wide changes in the production of goods and services.

The Components of Expenditure

Economists and policymakers care not only about the economy's total output of goods and services but also about the allocation of this output among alternative uses. The national accounts divide GDP into four broad categories of spending:

➤ Consumption (*C*)

➤ Investment (*I*)

➤ Government purchases (*G*)

➤ Net exports (*NX*).

Thus, letting *Y* stand for GDP,

$$Y = C + I + G + NX.$$

GDP is the sum of consumption, investment, government purchases, and net exports. Each dollar of GDP falls into one of these categories. This equation is an *identity*—an equation that must hold because of the way the variables are defined. It is called the **national accounts identity.**

TWO ARITHMETIC TRICKS FOR WORKING WITH PERCENTAGE CHANGES

For manipulating many relationships in economics, there is an arithmetic trick that is useful to know: *The percentage change of a product of two variables is approximately the sum of the percentage changes in each of the variables.*

To see how this trick works, consider an example. Let *P* denote the GDP deflator and *Y* denote real GDP. Nominal GDP is *P* × *Y*. The trick states that

Percentage Change in (*P* × *Y*)

≈ (Percentage Change in *P*)

+ (Percentage Change in *Y*).

For instance, suppose that in one year, real GDP is 100 and the GDP deflator is 2; the next year, real GDP is 103 and the GDP deflator is 2.1. We can calculate that real GDP rose by 3 percent and that the GDP deflator rose by 5 percent. Nominal GDP rose from 200 the first year to 216.3 the sec-

ond year, an increase of 8.15 percent. Notice that the growth in nominal GDP (8.15 percent) is approximately the sum of the growth in the GDP deflator (5 percent) and the growth in real GDP (3 percent).[1]

A second arithmetic trick follows as a corollary to the first: *The percentage change of a ratio is approximately the percentage change in the numerator minus the percentage change in the denominator.* Again, consider an example. Let *Y* denote GDP and *L* denote the population, so that *Y/L* is GDP per person. The second trick states

Percentage Change in (*Y/L*)

≈ (Percentage Change in *Y*)

− (Percentage Change in *L*).

For instance, suppose that in the first year, *Y* is 100,000 and *L* is 100, so *Y/L* is 1,000; in the second year, *Y* is 110,000 and *L* is 103, so *Y/L* is 1,068. Notice that the growth in GDP per person (6.8 percent) is approximately the growth in income (10 percent) minus the growth in population (3 percent).

---

[1]*Mathematical note:* The proof that this trick works begins with the chain rule from calculus:

$$d(PY) = Y\,dP + P\,dY.$$

Now divide both sides of this equation by *PY* to obtain:

$$d(PY)/(PY) = dP/P + dY/Y.$$

Notice that all three terms in this equation are percentage changes.

fyi

WHAT IS INVESTMENT?

Newcomers to macroeconomics are sometimes confused by how macroeconomists use familiar words in new and specific ways. One example is the term "investment." The confusion arises because what looks like investment for an individual may not be investment for the economy as a whole. The general rule is that the economy's investment does not include purchases that merely reallocate existing assets among different individuals. Investment, as macroeconomists use the term, creates new capital.

Let's consider some examples. Suppose we observe these two events:

➤ Smith buys for himself a 100-year-old Victorian house.

➤ Jones builds for herself a brand-new contemporary house.

What is total investment here? Two houses, one house, or zero?

A macroeconomist seeing these two transactions counts only the Jones house as investment.

Smith's transaction has not created new housing for the economy; it has merely reallocated existing housing. Smith's purchase is investment for Smith, but it is disinvestment for the person selling the house. By contrast, Jones has added new housing to the economy; her new house is counted as investment.

Similarly, consider these two events:

➤ Clarke buys $5 million in Air Canada stock from White on the Toronto Stock Exchange.

➤ General Motors sells $10 million in stock to the public and uses the proceeds to build a new car factory.

Here, investment is $10 million. In the first transaction, Clarke is investing in Air Canada stock, and White is disinvesting; there is no investment for the economy. By contrast, General Motors is using some of the economy's output of goods and services to add to its stock of capital; hence, its new factory is counted as investment.

Consumption consists of the goods and services bought by households. It is divided into three subcategories: durable goods, nondurable goods, and services. Durable goods are goods that last a long time, such as cars and TVs. Nondurable goods are goods that last only a short time, such as food and clothing. Services include the work done for consumers by individuals and firms, such as haircuts and doctor visits.

Investment consists of goods bought for future use. Investment is also divided into three subcategories: business fixed investment, residential construction, and inventory investment. Business fixed investment is the purchase of new plant and equipment by firms. Residential construction is the purchase of new housing by households and landlords. Inventory investment is the increase in firms' inventories of goods (if inventories are falling, inventory investment is negative).

Government purchases are the goods and services bought by federal, provincial, and municipal governments. This category includes such items as military equipment, highways, and the services that government workers provide. It does not include transfer payments to individuals, such as the Canada

Pension, employment insurance benefits, and welfare. Because transfer payments reallocate existing income and are not made in exchange for goods and services, they are not part of GDP.

The last category, **net exports,** takes into account trade with other countries. Net exports are the value of goods and services exported to other countries minus the value of goods and services that foreigners provide us. Net exports represent the net expenditure from abroad on our goods and services, which provides income for domestic producers.

CASE STUDY

GDP and Its Components

In 1998 the GDP of Canada totaled almost $895.8 billion. This number is so large that it is almost impossible to comprehend. We can make it easier to understand by dividing it by the 1998 Canadian population of 30.212 million. In this way, we obtain GDP per person—the amount of expenditure for the average Canadian—which equaled $29,650 in 1998.

How did we use this GDP? Table 2-1 shows that just under 60 percent of it, or $17,553 per person, was spent on consumption. Investment was $5,210 per person, and government purchases were $6,471 per person.

table 2-1

GDP and the Components of Expenditure: 1998

	Total (billions of dollars)	Per Person (dollars)
Gross Domestic Product	$895.8	$29,650
Consumption	530.3	17,553
Durables and nondurables	244.1	8,080
Services	286.2	9,473
Investment	157.4	5,210
Business fixed investment (factories, machinery)	107.8	3,568
Residential construction	44.9	1,486
Inventory investment	4.7	156
Government Purchases	195.5	6,471
Net Exports	12.6	417
Exports	370.0	12,247
Imports	357.4	11,830

Source: Statistics Canada, *National Income and Expenditure Accounts, Catalogue 13-001* (Quarterly Estimates, 1998).

The average person bought $11,830 of goods imported from abroad and produced $12,247 of goods that were exported to other countries. Thus, net exports were a small positive amount. Since we earned more from selling to foreigners than we spent on foreign goods, we used up the difference by paying a small part of the annual interest obligation that the average Canadian owed on the country's foreign debt. (Recall that over 3 percent of Canadian GDP was paid to foreigners in 1998; that is, GNP was less than GDP.)

It is interesting to compare how Canadians use their GDP to the spending patterns in other countries. Even when compared to Americans, there are significant differences. While Canadians spend 40 percent of per-capita GDP on imports, Americans limit spending on imports to 13 percent. Canadians leave almost 22 percent of per-capita GDP to be spent by various levels of government, while Americans limit this proportion to 18 percent.

Several Measures of Income

The national accounts include other measures of income that differ slightly in definition from GDP and GNP. It is important to be aware of the various measures, because economists and the press often refer to them.

We can see how the alternative measures of income relate to one another, by starting with GDP and subtracting various quantities. To obtain GNP from GDP, we subtract the net income of foreigners who own factors of production employed in Canada:

$$GNP = GDP - \text{Net Income of Foreigners.}$$

To obtain *net national product (NNP)*, we subtract the depreciation of capital—the amount of the economy's stock of plants, equipment, and residential structures that wears out during the year:

$$NNP = GNP - \text{Depreciation.}$$

In the national accounts, depreciation is called the *capital consumption allowances*. In 1998, it equaled about 13 percent of GNP. Since the depreciation of capital is a cost of producing the output of the economy, subtracting depreciation shows the net result of economic activity. For this reason, some economists believe that NNP is a better measure of economic well-being.

The next adjustment in the national accounts is for indirect business taxes, such as sales taxes. These taxes, which make up about 16 percent of NNP, place a wedge between the price that consumers pay for a good and the price that firms receive. Because firms never receive this tax wedge, it is not part of their income. Once we subtract indirect business taxes from NNP, we obtain a measure called *national income:*

$$\text{National Income} = NNP - \text{Indirect Business Taxes.}$$

National income is a measure of how much everyone in the economy has earned.

The national accounts divide national income into four components, depending on the way the income is earned. The four categories, and the percentage of national income that each comprises, in 1998, are:

> ➤ *Compensation of employees (72 percent)*. The wages and fringe benefits earned by workers

> ➤ *Corporate profits (12 percent)*. The income of corporations after payments to their workers and creditors

> ➤ *Nonincorporated business income (9 percent)*. The income of noncorporate businesses, such as small farms and law partnerships, and the income that landlords receive, including the imputed rent that homeowners "pay" to themselves, less expenses, such as depreciation

> ➤ *Net interest (7 percent)*. The interest domestic businesses pay minus the interest they receive, plus interest earned from foreigners.

A series of adjustments takes us from national income to *personal income*, the amount of income that households and noncorporate businesses receive. Three of these adjustments are most important. First, we reduce national income by the amount that corporations earn but do not pay out, either because the corporations are retaining earnings or because they are paying taxes to the government. This adjustment is made by subtracting corporate profits (which equals the sum of corporate taxes, dividends, and retained earnings) and adding back dividends. Second, we increase national income by the net amount the government pays out in transfer payments. This adjustment equals government transfers to individuals minus social insurance contributions paid to the government. Third, we adjust national income to include the interest that households earn rather than the interest that businesses pay. This adjustment is made by adding personal interest income and subtracting net interest. (The difference between personal interest and net interest arises in part from the interest on the government debt.) Thus, personal income is

$$
\begin{aligned}
\text{Personal Income} = \ &\text{National Income} \\
&- \text{Corporate Profits} \\
&- \text{Social Insurance Contributions} \\
&- \text{Net Interest} \\
&+ \text{Dividends} \\
&+ \text{Government Transfers to Individuals} \\
&+ \text{Personal Interest Income.}
\end{aligned}
$$

Next, if we subtract personal tax payments, we obtain *personal disposable income*:

$$
\begin{aligned}
\text{Personal Disposable Income} = \ &\text{Personal Income} \\
&- \text{Personal Tax Payments.}
\end{aligned}
$$

We are interested in personal disposable income because it is the amount households and noncorporate businesses have available to spend after satisfying their tax obligations to the government.

CASE STUDY

The Seasonal Cycle and Seasonal Adjustment

Because real GDP and the other measures of income reflect how well the economy is performing, economists are interested in studying the quarter-to-quarter fluctuations in these variables. Yet when we start to do so, one fact leaps out: all these measures of income exhibit a regular seasonal pattern. The output of the economy rises during the year, reaching a peak in the fourth quarter (October, November, and December), and then falling in the first quarter (January, February, and March) of the next year. These regular seasonal changes are substantial. From the fourth quarter to the first quarter, real GDP falls on average about 5 percent.[2]

It is not surprising that real GDP follows a seasonal cycle. Some of these changes are attributable to changes in our ability to produce: for example, building homes is more difficult during the cold weather of winter than during other seasons. In addition, people have seasonal tastes: they have preferred times for such activities as vacations and Christmas shopping.

When economists study fluctuations in real GDP and other economic variables, they often want to eliminate the portion of fluctuations due to predictable seasonal changes. You will find that most of the economic statistics reported in the newspaper are *seasonally adjusted*. This means that the data have been adjusted to remove the regular seasonal fluctuations. Therefore, when you observe a rise or fall in real GDP or any other data series, you must look beyond the seasonal cycle for the explanation.

2-2 | Measuring the Cost of Living: The Consumer Price Index

A dollar today doesn't buy as much as it did twenty years ago. The cost of almost everything has gone up. This increase in the overall level of prices is called *inflation*, and it is one of the primary concerns of economists and policymakers. In later chapters we examine in detail the causes and effects of inflation. Here we discuss how economists measure changes in the cost of living.

The Price of a Basket of Goods

The most commonly used measure of the level of prices is the **consumer price index (CPI).** Statistics Canada has the job of computing the CPI. It begins by collecting the prices of thousands of goods and services. Just as GDP

[2] Robert B. Barsky and Jeffrey A. Miron, "The Seasonal Cycle and the Business Cycle," *Journal of Political Economy* 97 (June 1989): 503–534.

turns the quantities of many goods and services into a single number measuring the value of production, the CPI turns the prices of many goods and services into a single index measuring the overall level of prices.

How should economists aggregate the many prices in the economy into a single index that reliably measures the price level? They could simply compute an average of all prices. Yet this approach would treat all goods and services equally. Because people buy more chicken than caviar, the price of chicken should have a greater weight in the CPI than the price of caviar. Statistics Canada weights different items by computing the price of a basket of goods and services purchased by a typical consumer. The CPI is the price of this basket of goods and services relative to the price of the same basket in some base year.

For example, suppose that the typical consumer buys 5 apples and 2 oranges every month. Then the basket of goods consists of 5 apples and 2 oranges, and the CPI is

$$\text{CPI} = \frac{(5 \times \text{Current Price of Apples}) + (2 \times \text{Current Price of Oranges})}{(5 \times \text{1992 Price of Apples}) + (2 \times \text{1992 Price of Oranges})}.$$

In this CPI, 1992 is the base year. The index tells us how much it costs now to buy 5 apples and 2 oranges relative to how much it cost to buy the same basket of fruit in 1992.

The consumer price index is the most closely watched index of prices, but it is not the only such index. Another is the producer price index, which measures the price of a typical basket of goods bought by firms rather than consumers. In addition to these overall price indices, Statistics Canada computes price indices for specific types of goods, such as food, housing, and energy.

The CPI Versus the GDP Deflator

Earlier in this chapter we saw another measure of prices—the implicit price deflator for GDP, which is the ratio of nominal GDP to real GDP. The GDP deflator and the CPI give somewhat different information about what's happening to the overall level of prices in the economy. There are three key differences between the two measures.

The first difference is that the GDP deflator measures the prices of all goods and services produced, whereas the CPI measures the prices of only the goods and services bought by consumers. Thus, an increase in the price of goods bought by firms or the government will show up in the GDP deflator but not in the CPI.

The second difference is that the GDP deflator includes only those goods produced domestically. Imported goods are not part of GDP and do not show up in the GDP deflator. Hence, an increase in the price of a Volkswagen made in Germany and sold in this country affects the CPI, because the Volkswagen is bought by consumers, but it does not affect the GDP deflator.

The third and most subtle difference results from the way the two measures aggregate the many prices in the economy. The CPI assigns fixed weights to the prices of different goods, whereas the GDP deflator assigns changing weights. In other words, the CPI is computed using a fixed basket of goods, whereas the GDP deflator allows the basket of goods to change over time as the composition of GDP changes. The following example shows how these approaches differ. Suppose that major frosts arrive early and destroy the nation's crop of apples. The quantity of apples produced falls to zero, and the price of the few apples that remain on grocers' shelves is driven sky-high. Because apples are no longer part of GDP, the increase in the price of apples does not show up in the GDP deflator. But because the CPI is computed with a fixed basket of goods that includes apples, the increase in the price of apples causes a substantial rise in the CPI.

Economists call a price index with a fixed basket of goods a *Laspeyres index* and a price index with a changing basket a *Paasche index*. Economic theorists have studied the properties of these different types of price indices to determine which is a better measure of the cost of living. The answer, it turns out, is that

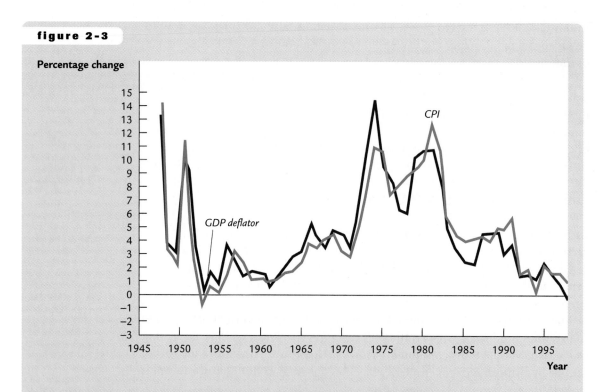

figure 2-3

Percentage change

The GDP Deflator and the CPI This figure shows the percentage change in the GDP deflator and in the CPI for every year since 1948. Although these two measures of prices diverge at times, they usually tell the same story about how quickly prices are rising. Both the CPI and the GDP deflator show that prices rose slowly in most of the 1950s and 1960s, that they rose much more quickly in the 1970s, and that they rose slowly again after the 1980s.

Source: Statistics Canada, CANSIM series P200000 and D15612.

neither is clearly superior. When prices of different goods are changing by different amounts, a Laspeyres (fixed basket) index tends to overstate the increase in the cost of living because it does not take into account that consumers have the opportunity to substitute less expensive goods for more expensive ones. By contrast, a Paasche (changing basket) index tends to understate the increase in the cost of living. While it accounts for the substitution of alternative goods, it does not reflect the reduction in consumers' welfare that may result from such substitutions.

The example of the destroyed apple crop shows the problems with Laspeyres and Paasche price indices. Because the CPI is a Laspeyres index, it overstates the impact of the increase in apple prices on consumers: by using a fixed basket of goods, it ignores consumers' ability to substitute other foods for apples. By contrast, because the GDP deflator is a Paasche index, it understates the impact on consumers: the GDP deflator shows no rise in prices, yet surely the higher price of apples makes consumers worse off.

Luckily, the difference between the GDP deflator and the CPI is usually not large in practice. Figure 2-3 shows the percentage change in the GDP deflator and the percentage change in the CPI for each year since 1948. Both measures usually tell the same story about how quickly prices are rising.

CASE STUDY

Difficulties in Measuring Inflation

From 1973 to 1976 prices in Canada rose at a very rapid pace. But exactly how much did they rise? This question was asked by public policymakers who had to judge the seriousness of the inflation problem. It was also asked by private decisionmakers: many private contracts, such as wage agreements and pensions, are indexed to correct for the effects of rising prices.

The magnitude of the price rise depends on which measure of prices one uses. According to the GDP deflator, prices rose an average of 10.5 percent per year during these four years. According to the CPI, prices rose 9.2 percent per year. Over the four-year period, the accumulated difference is over 5 percent.

This discrepancy is partly attributable to the large increase in the price of natural resources that occurred in the mid-1970s. A significant part of the Canadian economy involves primary commodity industries. As a result, big price increases in these commodities make a significant contribution to the overall inflation rate as measured by the GDP deflator. But since households spend a lower proportion of their incomes on these products, natural resource price increases have a smaller impact on inflation as measured by the CPI.

A similar discrepancy between the two price indices emerged in the 1990s. At this time, the relative prices for primary commodities had fallen to their lowest levels in 60 years. This development, which was particularly hard on many individuals, such as western farmers, caused the GDP deflator to increase at a slower rate than the CPI. During the 1990–1994 period, the cumulative difference in the two measures was 6 percent.

When price indices differ, as they did during these episodes of commodity price volatility, it is usually possible to identify the sources of the differences. Yet accounting for the differences is easier than deciding which index provides the better measure. Furthermore, which index one should use in practice is not merely a question of measurement; it also depends on one's purpose. In practice, government programs and private contracts usually use the CPI to measure the level of prices, despite the fact that we know the CPI is biased in the upward direction. The magnitude of that upward bias is about one-half of one percentage point.[3] Thus, we should interpret an annual inflation rate for the CPI in the 0.5 range as evidence that we have reached "zero" inflation.

In addition to the substitution bias, a second problem is the introduction of new goods. When a new good is introduced into the marketplace, consumers are better off, because they have more products from which to choose. In effect, the introduction of new goods increases the real value of the dollar. Yet this increase in the purchasing power of the dollar is not reflected in a lower CPI.

A third problem is unmeasured changes in quality. When a firm changes the quality of a good it sells, not all of the good's price change reflects a change in the cost of living. Statistics Canada does its best to account for changes in the quality of goods over time. For example, if Ford increases the horsepower of a particular car model from one year to the next, the CPI will reflect the change: the quality-adjusted price of the car will not rise as fast as the unadjusted price. Yet many changes in quality, such as comfort or safety, are hard to measure. If unmeasured quality improvement (rather than unmeasured quality deterioration) is typical, then the measured CPI rises faster than it should.

2-3 | Measuring Joblessness: The Unemployment Rate

One aspect of economic performance is how well an economy uses its resources. Because an economy's workers are its chief resource, keeping workers employed is a paramount concern of economic policymakers. The unemployment rate is the statistic that measures the percentage of those people wanting to work who do not have jobs.

Every month Statistics Canada computes the unemployment rate and many other statistics with which economists and policymakers monitor developments in the labour market. These statistics come from the Labour Force Survey of about 56,000 households. Based on the responses to survey questions, each

---

[3] Allan Crawford, "Measuring Biases in the Canadian CPI," in *Bank of Canada Technical Report No. 64*(1993), and Pierre Fortin, "Do We Measure Inflation Correctly?" in *Zero Inflation: The Goal of Price Stability*, R.G. Lipsey, ed. (Toronto: C.D. Howe Institute, 1990).

adult (15 years and older) in each household is placed into one of three categories: employed, unemployed, or not in the labour force. A person is employed if he or she spent most of the previous week working at a paid job, as opposed to keeping house, going to school, or doing something else. A person is unemployed if he or she is not employed and is waiting for the start date of a new job, is on temporary lay-off, or has been looking for a job. A person who fits into

"Well, so long, Eddie. The recession's over."

Drawing by M. Stevens; © 1980 The New Yorker Magazine, Inc.

neither of the first two categories, such as a student or retiree, is not in the labour force. A person who wants a job but has given up looking—a *discouraged worker*—is counted as not being in the labour force.

The **labour force** is defined as the sum of the employed and unemployed, and the **unemployment rate** is defined as the percentage of the labour force that is unemployed. That is,

$$\text{Labour Force} = \text{Number of Employed} + \text{Number of Unemployed},$$

and

$$\text{Unemployment Rate} = \frac{\text{Number of Unemployed}}{\text{Labour Force}} \times 100.$$

A related statistic is the **labour-force participation rate,** the percentage of the adult population that is in the labour force:

$$\text{Labour-Force Participation Rate} = \frac{\text{Labour Force}}{\text{Adult Population}} \times 100.$$

Statistics Canada computes these statistics for the overall population and for groups within the population: men and women, teenagers and prime-age workers.

Figure 2-4 shows the breakdown of the population into the three categories for 1998. The statistics broke down as follows:

$$\text{Labour Force} = 14.33 + 1.30 = 15.63 \text{ million.}$$
$$\text{Unemployment Rate} = (1.3/15.63) \times 100 = 8.3\%.$$
$$\text{Labour-Force Participation Rate} = (15.63/24.0) \times 100 = 65.1\%.$$

Hence, about two-thirds of the adult population was in the labour force, and 8.3 percent of those in the labour force did not have a job.

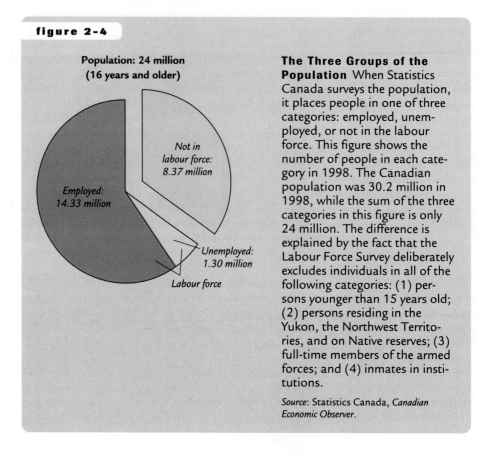

figure 2-4

Population: 24 million
(16 years and older)

Not in labour force:
8.37 million

Employed:
14.33 million

Unemployed:
1.30 million

Labour force

The Three Groups of the Population When Statistics Canada surveys the population, it places people in one of three categories: employed, unemployed, or not in the labour force. This figure shows the number of people in each category in 1998. The Canadian population was 30.2 million in 1998, while the sum of the three categories in this figure is only 24 million. The difference is explained by the fact that the Labour Force Survey deliberately excludes individuals in all of the following categories: (1) persons younger than 15 years old; (2) persons residing in the Yukon, the Northwest Territories, and on Native reserves; (3) full-time members of the armed forces; and (4) inmates in institutions.

Source: Statistics Canada, *Canadian Economic Observer*.

CASE STUDY

Unemployment, GDP, and Okun's Law

What relationship should we expect to find between unemployment and real GDP? Because employed workers help to produce goods and services and unemployed workers do not, increases in the unemployment rate should be associated with decreases in real GDP. This negative relationship between unemployment and GDP is called **Okun's law,** after Arthur Okun, the economist who first studied it.[4]

Figure 2-5 uses annual data for Canada to illustrate Okun's law. This figure is a scatterplot—a scatter of points where each point represents one observation (in this case, the data for a particular year). The vertical axis represents the change in the unemployment rate from the previous year, and the horizontal

---

[4] Arthur M. Okun, "Potential GNP: Its Measurement and Significance," in *Proceedings of the Business and Economics Statistics Section, American Statistical Association* (Washington, DC: American Statistical Association, 1962), 98–103; reprinted in Arthur M. Okun, *Economics for Policymaking* (Cambridge, MA: MIT Press, 1983), 145–158.

figure 2-5

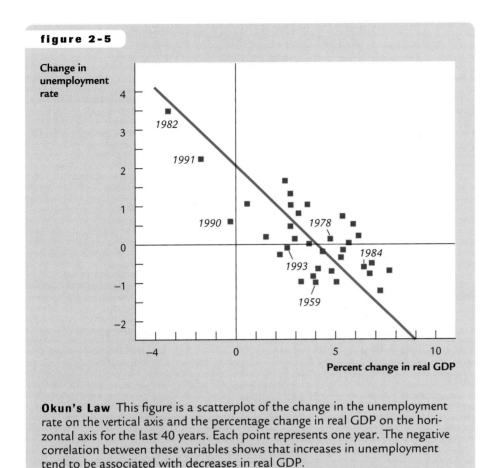

Okun's Law This figure is a scatterplot of the change in the unemployment rate on the vertical axis and the percentage change in real GDP on the horizontal axis for the last 40 years. Each point represents one year. The negative correlation between these variables shows that increases in unemployment tend to be associated with decreases in real GDP.

Source: Statistics Canada, CANSIM series D14872 and D984952.

axis represents the percentage change in GDP. This figure shows clearly that year-to-year changes in the unemployment rate are closely associated with year-to-year changes in real GDP.

We can be more precise about the magnitude of the Okun's law relationship. The summary line drawn through the scatter of points tells us that

$$\text{Change in the Unemployment Rate} = -0.5 \left[\left(\begin{array}{c} \text{Percent Change} \\ \text{in Real GDP} \end{array} \right) - 4 \right]$$

On average, real GDP has grown by about 4 percent each year since 1950; this normal growth is due to population growth, capital accumulation, and technological progress. Okun's law indicates that this is roughly the amount of growth that is necessary to keep the growth in the number of jobs in pace with the growing size of the labour force—so that the unemployment rate can stay constant. If, however, real GDP growth is only 3 percent, this relationship tells us that the unemployment rate will rise by about one-half of one percentage point.

The implications for unemployment are more dramatic in a recession (when real GDP growth is negative). For example, when real growth is −1 percent, unemployment rises by 0.5 (1 + 4) = 2.5 percentage points. Policymakers often try to stabilize GDP growth around its long-run average value, with a view toward minimizing these disruptive swings in the unemployment rate.

2-4 | Conclusion: From Economic Statistics to Economic Models

The three statistics discussed in this chapter—gross domestic product, the consumer price index, and the unemployment rate—quantify the performance of the economy. Public and private decisionmakers use these statistics to monitor changes in the economy and to formulate appropriate policies. Economists use these statistics to develop and test theories about how the economy works.

In the chapters that follow, we examine some of these theories. That is, we build models that explain how these variables are determined and how economic policy affects them. Chapters 3, 4, and 5 study models of GDP, Chapter 6 studies unemployment, and Chapter 7 studies inflation. Having learned how to measure economic performance, we now learn how to explain it.

Summary

1. Gross domestic product (GDP) measures both the total output of the economy and the total expenditure on the economy's output of goods and services. GNP, which is GDP minus the net income earned by foreigners operating in Canada, measures the total income of all Canadians.

2. Nominal GDP values goods and services at current prices. Real GDP values goods and services at constant prices. Real GDP rises only when the amount of goods and services has increased, whereas nominal GDP can rise either because output has increased or because prices have increased.

3. GDP is the sum of four categories of expenditure: consumption, investment, government purchases, and net exports.

4. The consumer price index (CPI) measures the price of a fixed basket of goods and services purchased by a typical consumer. Like the GDP deflator, which is the ratio of nominal GDP to real GDP, the CPI measures the overall level of prices.

5. The unemployment rate shows what fraction of those who would like to work do not have a job. When the unemployment rate rises, real GDP typically grows slower than its normal rate and may even fall.

KEY CONCEPTS

Gross domestic product (GDP)

Consumer price index (CPI)

Unemployment rate

Gross national product (GNP)

National accounting

Stocks and flows

Value added

Imputed value

Nominal versus real GDP

GDP deflator

National accounts identity

Consumption

Investment

Government purchases

Net exports

Labour force

Labour-force participation rate

Okun's law

QUESTIONS FOR REVIEW

1. List the two things that GDP measures. How can GDP measure two things at once?

2. What does the consumer price index measure?

3. List the three categories used by Statistics Canada to classify everyone in the economy. How is the unemployment rate calculated?

4. Explain Okun's law.

PROBLEMS AND APPLICATIONS

1. Look at the newspapers for the past few days. What new economic statistics have been released? How do you interpret these statistics?

2. A farmer grows some wheat and sells it to a miller for $1.00. The miller turns the wheat into flour and then sells the flour to a baker for $3.00. The baker uses the flour to make bread and sells the bread to an engineer for $6.00. The engineer eats the bread. What is the value added by each person? What is GDP?

3. Suppose that a woman marries her butler. After they are married, her husband continues to wait on her as before, and she continues to support him as before (but as a husband rather than as an employee). How does the marriage affect GDP? How should it affect GDP?

4. Place each of the following transactions in one of the four components of expenditure: consumption, investment, government purchases, and net exports.

   a. A domestic airline manufacturer sells an airplane to the government.

   b. A domestic airline manufacturer sells an airplane to a domestic airline operator.

   c. A domestic airline manufacturer sells an airplane to Air France.

   d. A domestic airline manufacturer sells an airplane to a Canadian golf professional.

   e. A domestic airline manufacturer builds an airplane to be sold next year.

5. Find data on GDP and its components, and compute the percentage of GDP for the following components for 1950, 1970, and 1990.

a. Personal consumption expenditures

b. Gross private domestic investment

c. Government purchases

d. Net exports

e. Federal government purchases

f. Provincial and municipal government purchases

g. Imports

Do you see any stable relationships in the data? Do you see any trends? (*Hint:* A good place to look for data is the Historical Statistical Supplement of the *Canadian Economic Observer*—an annual summary publication of Statistics Canada. Alternatively, you can access Statistics Canada over the internet. Follow the suggestions described in the preface to this book.

6. Consider an economy that produces and consumes bread and automobiles. In the table below are data for two different years.

	Year 2000	Year 2010
Price of an automobile	$50,000	$60,000
Price of a loaf of bread	$10	$20
Number of automobiles produced	100	120
Number of loaves of bread produced	500,000	400,000

a. Using the year 2000 as the base year, compute the following statistics for each year: nominal GDP, real GDP, the implicit price deflator for GDP, and a fixed-weight price index such as the CPI.

b. How much have prices risen between year 2000 and year 2010? Compare the answers given by the Laspeyres and Paasche price indices. Explain the difference.

c. Suppose you are a member of Parliament writing a bill to update the indexing provisions for the Canada Pension Plan. Would you use the GDP deflator or the CPI? Why?

7. Abby consumes only apples. In year 1, red apples cost $1 each, green apples cost $2 each, and Abby buys 10 red apples. In year 2, red apples cost $2, green apples cost $1, and Abby buys 10 green apples.

a. Compute a consumer price index for apples for each year. Assume that year 1 is the base year in which the consumer basket is fixed. How does your index change from year 1 to year 2?

b. Compute Abby's nominal spending on apples in each year. How does it change from year 1 to year 2?

c. Using year 1 as the base year, compute Abby's real spending on apples in each year. How does it change from year 1 to year 2?

d. Defining the implicit price deflator as nominal spending divided by real spending, compute the deflator for each year. How does the deflator change from year 1 to year 2?

e. Suppose that Abby is equally happy eating red or green apples. How much has the true cost of living increased for Abby? Compare this answer to your answers to parts (a) and (d). What does this example tell you about Laspeyres and Paasche price indices?

8. Consider how each of the following events is likely to affect real GDP. Do you think the change in real GDP reflects a similar change in economic well-being?

a. A hurricane in Ontario forces Canada's Wonderland to shut down for a month.

b. The discovery of a new, easy-to-grow strain of wheat increases farm harvests.

c. Increased hostility between unions and management sparks a rash of strikes.

d. Firms throughout the economy experience falling demand, causing them to lay off workers.

e. The government passes new environmental laws that prohibit firms from using production methods that emit large quantities of pollution.

f. More high-school students drop out of school to take jobs mowing lawns.

g. Fathers around the country reduce their workweeks to spend more time with their children.

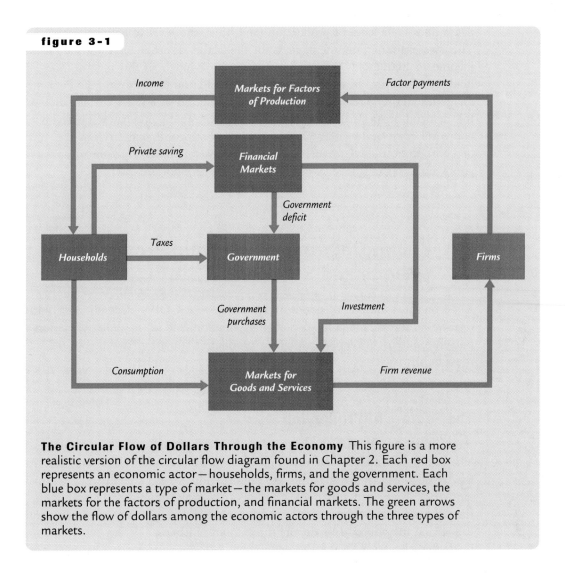

figure 3-1

The Circular Flow of Dollars Through the Economy This figure is a more realistic version of the circular flow diagram found in Chapter 2. Each red box represents an economic actor—households, firms, and the government. Each blue box represents a type of market—the markets for goods and services, the markets for the factors of production, and financial markets. The green arrows show the flow of dollars among the economic actors through the three types of markets.

households, firms, and the government—and how dollars flow among them through the various markets in the economy.

Let's look at the flow of dollars from the viewpoints of these economic actors. Households receive income and use it to pay taxes to the government, to consume goods and services, and to save through the financial markets. Firms receive revenue from the sale of goods and services and use it to pay for the factors of production. Both households and firms borrow in financial markets to buy investment goods, such as housing, plant, and equipment. The government receives revenue from taxes, uses it to pay for government purchases, and, if it spends more than it receives, borrows in the financial markets to cover the deficit.

In this chapter we develop a basic classical model to explain the economic interactions depicted in Figure 3-1. We begin with firms and look at what determines their level of production (and, thus, the level of national income). Then we examine how the markets for the factors of production distribute this income to households. Next, we consider how much of this income households consume and how much they save. In addition to discussing the demand for goods and services arising from the consumption of households, we discuss the demand arising from investment and government purchases. Finally, we come full circle and examine how the demand for goods and services (the sum of consumption, investment, and government purchases) and the supply of goods and services (the level of production) are brought into balance.

3-1 | What Determines the Total Production of Goods and Services?

An economy's output of goods and services—its GDP—depends on (1) its quantity of inputs, called the factors of production, and (2) its ability to turn inputs into output, as represented by the production function. We discuss each of these in turn.

The Factors of Production

Factors of production are the inputs used to produce goods and services. The two most important factors of production are capital and labour. Capital is the set of tools that workers use: the construction worker's crane, the accountant's calculator, and this book's authors' personal computers. Labour is the time people spend working. We use the symbol K to denote the amount of capital and the symbol L to denote the amount of labour.

In this chapter we take the economy's factors of production as given. In other words, we assume that the economy has a fixed amount of capital and a fixed amount of labour. We write

$$K = \overline{K}.$$
$$L = \overline{L}.$$

The overbar means that each variable is fixed at some level. In Chapter 4 we examine what happens when the factors of production change over time, as they do in the real world. For now, to keep our analysis simple, we assume fixed amounts of capital and labour.

We also assume here that the factors of production are fully utilized—that is, that no resources are wasted. Again, in the real world, part of the labour force is unemployed, and some capital lies idle. In Chapter 6 we examine the reasons for unemployment, but for now we assume that capital and labour are fully employed.

The Production Function

The available production technology determines how much output is produced from given amounts of capital and labour. Economists express the available technology using a **production function.** Letting Y denote the amount of output, we write the production function as

$$Y = F(K, L).$$

This equation states that output is a function of the amount of capital and the amount of labour.

The production function reflects the available technology for turning capital and labour into output. If someone invents a better way to produce a good, the result is more output from the same amounts of capital and labour. Thus, technological change alters the production function.

Many production functions have a property called **constant returns to scale.** A production function has constant returns to scale if an increase of an equal percentage in all factors of production causes an increase in output of the same percentage. If the production function has constant returns to scale, then we get 10 percent more output when we increase both capital and labour by 10 percent. Mathematically, a production function has constant returns to scale if

$$zY = F(zK, zL)$$

for any positive number z. This equation says that if we multiply both the amount of capital and the amount of labour by some number z, output is also multiplied by z. In the next section we see that the assumption of constant returns to scale has an important implication for how the income from production is distributed.

As an example of a production function, consider production at a bakery. The kitchen and its equipment are the bakery's capital, the workers hired to make the bread are its labour, and the loaves of bread are its output. The bakery's production function shows that the number of loaves produced depends on the amount of equipment and the number of workers. If the production function has constant returns to scale, then doubling the amount of equipment and the number of workers doubles the amount of bread produced.

The Supply of Goods and Services

We can now see that the factors of production and the production function together determine the quantity of goods and services supplied, which in turn equals the economy's output. To express this mathematically, we write

$$Y = F(\overline{K}, \overline{L})$$
$$= \overline{Y}.$$

In this chapter, because we assume that the supplies of capital and labour and the technology are fixed, output is also fixed (at a level denoted here as $\overline{Y}$).

When we discuss economic growth in Chapters 4 and 5, we will examine how increases in capital and labour and improvements in the production technology lead to growth in the economy's output.

3-2 | How Is National Income Distributed to the Factors of Production?

As we discussed in Chapter 2, the total output of an economy equals its total income. Because the factors of production and the production function together determine the total output of goods and services, they also determine national income. The circular flow diagram in Figure 3-1 shows that this national income flows from firms to households through the markets for the factors of production.

In this section we continue developing our model of the economy by discussing how these factor markets work. Economists have long studied factor markets to understand the distribution of income. (For example, Karl Marx, the noted nineteenth-century economist, spent much time trying to explain the incomes of capital and labour. The political philosophy of communism was in part based on Marx's now-discredited theory.) Here we examine the modern theory of how national income is divided among the factors of production. This theory, called the *neoclassical theory of distribution*, is accepted by most economists today.

Factor Prices

The distribution of national income is determined by factor prices. **Factor prices** are the amounts paid to the factors of production—the wage workers earn and the rent the owners of capital collect. As Figure 3-2 illustrates, the rental price each factor of production receives for its services is in turn determined by the supply and demand for that factor. Because we have assumed that the economy's factors of production are fixed, the factor supply curve in Figure 3-2 is vertical. The intersection of the downward-sloping factor demand curve and the vertical supply curve determines the equilibrium factor price.

To understand factor prices and the distribution of income, we must examine the demand for the factors of production. Because factor demand arises from the thousands of firms that use capital and labour, we now look at the decisions faced by a typical firm about how much of these factors to employ.

The Decisions Facing the Competitive Firm

The simplest assumption to make about a typical firm is that it is **competitive.** A competitive firm is small relative to the markets in which it trades, so it has little influence on market prices. For example, our firm produces a good and

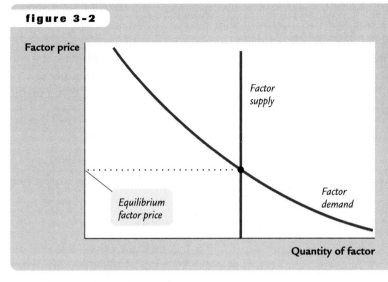

figure 3-2

Factor price

Factor supply

Equilibrium factor price

Factor demand

Quantity of factor

How a Factor of Production Is Compensated The price paid to any factor of production depends on the supply and demand for that factor's services. Because we have assumed that supply is fixed, the supply curve is vertical. The demand curve is downward sloping. The intersection of supply and demand determines the equilibrium factor price.

sells it at the market price. Because many firms produce this good, our firm can sell as much as it wants without causing the price of the good to fall, or it can stop selling altogether without causing the price of the good to rise. Similarly, our firm cannot influence the wages of the workers it employs because many other local firms also employ workers. The firm has no reason to pay more than the market wage, and if it tried to pay less, its workers would take jobs elsewhere. Therefore, the competitive firm takes the prices of its output and its inputs as given.

To make its product, the firm needs two factors of production, capital and labour. As we did for the aggregate economy, we represent the firm's production technology by the production function

$$Y = F(K, L),$$

where Y is the number of units produced (the firm's output), K the number of machines used (the amount of capital), and L the number of hours worked by the firm's employees (the amount of labour). The firm produces more output if it has more machines or if its employees work more hours.

The firm sells its output at a price P, hires workers at a wage W, and rents capital at a rate R. Notice that when we speak of firms renting capital, we are assuming that households own the economy's stock of capital. In this analysis, households rent out their capital, just as they sell their labour. The firm obtains both factors of production from the households that own them.[1]

---

[1] This is a simplification. In the real world, the ownership of capital is indirect because firms own capital and households own the firms. That is, real firms have two functions: owning capital and producing output. To help us understand how the factors of production are compensated, however, we assume that firms only produce output and that households own capital directly.

The goal of the firm is to maximize profit. *Profit* is revenue minus costs—it is what the owners of the firm keep after paying for the costs of production. Revenue equals $P \times Y$, the selling price of the good P multiplied by the amount of the good the firm produces Y. Costs include both labour costs and capital costs. Labour costs equal $W \times L$, the wage W times the amount of labour L. Capital costs equal $R \times K$, the rental price of capital R times the amount of capital K. We can write

$$\text{Profit} = \text{Revenue} - \text{Labour Costs} - \text{Capital Costs}$$
$$= PY - WL - RK.$$

To see how profit depends on the factors of production, we use the production function $Y = F(K, L)$ to substitute for Y to obtain

$$\text{Profit} = PF(K, L) - WL - RK.$$

This equation shows that profit depends on the product price P, the factor prices W and R, and the factor quantities L and K. The competitive firm takes the product price and the factor prices as given and chooses the amounts of labour and capital that maximize profit.

The Firm's Demand for Factors

We now know that our firm will hire labour and rent capital in the quantities that maximize profit. But how does it figure out what those profit-maximizing quantities are? To answer this question, we first consider the quantity of labour and then the quantity of capital.

The Marginal Product of Labour   The more labour the firm employs, the more output it produces. The **marginal product of labour (MPL)** is the extra amount of output the firm gets from one extra unit of labour, holding the amount of capital fixed. We can express this using the production function:

$$MPL = F(K, L + 1) - F(K, L).$$

The first term on the right-hand side is the amount of output produced with K units of capital and $L + 1$ units of labour; the second term is the amount of output produced with K units of capital and L units of labour. This equation states that the marginal product of labour is the difference between the amount of output produced with $L + 1$ units of labour and the amount produced with only L units of labour.

Most production functions have the property of **diminishing marginal product:** holding the amount of capital fixed, the marginal product of labour decreases as the amount of labour increases. For example, consider again the production of bread at a bakery. As a bakery hires more labour, it produces more bread. The *MPL* is the amount of extra bread produced when an extra unit of labour is hired. As more labour is added to a fixed amount of capital, however, the *MPL* falls. Fewer additional loaves are produced because workers are less productive when the kitchen is more crowded. In other words, holding the size of the kitchen fixed, each additional worker adds fewer loaves of bread to the bakery's output.

Figure 3-3 graphs the production function. It illustrates what happens to the amount of output when we hold the amount of capital constant and vary the amount of labour. This figure shows that the marginal product of labour is the slope of the production function. As the amount of labour increases, the production function becomes flatter, indicating diminishing marginal product.

From the Marginal Product of Labour to Labour Demand When the competitive, profit-maximizing firm is deciding whether to hire an additional unit of labour, it considers how that decision would affect profits. It therefore compares the extra revenue from the increased production that results from the added labour to the extra cost of higher spending on wages. The increase in revenue from

figure 3-3

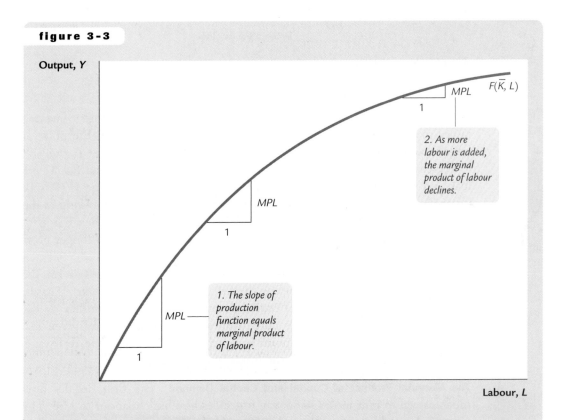

The Production Function This curve shows how output depends on labour input, holding the amount of capital constant. The marginal product of labour *MPL* is the change in output when the labour input is increased by 1 unit. As the amount of labour increases, the production function becomes flatter, indicating diminishing marginal product.

an additional unit of labour depends on two variables: the marginal product of labour and the price of the output. Because an extra unit of labour produces *MPL* units of output and each unit of output sells for *P* dollars, the extra revenue is *P* × *MPL*. The extra cost of hiring one more unit of labour is the wage *W*. Thus, the change in profit from hiring an additional unit of labour is

$$\Delta\text{Profit} = \Delta\text{Revenue} - \Delta\text{Cost}$$
$$= (P \times MPL) - W.$$

The symbol Δ (called *delta*) denotes the change in a variable.

We can now answer the question we asked at the beginning of this section: How much labour does the firm hire? The firm's manager knows that if the extra revenue *P* × *MPL* exceeds the wage *W*, an extra unit of labour increases profit. Therefore, the manager continues to hire labour until the next unit would no longer be profitable—that is, until the *MPL* falls to the point where the extra revenue equals the wage. The firm's demand for labour is determined by

$$P \times MPL = W.$$

We can also write this as

$$MPL = W/P.$$

W/P is the **real wage**—the payment to labour measured in units of output rather than in dollars. To maximize profit, the firm hires up to the point at which the marginal product of labour equals the real wage.

For example, again consider a bakery. Suppose the price of bread *P* is $2 per loaf, and a worker earns a wage *W* of $20 per hour. The real wage *W/P* is 10 loaves per hour. In this example, the firm keeps hiring workers as long as the additional worker would produce at least 10 loaves per hour. When the *MPL* falls to 10 loaves per hour or less, hiring additional workers is no longer profitable.

Figure 3-4 shows how the marginal product of labour depends on the amount of labour employed (holding the firm's capital stock constant). That is, this figure graphs the *MPL* schedule. Because the *MPL* diminishes as the amount of labour increases, this curve slopes downward. For any given real wage, the firm hires up to the point at which the *MPL* equals the real wage. Hence, the *MPL* schedule is also the firm's labour demand curve.

The Marginal Product of Capital and Capital Demand The firm decides how much capital to rent in the same way it decides how much labour to hire. The **marginal product of capital (MPK)** is the amount of extra output the firm gets from an extra unit of capital, holding the amount of labour constant:

$$MPK = F(K + 1, L) - F(K, L).$$

Thus, the marginal product of capital is the difference between the amount of output produced with *K* + 1 units of capital and that produced with only *K* units of capital. Like labour, capital is subject to diminishing marginal product.

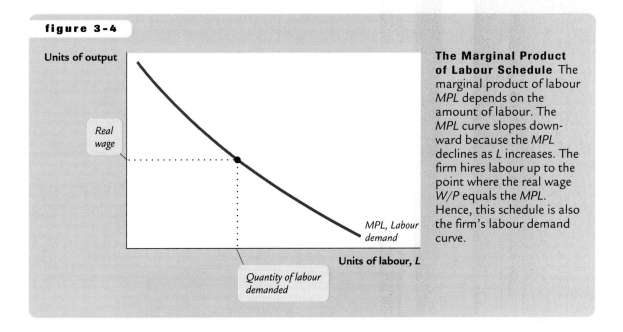

figure 3-4

Units of output

Real wage

MPL, Labour demand

Units of labour, *L*

Quantity of labour demanded

The Marginal Product of Labour Schedule The marginal product of labour *MPL* depends on the amount of labour. The *MPL* curve slopes downward because the *MPL* declines as *L* increases. The firm hires labour up to the point where the real wage *W/P* equals the *MPL*. Hence, this schedule is also the firm's labour demand curve.

The increase in profit from renting an additional machine is the extra revenue from selling the output of that machine minus the machine's rental price:

$$\Delta\text{Profit} = \Delta\text{Revenue} - \Delta\text{Cost}$$
$$= (P \times MPK) - R.$$

To maximize profit, the firm continues to rent more capital until the *MPK* falls to equal the real rental price:

$$MPK = R/P.$$

The **real rental price of capital** is the rental price measured in units of goods rather than in dollars.

To sum up, the competitive, profit-maximizing firm follows a simple rule about how much labour to hire and how much capital to rent. *The firm demands each factor of production until that factor's marginal product falls to equal its real factor price.*

The Division of National Income

Having analyzed how a firm decides how much of each factor to employ, we can now explain how the markets for the factors of production distribute the economy's total income. If all firms in the economy are competitive and profit-maximizing, then each factor of production is paid its marginal contribution to the production process. The real wage paid to each worker equals the *MPL*, and the real rental price paid to each owner of capital equals the *MPK*. The total real wages paid to labour are therefore *MPL* × *L*, and the total real return paid to capital owners is *MPK* × *K*.

The income that remains after the firms have paid the factors of production is the **economic profit** of the owners of the firms. Real economic profit is

$$\text{Economic Profit} = Y - (MPL \times L) - (MPK \times K).$$

Because we want to examine the distribution of national income, we rearrange the terms as follows:

$$Y = (MPL \times L) + (MPK \times K) + \text{Economic Profit}.$$

Total income is divided among the return to labour, the return to capital, and economic profit.

How large is economic profit? The answer is surprising: if the production function has the property of constant returns to scale, as is often thought to be the case, then economic profit must be zero. That is, nothing is left after the factors of production are paid. This conclusion follows from a famous mathematical result called *Euler's theorem,*[2] which states that if the production function has constant returns to scale, then

$$F(K, L) = (MPK \times K) + (MPL \times L).$$

If each factor of production is paid its marginal product, then the sum of these factor payments equals total output. In other words, constant returns to scale, profit maximization, and competition together imply that economic profit is zero.

If economic profit is zero, how can we explain the existence of "profit" in the economy? The answer is that the term "profit" as normally used is different from economic profit. We have been assuming that there are three types of agents: workers, owners of capital, and owners of firms. Total income is divided among wages, return to capital, and economic profit. In the real world, however, most firms own rather than rent the capital they use. Because firm owners and capital owners are the same people, economic profit and the return to capital are often lumped together. If we call this alternative definition **accounting profit,** we can say that

$$\text{Accounting Profit} = \text{Economic Profit} + (MPK \times K).$$

Under our assumptions—constant returns to scale, profit maximization, and competition—economic profit is zero. If these assumptions approximately describe the world, then the "profit" in the national income accounts must be mostly the return to capital.

We can now answer the question posed at the beginning of this chapter about how the income of the economy is distributed from firms to households. Each factor of production is paid its marginal product, and these factor payments exhaust total output. *Total output is divided between the payments to capital and the payments to labour, depending on their marginal productivities.*

---

[2] *Mathematical note:* To prove Euler's theorem, begin with the definition of constant returns to scale: $zY = F(zK, zL)$. Now differentiate with respect to z and then evaluate at $z = 1$.

CASE STUDY

The Black Death and Factor Prices

As we have just learned, in the neoclassical theory of distribution, factor prices equal the marginal products of the factors of production. Because the marginal products depend on the quantities of the factors, a change in the quantity of any one factor alters the marginal products of all the factors. Therefore, a change in the supply of a factor alters equilibrium factor prices.

Fourteenth-century Europe provides a vivid example of how factor quantities affect factor prices. The outbreak of the bubonic plague—the Black Death—in 1348 reduced the population of Europe by about one-third within a few years. Because the marginal product of labour increases as the amount of labour falls, this massive reduction in the labour force raised the marginal product of labour. (The economy moved to the left along the curves in Figures 3-3 and 3-4.) Real wages did increase substantially during the plague years—doubling, by some estimates. The peasants who were fortunate enough to survive the plague enjoyed economic prosperity.

The reduction in the labour force caused by the plague also affected the return to land, the other major factor of production in medieval Europe. With fewer workers available to farm the land, an additional unit of land produced less additional output. This fall in the marginal product of land led to a decline in real rents of 50 percent or more. Thus, while the peasant classes prospered, the landed classes suffered reduced incomes.[3]

3-3 | What Determines the Demand for Goods and Services?

We have seen what determines the level of production and how the income from production is distributed to workers and owners of capital. We now continue our tour of the circular flow diagram, Figure 3-1, and examine how the output from production is used.

In Chapter 2 we identified the four components of GDP:

➤ Consumption (C)

➤ Investment (I)

➤ Government purchases (G)

➤ Net exports (NX).

---

[3] Carlo M. Cipolla, *Before the Industrial Revolution: European Society and Economy, 1000–1700,* 2d ed. (New York: Norton, 1980), 200–202.

The circular flow diagram contains only the first three components. For now, to simplify the analysis, we assume a *closed economy*—a country that does not trade with other countries. Thus, net exports are always zero. (We examine the macroeconomics of *open economies* in Chapter 8.)

A closed economy has three uses for the goods and services it produces. These three components of GDP are expressed in the national accounts identity:

$$Y = C + I + G.$$

Households consume some of the economy's output; firms and households use some of the output for investment; and the government buys some of the output for public purposes. We want to see how GDP is allocated among these three uses.

Consumption

When we eat food, wear clothing, or go to a movie, we are consuming some of the output of the economy. All forms of consumption together make up 59 percent of GDP. Because consumption is so large, macroeconomists have devoted much energy to studying how households decide how much to consume. Chapter 16 examines this work in detail. Here we consider the simplest story of consumer behaviour.

Households receive income from their labour and their ownership of capital, pay taxes to the government, and then decide how much of their after-tax income to consume and how much to save. As we discussed in Section 3-2, the income that households receive equals the output of the economy Y. The government then taxes households an amount T. (Although the government imposes many kinds of taxes, such as personal and corporate income taxes and sales taxes, for our purposes we can lump all these taxes together.) We define income after the payment of all taxes, $Y - T$, as **disposable income.** Households divide their disposable income between consumption and saving.

We assume that the level of consumption depends directly on the level of disposable income. The higher is disposable income, the greater is consumption. Thus,

$$C = C(Y - T).$$

This equation states that consumption is a function of disposable income. The relationship between consumption and disposable income is called the **consumption function.**

The **marginal propensity to consume (*MPC*)** is the amount by which consumption changes when disposable income increases by one dollar. The *MPC* is between zero and one: an extra dollar of income increases consumption, but by less than one dollar. Thus, if households obtain an extra dollar of income, they save a portion of it. For example, if the *MPC* is 0.7, then households spend 70 cents of each additional dollar of disposable income on consumer goods and services and save 30 cents.

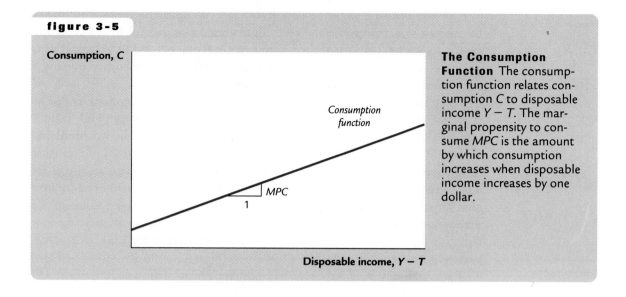

figure 3-5

Consumption, C

Consumption function

MPC

1

Disposable income, Y − T

The Consumption Function The consumption function relates consumption C to disposable income Y − T. The marginal propensity to consume MPC is the amount by which consumption increases when disposable income increases by one dollar.

Figure 3-5 illustrates the consumption function. The slope of the consumption function tells us how much consumption increases when disposable income increases by one dollar. That is, the slope of the consumption function is the *MPC*.

Investment

Both firms and households purchase investment goods. Firms buy investment goods to add to their stock of capital and to replace existing capital as it wears out. Households buy new houses, which are also part of investment. Total investment in Canada averages about 17 percent of GDP.

The quantity of investment goods demanded depends on the interest rate, which measures the cost of the funds used to finance investment. For an investment project to be profitable, its return (the revenue from increased future production of goods and services) must exceed its cost (the payments for borrowed funds). If the interest rate rises, fewer investment projects are profitable, and the quantity of investment goods demanded falls.

For example, suppose that a firm is considering whether it should build a $1 million factory that would yield a return of $100,000 per year, or 10 percent. The firm compares this return to the cost of borrowing the $1 million. If the interest rate is below 10 percent, the firm borrows the money in financial markets and makes the investment. If the interest rate is above 10 percent, the firm forgoes the investment opportunity and does not build the factory.

The firm makes the same investment decision even if it does not have to borrow the $1 million but rather uses its own funds. The firm can always deposit this money in a bank or a money market fund and earn interest on it. Building the factory is more profitable than the deposit if and only if the interest rate is less than the 10 percent return on the factory.

A person wanting to buy a new house faces a similar decision. The higher the interest rate, the greater the cost of carrying a mortgage. A $100,000 mortgage costs $8,000 per year if the interest rate is 8 percent and $10,000 per year if the interest rate is 10 percent. As the interest rate rises, the cost of owning a home rises, and the demand for new homes falls.

When studying the role of interest rates in the economy, economists distinguish between the nominal interest rate and the real interest rate. This distinction is relevant when the overall level of prices is changing. The **nominal interest rate** is the interest rate as usually reported: it is the rate of interest that investors pay to borrow money. The **real interest rate** is the nominal interest rate corrected for the effects of inflation. To see how nominal and real interest rates differ, consider a firm that decides to build a new factory and borrows the money from a bank at an interest rate of 8 percent. The nominal interest rate is therefore 8 percent—that is, the amount the firm owes to the bank grows by 8 percent per year.

If prices are rising by 3 percent per year, the dollars with which the firm will repay the bank are losing 3 percent of their value per year. Each year the firm owes 8 percent more dollars, but the dollars are worth 3 percent less. Since the firm got to spend the original dollars and then only has to pay back dollars with lower purchasing power, the real burden to the firm is only growing at 5 percent. Thus, the real interest rate is 5 percent, the difference between the nominal interest rate and the rate of inflation. In Chapter 7 we discuss the relation between nominal and real interest rates in detail. Here it is sufficient to note that the real interest rate measures the true cost of borrowing and, thus, determines the quantity of investment.

We can summarize this discussion with an equation relating investment I to the real interest rate r:

$$I = I(r).$$

Figure 3-6 shows this investment function. It slopes downward, because as the interest rate rises, the quantity of investment demanded falls.

figure 3-6

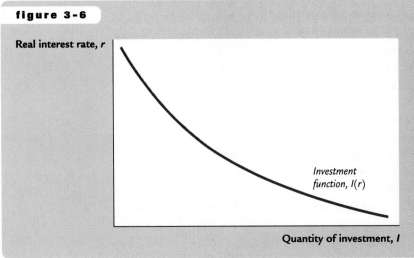

Real interest rate, r

Investment function, $I(r)$

Quantity of investment, I

The Investment Function The investment function relates the quantity of investment I to the real interest rate r. Investment depends on the real interest rate because the interest rate is the cost of borrowing. The investment function slopes downward: when the interest rate rises, fewer investment projects are profitable.

f y i

THE MANY DIFFERENT INTEREST RATES

If you look in the business section of a newspaper, you will find many different interest rates reported. By contrast, throughout this book, we will talk about "the" interest rate, as if there were only one interest rate in the economy. The only distinction we will make is between the nominal interest rate (which is not corrected for inflation) and the real interest rate (which is corrected for inflation). Almost all of the interest rates reported in the newspaper are nominal.

Why does the newspaper report so many interest rates? The various interest rates differ in three ways:

➤ *Term.* Some loans in the economy are for short periods of time, even as short as overnight. Other loans are for thirty years or even longer. The interest rate on a loan depends on its term. Long-term interest rates are usually, but not always, higher than short-term interest rates.

➤ *Credit risk.* In deciding whether to make a loan, a lender must take into account the probability that the borrower will repay. The law allows borrowers to default on their loans by declaring bankruptcy. The higher the perceived probability of default, the higher the interest rate. The safest credit risk is the government, and so government bonds tend to pay a low interest rate. At the other extreme, financially shaky corporations can raise funds only by issuing *junk bonds*, which pay a high interest rate to compensate for the high risk of default.

➤ *Currency denomination.* A lender must be concerned about possible changes in international exchange rates. For example, an American who lends money to a provincial government by buying a bond denominated in Canadian dollars will form expectations concerning the likely change in the value of the Canadian dollar over the period she is making this loan. If the Canadian dollar is expected to fall in value, perhaps due to uncertainty concerning Quebec separation, Canadian borrowers have to pay a higher interest rate than do borrowers in the United States. Thus, the spread between Canadian and American interest rates widens whenever the Canadian dollar is perceived as "weak."

When you see two different interest rates in the newspaper, you can almost always explain the difference by considering the term, credit risk, and currency denomination of the loan.

Although there are many different domestic interest rates, macroeconomists can usually ignore these distinctions. The various interest rates tend to move up and down together. The assumption that there is only one domestic interest rate is, for our purposes, a useful simplification.

Government Purchases

Government purchases are the third component of the demand for goods and services. The federal government buys helicopters, computers, and the services of government employees. Provincial and municipal governments buy library books, build schools and hospitals, and hire teachers and doctors. Governments at all levels build roads and other public works. All these transactions make up government purchases of goods and services, which account for about 22 percent of GDP in Canada.

These purchases are only one type of government spending. The other type is transfer payments to households, such as welfare for the poor and Canada

Pension payments for the elderly. Unlike government purchases, transfer payments are not made in exchange for some of the economy's output of goods and services. Therefore, they are not included in the variable G.

Transfer payments do affect the demand for goods and services indirectly. Transfer payments are the opposite of taxes: they increase households' disposable income, just as taxes reduce disposable income. Thus, an increase in transfer payments financed by an increase in taxes leaves disposable income unchanged. We can now revise our definition of T to equal taxes minus transfer payments. Disposable income, $Y - T$, includes both the negative impact of taxes and the positive impact of transfer payments.

If government purchases equal taxes minus transfers, then $G = T$, and the government has a *balanced budget*. If G exceeds T, the government runs a *budget deficit*, which it funds by issuing government debt—that is, by borrowing in the financial markets. If G is less than T, the government runs a *budget surplus*, which it can use to repay some of its outstanding debt.

Here we do not try to explain the political process that leads to a particular fiscal policy—that is, to the level of government purchases and taxes. Instead, we take government purchases and taxes as exogenous variables. To denote that these variables are fixed outside of our model of national income, we write

$$G = \overline{G}.$$
$$T = \overline{T}.$$

We do, however, want to examine the impact of fiscal policy on the variables determined within the model, the endogenous variables. The endogenous variables here are consumption, investment, and the interest rate.

To see how the exogenous variables affect the endogenous variables, we must complete the model. This is the subject of the next section.

3-4 | What Brings the Supply and Demand for Goods and Services Into Equilibrium?

We have now come full circle in the circular flow diagram, Figure 3-1. We began by examining the supply of goods and services, and we have just discussed the demand for them. How can we be certain that all these flows balance? In other words, what ensures that the sum of consumption, investment, and government purchases equals the amount of output produced? We will see that in this classical model, the interest rate has the crucial role of equilibrating supply and demand.

There are two ways to think about the role of the interest rate in the economy. We can consider how the interest rate affects the supply and demand for goods or services. Or we can consider how the interest rate affects the supply and demand for loanable funds. As we will see, these two approaches are two sides of the same coin.

Equilibrium in the Market for Goods and Services: The Supply and Demand for the Economy's Output

The following equations summarize the discussion of the demand for goods and services in Section 3-3:

$$Y = C + I + G.$$
$$C = C(Y - T).$$
$$I = I(r).$$
$$G = \overline{G}.$$
$$T = \overline{T}.$$

The demand for the economy's output comes from consumption, investment, and government purchases. Consumption depends on disposable income; investment depends on the real interest rate; and government purchases and taxes are the exogenous variables set by fiscal policymakers.

To this analysis, let's add what we learned about the supply of goods and services in Section 3-1. There we saw that the factors of production and the production function determine the quantity of output supplied to the economy:

$$Y = F(\overline{K}, \overline{L})$$
$$= \overline{Y}.$$

Now let's combine these equations describing the supply and demand for output. If we substitute the consumption function and the investment function into the national accounts identity, we obtain

$$Y = C(Y - T) + I(r) + G.$$

Because the variables G and T are fixed by policy, and the level of output Y is fixed by the factors of production and the production function, we can write

$$\overline{Y} = C(\overline{Y} - \overline{T}) + I(r) + \overline{G}.$$

This equation states that the supply of output equals its demand, which is the sum of consumption, investment, and government purchases.

Notice that the interest rate r is the only variable not already determined in the last equation. This is because the interest rate still has a key role to play: it must adjust to ensure that the demand for goods equals the supply. The greater the interest rate, the lower the level of investment, and thus the lower the demand for goods and services, $C + I + G$. If the interest rate is too high, investment is too low, and the demand for output falls short of the supply. If the interest rate is too low, investment is too high, and the demand exceeds the supply. *At the equilibrium interest rate, the demand for goods and services equals the supply.*

This conclusion may seem somewhat mysterious. One might wonder how the interest rate gets to the level that balances the supply and demand for goods and services. The best way to answer this question is to consider how financial markets fit into the story.

Equilibrium in the Financial Markets: The Supply and Demand for Loanable Funds

Because the interest rate is the cost of borrowing and the return to lending in financial markets, we can better understand the role of the interest rate in the economy by thinking about the financial markets. To do this, rewrite the national accounts identity as

$$Y - C - G = I.$$

The term $Y - C - G$ is the output that remains after the demands of consumers and the government have been satisfied; it is called **national saving** or simply **saving (S).** In this form, the national accounts identity shows that saving equals investment.

To understand this identity more fully, we can split national saving into two parts—one part representing the saving of the private sector and the other representing the saving of the government:

$$(Y - T - C) + (T - G) = I.$$

The term $(Y - T - C)$ is disposable income minus consumption, which is **private saving.** The term $(T - G)$ is government revenue minus government spending, which is **public saving.** (If government spending exceeds government revenue, the government runs a budget deficit, and public saving is negative.) National saving is the sum of private and public saving. The circular flow diagram in Figure 3-1 reveals an interpretation of this equation: this equation states that the flows into the financial markets (private and public saving) must balance the flows out of the financial markets (investment).

To see how the interest rate brings financial markets into equilibrium, substitute the consumption function and the investment function into the national accounts identity:

$$Y - C(Y - T) - G = I(r).$$

Next, note that G and T are fixed by policy and Y is fixed by the factors of production and the production function:

$$\overline{Y} - C(\overline{Y} - \overline{T}) - \overline{G} = I(r).$$
$$\overline{S} = I(r).$$

The left-hand side of this equation shows that national saving depends on income Y and the fiscal policy variables G and T. For fixed values of Y, G, and T, national saving S is also fixed. The right-hand side of the equation shows that investment depends on the interest rate.

Figure 3-7 graphs saving and investment as a function of the interest rate. The saving function is a vertical line because in this model saving does not depend on the interest rate (although we relax this assumption later). The investment function slopes downward: the higher the interest rate, the fewer investment projects are profitable.

From a quick glance at Figure 3-7, one might think it was a supply and demand diagram for a particular good. In fact, saving and investment can be in-

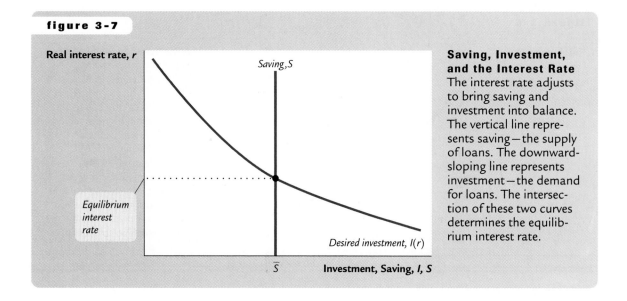

figure 3-7

Real interest rate, *r*

Saving, *S*

Equilibrium interest rate

Desired investment, *I(r)*

$\overline{S}$

Investment, Saving, *I, S*

Saving, Investment, and the Interest Rate The interest rate adjusts to bring saving and investment into balance. The vertical line represents saving—the supply of loans. The downward-sloping line represents investment—the demand for loans. The intersection of these two curves determines the equilibrium interest rate.

terpreted in terms of supply and demand. In this case, the "good" is **loanable funds,** and its "price" is the interest rate. Saving is the supply of loanable funds—households lend their saving to investors or deposit their saving in a bank that then loans the funds out. Investment is the demand for loanable funds—investors borrow from the public directly by selling bonds or indirectly by borrowing from banks. Because investment depends on the interest rate, the quantity of loanable funds demanded also depends on the interest rate.

The interest rate adjusts until the amount that firms want to invest equals the amount that households want to save. If the interest rate is too low, investors want more of the economy's output than households want to save. Equivalently, the quantity of loans demanded exceeds the quantity supplied. When this happens, the interest rate rises. Conversely, if the interest rate is too high, households want to save more than firms want to invest; because the quantity of loans supplied is greater than the quantity demanded, the interest rate falls. The equilibrium interest rate is found where the two curves cross. *At the equilibrium interest rate, households' desire to save balances firms' desire to invest, and the quantity of loans supplied equals the quantity demanded.*

Changes in Saving: The Effects of Fiscal Policy

We can use our model to show how fiscal policy affects the economy. When the government changes its spending or the level of taxes, it affects the demand for the economy's output of goods and services and alters national saving, investment, and the equilibrium interest rate.

An Increase in Government Purchases Consider first the effects of an increase in government purchases of an amount ΔG. The immediate impact is to increase the demand for goods and services by ΔG. But since total output is fixed by the factors of production, the increase in government purchases must be met by a

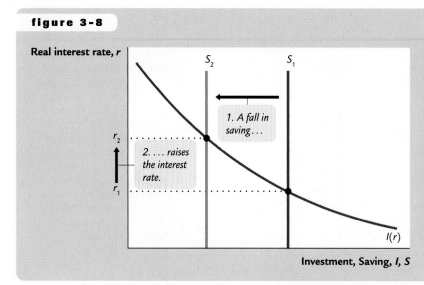

figure 3-8

Real interest rate, r

S_2 S_1

1. A fall in saving...

r_2

2. ... raises the interest rate.

r_1

$I(r)$

Investment, Saving, I, S

A Reduction in Saving
A reduction in saving, possibly the result of a change in fiscal policy, shifts the saving schedule to the left. The new equilibrium is the point at which the new saving schedule crosses the investment schedule. A reduction in saving lowers the amount of investment and raises the interest rate. Fiscal-policy actions that reduce saving are said to crowd out investment.

decrease in some other category of demand. Since disposable income $Y - T$ is unchanged, consumption C is unchanged. The increase in government purchases must be met by an equal decrease in investment.

To induce investment to fall, the interest rate must rise. Hence, the increase in government purchases causes the interest rate to increase and investment to decrease. Government purchases are said to **crowd out** investment.

To grasp the effects of an increase in government purchases, consider the impact on the market for loanable funds. Since the increase in government purchases is not accompanied by an increase in taxes, the government finances the additional spending by borrowing—that is, by reducing public saving. Since private saving is unchanged, this government borrowing reduces national saving. As Figure 3-8 shows, a reduction in national saving is represented by a leftward shift in the supply of loanable funds available for investment. At the initial interest rate, the demand for loans exceeds the supply. The equilibrium interest rate rises to the point where the investment schedule crosses the new saving schedule. Thus, an increase in government purchases causes the interest rate to rise from r_1 to r_2.

CASE STUDY

Wars and Interest Rates in the United Kingdom, 1730–1920

Wars are traumatic—both for those who fight them and for a nation's economy. Because the economic changes accompanying them are often large, wars provide a natural experiment with which economists can test their theories. We can learn about the economy by seeing how in wartime the endogenous variables respond to the major changes in the exogenous variables.

One exogenous variable that changes substantially in wartime is the level of government purchases. Figure 3-9 shows military spending as a percentage of GDP for the United Kingdom from 1730 to 1919. This graph shows, as one

figure 3-13

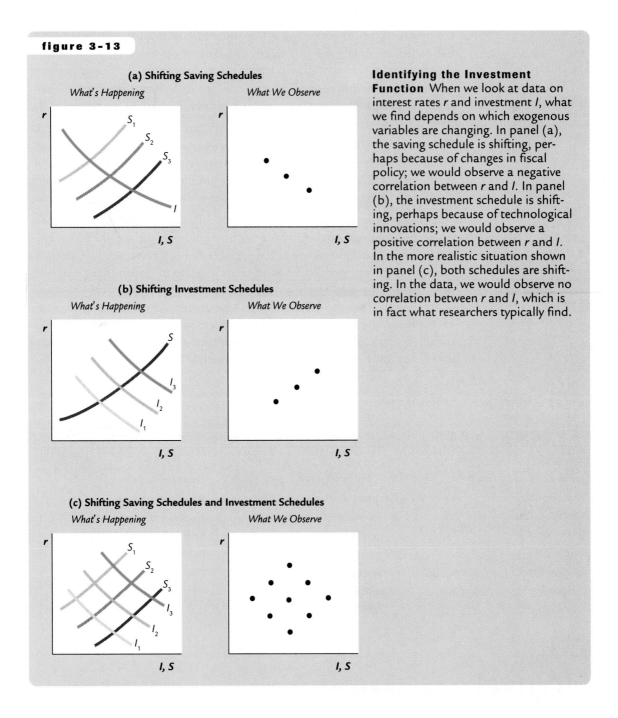

(a) Shifting Saving Schedules

What's Happening

What We Observe

(b) Shifting Investment Schedules

What's Happening

What We Observe

(c) Shifting Saving Schedules and Investment Schedules

What's Happening

What We Observe

Identifying the Investment Function When we look at data on interest rates r and investment I, what we find depends on which exogenous variables are changing. In panel (a), the saving schedule is shifting, perhaps because of changes in fiscal policy; we would observe a negative correlation between r and I. In panel (b), the investment schedule is shifting, perhaps because of technological innovations; we would observe a positive correlation between r and I. In the more realistic situation shown in panel (c), both schedules are shifting. In the data, we would observe no correlation between r and I, which is in fact what researchers typically find.

Summary

1. The factors of production and the production technology determine the economy's output of goods and services. An increase in one of the factors of production or a technological advance raises output.

2. Competitive, profit-maximizing firms hire labour until the marginal product of labour equals the real wage. Similarly, these firms rent capital until the marginal product of capital equals the real rental price. Therefore, each factor of production is paid its marginal product. If the production function has constant returns to scale, all output is used to compensate the inputs.

3. The economy's output is used for consumption, investment, and government purchases. Consumption depends positively on disposable income. Investment depends negatively on the real interest rate. Government purchases and taxes are the exogenous variables of fiscal policy.

4. The real interest rate adjusts to equilibrate the supply and demand for the economy's output—or, equivalently, to equilibrate the supply of loanable funds (saving) and the demand for loanable funds (investment). A decrease in national saving, perhaps because of an increase in government purchases or a decrease in taxes, reduces the equilibrium amount of investment and raises the interest rate. An increase in investment demand, perhaps because of a technological innovation or a tax incentive for investment, also raises the interest rate. An increase in investment demand increases the quantity of investment only if higher interest rates stimulate additional saving.

KEY CONCEPTS

Factors of production	Marginal product of capital (*MPK*)	Nominal interest rate
Production function	Real rental price of capital	Real interest rate
Constant returns to scale	Economic profit versus account-	National saving (saving) (*S*)
Factor prices	ing profit	Private saving
Competition	Disposable income	Public saving
Marginal product of labour (*MPL*)	Consumption function	Loanable funds
Diminishing marginal product	Marginal propensity to consume	Crowding out
Real wage	(*MPC*)	

QUESTIONS FOR REVIEW

1. What determines the amount of output an economy produces?

2. Explain how a competitive, profit-maximizing firm decides how much of each factor of production to demand.

3. What is the role of constant returns to scale in the distribution of income?

4. What determines consumption and investment?

5. Explain the difference between government pur-

$(1 - \alpha)Y$. Therefore, $(1 - \alpha)$ is labour's share of output. Similarly, the total return to capital, $MPK \times K$, is αY, and α is capital's share of output. The ratio of labour income to capital income is a constant, $(1 - \alpha)/\alpha$, just as Douglas observed. The factor shares depend only on the parameter α, not on the amounts of capital or labour or on the state of technology as measured by the parameter A.

More recent data are also consistent with the Cobb–Douglas production function. Figure 3-14 shows the ratio of labour income to total income in Canada from 1945 to 1998. Despite the many changes in the economy over this half century, this ratio has remained about 0.67. This division of income is easily explained by a Cobb–Douglas production function in which the parameter α is about 0.33.

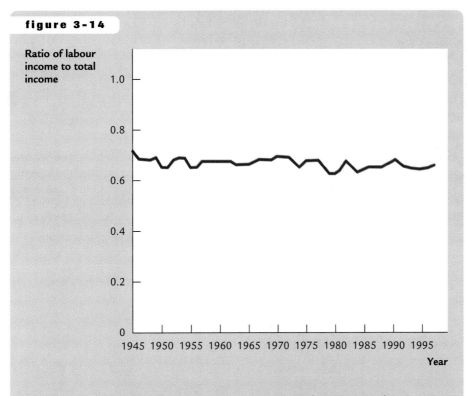

figure 3-14

Ratio of labour income to total income

The Ratio of Labour Income to Total Income Labour income has remained about 0.67 of total income over a long period of time. This approximate constancy of factor shares is evidence for the Cobb–Douglas production function. (This figure is produced from Canadian national accounts data. Labour income is wages. Total income is the sum of labour income (D15654), corporate profits before taxes (D15655), interest and investment income (D15657), and capital consumption allowances (D15663)).

Source: Statistics Canada, CANSIM series labels given above.

MORE PROBLEMS AND APPLICATIONS |

1. Suppose that the production function is Cobb–Douglas with parameter $\alpha = 0.3$.

   a. What fractions of income do capital and labour receive?

   b. Suppose that immigration raises the labour force by 10 percent. What happens to total output (in percent)? The rental price of capital? The real wage?

   c. Suppose that a gift of capital from abroad raises the capital stock by 10 percent. What happens to total output (in percent)? The rental price of capital? The real wage?

   d. Suppose that a technological advance raises the value of the parameter A by 10 percent. What happens to total output (in percent)? The rental price of capital? The real wage?

2. (This problem requires the use of calculus.) Consider a Cobb–Douglas production function with three inputs. K is capital (the number of machines), L is labour (the number of workers), and H is human capital (the number of college degrees among the workers). The production function is

   $$Y = K^{1/3}L^{1/3}H^{1/3}.$$

   a. Derive an expression for the marginal product of labour. How does an increase in the amount of human capital affect the marginal product of labour?

   b. Derive an expression for the marginal product of human capital. How does an increase in the amount of human capital affect the marginal product of human capital?

   c. What is the income share paid to labour? What is the income share paid to human capital? In the national accounts of this economy, what share of total income do you think workers would appear to receive? (*Hint:* Consider where the return to human capital shows up.)

   d. An unskilled worker earns the marginal product of labour, whereas a skilled worker earns the marginal product of labour plus the marginal product of human capital. Using your answers to parts (a) and (b), find the ratio of the skilled wage to the unskilled wage. How does an increase in the amount of human capital affect this ratio? Explain.

   e. Some people advocate government funding of university scholarships as a way of creating a more egalitarian society. Others argue that scholarships help only those who are able to go to university. Do your answers to the above questions shed light on this debate?

Economic Growth I

The question of growth is nothing new but a new disguise for an age-old issue, one which has always intrigued and preoccupied economics: the present versus the future.

—*James Tobin*

If you have ever spoken with your grandparents about what their lives were like when they were young, most likely you learned an important lesson about economics: material standards of living have improved substantially over time for most families in most countries. This advance comes from rising incomes, which have allowed people to consume greater quantities of goods and services.

To measure economic growth, economists use data on gross domestic product, which measures the total income of everyone in the economy. The real GDP of Canada in 1998 was 6.5 times its 1950 level, and real GDP per person was 2.9 times its 1950 level. In any given year, we can also observe large differences in the standard of living among countries. Table 4-1 shows income per person in 1997 of the world's 12 most populous countries. The United States tops the list with an income of $28,740 per person. Nigeria has an income per person of only $880—about 3 percent of the figure for the United States. (While not included in Table 4-1 since we are not one of the more populated countries, it is interesting to note that Canada's GDP per person—in U.S. dollars—was $21,860.)

Our goal in this and the next chapter is to understand what causes these differences in income over time and across countries. In Chapter 3 we identified the factors of production—capital and labour—and the production technology as the sources of the economy's output and, thus, of its total income. Differences in income, then, must come from differences in capital, labour, and technology.

Our primary task is to develop a theory of economic growth called the **Solow growth model.** Our analysis in Chapter 3 enabled us to describe how the economy produces and uses its output at one point in time. The analysis was static—a snapshot of the economy. To explain why our national income grows, and why some economies grow faster than others, we must broaden our analysis so that it describes changes in the economy over time.

table 4-1

International Differences in the Standard of Living, 1997

Country	Income per Person (in U.S. dollars)
United States	$28,740
Japan	23,400
Germany	21,300
Mexico	8,120
Brazil	6,240
Russian Federation	4,190
China	3,570
Indonesia	3,450
India	1,650
Pakistan	1,590
Bangladesh	1,050
Nigeria	880

Source: World Bank.

By developing such a model, we make our analysis dynamic—more like a movie than a photograph. The Solow growth model shows how saving, population growth, and technological progress affect the level of an economy's output and its growth over time. In this chapter we analyze the roles of saving and population growth. In the next chapter we introduce technological progress.[1]

4-1 | The Accumulation of Capital

The Solow growth model is designed to show how growth in the capital stock, growth in the labour force, and advances in technology interact in an economy, and how they affect a nation's total output of goods and services. We build this model in steps. Our first step is to examine how the supply and demand for goods determine the accumulation of capital. In this first step, we assume that the labour force and technology are fixed. We then relax these assumptions, by introducing changes in the labour force later in this chapter and by introducing changes in technology in the next.

---

[1] The Solow growth model is named after economist Robert Solow and was developed in the 1950s and 1960s. In 1987 Solow won the Nobel Prize in economics for his work in economic growth. The model was introduced in Robert M. Solow, "A Contribution to the Theory of Economic Growth," *Quarterly Journal of Economics* (February 1956): 65–94.

The Supply and Demand for Goods

The supply and demand for goods played a central role in our static model of the economy in Chapter 3. The same is true for the Solow model. By considering the supply and demand for goods, we can see what determines how much output is produced at any given time and how this output is allocated among alternative uses.

The Supply of Goods and the Production Function The supply of goods in the Solow model is based on the now-familiar production function, which states that output depends on the capital stock and the labour force:

$$Y = F(K, L).$$

The Solow growth model assumes that the production function has constant returns to scale. This assumption is often considered realistic, and as we will see shortly, it helps simplify the analysis. Recall that a production function has constant returns to scale if

$$zY = F(zK, zL)$$

for any positive number z. That is, if we multiply both capital and labour by z, we also multiply the amount of output by z.

Production functions with constant returns to scale allow us to analyze all quantities in the economy relative to the size of the labour force. To see that this is true, set $z = 1/L$ in the equation above to obtain

$$Y/L = F(K/L, 1).$$

This equation shows that the amount of output per worker Y/L is a function of the amount of capital per worker K/L. (The number "1" is, of course, constant and thus can be ignored.) The assumption of constant returns to scale implies that the size of the economy—as measured by the number of workers—does not affect the relationship between output per worker and capital per worker.

Because the size of the economy does not matter, it will prove convenient to denote all quantities in per-worker terms. We designate these with lower-case letters, so $y = Y/L$ is output per worker, and $k = K/L$ is capital per worker. We can then write the production function as

$$y = f(k),$$

where we define $f(k) = F(k,1)$. Figure 4-1 illustrates this production function.

The slope of this production function shows how much extra output a worker produces when given an extra unit of capital. This amount is the marginal product of capital MPK. Mathematically, we write

$$MPK = f(k + 1) - f(k).$$

Note that in Figure 4-1, as the amount of capital increases, the production function becomes flatter, indicating that the production function exhibits diminishing marginal product of capital. When k is low, the average worker has only a little capital to work with, so an extra unit of capital is very useful and

figure 4-1

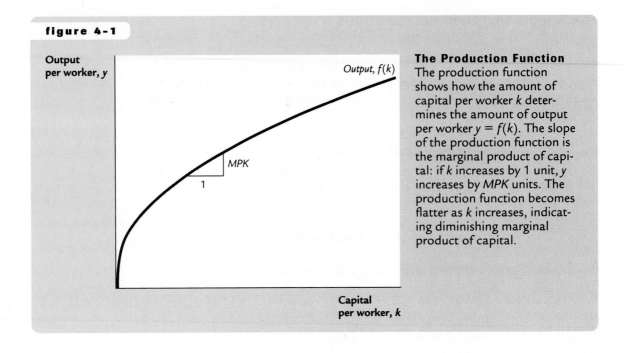

Output per worker, y

Output, $f(k)$

MPK

1

Capital per worker, k

The Production Function
The production function shows how the amount of capital per worker k determines the amount of output per worker $y = f(k)$. The slope of the production function is the marginal product of capital: if k increases by 1 unit, y increases by *MPK* units. The production function becomes flatter as k increases, indicating diminishing marginal product of capital.

produces a lot of additional output. When k is high, the average worker has a lot of capital, so an extra unit increases production only slightly.

The Demand for Goods and the Consumption Function   The demand for goods in the Solow model comes from consumption and investment. In other words, output per worker y is divided between consumption per worker c and investment per worker i:

$$y = c + i.$$

This equation is the per-worker version of the national accounts identity for the economy. Notice that it omits government purchases (which for present purposes we can ignore) and net exports (because we are assuming a closed economy).

The Solow model assumes that each year people save a fraction s of their income and consume a fraction $(1 - s)$. We can express this idea with a consumption function with the simple form

$$c = (1 - s)y,$$

where s, the saving rate, is a number between zero and one. Keep in mind that various government policies can potentially influence a nation's saving rate, so one of our goals is to find what saving rate is desirable. For now, however, we just take the saving rate s as given.

To see what this consumption function implies for investment, substitute $(1 - s)y$ for c in the national accounts identity:

$$y = (1 - s)y + i.$$

Rearrange the terms to obtain

$$i = sy.$$

This equation shows that investment equals saving, as we first saw in Chapter 3. Thus, the rate of saving s is also the fraction of output devoted to investment.

We have now introduced the two main ingredients of the Solow model—the production function and the consumption function—which describe the economy at any moment in time. For any given capital stock k, the production function $y = f(k)$ determines how much output the economy produces, and the saving rate s determines the allocation of that output between consumption and investment.

Growth in the Capital Stock and the Steady State

At any moment, the capital stock is a key determinant of the economy's output, but the capital stock can change over time, and those changes can lead to economic growth. In particular, two forces influence the capital stock: investment and depreciation. *Investment* refers to the expenditure on new plant and equipment, and it causes the capital stock to rise. *Depreciation* refers to the wearing out of old capital, and it causes the capital stock to fall. Let's consider each of these in turn.

As we have already noted, investment per worker i equals sy. By substituting the production function for y, we can express investment per worker as a function of the capital stock per worker:

$$i = sf(k).$$

figure 4-2

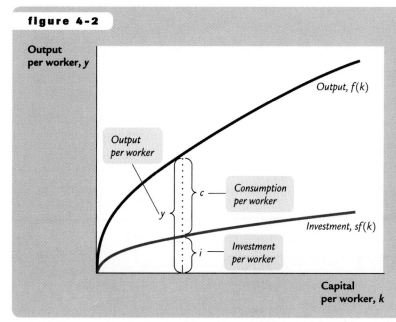

Output, Consumption, and Investment The saving rate s determines the allocation of output between consumption and investment. For any level of capital k, output is $f(k)$, investment is $sf(k)$, and consumption is $f(k) - sf(k)$.

This equation relates the existing stock of capital *k* to the accumulation of new capital *i*. Figure 4-2 shows this relationship. This figure illustrates how, for any value of *k*, the amount of output is determined by the production function *f*(*k*), and the allocation of that output between consumption and saving is determined by the saving rate *s*.

To incorporate depreciation into the model, we assume that a certain fraction δ of the capital stock wears out each year. Here δ (the lowercase Greek letter delta) is called the *depreciation rate*. For example, if capital lasts an average of 25 years, then the depreciation rate is 4 percent per year ($\delta = 0.04$). The amount of capital that depreciates each year is δk. Figure 4-3 shows how the amount of depreciation depends on the capital stock.

We can express the impact of investment and depreciation on the capital stock with this equation:

$$\text{Change in Capital Stock} = \text{Investment} - \text{Depreciation}$$
$$\Delta k = i - \delta k,$$

where Δk is the change in the capital stock between one year and the next. Because investment *i* equals *sf*(*k*), we can write this as

$$\Delta k = sf(k) - \delta k.$$

Figure 4-4 graphs the terms of this equation—investment and depreciation—for different levels of the capital stock *k*. The higher the capital stock, the greater the amounts of output and investment. Yet the higher the capital stock, the greater also the amount of depreciation.

As Figure 4-4 shows, there is a single capital stock k^* at which the amount of investment equals the amount of depreciation. If the economy ever finds it-

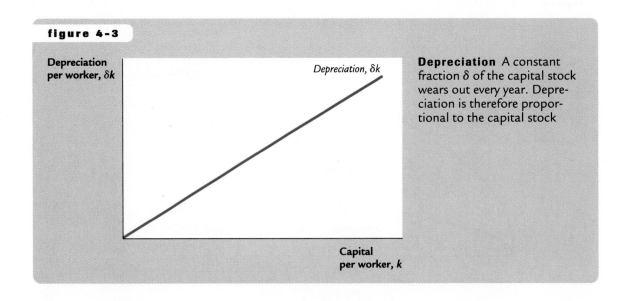

figure 4-3

Depreciation per worker, δk

Depreciation, δk

Capital per worker, *k*

Depreciation A constant fraction δ of the capital stock wears out every year. Depreciation is therefore proportional to the capital stock

figure 4-4

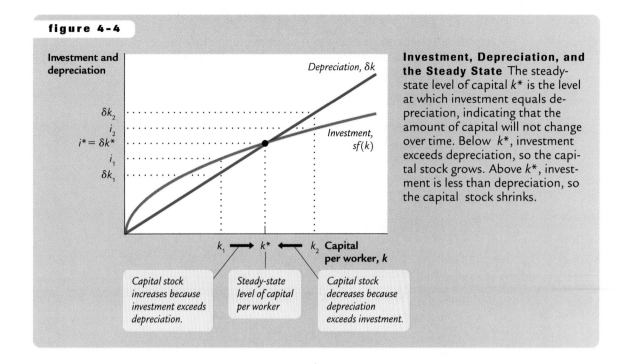

Investment, Depreciation, and the Steady State The steady-state level of capital k^* is the level at which investment equals depreciation, indicating that the amount of capital will not change over time. Below k^*, investment exceeds depreciation, so the capital stock grows. Above k^*, investment is less than depreciation, so the capital stock shrinks.

self at this level of the capital stock, the capital stock will not change because the two forces acting on it—investment and depreciation—just balance. That is, at k^*, $\Delta k = 0$, so the capital stock k and output $f(k)$ are steady over time (rather than growing or shrinking). We therefore call k^* the **steady-state** level of capital.

The steady state is significant for two reasons. As we have just seen, an economy at the steady state will stay there. In addition, and just as important, an economy not at the steady state will go there. That is, regardless of the level of capital with which the economy begins, it ends up with the steady-state level of capital. In this sense, *the steady state represents the long-run equilibrium of the economy*.

To see why an economy always ends up at the steady state, suppose that the economy starts with less than the steady-state level of capital, such as level k_1 in Figure 4-4. In this case, the level of investment exceeds the amount of depreciation. Over time, the capital stock will rise and will continue to rise—along with output $f(k)$—until it approaches the steady state k^*.

Similarly, suppose that the economy starts with more than the steady-state level of capital, such as level k_2. In this case, investment is less than depreciation: capital is wearing out faster than it is being replaced. The capital stock will fall, again approaching the steady-state level. Once the capital stock reaches the steady state, investment equals depreciation, and there is no pressure for the capital stock to increase or decrease.

Approaching the Steady State: A Numerical Example

Let's use a numerical example to see how the Solow model works and how the economy approaches the steady state. For this example, we assume that the production function is[2]

$$Y = K^{1/2}L^{1/2}.$$

To derive the per-worker production function $f(k)$, divide both sides of the production function by the labour force L:

$$\frac{Y}{L} = \frac{K^{1/2}L^{1/2}}{L}.$$

Rearrange to obtain

$$\frac{Y}{L} = \left(\frac{K}{L}\right)^{1/2}.$$

Because $y = Y/L$ and $k = K/L$, this becomes

$$y = k^{1/2}.$$

This equation can also be written as

$$y = \sqrt{k}.$$

This form of the production function states that output per worker is equal to the square root of the amount of capital per worker.

To complete the example, let's assume that 30 percent of output is saved ($s = 0.3$), that 10 percent of the capital stock depreciates every year ($\delta = 0.1$), and that the economy starts off with 4 units of capital per worker ($k = 4$). Given these numbers, we can now examine what happens to this economy over time.

We begin by looking at the production and allocation of output in the first year. According to the production function, the 4 units of capital per worker produce 2 units of output per worker. Because 30 percent of output is saved and invested and 70 percent is consumed, $i = 0.6$ and $c = 1.4$. Also, because 10 percent of the capital stock depreciates, $\delta k = 0.4$. With investment of 0.6 and depreciation of 0.4, the change in the capital stock is $\Delta k = 0.2$. The second year begins with 4.2 units of capital per worker.

Table 4-2 shows how the economy progresses year by year. Every year, new capital is added and output grows. Over many years, the economy approaches a steady state with 9 units of capital per worker. In this steady state, investment of 0.9 exactly offsets depreciation of 0.9, so that the capital stock and output are no longer growing.

---

[2] If you read the appendix to Chapter 3, you will recognize this as the Cobb–Douglas production function with the parameter α equal to $1/2$.

table 4-2						
Approaching the Steady State: A Numerical Example						
Assumptions: $y = \sqrt{k}$; $s = 0.3$; $\delta = 0.1$; initial $k = 4.0$						
Year	k	y	c	i	δk	Δk
1	4.000	2.000	1.400	0.600	0.400	0.200
2	4.200	2.049	1.435	0.615	0.420	0.195
3	4.395	2.096	1.467	0.629	0.440	0.189
4	4.584	2.141	1.499	0.642	0.458	0.184
5	4.768	2.184	1.529	0.655	0.477	0.178
⋮						
10	5.602	2.367	1.657	0.710	0.560	0.150
⋮						
25	7.321	2.706	1.894	0.812	0.732	0.080
⋮						
100	8.962	2.994	2.096	0.898	0.896	0.002
⋮						
∞	9.000	3.000	2.100	0.900	0.900	0.000

Following the progress of the economy for many years is one way to find the steady-state capital stock, but there is another way that requires fewer calculations. Recall that

$$\Delta k = sf(k) - \delta k.$$

This equation shows how k evolves over time. Because the steady state is (by definition) the value of k at which $\Delta k = 0$, we know that

$$0 = sf(k^*) - \delta k^*,$$

or, equivalently,

$$\frac{k^*}{f(k^*)} = \frac{s}{\delta}.$$

This equation provides a way of finding the steady-state level of capital per worker, k^*. Substituting in the numbers and production function from our example, we obtain

$$\frac{k^*}{\sqrt{k^*}} = \frac{0.3}{0.1}.$$

Now square both sides of this equation to find

$$k^* = 9.$$

The steady-state capital stock is 9 units per worker. This result confirms the calculation of the steady state in Table 4-2.

CASE STUDY

The Miracle of Japanese and German Growth

Japan and Germany are two success stories of economic growth. Although today they are economic superpowers, in 1945 the economies of both countries were in shambles. World War II had destroyed much of their capital stocks. In the decades after the war, however, these two countries experienced some of the most rapid growth rates on record. Between 1948 and 1972, output per person grew at 8.2 percent per year in Japan and 5.7 percent per year in Germany, compared to only 4.1 percent per year in Canada.

Are the postwar experiences of Japan and Germany so surprising from the standpoint of the Solow growth model? Consider an economy in steady state. Now suppose that a war destroys some of the capital stock. (That is, suppose the capital stock drops from k^* to k_1 in Figure 4-4.) Not surprisingly, the level of output immediately falls. But if the saving rate—the fraction of output devoted to saving and investment—is unchanged, the economy will then experience a period of high growth. Output grows because, at the lower capital stock, more capital is added by investment than is removed by depreciation. This high growth continues until the economy approaches its former steady state. Hence, although destroying part of the capital stock immediately reduces output, it is followed by higher than normal growth. The "miracle" of rapid growth in Japan and Germany, as it is often described in the business press, is what the Solow model predicts for countries in which war has greatly reduced the capital stock.

How Saving Affects Growth

The explanation of Japanese and German growth after World War II is not quite as simple as suggested in the preceding case study. Another relevant fact is that both Japan and Germany save and invest a higher fraction of their output than does the United States—the country to which the performance of others is usually compared. To understand more fully the international differences in economic performance, we must consider the effects of different saving rates.

Consider what happens to an economy when its saving rate increases. Figure 4-5 shows such a change. The economy is assumed to begin in a steady state with saving rate s_1 and capital stock k_1^*. When the saving rate increases from s_1 to s_2, the $sf(k)$ curve shifts upward. At the initial saving rate s_1 and the initial capital stock k_1^*, the amount of investment just offsets the amount of depreciation. Immediately after the saving rate rises, investment is higher, but the capital stock and depreciation are unchanged. Therefore, investment exceeds depreciation. The capital stock will gradually rise until the economy reaches the

figure 4-5

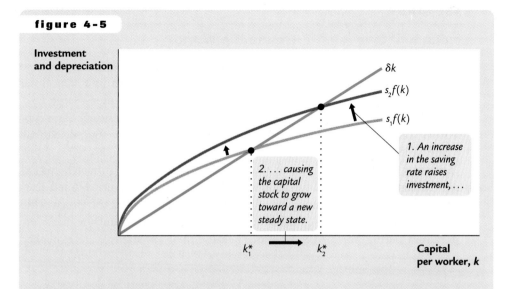

An Increase in the Saving Rate An increase in the saving rate *s* implies that the amount of investment for any given capital stock is higher. It therefore shifts the saving function upward. At the initial steady state k_1^*, investment now exceeds depreciation. The capital stock rises until the economy reaches a new steady state k_2^*, with more capital and output.

new steady state k_2^*, which has a higher capital stock and a higher level of output than the old steady state.

The Solow model shows that the saving rate is a key determinant of the steady-state capital stock. *If the saving rate is high, the economy will have a large capital stock and a high level of output. If the saving rate is low, the economy will have a small capital stock and a low level of output.* This conclusion sheds light on many discussions of fiscal policy. As we saw in Chapter 3, a government budget deficit can reduce national saving and crowd out investment. Now we can see that the long-run consequences of a reduced saving rate are a lower capital stock and lower national income. This is why many economists are critical of persistent budget deficits.

What does the Solow model say about the relationship between saving and economic growth? Higher saving leads to faster growth in the Solow model, but only temporarily. An increase in the rate of saving raises growth until the economy reaches the new steady state. If the economy maintains a high saving rate, it will also maintain a large capital stock and a high level of output, but it will not maintain a high rate of growth forever.

Now that we understand how saving affects growth, we can more fully explain the impressive economic performance of Germany and Japan after World War II. Not only were their initial capital stocks low because of the war, but their steady-state capital stocks were high because of their high saving rates. Both of these facts help explain the rapid growth of these two countries in the 1950s and 1960s.

CASE STUDY

Saving and Investment Around the World

We started this chapter with an important question: Why are some countries so rich while others are mired in poverty? Our analysis has taken us a step closer to the answer. According to the Solow model, if a nation devotes a large fraction of its income to saving and investment, it will have a high steady-state capital stock and a high level of income. If a nation saves and invests only a small fraction of its income, its steady-state capital and income will be low.

Let's now look at some data to see if this theoretical result in fact helps explain the large international variation in standards of living. Figure 4-6 is a scatterplot of data from 84 countries. (The figure includes most of the world's economies. It excludes major oil-producing countries and countries that were communist during much of this period, because their experiences are explained

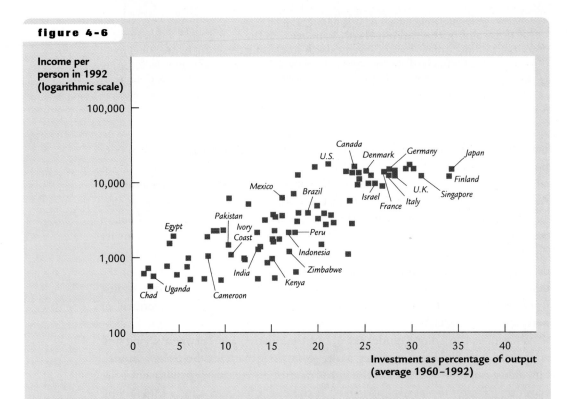

figure 4-6

International Evidence on Investment Rates and Income per Person This scatterplot shows the experience of 84 countries, each represented by a single point. The horizontal axis shows the country's rate of investment, and the vertical axis shows the country's income per person. High investment is associated with high income per person, as the Solow model predicts.

Source: Robert Summers and Alan Heston, Supplement (Mark 5.6) to "The Penn World Table (Mark 5): An Expanded Set of International Comparisons 1950–1988," *Quarterly Journal of Economics* (May 1991): 327–368.

by their special circumstances.) The data show a positive relationship between the fraction of output devoted to investment and the level of income per person. That is, countries with high rates of investment, such as Canada and Japan, usually have high incomes, whereas countries with low rates of investment, such as Uganda and Chad, have low incomes. Thus, the data are consistent with the Solow model's prediction that the investment rate is a key determinant of whether a country is rich or poor.

The strong correlation shown in this figure is an important fact, but it raises as many questions as it resolves. One might naturally ask, why do rates of saving and investment vary so much from country to country? There are many potential answers, such as tax policy, retirement patterns, the development of financial markets, and cultural differences. In addition, political stability may play a role: not surprisingly, rates of saving and investment tend to be low in countries with frequent wars, revolutions, and coups. Saving and investment also tend to be low in countries with poor political institutions, as measured by estimates of official corruption. A final interpretation of the evidence in Figure 4-6 is reverse causation: perhaps high levels of income somehow foster high rates of saving and investment. Unfortunately, there is no consensus among economists about which of the many possible explanations is most important.

The association between investment rates and income per person is strong, and it is an important clue as to why some countries are rich and others poor, but it is not the whole story. The correlation between these two variables is far from perfect. Mexico and Zimbabwe, for instance, have had similar investment rates, but income per person is more than three times higher in Mexico. There must be other determinants of living standards beyond saving and investment. We therefore return to the international differences later in the chapter to see what other variables enter the picture.

4-2 | The Golden Rule Level of Capital

So far, we have used the Solow model to examine how an economy's rate of saving and investment determines its steady-state levels of capital and income. This analysis might lead you to think that higher saving is always a good thing, for it always leads to greater income. Yet suppose a nation had a saving rate of 100 percent. That would lead to the largest possible capital stock and the largest possible income. But if all of this income is saved and none is ever consumed, what good is it?

This section uses the Solow model to discuss what amount of capital accumulation is optimal from the standpoint of economic well-being. In the next chapter, we discuss how government policies influence a nation's saving rate. But first, in this section, we present the theory behind these policy decisions.

Comparing Steady States

To keep our analysis simple, let's assume that a policymaker can set the economy's saving rate at any level. By setting the saving rate, the policymaker determines the economy's steady state. What steady state should the policymaker choose?

When choosing a steady state, the policymaker's goal is to maximize the well-being of the individuals who make up the society. Individuals themselves do not care about the amount of capital in the economy, or even the amount of output. They care about the amount of goods and services they can consume. Thus, a benevolent policymaker would want to choose the steady state with the highest level of consumption. The steady-state value of k that maximizes consumption is called the **Golden Rule level of capital** and is denoted k^*_{gold}.[3]

How can we tell whether an economy is at the Golden Rule level? To answer this question, we must first determine steady-state consumption per worker. Then we can see which steady state provides the most consumption.

To find steady-state consumption per worker, we begin with the national accounts identity

$$y = c + i$$

and rearrange it as

$$c = y - i.$$

Consumption is simply output minus investment. Because we want to find steady-state consumption, we substitute steady-state values for output and investment. Steady-state output per worker is $f(k^*)$, where k^* is the steady-state capital stock per worker. Furthermore, because the capital stock is not changing in the steady state, investment is equal to depreciation δk^*. Substituting $f(k^*)$ for y and δk^* for i, we can write steady-state consumption per worker as

$$c^* = f(k^*) - \delta k^*.$$

According to this equation, steady-state consumption is what's left of steady-state output after paying for steady-state depreciation. This equation shows that an increase in steady-state capital has two opposing effects on steady-state consumption. On the one hand, more capital means more output. On the other hand, more capital also means that more output must be used to replace capital that is wearing out.

Figure 4-7 graphs steady-state output and steady-state depreciation as a function of the steady-state capital stock. Steady-state consumption is the gap between output and depreciation. This figure shows that there is one level of the capital stock—the Golden Rule level k^*_{gold}—that maximizes consumption.

When comparing steady states, we must keep in mind that higher levels of capital affect both output and depreciation. If the capital stock is below the

---

[3] Edmund Phelps, "The Golden Rule of Accumulation: A Fable for Growthmen," *American Economic Review* 51 (September 1961): 638–643.

figure 4-7

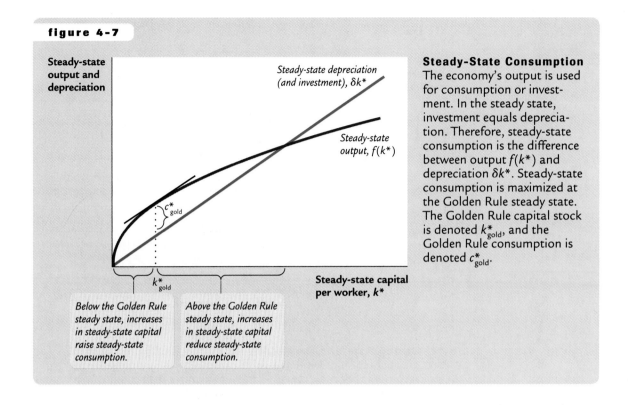

Steady-state output and depreciation

Steady-state depreciation (and investment), δk^*

Steady-state output, $f(k^*)$

c^*_{gold}

k^*_{gold}

Steady-state capital per worker, k^*

Below the Golden Rule steady state, increases in steady-state capital raise steady-state consumption.

Above the Golden Rule steady state, increases in steady-state capital reduce steady-state consumption.

Steady-State Consumption The economy's output is used for consumption or investment. In the steady state, investment equals depreciation. Therefore, steady-state consumption is the difference between output $f(k^*)$ and depreciation δk^*. Steady-state consumption is maximized at the Golden Rule steady state. The Golden Rule capital stock is denoted k^*_{gold}, and the Golden Rule consumption is denoted c^*_{gold}.

Golden Rule level, an increase in the capital stock raises output more than depreciation, so that consumption rises. In this case, the production function is steeper than the δk^* line, so the gap between these two curves—which equals consumption—grows as k^* rises. By contrast, if the capital stock is above the Golden Rule level, an increase in the capital stock reduces consumption, since the increase in output is smaller than the increase in depreciation. In this case, the production function is flatter than the δk^* line, so the gap between the curves—consumption—shrinks as k^* rises. At the Golden Rule level of capital, the production function and the δk^* line have the same slope, and consumption is at its greatest level.

We can now derive a simple condition that characterizes the Golden Rule level of capital. Recall that the slope of the production function is the marginal product of capital MPK. The slope of the δk^* line is δ. Because these two slopes are equal at k^*_{gold}, the Golden Rule is described by the equation

$$MPK = \delta.$$

At the Golden Rule level of capital, the marginal product of capital equals the depreciation rate.

To make the point somewhat differently, suppose that the economy starts at some steady-state capital stock k^* and that the policymaker is considering increasing the capital stock to $k^* + 1$. The amount of extra output from this increase in capital would be $f(k^* + 1) - f(k^*)$, which is the marginal product of capital MPK. The amount of extra depreciation from having 1 more unit

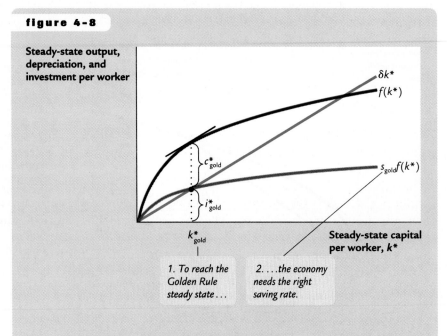

figure 4-8

Steady-state output, depreciation, and investment per worker

δk^*

$f(k^*)$

c^*_{gold}

$s_{gold} f(k^*)$

i^*_{gold}

k^*_{gold}

Steady-state capital per worker, k^*

1. To reach the Golden Rule steady state . . .

2. . . . the economy needs the right saving rate.

The Saving Rate and the Golden Rule There is only one saving rate that produces the Golden Rule level of capital k^*_{gold}. Any change in the saving rate would shift the $sf(k)$ curve and would move the economy to a steady state with a lower level of consumption.

of capital is the depreciation rate δ. Thus, the net effect of this extra unit of capital on consumption is then $MPK - \delta$. If $MPK - \delta > 0$, then increases in capital increase consumption, so k^* must be below the Golden Rule level. If $MPK - \delta < 0$, then increases in capital decrease consumption, so k^* must be above the Golden Rule level. Therefore, the following condition describes the Golden Rule:

$$MPK - \delta = 0.$$

At the Golden Rule level of capital, the marginal product of capital net of depreciation ($MPK - \delta$) equals zero. As we will see, a policymaker can use this condition for figuring out the Golden Rule capital stock for any given economy.[4]

Keep in mind that the economy does not automatically gravitate toward the Golden Rule steady state. If we want any particular steady-state capital stock, such as the Golden Rule, we need a particular saving rate to support it. Figure 4-8 shows the steady state if the saving rate is set to produce the Golden Rule level of capital. If the saving rate is higher than the one used in

---

[4] *Mathematical note:* Another way to derive the condition for the Golden Rule uses a bit of calculus. Recall that $c^* = f(k^*) - \delta k^*$. To find the k^* that maximizes c^*, differentiate to find $dc^*/dk^* = f'(k^*) - \delta$ and set this derivative equal to zero. Noting that $f'(k^*)$ is the marginal product of capital, we obtain the Golden Rule condition in the text.

We can now see that the return to capital ($MPK - \delta = 7.67$ percent per year) is well in excess of the economy's average growth rate ($n + g = 4$ percent per year). This fact, together with our previous analysis, indicates that the capital stock in the Canadian economy is well below the Golden Rule level. In other words, if Canada saved and invested a higher fraction of its income, it would grow more rapidly and eventually reach a steady state with higher consumption. This finding suggests that policymakers should want to increase the rate of saving and investment. In fact, for many years, increasing capital formation has been a high priority of economic policy.

Changing the Rate of Saving

The preceding calculations show that to move the Canadian economy toward the Golden Rule steady state, policymakers should increase national saving. But how can they do that? We saw in Chapter 3 that, as a matter of sheer accounting, higher national saving means higher public saving, higher private saving, or some combination of the two. Much of the debate over policies to increase growth centers on which of these is likely to be most effective.

The most direct way in which the government affects national saving is through public saving—the difference between what the government receives in tax revenue and what it spends. When the government's spending exceeds its revenue, the government is said to run a *budget deficit,* which represents negative public saving. As we saw in Chapter 3, a budget deficit raises interest rates and crowds out investment; the resulting reduction in the capital stock is part of the burden of the national debt on future generations. Conversely, if the government spends less than it raises in revenue, it is said to run a *budget surplus.* It can then retire some of the national debt and stimulate investment. This influence of government budget policy on capital accumulation explains why the Liberal party made reducing the budget deficit an important priority when it formed the government in 1993.

The government also affects national saving by influencing private saving—the saving done by households and firms. In particular, how much people decide to save depends on the incentives they face, and these incentives are altered by a variety of public policies. Many economists argue that high tax rates on capital income—including the corporate income tax and the personal income tax—discourage private saving by reducing the rate of return that savers earn. On the other hand, tax-exempt retirement savings plans, such as RRSPs, are designed to encourage private saving by giving preferential treatment to income that is saved.

Many disagreements among economists over public policy are rooted in different views about how much private saving responds to incentives. For example, suppose that the government were to expand the amount that people can put into RRSPs. Would people respond to the increased incentive to save by saving more? Or would people merely transfer saving done in other forms into this form—reducing tax revenue and thus public saving without any stimulus to private saving? Clearly, the desirability of the policy depends on the answers to these questions. Unfortunately, despite much research on this issue, no consensus has emerged.

CASE STUDY

Tax Incentives for Saving and Investment

The Canadian government has long believed that Canada's capital/labour ratio is below the Golden Rule value. This has been the motivation behind a series of policies that were designed to raise domestic saving and to make investment more profitable for firms.

On the saving side, we have had RRSPs, the goods and services tax (GST), and the capital gains exemption from income taxes. All savings that are deposited within an RRSP involve two tax breaks. First, the amount contributed can be deducted from taxable income (so individuals in a 50 percent tax bracket are effectively earning interest on twice the funds that they would have without an RRSP). Second, all interest earned within the plan is tax deferred. Eventually, when the RRSP is closed out, the individuals must pay taxes on all funds withdrawn. But this does not remove the tax advantage. For one thing, the tax rate is often lower during one's retirement. For another thing, even when this is not the case, people prefer to pay taxes later. By allowing people to defer taxes, RRSPs involve the government in extending an interest-free loan to individuals (for many years). The government has been willing to give up all the associated revenue in an attempt to increase national saving.

The GST was introduced in 1988. One rationale for this tax is that sales taxes stimulate saving (compared to income taxes). With an income tax, individuals pay taxes whether they spend their income on consumption or saving. With a sales tax, people can avoid the tax by saving, since the tax is only levied when people spend.

The tax exemption on capital gains income was removed in the 1994 federal budget. With the government budget deficit running out of control, the government felt it had no option but to end this tax incentive. But its original intent was the same as with RRSPs. Prior to the 1994 budget, all individuals were exempt from tax on the first $100,000 of capital gains they had received on their saving.

Although many government policies are designed to encourage saving, one important policy is often thought to reduce saving: the public pension system. These transfers to the elderly are financed with a payroll tax on the working-age population. This system is thought to reduce private saving because it reduces individuals' need to provide for their own retirement.

To counteract the reduction in national saving attributed to public pensions, many economists have proposed reforms. The system is now largely *pay-as-you-go:* most of the current tax receipts are paid out to the current elderly population. One suggestion is that the system should be *fully funded*. Under this plan, the government would put aside in a trust fund the payments a generation makes when it is young and working; the government would then pay out the principal and accumulated interest to this same generation when it is older and retired. Under a fully funded pension system, an increase in public saving would offset the reduction in private saving.

A closely related proposal is *privatisation,* which means turning this government program for the elderly into a system of mandatory private savings accounts, much like private pension plans. In principle, the issues of funding and privatisation are distinct. A fully funded system could be either public (in which case the government holds the funds) or private (in which case private financial institutions hold the funds). In practice, however, the issues are often linked. Some economists have argued that a fully funded public system is problematic. They note that such a system would end up holding a large share of the nation's wealth, which would increase the role of the government in allocating capital. In addition, they fear that a large publicly controlled fund would tempt politicians to cut taxes or increase spending, which could deplete the fund and cause the system to revert to pay-as-you-go status.

These issues rose to prominence in the late 1990s, as policymakers became aware that the current public pension system was not sustainable. That is, the amount of revenue being raised by the payroll tax appeared insufficient to pay all the benefits being promised. According to most projections, this problem was to become acute as the large baby-boom generation retired during the early decades of the twenty-first century. Various solutions were proposed. One possibility was to maintain the current system with some combination of smaller benefits and higher taxes. Other possibilities included movements toward a fully funded system, perhaps also including private accounts. The federal government opted for higher payroll taxes.

In addition to its attempts to stimulate private saving, the government also tries to raise investment by giving interest-free loans directly to firms, in the form of "accelerated depreciation allowances." Again, the purpose is to increase capital accumulation in the economy. When firms fill out their corporate tax forms, they deduct expenses from gross sales to calculate their tax base (profits). One aspect of these calculations is particularly arbitrary—how the expenses of the firm's machines and equipment are treated. Firms would like to claim (for tax purposes) that equipment fully wears out (depreciates) during the purchase year. Firms can then claim the entire cost of the equipment immediately. This makes recorded profits low, and so keeps initial tax payments low. In fact, equipment wears out over a period of years. By having no equipment-purchase expenses left to claim in those later years, firms have bigger tax obligations later on. But, as with households, firms like paying taxes later, since by doing so they have received an interest-free loan from the government.

Vast amounts of tax revenue are forgone because of these tax incentives, so it should not be surprising to learn that some have been controversial. One class of policies that is particularly "expensive" is the set of corporate tax breaks that are available to all firms operating in Canada, whether or not they are branch plants of multinational companies. International tax agreements make our tax initiatives useless for these firms. Multinationals are allowed a tax credit for taxes already paid in other countries when they calcuate their corporate tax obligations in the country where the parent company is based. For example, a company based in the United States is allowed to deduct the taxes its affiliate has already paid in Canada from what taxes it would otherwise owe to the U.S. government. Thus, a tax break offered by the Canadian government makes the tax credit in the United States precisely that much smaller. The Canadian government is simply transferring revenue to the U.S. government. Since these firms are no better off as a result of the Canadian government's generosity, we cannot expect the policy to stimulate investment spending on the part of these firms.

This is not the place to evaluate more fully the Canadian attempts to raise saving and investment. However successful these schemes have been, the main point to be appreciated is *why* these initiatives were taken. The purpose has been to move Canada closer to the Golden Rule outcome.

Allocating the Economy's Investment

The Solow model makes the simplifying assumption that there is only one type of capital. In the world, of course, there are many types. Private businesses invest in traditional types of capital, such as bulldozers and steel plants, and newer types of capital, such as computers and robots. The government invests in various forms of public capital, called *infrastructure,* such as roads, bridges, and sewer systems.

In addition, there is *human capital*—the knowledge and skills that workers acquire through education, from early childhood programs to on-the-job training for adults in the labour force. Although the basic Solow model includes only physical capital and does not try to explain the efficiency of labour, in many ways human capital is analogous to physical capital. Like physical capital, human capital raises our ability to produce goods and services. Raising the level of human capital requires investment in the form of teachers, libraries, and student time. Recent research on economic growth has emphasized that human capital is at least as important as physical capital in explaining international differences in standards of living.[2]

Policymakers trying to stimulate economic growth must confront the issue of what kinds of capital the economy needs most. In other words, what kinds of capital yield the highest marginal products? To a large extent, policymakers can rely on the marketplace to allocate the pool of saving to alternative types of investment. Those industries with the highest marginal products of capital will naturally be most willing to borrow at market interest rates to finance new investment. Many economists advocate that the government should merely create a "level playing field" for different types of capital—for example, by ensuring that the tax system treats all forms of capital equally. The government can then rely on the market to allocate capital efficiently.

---

[2] N. Gregory Mankiw, David Romer, and David N. Weil, "A Contribution to the Empirics of Economic Growth," *Quarterly Journal of Economics* (May 1992): 407–437.

Other economists have suggested that the government should actively encourage particular forms of capital. Suppose, for instance, that technological advance occurs as a by-product of certain economic activities. This would happen if new and improved production processes are devised during the process of building capital (a phenomenon called *learning by doing*) and if these ideas become part of society's pool of knowledge. Such a by-product is called a *technological externality* (or a *knowledge spillover*). In the presence of such externalities, the social returns to capital exceed the private returns, and the benefits of increased capital accumulation to society are greater than the Solow model suggests.[3] Moreover, some types of capital accumulation may yield greater externalities than others. If, for example, installing robots yields greater technological externalities than building a new steel mill, then perhaps the government should use the tax laws to encourage investment in robots. The success of such an *industrial policy,* as it is sometimes called, requires that the government be able to measure the externalities of different economic activities so it can give the correct incentive to each activity.

Most economists are skeptical about industrial policies, for two reasons. First, measuring the externalities from different sectors is so difficult as to be virtually impossible. If policy is based on poor measurements, its effects might be close to random and, thus, worse than no policy at all. Second, the political process is far from perfect. Once the government gets in the business of rewarding specific industries with subsidies and tax breaks, the rewards are as likely to be based on political clout as the magnitude of externalties.

One type of capital that necessarily involves the government is public capital. Municipal, provincial, and federal governments are always deciding whether to borrow to finance new roads, bridges, and transit systems. During both his election campaigns in the 1990s, Prime Minister Jean Chrétien argued that Canada had been investing too little in infrastructure. He claimed that a higher level of infrastructure investment would make the economy substantially more productive. Among economists, this claim had both defenders and critics. Yet all of them agree that measuring the marginal product of public capital is difficult. Private capital generates an easily measured rate of profit for the firm owning the capital, whereas the benefits of public capital are more diffuse.

Encouraging Technological Progress

The Solow model shows that sustained growth in income per worker must come from technological progress. The Solow model, however, takes technological progress as exogenous; it does not explain it. Unfortunately, the determinants of technological progress are not well understood.

Despite this limited understanding, many public policies are designed to stimulate technological progress. Most of these policies encourage the private

---

[3] Paul Romer, "Crazy Explanations for the Productivity Slowdown," *NBER Macroeconomics Annual* 2 (1987): 163–201.

sector to devote resources to technological innovation. For example, the patent system gives a temporary monopoly to inventors of new products; the tax code offers tax breaks for firms engaging in research and development; and government funding agencies directly subsidize basic research. In addition, as discussed above, proponents of industrial policy argue that the government should take a more active role in promoting specific industries that are key for rapid technological progress.

CASE STUDY

The Worldwide Slowdown in Economic Growth

One of the most perplexing problems that policymakers have faced in recent decades is the worldwide slowdown in economic growth that began in the early 1970s. Table 5-2 presents data on the growth in real GDP per person for the seven major world economies. Growth in Canada fell from 2.9 percent to 1.8 percent. (Note that Table 5-2 focuses on growth in output *per person*. Since Canada's population has grown more rapidly than our real GDP, these growth rates are lower than the 4 percent output growth rate discussed earlier.) Other countries experienced similar or more severe declines.

Studies have shown that the slowdown in growth is attributable to a slowdown in the rate at which the production function is improving over time. The appendix to this chapter explains how economists measure changes in the production function with a variable called *total factor productivity*, which is closely related to the efficiency of labour in the Solow model. Accumulated over many years, even a small change in the rate of productivity growth has a large effect on economic welfare. Real income in Canada today is 35 percent

---

table 5-2

The Slowdown in Growth Around the World

Country	GROWTH IN OUTPUT PER PERSON (PERCENT PER YEAR)	
	1948–1972	1972–1995
Canada	2.9	1.8
France	4.3	1.6
West Germany	5.7	2.0
Italy	4.9	2.3
Japan	8.2	2.6
United Kingdom	2.4	1.8
United States	2.2	1.5

Source: Angus Maddison, *Phases of Capitalist Development* (Oxford: Oxford University Press, 1982); *OECD National Accounts.*

Does total factor productivity increase, decrease, or stay the same?

b. In year 1, the capital stock was 6, the labour input was 3, and output was 12. In year 2, the capital stock was 7, the labour input was 4, and output was 14. What happened to total factor productivity between the two years?

2. Labour productivity is defined as Y/L, the amount of output divided by the amount of labour input. Start with the growth-accounting equation and show that the growth in labour productivity depends on growth in total factor productivity and growth in the capital–labour ratio. In particular, show that

$$\frac{\Delta(Y/L)}{Y/L} = \frac{\Delta A}{A} + \alpha \frac{\Delta(K/L)}{K/L}.$$

(*Hint:* You may find the following mathematical trick helpful. If $z = wx$, then the growth rate of z is approximately the growth rate of w plus the growth rate of x. That is,

$$\Delta z/z \approx \Delta w/w + \Delta x/x.)$$

3. Suppose an economy described by the Solow model is in a steady state with population growth n of 1.0 percent per year and technological progress g of 2.0 percent per year. Total output and total capital grow at 3.0 percent per year. Suppose further that the capital share of output is 0.3. If you used the growth-accounting equation to divide output growth into three sources—capital, labour, and total factor productivity—how much would you attribute to each source?

chapter 6

Unemployment

A man willing to work, and unable to find work, is perhaps the saddest
sight that fortune's inequality exhibits under the sun.

— *Thomas Carlyle*

Unemployment is the macroeconomic problem that affects people most directly and severely. For most people, the loss of a job means a reduced living standard and psychological distress. It is no surprise that unemployment is a frequent topic of political debate and that politicians often claim that their proposed policies would help create jobs.

Economists study unemployment to identify its causes and to help improve the public policies that affect the unemployed. Some of these policies, such as job-training programs, assist people in finding employment. Others, such as employment insurance, alleviate some of the hardships that the unemployed face. Still other policies affect the prevalence of unemployment inadvertently. Laws mandating a high minimum wage, for instance, are widely thought to raise unemployment among the least skilled and experienced members of the labour force. By showing the effects of various policies, economists help policy-makers evaluate their options.

In our discussions of the labour market in the previous three chapters, we ignored unemployment. Our models of national income (Chapter 3) and economic growth (Chapters 4 and 5) were built with the assumption that the economy was always at full employment. In reality, of course, not everyone in the labour force has a job all the time: all free-market economies experience some unemployment.

Figure 6-1 shows the rate of unemployment—the percentage of the labour force unemployed—in Canada since 1950. The figure shows that there is always some unemployment, although the amount fluctuates from year to year.

In this chapter we begin our study of unemployment by discussing why there is always some unemployment and what determines its level. We do not study what determines the year-to-year fluctuations in the rate of unemployment until Part Three of this book, where we examine short-run economic fluctuations. Here we examine the determinants of the **natural rate of unemployment**—the average rate of unemployment around which the econ-

at increasing the rate of job finding, they decrease the natural rate of unemployment.

Other government programs inadvertently increase the amount of frictional unemployment. One of these is **employment insurance (EI).** Under this program, unemployed workers can collect a fraction of their wages for a certain period after losing their jobs. Although the precise terms of the program differ from year to year and from province to province, a typical worker covered by employment insurance in Canada has received about 50 percent of his or her former wages for about half a year. Before change in the EI program in the mid-1990s, Canada's insurance system was one of the most generous in the world.

By softening the economic hardship of unemployment, employment insurance increases the amount of frictional unemployment and raises the natural rate. The unemployed who receive employment-insurance benefits are less pressed to search for new employment and are more likely to turn down unattractive job offers. Both of these changes in behaviour reduce the rate of job finding. In addition, because workers know that their incomes are partially protected by employment insurance, they are less likely to seek jobs with stable employment prospects and are less likely to bargain for guarantees of job security. These behavioral changes raise the rate of job separation.

That employment insurance raises the natural rate of unemployment does not necessarily imply that the policy is ill advised. The program has the benefit of reducing workers' uncertainty about their incomes. Moreover, inducing workers to reject unattractive job offers may lead to a better matching between workers and jobs. Evaluating the costs and benefits of different systems of employment insurance is a difficult task that continues to be a topic of much research.

Economists who study employment insurance often propose reforms that would reduce the amount of unemployment. One common proposal is to require a firm that lays off a worker to bear the full cost of that worker's employment benefits. Such a system is called *100 percent experience rated,* because the rate that each firm pays into the employment-insurance system fully reflects the unemployment experience of its own workers. The programs in many countries are *partially experience rated.* Under this system, when a firm lays off a worker, it is charged for only part of the worker's employment benefits; the remainder comes from the program's general revenue. Because a firm pays only a fraction of the cost of the unemployment it causes, it has an incentive to lay off workers when its demand for labour is temporarily low. Canada's system has no experience rating, so this incentive problem is acute. By reducing that incentive, the proposed reform may reduce the prevalence of temporary layoffs.

CASE STUDY

Interwar British Unemployment

Between World War I and World War II, Britain experienced persistently high unemployment. From 1920 to 1938 the unemployment rate in Britain averaged 14 percent and never fell below 9 percent.

Economists Daniel Benjamin and Levis Kochin have suggested that Britain's generous unemployment benefits can largely explain this high rate of unemployment. They cite three pieces of evidence to support their view. First, during this period, increases in British unemployment benefits coincided with increases in the economy's unemployment rate. Second, teenagers, who received few or no unemployment benefits, had much lower unemployment rates than adults. Third, when the benefits for married women were reduced in 1932, their unemployment rate dropped significantly relative to that for men. All three pieces of evidence suggest a connection between unemployment benefits and unemployment rates.

This explanation of interwar British unemployment is controversial among economists who study this period. One difficulty in interpreting the evidence is that the data on unemployment benefits and unemployment rates may reflect two different relationships—one economic and one political. On the one hand, the higher the level of benefits, the more likely it is that an unemployed person will turn down an unattractive job offer, and the higher the level of frictional unemployment. On the other hand, the higher the rate of unemployment, the more pressing unemployment becomes as a political issue, and the higher the level of benefits the government chooses to offer. Hence, high unemployment rates may have caused high unemployment benefits, rather than the other way around. When we observe an empirical relationship between unemployment rates and unemployment benefits, we cannot tell whether we have identified an economic connection, a political connection, or some combination of the two.[2]

CASE STUDY

Employment Insurance and the Rate of Job Finding

Another way to demonstrate the effect of employment insurance on job search is to examine how the economic incentives facing unemployed workers influence their rate of job finding. To do this, one needs to examine data on uemployed individuals, rather than data on economy-wide rates of unemployment. Individual data sometimes provide evidence that is less open to alternative interpretations.

One finding from individual data is that when unemployed workers become ineligible for employment insurance, the probability of their finding a new job rises markedly. Canadian evidence shows that the probability of an unemployed person finding employment varies—depending on how many weeks that person has been unemployed and how many weeks of employment-insurance

---

[2] Daniel Benjamin and Levis Kochin, "Searching for an Explanation of Unemployment in Interwar Britain," *Journal of Political Economy* 87 (June 1979): 441–478. For critical comments on this article and a reply by the authors, see *Journal of Political Economy* 90 (April 1982): 369–436.

twice that of the United States, but unions play a greater role in many European countries.

The wages of unionized workers are determined not by the equilibrium of supply and demand but by collective bargaining between union leaders and firm management. Often, the final agreement raises the wage above the equilibrium level and allows the firm to decide how many workers to employ. The result is a reduction in the number of workers hired, a lower rate of job finding, and an increase in wait unemployment.

Unions can also influence the wages paid by firms whose work forces are not unionized because the threat of unionization can keep wages above the equilibrium level. Most firms dislike unions. Unions not only raise wages but also increase the bargaining power of labour on many other issues, such as hours of employment and working conditions. A firm may choose to pay its workers high wages to keep them happy in order to discourage them from forming a union.

The unemployment caused by unions and by the threat of unionization is an instance of conflict between different groups of workers—**insiders** and **outsiders.** Those workers already employed by a firm, the insiders, typically try to keep their firm's wages high. The unemployed, the outsiders, bear part of the cost of higher wages because at a lower wage they might be hired. These two groups inevitably have conflicting interests. The effect of any bargaining process on wages and employment depends crucially on the relative influence of each group.

The conflict between insiders and outsiders is resolved differently in different countries. In some countries, such as those in North America, wage bargaining takes place at the level of the firm or plant. In other countries, such as Sweden, wage bargaining takes place at the national level—with the government often playing a key role. Despite a highly unionized labour force, Sweden has not experienced extraordinarily high unemployment throughout its history. One possible explanation is that the centralization of wage bargaining and the role of the government in the bargaining process give more influence to the outsiders, which keeps wages closer to the equilibrium level.

CASE STUDY

Unionization and Unemployment in the United States and Canada

Throughout the 1960s the United States and Canada had similar labour markets. The rates of unemployment in the two countries were about the same on average, and they fluctuated together. In the mid-1970s, the experiences of the two countries began to diverge. Unemployment became much more prevalent in Canada than in the United States. Since the early 1980s, the Canadian unemployment rate has been about 3 to 4 percentage points above the U.S. rate, and only 0.7 percentage point can be explained by the stricter definition of unemployment used in the United States.

The changing roles of unions in the two countries is one possible explanation for this divergence. In the 1960s, about 30 percent of the labour force was unionized in each country. But Canadian labour laws did more to foster union-ization than U.S. laws did. Unionization rose in Canada while it fell in the United States.

As one might have predicted, changes in real wages accompanied the change in unionization. The real wage in Canada increased by about 30 percent rela-tive to the real wage in the United States. This evidence suggests that unions in Canada pushed the real wage further above the equilibrium level, leading to more wait unemployment.

The divergence in the two unemployment rates may also be attributable to the increase in the availability of employment-insurance benefits in Canada. Not only does employment insurance raise search times and the amount of fric-tional unemployment, but it also interacts with the effects of unionization in two ways. First, employment insurance makes unemployed workers more will-ing to wait for a high-wage job in a unionized firm rather than take a lower-wage job in a nonunion firm. Second, because employment insurance partially protects the incomes of unemployed workers, it makes unions more willing to press for high wages at the expense of lower employment.[7]

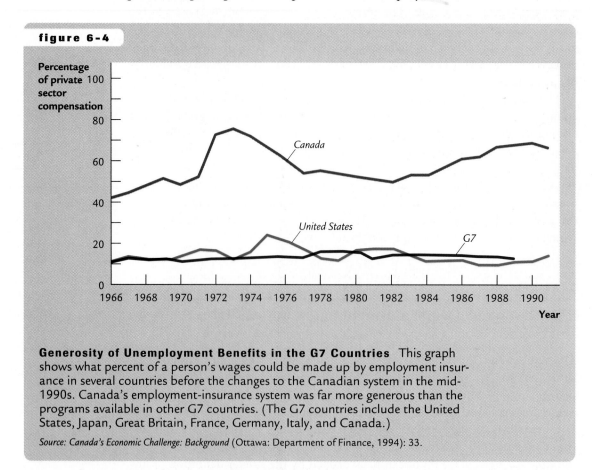

figure 6-4

Generosity of Unemployment Benefits in the G7 Countries This graph shows what percent of a person's wages could be made up by employment insur-ance in several countries before the changes to the Canadian system in the mid-1990s. Canada's employment-insurance system was far more generous than the programs available in other G7 countries. (The G7 countries include the United States, Japan, Great Britain, France, Germany, Italy, and Canada.)

Source: Canada's Economic Challenge: Background (Ottawa: Department of Finance, 1994): 33.

---

[7] Herbert G. Grubel, "Drifting Apart: Canadian and U.S. Labor Markets," *Contemporary Policy Issues* 6 (January 1988): 39–55, also in *Journal of Economic and Monetary Affairs* 2 (Winter 1988): 59–75.

As a matter of history, the relative generosity of Canada's employment-insurance system is shown in Figure 6-4. The data in this graph give conflicting messages concerning the role played by employment insurance in determining unemployment. On the one hand, Canada's insurance program is dramatically more generous than that of the United States. This fact is consistent with the proposition that the availability of employment insurance raises unemployment (since the U.S. unemployment rate is much lower than Canada's). On the other hand, Canada's insurance program is far more generous than that of the other Group of 7 (G7) countries (the United States, Japan, Great Britain, France, Germany, Italy, and Canada) as well, and the unemployment rate in the European countries of this group has been just as high (or higher) as it has been in Canada.

Efficiency Wages

Efficiency-wage theories propose a third cause of wage rigidity in addition to minimum-wage laws and unionization. These theories hold that high wages make workers more productive. The influence of wages on worker efficiency may explain the failure of firms to cut wages despite an excess supply of labour. Even though a wage reduction would lower a firm's wage bill, it would also—if these theories are correct—lower worker productivity and the firm's profits.

Economists have proposed various theories to explain how wages affect worker productivity. One efficiency-wage theory, which is applied mostly to poorer countries, holds that wages influence nutrition. Better-paid workers can afford a more nutritious diet, and healthier workers are more productive. A firm may decide to pay a wage above the equilibrium level to maintain a healthy work force. Obviously, this consideration is not important for employers in wealthy countries, such as Canada, the United States, and most of Europe, since the equilibrium wage is well above the level necessary to maintain good health.

A second efficiency-wage theory, which is more relevant for developed countries, holds that high wages reduce labour turnover. Workers quit jobs for many reasons—to accept better positions at other firms, to change careers, or to move to other parts of the country. The more a firm pays its workers, the greater their incentive to stay with the firm. By paying a high wage, a firm reduces the frequency of quits, thereby decreasing the time spent hiring and training new workers.

A third efficiency-wage theory holds that the average quality of a firm's work force depends on the wage it pays its employees. If a firm reduces its wage, the best employees may take jobs elsewhere, leaving the firm with inferior employees who have fewer alternative opportunities. Economists recognize this unfavourable sorting as an example of *adverse selection*—the tendency of people with more information (in this case, the workers, who know their own outside opportunities) to self-select in a way that disadvantages people with less information (the firm). By paying a wage above the equilibrium level, the firm may reduce adverse selection, improve the average quality of its work force, and thereby increase productivity.

A fourth efficiency-wage theory holds that a high wage improves worker effort. This theory posits that firms cannot perfectly monitor their employees' work effort, and that employees must themselves decide how hard to work. Workers can choose to work hard, or they can choose to shirk and risk getting caught and fired. Economists recognize this possibility as an example of *moral hazard*—the tendency of people to behave inappropriately when their behaviour is imperfectly monitored. The firm can reduce the problem of moral hazard by paying a high wage. The higher the wage, the greater the cost to the worker of getting fired. By paying a higher wage, a firm induces more of its employees not to shirk and thus increases their productivity.

Although these four efficiency-wage theories differ in detail, they share a common theme: because a firm operates more efficiently if it pays its workers a high wage, the firm may find it profitable to keep wages above the level that balances supply and demand. The result of this higher-than-equilibrium wage is a lower rate of job finding and greater wait unemployment.[8]

CASE STUDY

Henry Ford's $5 Workday

In 1914 the Ford Motor Company started paying its U.S. workers $5 per day. Since the prevailing wage at the time was between $2 and $3 per day, Ford's wage was well above the equilibrium level. Not surprisingly, long lines of job seekers waited outside the Ford plant gates hoping for a chance to earn this high wage.

What was Ford's motive? Henry Ford later wrote, "We wanted to pay these wages so that the business would be on a lasting foundation. We were building for the future. A low wage business is always insecure . . . . The payment of five dollars a day for an eight hour day was one of the finest cost cutting moves we ever made."

From the standpoint of traditional economic theory, Ford's explanation seems peculiar. He was suggesting that *high* wages imply *low* costs. But perhaps Ford had discovered efficiency-wage theory. Perhaps he was using the high wage to increase worker productivity.

Evidence suggests that paying such a high wage did benefit the company. According to an engineering report written at the time, "The Ford high wage does away with all the inertia and living force resistance. . . . The workingmen are absolutely docile, and it is safe to say that since the last day of 1913, every single day has seen major reductions in Ford shops' labor costs." Absenteeism fell by 75 percent, suggesting a large increase in worker effort. Alan Nevins, a historian who studied the early Ford Motor Company, wrote, "Ford and his

---

[8] For more extended discussions of efficiency wages, see Janet Yellen, "Efficiency Wage Models of Unemployment," *American Economic Review Papers and Proceedings* (May 1984): 200–205; and Lawrence Katz, "Efficiency Wages: A Partial Evaluation," *NBER Macroeconomics Annual* (1986): 235–276.

associates freely declared on many occasions that the high wage policy had turned out to be good business. By this they meant that it had improved the discipline of the workers, given them a more loyal interest in the institution, and raised their personal efficiency."[9]

6-4 | Patterns of Unemployment

So far we have developed the theory behind the natural rate of unemployment. We began by showing that the economy's steady-state unemployment rate depends on the rates of job separation and job finding. Then we discussed two reasons why job finding is not instantaneous: the process of job search (which leads to frictional unemployment) and wage rigidity (which leads to wait unemployment). Wage rigidity, in turn, arises from minimum-wage laws, unionization, and efficiency wages.

With these theories as background, we now examine some additional facts about unemployment. These facts will help us to evaluate our theories and assess public policies aimed at reducing unemployment.

The Duration of Unemployment

When a person becomes unemployed, is the spell of unemployment likely to be short or long? The answer to this question is important because it indicates the reasons for the unemployment and what policy response is appropriate. On the one hand, if most unemployment is short-term, one might argue that it is frictional and perhaps unavoidable. Unemployed workers may need some time to search for the job that is best suited to their skills and tastes. On the other hand, long-term unemployment cannot easily be attributed to the time it takes to match jobs and workers: we would not expect this matching process to take many months. Long-term unemployment is more likely to be wait unemployment. Thus, data on the duration of unemployment can affect our view about the reasons for unemployment.

In any one month, a lot of action takes place within Canada's labour market. Over the last 25 years, during an average month, about 1.1 million Canadians were unemployed. About 22 percent of these individuals became employed the next month, and another 17 percent left the labour force altogether. Of the two-thirds that remained unemployed, it was typical for about one-third of these to remain unemployed six months later. But changes have occurred in the makeup of the unemployed during this period. Compared to earlier times, a smaller proportion of unemployment is due to short unemployment spells

---

[9] Jeremy I. Bulow and Lawrence H. Summers, "A Theory of Dual Labor Markets With Application to Industrial Policy, Discrimination, and Keynesian Unemployment," *Journal of Labor Economics* 4 (July 1986): 376–414; Daniel M. G. Raff and Lawrence H. Summers, "Did Henry Ford Pay Efficiency Wages?" *Journal of Labor Economics* 5 (October 1987, Part 2): S57–S86.

spread across a large number of people, and a bigger proportion of the problem is due to a particular group of individuals' remaining unemployed longer. Policymakers speak in terms of the "incidence" of unemployment across the population being reduced but the "duration" of each unemployment spell having been increased (doubled from the mid-1970s to the mid-1990s). Statistics Canada has estimated that about two-thirds of any increase in the unemployment rate is due to longer duration and one-third to higher incidence.[10]

This evidence on the duration of unemployment has an important implication for public policy. If the goal is to lower substantially the natural rate of unemployment, policies must aim at the long-term unemployed, because these individuals account for a large amount of unemployment. Yet policies must be carefully targeted, because the long-term unemployed still constitute a minority of those who become unemployed at some point during the year. It is still the case that most people who become unemployed find work within a fairly short time.

Variation in the Unemployment Rate Across Age Groups and Regions

The rate of unemployment varies substantially across different groups within the population. Table 6-2 presents the unemployment rates for different age groups during the fall of 1992, the peak year for unemployment in the last ten years. While the country's overall unemployment rate was 11.3 percent in 1992, this unemployment was not equally distributed by age. The unemployment rate for teenagers was a full 2.5 times that of people in the 45–54 age category. Not surprisingly, education affects employment prospects as well. Over the last 25 years, the unemployment rate for those with only primary-level education has been 2.75 times that facing those with a university education. Most analysts expect this gap to widen in years to come.

table 6-2

Unemployment by Age Groups: October 1992

Age	Unemployment Rate (%)
15–19	19.0
20–24	14.2
25–34	11.4
35–44	8.6
45–54	7.5
55–64	8.9
65 and over	5.4

Source: Statistics Canada, *Catalogue 71-001* (October 1992): B7.

[10] Mike Corak, "The Duration of Unemployment During Boom and Bust," *Canadian Economic Observer* (September 1993): 4.9.

To explain the differences in unemployment across age groups, recall our model of the natural rate of unemployment. The model isolates two possible causes for a high rate of unemployment: a low rate of job finding, or a high rate of job separation. When economists study data on the transition of individuals between employment and unemployment, they find that those groups with high unemployment tend to have high rates of job separation. They find less variation across groups in the rate of job finding.

These findings help explain the higher unemployment rates for younger workers. Younger workers have only recently entered the labour market, and they are often uncertain about their career plans. It may be best for them to try different types of jobs before making a long-term commitment to a specific occupation. If so, we should expect a higher rate of job separation and a higher rate of frictional unemployment for this group.

Finally, unemployment varies significantly across Canadian regions. Again considering 1992, the last time the overall unemployment rate peaked (at 11.3 percent) the regional unemployment rates were: the Atlantic provinces—15 percent, Quebec—12.5 percent, Ontario—11 percent, the Prairie provinces—9 percent, and British Columbia—10 percent. This regional variation helps explain why it is difficult to reform the employment-insurance system so that it operates as a true insurance policy instead of being a means for performing *ongoing* income redistribution. Without some other policies to support those in the depressed regions, many policymakers oppose changes and cuts in the current employment-insurance system. There is a certain irony in this outcome. It is concern for the welfare of Canadians living in the depressed regions in the *short run* that limits reforms to employment insurance from being implemented. Nevertheless, it can hurt the welfare of those same individuals in the *long run* if employment insurance is not reformed. Without reform, these regions can never escape the long-run dependency trap.

The Upward Drift in Unemployment   Over the past 50 years, the rate of unemployment in Canada has drifted upward. As Figure 6-5 shows, unemployment averaged well below 5 percent in the 1950s and 1960s, and above 9 percent in the 1980s and 1990s. Although economists do not have a conclusive explanation for this trend, and there are some signs that the trend may be coming to an end, they have proposed various hypotheses.

One explanation stresses the changing composition of the Canadian labour force. After World War II, birth rates rose dramatically, producing a baby-boom generation that began entering the labour force around 1970. Because younger workers have higher unemployment rates, this influx of baby boomers into the labour force increased the average level of unemployment. At roughly the same time, the participation of women in the labour force also was increasing significantly. Since 1966, the labour-force participation rate for women has risen from 35 percent to 58 percent. Since women historically have had higher unemployment rates than men (a difference that has disappeared since the early 1980s), the increasing proportion of women in the labour force may have raised the average unemployment rate, at least in the 1970s.

These two demographic changes, however, cannot fully explain the upward trend in unemployment because the trend also was apparent for fixed demo-

figure 6-5

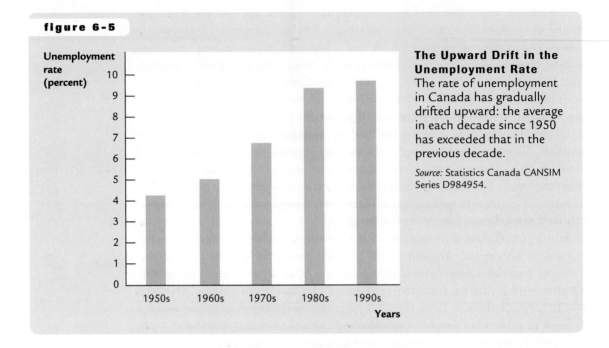

The Upward Drift in the Unemployment Rate
The rate of unemployment in Canada has gradually drifted upward: the average in each decade since 1950 has exceeded that in the previous decade.

Source: Statistics Canada CANSIM Series D984954.

graphic groups. For example, for prime-aged males (men aged 25 years or more), the average unemployment rate rose from below 3 percent in the 1950s and 1960s to 4.2 percent in the 1970s, 7.1 percent in the 1980s, and 9.1 percent in the 1990s.

Another point to bear in mind is that some of the demographic shifts and microeconomic rigidities that can explain rising unemployment in the 1970s have since reversed—without a corresponding decrease in unemployment. For example, as a proportion of the population, the 15–24 age group dropped from 26 percent of the population in the mid-1970s to under 18 percent in 1992. Also the *ratio* of the minimum wage to the average hourly wage available in Canada *fell* by 15 percent over this same period.[11]

A second possible explanation for the upward trend in unemployment is that sectoral shifts have become more prevalent. The greater the amount of sectoral reallocation, the greater the rate of job separation and the higher the level of frictional unemployment.[12] One source of sectoral shifts has been the increased pace of technological change involving robotics and major breakthroughs in the methods of information storage and transfer. Another series of sectoral shifts has resulted from the major shifts in natural resource prices. The world price of oil has been *far* more volatile since the mid-1970s, and the relative price of most of the natural resources that Canada exports has fallen by a factor of 50

---

[11] Pierre Fortin, "Slow Growth, Unemployment and Debt: What Happened? What Can We Do?" in *The Bell Canada Papers on Economic and Public Policy* (Kingston: John Deutsch Institute for the Study of Economic Policy, 1994).

[12] David M. Lilien, "Sectoral Shifts and Cyclical Unemployment," *Journal of Political Economy* 90 (August 1982): 777–793.

Unemployment, Inequality, and Government Policy

The efficiency-wage model is one theory of unemployment that was discussed in the main body of this chapter. In this appendix, we describe a specific version of this model that can be used as a vehicle to assess some common presumptions—such as "payroll taxes are job killers" and "globalization makes rising income inequality inevitable."

As explained earlier, one common version of the efficiency-wage model is based on the assumption of asymmetric information. Employees know whether they are shirking, but employers cannot be sure. To mention just one consideration, it is impossible for employers to verify fully whether individual employees can be believed when they call in sick. Firms can lessen this worker-productivity problem by making it more expensive for employees to lose their jobs. By paying a wage that exceeds each worker's alternative option, employers can ensure that their employees work hard to avoid being fired. But when all firms raise payments in this way, the overall level of wages exceeds what would obtain in a competitive market. With labour more expensive, firms hire fewer workers in total, and there is unemployment, as shown in Figure 6-3.

It is worthwhile formalizing this model of the labour market. Let w and b stand for the wage a worker receives from her employer and the income she can expect if she leaves that firm, respectively. With the firm's incomplete monitoring process, there is a probability that the worker can be fired for low productivity. That probability can be reduced by putting forth more effort, but this effort decreases the utility that the employee receives while at work. Let fraction a times the wage represent the income equivalent of the loss in utility that stems from this extra effort.

The worker faces two options: either she stays on the job with a net return of $(1 - a)w$, or she is fired, in which case she receives b. Firms will get high productivity from workers as long as $(1 - a)w$ is greater than or equal to b. But in the interest of minimizing wage costs, firms do not want to meet this constraint with any unnecessary payment, so they set

$$w = b/(1 - a).$$

Since a is a fraction, this equation verifies that firms set wages above the workers' alternative.

How is b, the workers' alternative, determined? Again, there are two options. A fired worker may get employed by another firm (and the probability of this outcome is the economy's employment rate, $(1 - u)$), or she may go without work (and the probability of this happening is the unemployment rate, u). In a full equilibrium, all firms have to pay the same wage to keep their workers.

Finally, for simplicity, let us assume that there is an employment-insurance program that pays workers fraction c of their former wage if they are out of work. All this means that each worker's alternative is

$$b = (1 - u)w + u(cw).$$

When this definition of the alternative option is substituted into the wage-setting rule, $w = b/(1 - a)$, the result can be simplified to

$$u = a/(1 - c).$$

This expression for the steady-state unemployment rate indicates three things. First, if workers did not find hard work distasteful at all (that is, if $a = 0$), firms would not need to set wages above the competitive level to limit any shirking problem, so there would be no unemployment. (Implicitly, this is what we assumed in Chapter 3.) Second, since there is no variable relating to worker skill or education levels in the unemployment-rate equation, changes in these factors do *not* affect employment. If workers are more skilled, both their current employer and other potential employers are prepared to pay them more. So wages rise generally and there are no changes in the incentive to shirk. The model is consistent with experience in this regard. Labour productivity increased dramatically over the twentieth century and, just as the model predicts, we observed a vast increase in real wages and no long-term trend in the unemployment rate.

The third implication of this model is that the unemployment problem is accentuated by a more generous employment-insurance program (a higher value for c). The reason? More generous support for unemployment lowers the cost of being fired. Workers react by shirking more, so firms react by raising wages. With higher wages, firms find it profitable to hire fewer workers. Since unemployment insurance is a form of income redistribution, the model illustrates the standard tradeoff involved: the size of the overall economic pie shrinks when we try to redistribute. This fact does not mean that redistribution should be rejected. Society may prefer a higher unemployment rate if each individual involved is better protected from hardship.

Let us extend this model to allow for payroll and personal income taxes. Employees pay tax rate t times their wages, while employment-insurance receipts are not taxed. Since workers keep only proportion $(1 - t)$ of each dollar earned on the job, the revised expressions are $w(1 - t)(1 - a) = b$ and $b = (1 - u)w(1 - t) + u(cw)$. These relationships lead to a revised expression for the steady-state unemployment rate:

$$u = a(1 - t)/(1 - c - t).$$

We see that the unemployment rate depends on the tax rate faced by employees. Higher taxes lower the return from working. To counteract the resulting increased propensity to shirk, firms raise wages and fewer individuals find jobs.

An important insight can be gained by inserting representative numerical values for each term in the unemployment-rate equation. Initially, let us assume a tax rate of 15 percent ($t = 0.15$), an employment insurance program that pays each former worker one-half of what she previously earned ($c = 0.5$), and a shirking parameter value ($a = 0.02$) that yields a representative value for unemployment of 5 percent ($u = 0.05$). Now we investigate how much the unemployment rate rises as we consider higher values for the tax rate (and the other parameters, c and a, are fixed). You can verify that as the tax rate rises by equal amounts, first from 15 to 25 percent and then from 25 to 35 percent, the unemployment rate rises, first by 1 percentage point, from 5 to 6 percent, and then by 2.67 percentage points, from 6 to 8.67 percent. Clearly, the unemployment rate rises much more when taxes are already high. The model is consistent with the widespread drive to lower taxes.

It is noteworthy that the *employer* payroll tax rate does not affect unemployment. Just like an increase in general productivity, a lower employer payroll tax rate raises both the firms' willingness to pay higher wages and the workers' wage claims. As a result, unemployment can be reduced by a revenue-neutral cut in the employee payroll tax rate (financed by an increase in the employer payroll tax rate).

The major payroll taxes in Canada are the contributions to employment insurance (EI) and to the public pension programs (the CPP and QPP). During the late 1990s, the contributions to EI were reduced by a small amount each year (because the EI account was in surplus), but the contributions to the CPP/QPP were increased a great deal more (because this is how the government means to keep the public pension system from going bankrupt as the baby-boom generation ages). Since, on balance, payroll taxes have risen and will continue to rise, there will remain upward pressure on unemployment. It is unfortunate that the government has not decreased its reliance on the employee portion of this levy, since (as this model illustrates) such a change in policy could reverse this upward pressure on the unemployment rate.

Inequality Increased taxation is not the only basis for anticipating rising unemployment. Globalization is another. Compared to many low-wage countries, Canada has an abundance of skilled workers and a relatively small proportion of the population in the unskilled category. The opposite is the case in the developing countries. With increased integration among the world economies, Canada specializes in the production of goods that emphasize our relatively abundant factor, skilled labour, so it is the wages of skilled workers that are bid up by increased foreign trade. The other side of this development is that Canada relies more on imports to supply goods that only require unskilled labour, and this means that the demand for unskilled labour falls in Canada. The result is either lower wages for the unskilled in Canada (if there is no legislation that puts a floor on wages here) or rising unemployment among the unskilled (if there is a floor on wages—such as that imposed by minimum-wage laws). In either case, unskilled individuals can lose in the new global economy.

A second hypothesis concerning rising income inequality is that, during the last 30 years, technological change has been decidedly skill-biased—with the result that the demand for skilled workers has risen while that for the unskilled has fallen. Just as with the globalization hypothesis, the effects of these shifts in demand depend on whether it is possible for wages in the unskilled sector to fall.

The United States and Europe are often cited as illustrations of the possible outcomes. The United States has only a limited welfare state, so there is little to stop increased wage inequality from emerging, as indeed it has in recent decades. European governments, on the other hand, maintain floors below which the wages of the unskilled cannot be pushed. When technological change decreases the demand for unskilled labour, firms have no freedom to do anything but reduce their employment of these individuals. Thus, Europe has avoided large increases in wage inequality, but the unemployment rate has been very high there for many years.

Government Policy Most economists favour the second hypothesis for explaining rising income inequality. This is because inequality has increased so much *within* each industry and occupation, in ways that are unrelated to foreign trade. But whatever the cause, the plight of the less skilled is a dire one. Figure 6-6 allows us to consider policy options.

Panel (a) in Figure 6-6 depicts the skilled labour market, while panel (b) illustrates the unskilled market. There is unemployment in both sectors. In the skilled labour market, unemployment is due to incomplete information and efficiency wages. In the unskilled market, unemployment is due to minimum wages. Let us consider a reduction in employer payroll taxes. Cutting the tax that employers must pay when hiring skilled workers results in a shift up in the demand for skilled labour. But since all firms react in this same way, the workers' outside option rises to the same extent, so the market outcome moves from

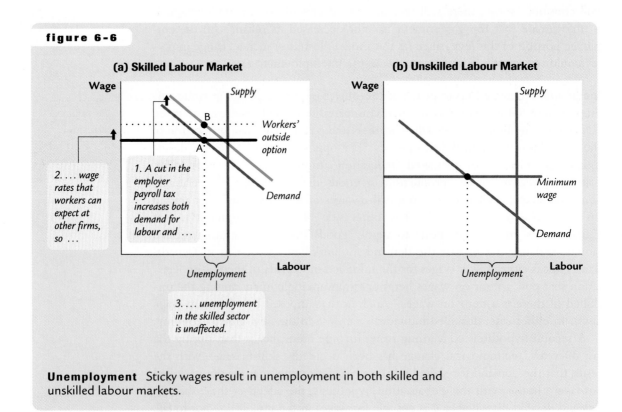

figure 6-6

(a) Skilled Labour Market

(b) Unskilled Labour Market

Unemployment Sticky wages result in unemployment in both skilled and unskilled labour markets.

Once we admit the logic of including demand deposits in the measured money stock, many other assets become candidates for inclusion. Funds in savings accounts, for example, can be easily transferred into chequing accounts; these assets are almost as convenient for transactions. Further, funds in similar accounts in trust companies and the Caisses Populaires in Quebec can be easily used for transactions. Thus, they could be included in the quantity of money.

Because it is hard to judge exactly which assets should be included in the money stock, various measures are available. Table 7-1 presents the five measures of the money stock that the Bank of Canada calculates for the Canadian economy, together with a list of which assets are included in each measure. From the smallest to the largest, they are designated $B, M1, M2, M3$, and $M2+$. The most commonly used measures for studying the effects of money on the economy are $M1$ and $M2$. There is no consensus, however, about which measure of the money stock is best. Disagreements about monetary policy sometimes arise because different measures of money are moving in different directions.

Luckily, the different measures normally move together and so tell the same story about whether the quantity of money is growing quickly or slowly.

7-2 | The Quantity Theory of Money

Having defined what money is and described how it is controlled and measured, we can now examine how the quantity of money affects the economy. To do this, we must see how the quantity of money is related to other economic variables, such as prices and incomes.

Transactions and the Quantity Equation

People hold money to buy goods and services. The more money they need for such transactions, the more money they hold. Thus, the quantity of money in the economy is closely related to the number of dollars exchanged in transactions.

The link between transactions and money is expressed in the following equation, called the **quantity equation:**

$$\text{Money} \times \text{Velocity} = \text{Price} \times \text{Transactions}$$
$$M \quad \times \quad V \quad = \quad P \quad \times \quad T.$$

Let's examine each of the four variables in this equation.

The right-hand side of the quantity equation tells us about transactions. T represents the total number of transactions during some period of time, say, a year. In other words, T is the number of times in a year that goods or services are exchanged for money. P is the price of a typical transaction—the number of dollars exchanged. The product of the price of a transaction and the number of transactions, PT, equals the number of dollars exchanged in a year.

The left-hand side of the quantity equation tells us about the money used to make the transactions. M is the quantity of money. V is called the **transactions velocity of money** and measures the rate at which money circulates in the economy. In other words, velocity tells us the number of times a dollar bill changes hands in a given period of time.

For example, suppose that 60 loaves of bread are sold in a given year at $0.50 per loaf. Then T equals 60 loaves per year, and P equals $0.50 per loaf. The total number of dollars exchanged is

$$PT = \$0.50/\text{loaf} \times 60 \text{ loaves/year} = \$30/\text{year}.$$

The right-hand side of the quantity equation equals $30 per year, which is the dollar value of all transactions.

Suppose further that the quantity of money in the economy is $10. By rearranging the quantity equation, we can compute velocity as

$$
\begin{aligned}
V &= PT/M \\
&= (\$30/\text{year})/(\$10) \\
&= 3 \text{ times per year.}
\end{aligned}
$$

That is, for $30 of transactions per year to take place with $10 of money, each dollar must change hands 3 times per year.

The quantity equation is an *identity:* the definitions of the four variables make it true. The equation is useful because it shows that if one of the variables changes, one or more of the others must also change to maintain the equality. For example, if the quantity of money increases and the velocity of money stays unchanged, then either the price or the number of transactions must rise.

From Transactions to Income

When studying the role of money in the economy, economists usually use a slightly different version of the quantity equation than the one just introduced. The problem with the first equation is that the number of transactions is difficult to measure. To solve this problem, the number of transactions T is replaced by the total output of the economy Y.

Transactions and output are closely related, because the more the economy produces, the more goods are bought and sold. They are not the same, however. When one person sells a used car to another person, for example, they make a transaction using money, even though the used car is not part of current output. Nonetheless, the dollar value of transactions is roughly proportional to the dollar value of output.

If Y denotes the amount of output and P denotes the price of one unit of output, then the dollar value of output is PY. We encountered measures for these variables when we discussed the national accounts in Chapter 2: Y is real GDP, P the GDP deflator, and PY nominal GDP. The quantity equation becomes

$$\text{Money} \times \text{Velocity} = \text{Price} \times \text{Output}$$
$$M \quad \times \quad V \quad = \quad P \quad \times \quad Y.$$

Because Y is also total income, V in this version of the quantity equation is called the **income velocity of money.** The income velocity of money tells us the number of times a dollar bill enters someone's income in a given period of time. This version of the quantity equation is the most common, and it is the one we use from now on.

The Money Demand Function and the Quantity Equation

When we analyze how money affects the economy, it is often useful to express the quantity of money in terms of the quantity of goods and services it can buy. This amount, M/P, is called **real money balances.**

Real money balances measure the purchasing power of the stock of money. For example, consider an economy that produces only bread. If the quantity of money is $10, and the price of a loaf is $0.50, then real money balances are 20 loaves of bread. That is, at current prices, the stock of money in the economy is able to buy 20 loaves.

A **money demand function** is an equation that shows what determines the quantity of real money balances people wish to hold. A simple money demand function is

$$(M/P)^\text{d} = kY,$$

where k is a constant that tells us how much money people want to hold for every dollar of income. This equation states that the quantity of real money balances demanded is proportional to real income.

The money demand function is like the demand function for a particular good. Here the "good" is the convenience of holding real money balances. Just as owning an automobile makes it easier for a person to travel, holding money makes it easier to make transactions. Therefore, just as higher income leads to a greater demand for automobiles, higher income also leads to a greater demand for real money balances.

This money demand function offers another way to view the quantity equation. To see this, add to the money demand function the condition that the demand for real money balances $(M/P)^\text{d}$ must equal the supply M/P. Therefore,

$$(M/P) = kY.$$

A simple rearrangement of terms changes this equation into

$$M(1/k) = PY,$$

which can be written as

$$MV = PY,$$

where $V = 1/k$. This simple mathematics shows the link between the demand for money and the velocity of money. When people want to hold a lot of money for each dollar of income (k is large), money changes hands infrequently (V is small). Conversely, when people want to hold only a little money (k is small), money changes hands frequently (V is large). In other words, the money demand parameter k and the velocity of money V are opposite sides of the same coin.

The Assumption of Constant Velocity

The quantity equation can be viewed as merely a definition: it defines velocity V as the ratio of nominal GDP, PY, to the quantity of money M. Yet if we make the additional assumption that the velocity of money is constant, then the quantity equation becomes a useful theory of the effects of money, called the **quantity theory of money.**

As with many of the assumptions in economics, the assumption of constant velocity is only an approximation to reality. Velocity does change if the money demand function changes. For example, when automatic teller machines were introduced, people could reduce their average money holdings, which meant a fall in the money demand parameter k and an increase in velocity V. Nonetheless, experience shows that the assumption of constant velocity provides a good approximation in many situations. Let's therefore assume that velocity is constant and see what this assumption implies about the effects of the money supply on the economy.

Once we assume that velocity is constant, the quantity equation can be seen as a theory of what determines nominal GDP. The quantity equation says

$$M\bar{V} = PY,$$

where the bar over V means that velocity is fixed. Therefore, a change in the quantity of money (M) must cause a proportionate change in nominal GDP (PY). That is, if velocity is fixed, the quantity of money determines the dollar value of the economy's output.

Money, Prices, and Inflation

We now have a theory to explain what determines the economy's overall level of prices. The theory has three building blocks:

1. The factors of production and the production function determine the level of output Y. We borrow this conclusion from Chapter 3.

2. The money supply determines the nominal value of output, PY. This conclusion follows from the quantity equation and the assumption that the velocity of money is fixed.

3. The price level P is then the ratio of the nominal value of output, PY, to the level of output Y.

In other words, the productive capability of the economy determines real GDP, the quantity of money determines nominal GDP, and the GDP deflator is the ratio of nominal GDP to real GDP.

This theory explains what happens when the Bank of Canada changes the supply of money. Because velocity is fixed, any change in the supply of money leads to a proportionate change in nominal GDP. Because the factors of production and the production function have already determined real GDP, the change in nominal GDP must represent a change in the price level. Hence, the quantity theory implies that the price level is proportional to the money supply.

Because the inflation rate is the percentage change in the price level, this theory of the price level is also a theory of the inflation rate. The quantity equation, written in percentage-change form, is

% Change in M + % Change in V = % Change in P + % Change in Y.

Consider each of these four terms. First, the percentage change in the quantity of money M is under the control of the central bank. Second, the percentage change in velocity V reflects shifts in money demand; we have assumed that velocity is constant, so the percentage change in velocity is zero. Third, the percentage change in the price level P is the rate of inflation; this is the variable in the equation that we would like to explain. Fourth, the percentage change in output Y depends on growth in the factors of production and on technological progress, which for our present purposes we can take as given. This analysis tells us that (except for a constant that depends on exogenous growth in output) the growth in the money supply determines the rate of inflation.

Thus, the quantity theory of money states that the central bank, which controls the money supply, has ultimate control over the rate of inflation. If the central bank keeps the money supply stable, the price level will be stable. If the central bank increases the money supply rapidly, the price level will rise rapidly.

CASE STUDY

Inflation and Money Growth

"Inflation is always and everywhere a monetary phenomenon." So wrote Milton Friedman, the great economist who won the Nobel Prize in economics in 1976. The quantity theory of money leads us to agree that the growth in the quantity of money is the primary determinant of the inflation rate. Yet Friedman's claim is empirical, not theoretical. To evaluate his claim, and to judge the usefulness of our theory, we need to look at data on money and prices.

Friedman, together with fellow economist Anna Schwartz, wrote two treatises on monetary history that documented the sources and effects of changes in the quantity of money over the past century.[4] Figure 7-1 uses some of their

---

[4] Milton Friedman and Anna J. Schwartz, *A Monetary History of the United States, 1867–1960* (Princeton, NJ: Princeton University Press, 1963); Milton Friedman and Anna J. Schwartz, *Monetary Trends in the United States and the United Kingdom: Their Relation to Income, Prices, and Interest Rates, 1867–1975* (Chicago: University of Chicago Press, 1982).

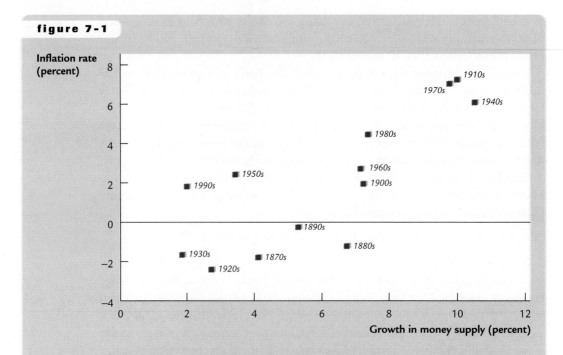

figure 7-1

Historical Data on U.S. Inflation and Money Growth In this scatterplot of money growth and inflation, each point represents a decade. The horizontal axis shows the average growth in the money supply (as measured by *M2*) over the decade, and the vertical axis shows the average rate of inflation (as measured by the GDP deflator). The positive correlation between money growth and inflation is evidence for the quantity theory's prediction that high money growth leads to high inflation.

Source: For the data through the 1960s: Milton Friedman and Anna J. Schwartz, *Monetary Trends in the United States and the United Kingdom: Their Relation to Income, Prices, and Interest Rates 1867–1975* (Chicago: University of Chicago Press, 1982). For recent data: U.S. Department of Commerce, Federal Reserve Board.

data and plots the average rate of money growth and the average rate of inflation in the United States over each decade since the 1870s. The data verify the link between inflation and growth in the quantity of money. Decades with high money growth tend to have high inflation, and decades with low money growth tend to have low inflation.

Figure 7-2 examines the same question with international data. It shows the average rate of inflation and the average rate of money growth in 34 countries during the 1980s. Again, the link between money growth and inflation is clear. Countries with high money growth tend to have high inflation, and countries with low money growth tend to have low inflation.

If we looked at monthly data on money growth and inflation, rather than data for 10-year periods, we would not see as close a connection between

figure 7-2

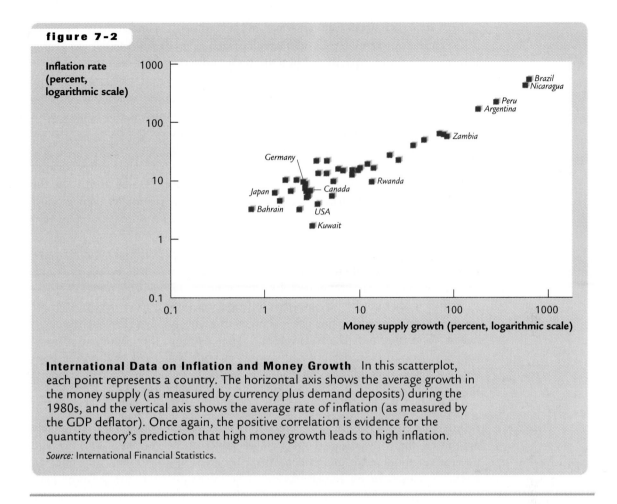

International Data on Inflation and Money Growth   In this scatterplot, each point represents a country. The horizontal axis shows the average growth in the money supply (as measured by currency plus demand deposits) during the 1980s, and the vertical axis shows the average rate of inflation (as measured by the GDP deflator). Once again, the positive correlation is evidence for the quantity theory's prediction that high money growth leads to high inflation.

Source: International Financial Statistics.

these two variables. This is because real GDP is not independent of the money supply in the short run. Thus, the quantity theory of inflation works best in the long run, not in the short run. We examine the short-run impact of changes in the quantity of money when we turn to economic fluctuations in Part Three of this book.

7-3 | Seigniorage: The Revenue From Printing Money

So far, we have seen how growth in the money supply causes inflation. But what might ever induce the government to increase the money supply? Here we examine one answer to this question.

Let's start with an indisputable fact: all governments spend money. Some of this spending is to buy goods and services (such as roads and police), and some is to provide transfer payments (for the poor and elderly, for example). A government can finance its spending in three ways. First, it can raise revenue through taxes, such as personal and corporate income taxes. Second, it can borrow from the public by selling government bonds. Third, it can simply print money. It does this indirectly—by selling bonds to the central bank and having the central bank issue new money to pay for the bonds.

The revenue raised through the printing of money is called **seigniorage.** The term comes from *seigneur,* the French word for "feudal lord." In the Middle Ages, the lord had the exclusive right on his manor to coin money. Today this right belongs to the central government, and it is one source of revenue.

When the government prints money to finance expenditure, it increases the money supply. The increase in the money supply, in turn, causes inflation. Printing money to raise revenue is like imposing an *inflation tax.*

At first it may not be obvious that inflation can be viewed as a tax. After all, no one receives a bill for this tax—the government merely prints the money it needs. Who then pays the inflation tax? The answer is the holders of money. As prices rise, the real value of the money in your wallet falls. When the government prints new money for its use, it makes the old money in the hands of the public less valuable. Thus, inflation is like a tax on holding money.

The amount raised by printing money varies substantially from country to country. In North America, the amount has been small: seigniorage has usually accounted for only about 1 percent of government revenue. In Italy and Greece, seigniorage has often been over 10 percent of government revenue.[5] In countries experiencing hyperinflation, seigniorage is often the government's chief source of revenue—indeed, the need to print money to finance expenditure is a primary cause of hyperinflation.

CASE STUDY

American and Russian Inflations

Although seigniorage has not been a major source of revenue for either the Canadian or the American government in recent history, the situation was very different two centuries ago in the United States, and it has been very different in Russia recently. We consider first the American history.

Beginning in 1775 the Continental Congress needed to find a way to finance the Revolution, but it had limited ability to raise revenue through taxa-

[5] William Scarth, "A Note on the Desirability of a Separate Quebec Currency," in David Laidler and William Robson, *Two Nations, One Money?* (Toronto: C.D. Howe Institute, 1991): 76; Stanley Fischer, "Seigniorage and the Case for a National Money," *Journal of Political Economy* 90 (April 1982): 295–313.

tion. It therefore relied heavily on the printing of fiat money to help pay for the war. The Continental Congress's reliance on seigniorage increased over time. In 1775 new issues of continental currency were approximately $6 million. This amount increased to $19 million in 1776, $13 million in 1777, $63 million in 1778, and $125 million in 1779.

Not surprisingly, this rapid growth in the money supply led to massive inflation. At the end of the war, the price of gold measured in continental dollars was more than 100 times its level of only a few years earlier. The large quantity of the continental currency made the continental dollar nearly worthless. This experience also gave birth to a once popular expression: people used to say something was "not worth a continental" to mean that the item had little real value.

The Russian ruble is another currency that has fallen precipitously in value. During the early 1990s, the former system of central planning was abandoned. But without a well-developed market system that already was flourishing and without the trade that had taken place earlier with the other former Soviet republics, many factories found that there was no demand for their output. To avoid massive layoffs, the government simply printed up vast quantities of money to subsidize the operation of the factories. As the quantity theory predicts, prices began to soar. In the final months of 1992, inflation was running at a rate of 1,300 percent per year.

7-4 | Inflation and Interest Rates

As we first discussed in Chapter 3, interest rates are among the most important macroeconomic variables. In essence, they are the prices that link the present and the future. Here we discuss the relationship between inflation and interest rates.

Two Interest Rates: Real and Nominal

Suppose you deposit your savings in a bank account that pays 8 percent interest annually. Next year, you withdraw your savings and the accumulated interest. Are you 8 percent richer than you were when you made the deposit a year earlier?

The answer depends on what "richer" means. Certainly, you have 8 percent more dollars than you had before. But if prices have risen, so that each dollar buys less, then your purchasing power has not risen by 8 percent. If the inflation rate was 5 percent, then the amount of goods you can buy has increased by only 3 percent. And if the inflation rate was 10 percent, then your purchasing power actually fell by 2 percent.

Economists call the interest rate that the bank pays the **nominal interest rate** and the increase in your purchasing power the **real interest rate.** If i denotes the nominal interest rate, r the real interest rate, and π the rate of inflation, then the relationship among these three variables can be written as

$$r = i - \pi.$$

The real interest rate is the difference between the nominal interest rate and the rate of inflation.[6]

The Fisher Effect

Rearranging terms in our equation for the real interest rate, we can show that the nominal interest rate is the sum of the real interest rate and the inflation rate:

$$i = r + \pi.$$

The equation written in this way is called the **Fisher equation,** after economist Irving Fisher (1867–1947). It shows that the nominal interest rate can change for two reasons: because the real interest rate changes or because the inflation rate changes.

Once we separate the nominal interest rate into these two parts, we can use this equation to develop a theory that explains the nominal interest rate. Chapter 3 showed that the real interest rate adjusts to equilibrate saving and investment. The quantity theory of money shows that the rate of money growth determines the rate of inflation. The Fisher equation then tells us to add the real interest rate and the inflation rate together to determine the nominal interest rate.

The quantity theory and the Fisher equation together tell us how money growth affects the nominal interest rate. *According to the quantity theory, an increase in the rate of money growth of 1 percent causes a 1 percent increase in the rate of inflation. According to the Fisher equation, a 1 percent increase in the rate of inflation in turn causes a 1 percent increase in the nominal interest rate.* The one-for-one relation between the inflation rate and the nominal interest rate is called the **Fisher effect.**

CASE STUDY

Inflation and Nominal Interest Rates

How useful is the Fisher effect in explaining interest rates? To answer this question we look at two types of data on inflation and nominal interest rates.

---

[6] *Mathematical note:* This equation relating the real interest rate, nominal interest rate, and inflation rate is only an approximation. The exact formula is $(1 + r) = (1 + i)/(1 + \pi)$. The approximation in the text is reasonably accurate as long as r, i, and π are relatively small (say, less than 20 percent per year).

ity in relative prices. For example, suppose a firm issues a new catalogue every January. If there is no inflation, then the firm's prices relative to the overall price level are constant over the year. Yet if inflation is 1 percent per month, then from the beginning to the end of the year the firm's relative prices fall by 12 percent. Sales from this catalogue will tend to be low early in the year (when its prices are relatively high) and high later in the year (when its prices are relatively low). Hence, when inflation induces variability in relative prices, it leads to microeconomic inefficiencies in the allocation of resources.

A fourth cost of inflation results from the tax laws. Many provisions of the tax code do not take into account the effects of inflation. Inflation can alter individuals' tax liability, often in ways that lawmakers did not intend.

One example of the failure of the tax code to deal with inflation is the tax treatment of capital gains. Suppose you buy some stock today and sell it a year from now at the same real price. It would seem reasonable for the government not to levy a tax, since you have earned no real income from this investment. Indeed, if there is no inflation, a zero tax liability would be the outcome. But suppose the rate of inflation is 12 percent and you initially paid $100 per share for the stock; for the real price to be the same a year later, you must sell the stock for $112 per share. In this case the tax code, which ignores the effects of inflation, says that you have earned $12 per share in income, and the government taxes you on this capital gain. The problem, of course, is that the tax code measures income as the nominal rather than the real capital gain. In this example, and in many others, inflation distorts how taxes are levied.

A similar problem occurs with interest-income taxes. Because the Canadian tax system was designed for a zero-inflation environment, it does not work well when inflation occurs. It turns out that when inflation and the tax system interact, the result is a powerful disincentive to save and invest. And worse still, this problem occurs even for mild inflations and even when all individuals anticipate inflation perfectly. Let us see how this problem develops, by adding interest-income taxes to our discussion of the Fisher equation.

If t stands for the tax rate that an individual must pay on her interest income, the *after-tax* real yield is

$$\text{After-tax } r = i\,(1 - t) - \pi.$$

Consider what happens to this effective yield on savings if inflation rises from 0 percent to 10 percent. Assume that the nominal interest rate rises by the same 10 percentage points—enough to compensate lenders fully for the inflation, if it were not for the tax system. The revised Fisher equation makes clear that the after-tax real yield must fall by t times 10 percent in this case. If the individual's marginal tax rate is 50 percent, the reduction in the real return to saving is a full $t\pi = 5$ percentage points. Most economists believe that this represents a significant disincentive to save, and so inflation reduces capital accumulation and future living standards.

The problem is that the tax system taxes nominal interest income instead of real interest income. During an inflationary time, much of an individual's nominal interest receipts are just a compensation for the fact that the loan's principal value is shrinking. Since that "inflation premium" part of interest is not income at all, it should not be taxed. If the tax system were fully indexed, it would not be taxed. In that case, the after-tax real yield would be given by

$$\text{After-tax } r = (i - \pi)(1 - t).$$

In this case, as long as the nominal interest rate rises one-for-one with inflation (as we discussed in the nonindexed tax case), the after-tax real yield is *not* reduced at all by inflation. The disincentive for saving and investment is removed.

Nevertheless, because our tax system does not limit taxes on interest earnings to just real returns, one of the central costs of inflation is that it lowers the economy's accumulation of capital, and so it reduces the standard of living for all members of future generations.

A fifth cost of inflation is the inconvenience of living in a world with a changing price level. Money is the ruler with which we measure economic transactions. When there is inflation, that ruler is changing in length. To continue the analogy, suppose that Parliament passed a law specifying that a metre would equal 100 centimetres in 2001, 95 centimetres in 2002, 90 centimetres in 2003, and so on. Although the law would result in no ambiguity, it would be highly inconvenient. When someone measured a distance in metres, it would be necessary to specify whether the measurement was in 2001 metres or 2002 metres; to compare distances measured in different years, one would need to make an "inflation" correction. Similarly, the dollar is a less useful measure when its value is always changing.

For example, a changing price level complicates personal financial planning. One important decision that all households face is how much of their income to consume today and how much to save for retirement. A dollar saved today and invested at a fixed nominal interest rate will yield a fixed dollar amount in the future. Yet the real value of that dollar amount—which will determine the retiree's living standard—depends on the future price level. Deciding how much to save would be much simpler if people could count on the price level in 30 years being similar to its level today.

The Costs of Unexpected Inflation

Unexpected inflation has an effect that is more pernicious than any of the costs of steady, anticipated inflation: it arbitrarily redistributes wealth among individuals. You can see how this works by examining long-term loans. Loan agreements typically specify a nominal interest rate, which is based on the rate of inflation expected at the time of the agreement. If inflation turns out differently from what was expected, the *ex post* real return that the debtor pays to the creditor differs from what both parties anticipated. On the one hand, if inflation turns out to be higher than expected, the debtor wins and the creditor loses because the debtor repays the loan with less valuable dollars. On the other hand, if inflation turns out to be lower than expected, the creditor wins and the debtor loses because the repayment is worth more than the two parties anticipated.

Consider, for example, a person taking out a mortgage in 1960. At the time, a 30-year mortgage had an interest rate of about 6 percent per year. This rate was based on a low rate of expected inflation—inflation over the previous decade had averaged only 2.5 percent. The creditor probably expected to receive a real return of about 3.5 percent, and the debtor expected to pay this real return. In fact, over the life of the mortgage, the inflation rate averaged 5.5 percent, so the *ex post* real return was only 0.5 percent. This unanticipated inflation benefited the debtor at the expense of the creditor.

Unanticipated inflation also hurts individuals on fixed pensions. Workers and firms often agree on a fixed nominal pension when the worker retires (or even earlier). Since the pension is deferred earnings, the worker is essentially providing the firm a loan: the worker provides labour services to the firm while young but does not get fully paid until old age. Like any creditor, the worker is hurt when inflation is higher than anticipated. Like any debtor, the firm is hurt when inflation is lower than anticipated. The magnitudes involved in these arbitrary redistributions of income can be very large. For example, with inflation of just 5 percent per year, the purchasing power of money *halves* in value in fewer than 15 years. So in a period when inflation is underpredicted by 5 percent, pensioners' real income is cut in half well before they are expected to die. This reduction in real income can be devastating.

These situations provide a clear argument against highly variable inflation. The more variable the rate of inflation, the greater the uncertainty that both debtors and creditors face. Since most people are *risk averse*—they dislike uncertainty—the unpredictability caused by highly variable inflation hurts almost everyone.

Given these effects of uncertain inflation, it is puzzling that nominal contracts are so prevalent. One might expect debtors and creditors to protect themselves from this uncertainty by writing contracts in real terms—that is, by indexing to some measure of the price level. In economies with extremely high and variable inflation, indexation is often widespread; sometimes this indexation takes the form of writing contracts using a more stable foreign currency. In economies with moderate inflation, such as Canada, indexation is less common. Yet even in Canada, some long-term obligations are indexed. For example, Canada Pension benefits for the elderly are adjusted annually in response to changes in the consumer price index, as is the basic personal exemption in the income tax system.

Finally, in thinking about the costs of inflation, it is important to note a widely documented but little understood fact: high inflation is variable inflation. That is, countries with high average inflation also tend to have inflation rates that change greatly from year to year. The implication is that if a country decides to pursue a high-inflation monetary policy, it will likely have to accept highly variable inflation as well. As we have just discussed, highly variable inflation increases uncertainty for both creditors and debtors by subjecting them to arbitrary and potentially large redistributions of wealth.

CASE STUDY

The Wizard of Oz

The redistributions of wealth caused by unexpected changes in the price level are often a source of political turmoil, as evidenced by the Free Silver movement in the late nineteenth century in the United States. From 1880 to 1896 the price level in the United States fell 23 percent. This deflation was good for creditors, primarily the bankers of the Northeast, but it was bad for debtors, primarily the farmers of the South and West. One proposed solution to this problem was to replace the gold standard with a bimetallic standard, under which both gold and silver could be minted into coin. The move to a bimetallic standard would increase the money supply and stop the deflation.

The silver issue dominated the presidential election of 1896. William McKinley, the Republican nominee, campaigned on a platform of preserving the gold standard. William Jennings Bryan, the Democratic nominee, supported the bimetallic standard. In a famous speech, Bryan proclaimed, "You shall not press down upon the brow of labor this crown of thorns, you shall not crucify mankind upon a cross of gold." Not surprisingly, McKinley was the candidate of the conservative eastern establishment, while Bryan was the candidate of the southern and western populists.

This debate over silver found its most memorable expression in a children's book, *The Wizard of Oz*. Written by a midwestern journalist, L. Frank Baum, just after the 1896 election, it tells the story of Dorothy, a girl lost in a strange land far from her home in Kansas. Dorothy (representing traditional American values) makes three friends: a scarecrow (the farmer), a tin woodman (the industrial worker), and a lion whose roar exceeds his might (William Jennings Bryan). Together, the four of them make their way along a perilous yellow brick road (the gold standard), hoping to find the Wizard who will help Dorothy return home. Eventually they arrive in Oz (Washington), where everyone sees the world through green glasses (money). The Wizard (William McKinley) tries to be all things to all people but turns out to be a fraud. Dorothy's problem is solved only when she learns about the magical power of her silver slippers.[10]

Although the Republicans won the election of 1896 and the United States stayed on a gold standard, the Free Silver advocates got what they ultimately wanted: inflation. Around the time of the election, gold was discovered in Alaska, Australia, and South Africa. In addition, gold refiners devised the cyanide process, which facilitated the extraction of gold from ore. These developments led to increases in the money supply and in prices. From 1896 to 1910 the price level rose 35 percent.

---

[10] The movie made forty years later hid much of the allegory by changing Dorothy's slippers from silver to ruby. For more on this topic, see Henry M. Littlefield, "The Wizard of Oz: Parable on Populism," *American Quarterly* 16 (Spring 1964): 47–58; and Hugh Rockoff, "The Wizard of Oz as a Monetary Allegory," *Journal of Political Economy* 98 (August 1990): 739–760.

7-7 | Hyperinflation

Hyperinflation is often defined as inflation that exceeds 50 percent per month, which is just over 1 percent per day. Compounded over many months, this rate of inflation leads to very large increases in the price level. An inflation rate of 50 percent per month implies a more than 100-fold increase in the price level over a year, and a more than 2-million-fold increase over three years. Here we consider the costs and causes of such extreme inflation.

The Costs of Hyperinflation

Although economists debate whether the costs of moderate inflation are large or small, no one doubts that hyperinflation extracts a high toll on society. The costs are qualitatively the same as those we discussed earlier. When inflation reaches extreme levels, however, these costs are more apparent because they are so severe.

The shoeleather costs associated with reduced money holding, for instance, are serious under hyperinflation. Business executives devote much time and

KEYNES (AND LENIN) ON THE COST OF INFLATION

The great economist John Maynard Keynes was no friend of inflation, as this chapter's opening quotation indicates. Here is the more complete passage from his famous book, *The Economic Consequences of the Peace,* in which Keynes predicted (correctly) that the treaty imposed on Germany after World War I would lead to economic hardship and renewed international tensions:

> Lenin is said to have declared that the best way to destroy the Capitalist System was to debauch the currency. By a continuing process of inflation, governments can confiscate, secretly and unobserved, an important part of the wealth of their citizens. By this method they not only confiscate, but they confiscate *arbitrarily;* and, while the process impoverishes many, it actually enriches some. The sight of this arbitrary rearrangement of riches strikes not only at security, but at confidence in the equity of the existing distribution of wealth. Those to whom the system brings windfalls, beyond their deserts and even beyond their expectations or desires, become "profiteers," who are the object of the hatred of the bourgeoisie, whom the inflationism has impoverished, not less than of the proletariat. As the inflation proceeds and the real value of the currency fluctuates wildly from month to month, all permanent relations between debtors and creditors, which form the ultimate foundation of capitalism, become so utterly disordered as to be almost meaningless; and the process of wealth-getting degenerates into a gamble and a lottery.
>
> Lenin was certainly right. There is no subtler, no surer means of overturning the existing basis of society than to debauch the currency. The process engages all the hidden forces of economic law on the side of destruction, and does it in a manner which not one man in a million is able to diagnose.*

History has given ample support to this assessment. A recent example occurred in Russia in 1998, where many citizens saw high rates of inflation wipe out their ruble-denominated savings. And, as Lenin would have predicted, this inflation put the country's burgeoning capitalist system in serious jeopardy.

* John Maynard Keynes, *The Economic Consequences of the Peace* (London: Macmillan, 1920): 219–220.

energy to cash management when cash loses its value quickly. By diverting this time and energy from more socially valuable activities, such as production and investment decisions, hyperinflation makes the economy run less efficiently.

Menu costs also become larger under hyperinflation. Firms have to change prices so often that normal business practices, such as printing and distributing catalogues with fixed prices, become impossible. In one restaurant during the German hyperinflation of the 1920s, a waiter would stand up on a table every 30 minutes to call out the new prices.

Similarly, relative prices do not do a good job of reflecting true scarcity during hyperinflations. When prices change frequently by large amounts, it is hard for customers to shop around for the best price. Highly volatile and rapidly rising prices can alter behaviour in many ways. According to one report, when patrons entered a pub during the German hyperinflation, they would often buy two pitchers of beer. Although the second pitcher would lose value by getting warm over time, it would lose value less rapidly than the money left sitting in the patron's wallet.

Tax systems are also distorted by hyperinflation—but in ways that are quite different from those under moderate inflation. In most tax systems there is a delay between the time when a tax is levied and the time when the tax is paid to the government. In Canada, for example, taxpayers are required to make estimated income tax payments every three months. This short delay does not matter much under low inflation. By contrast, during hyperinflation, even a short delay greatly reduces real tax revenue. By the time the government gets the money it is due, the money has fallen in value. As a result, once hyperinflations start, the real tax revenue of the government often falls substantially.

Finally, no one should underestimate the sheer inconvenience of living with hyperinflation. When carrying money to the grocery store is as burdensome as carrying the groceries back home, the monetary system is not doing its best to facilitate exchange. The government tries to overcome this problem by adding more and more zeros to the paper currency, but often it cannot keep up with the exploding price level.

Eventually, these costs of hyperinflation become intolerable. Over time, money loses its role as a store of value, unit of account, and medium of exchange. Barter becomes more common. And more stable unofficial monies—cigarettes or the U.S. dollar—naturally start to replace the official money.

CASE STUDY

Life During the Bolivian Hyperinflation

The following article from the *Wall Street Journal* shows what life was like during the Bolivian hyperinflation of 1985.[11] What costs of inflation does this article emphasize?

---

[11] Reprinted by permission of the *Wall Street Journal,* © August 13, 1985, page 1, Dow Jones & Company, Inc. All Rights Reserved Worldwide.

$$NX = [\overline{Y} - C(\overline{Y} - T) - G] - I(r^*)$$
$$= \underbrace{\phantom{[\overline{Y} - C(\overline{Y} - T) - G]}}_{S} - I(r^*).$$

This equation shows what determines saving S and investment I—and thus the trade balance NX. Remember that saving depends on fiscal policy: lower government purchases G or higher taxes T raise national saving. Investment depends on the world real interest rate r^*: high interest rates make some investment projects unprofitable. Therefore, the trade balance depends on these variables as well.

In Chapter 3 we graphed saving and investment as in Figure 8-3. In the closed economy studied in that chapter, the real interest rate adjusts to equilibrate saving and investment—that is, the real interest rate is found where the saving and investment curves cross. In the small open economy, however, the real interest rate equals the world real interest rate. *The trade balance is determined by the difference between saving and investment at the world interest rate.*

At this point, you might wonder about the mechanism that causes the trade balance to equal net foreign investment. The determinants of net foreign investment are easy to understand. When domestic saving falls short of domestic investment, domestic investors borrow from abroad; when saving exceeds investment, the excess is lent to other countries. But what causes those who import and export to behave in a way that ensures that the international flow of goods exactly balances this international flow of capital? For now we leave this question unanswered, but we return to it in Section 8-3 when we discuss the determination of exchange rates.

figure 8-3

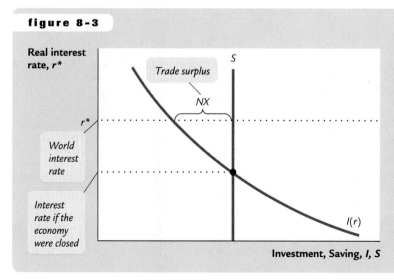

Real interest rate, r^*

Trade surplus

NX

r^* ....

World interest rate

Interest rate if the economy were closed

S

$I(r)$

Investment, Saving, *I, S*

Saving and Investment in a Small Open Economy In a closed economy, the real interest rate adjusts to equilibrate saving and investment. In a small open economy, the interest rate is determined in world financial markets. The difference between saving and investment determines the trade balance. Here there is a trade surplus, because at the world interest rate, saving exceeds investment.

How Policies Influence the Trade Balance

Suppose that the economy begins in a position of balanced trade. That is, at the world interest rate, investment I equals saving S, and net exports NX equal zero. Let's use our model to predict the effects of government policies at home and abroad.

Fiscal Policy at Home Consider first what happens to the small open economy if the government expands domestic spending by increasing government purchases. The increase in G reduces national saving, because $S = Y - C - G$. With an unchanged world real interest rate, investment remains the same. Therefore, saving falls below investment, and some investment must now be financed by borrowing from abroad. Since $NX = S - I$, the fall in S implies a fall in NX. The economy now runs a trade deficit.

The same logic applies to a decrease in taxes. A tax cut lowers T, raises disposable income $Y - T$, stimulates consumption, and reduces national saving. (Even though some of the tax cut finds its way into private saving, public saving falls by the full amount of the tax cut; in total, saving falls.) Since $NX = S - I$, the reduction in national saving in turn lowers NX.

Figure 8-4 illustrates these effects. A fiscal policy change that increases private consumption C or public consumption G reduces national saving $(Y - C - G)$ and, therefore, shifts the vertical line that represents saving from S_1 to S_2. Because NX is the distance between the saving schedule and the investment schedule at the world interest rate, this shift reduces NX. *Hence, starting from balanced trade, a change in fiscal policy that reduces national saving leads to a trade deficit.*

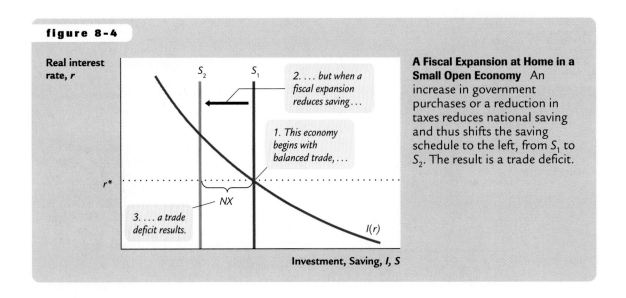

figure 8-4

A Fiscal Expansion at Home in a Small Open Economy An increase in government purchases or a reduction in taxes reduces national saving and thus shifts the saving schedule to the left, from S_1 to S_2. The result is a trade deficit.

2. ... but when a fiscal expansion reduces saving ...

1. This economy begins with balanced trade, ...

3. ... a trade deficit results.

NX

$I(r)$

Investment, Saving, I, S

CASE STUDY

The Twin Deficits

Government budget deficits and trade deficits are linked by the fundamental accounting identity: the trade surplus equals the excess of national saving over domestic investment. Since national saving is the sum of private saving $(Y - T - C)$ and public saving $(T - G)$, this fundamental identity can be rephrased as

Trade Deficit = Government Budget Deficit
+ The Excess of Investment Over Private Saving.

Many governments ran up large budget deficits during the 1980s without a corresponding increase in private saving relative to investment. Given these developments, we should expect to see these countries with large trade deficits in the early 1990s. Moreover, it should be the case that the larger a country's government budget deficit, the larger its trade deficit.

A country's trade with other countries is recorded in what are called the *balance of payments* accounts. Trades in goods and services are listed in the *current account* of this table, while trades in financial assets are listed in the *capital account* section. The twin deficits relationship that we have just noted should be evident if we compare government budget deficits and current account deficits (from the balance of payments records) across countries.

When the Liberal government took power in 1993, Finance Minister Paul Martin arranged that his department publish a booklet entitled *Canada's Economic Challenge*. The twin deficits relationship was one of the items stressed in this document, and Figure 8-5 is reproduced from that publication. This

figure 8-5

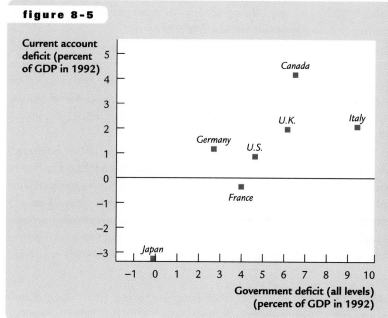

The Twin Deficits
This scatterplot shows the joint observation on the twin deficits for all G7 countries in 1992. The positive correlation is evident from the graph, and this supports the basic proposition that if a country's citizens "spend beyond their means," they must increase their indebtedness with the rest of the world.

Source: Canada's Economic Challenge: Background (Ottawa: Department of Finance, 1994): 40, 43.

scatterplot shows the joint observation (in 1992) on the twin deficits for all G7 countries. The positive correlation is evident in the graph. It follows that no country can "solve" its trade deficit "problem" without achieving some combination of reducing its government budget deficit, increasing its rate of private saving, and decreasing its rate of investment spending.

It is interesting to interpret the rhetoric on both sides concerning the massive trade imbalance between the Japanese and the Americans. Japan needs a trading surplus in manufactured goods to finance its trade deficit in the area of primary commodities (which Japan must import, given its natural geography). But the United States is concerned about the large magnitude of the net surplus Japan has in the trade between the two nations. American politicians argue that the Japanese should raise government spending to stimulate Japanese imports from the United States and to force a government budget deficit there. Given the connection between the twin deficits, this would help reduce the U.S. trade deficit, without the Americans' having to make painful choices themselves. Like everyone else, the Americans find it difficult to make large cuts in their own government budget deficit or to make cuts in domestic investment (since these cuts lower capital accumulation and future living standards within the country). Knowledge of the twin deficits relationship allows us to understand the logic behind these trade disputes.

Fiscal Policy Abroad Consider now what happens to a small open economy when foreign governments increase their government purchases. If these foreign countries are a small part of the world economy, then their fiscal change has a negligible impact on other countries. But if these foreign countries are a large part of the world economy, their increase in government purchases reduces world saving and causes the world interest rate to rise.

The increase in the world interest rate raises the cost of borrowing and, thus, reduces investment in our small open economy. Because there has been no change in domestic saving, saving S now exceeds investment I, and some of our saving begins to flow abroad. Since $NX = S - I$, the reduction in I must also increase NX. Hence, reduced saving abroad leads to a trade surplus at home.

Figure 8-6 illustrates how a small open economy starting from balanced trade responds to a foreign fiscal expansion. Because the policy change is occurring abroad, the domestic saving and investment schedules remain the same. The only change is an increase in the world interest rate from r_1^* to r_2^*. The trade balance is the difference between the saving and investment schedules; because saving exceeds investment at r_2^*, there is a trade surplus. *Hence, an increase in the world interest rate due to a fiscal expansion abroad leads to a trade surplus.*

Shifts in Investment Demand Consider what happens to our small open economy if its investment schedule shifts outward—that is, if the demand for investment goods at every interest rate increases. This shift would occur if, for

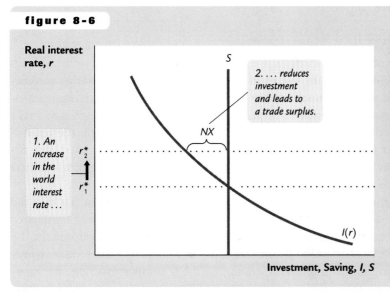

figure 8-6

1. An increase in the world interest rate ...

2. ... reduces investment and leads to a trade surplus.

A Fiscal Expansion Abroad in a Small Open Economy A fiscal expansion in a foreign economy large enough to influence world saving and investment raises the world interest rate from r_1^* to r_2^*. The higher world interest rate reduces investment in this small open economy, causing a trade surplus.

example, the government changed the tax laws to encourage investment by providing an investment tax credit. Figure 8-7 illustrates the impact of a shift in the investment schedule. At a given world interest rate, investment is now higher. Because saving is unchanged, some investment must now be financed by borrowing from abroad, which means net foreign investment is negative. Put differently, because $NX = S - I$, the increase in I implies a decrease in NX. Hence, *an outward shift in the investment schedule causes a trade deficit.*

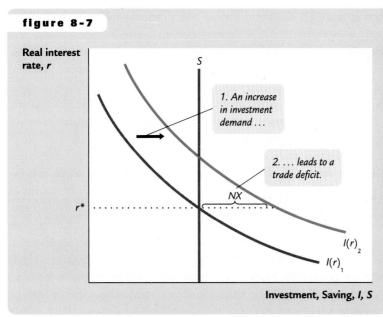

figure 8-7

1. An increase in investment demand ...

2. ... leads to a trade deficit.

A Shift in the Investment Schedule in a Small Open Economy An outward shift in the investment schedule from $I(r)_1$ to $I(r)_2$ increases the amount of investment at the world interest rate r^*. As a result, investment now exceeds saving, which means the economy is borrowing from abroad and running a trade deficit.

CASE STUDY

Fiscal Policy and the Canadian Economy

Several instances of major fiscal expansion in the rest of the world have occurred in the last 20 years. For example, the United States ran a large government budget deficit throughout the 1980s, as President Ronald Reagan introduced major tax cuts without, at the same time, persuading Congress to make
similar reductions in government spending. Also in the late 1980s, the reunification of Germany led that country's government to run up a series of large fiscal deficits, as officials tried to raise opportunities for those living in the former
East Germany in just a few years.

These events pushed up the general level of world interest rates, but they did
not produce a trade surplus for Canada, because these events were dominated
(in Canada) by the large increase in Canadian government budget deficits. By
raising world interest rates, the international developments did reduce investment spending in Canada. Overspending by the Canadian governments, however, decreased national saving by an even bigger amount, so Canada's trade
balance deteriorated.

Evaluating Economic Policy

Our model of the open economy shows that the flow of goods and services
measured by the trade balance is inextricably connected to the flow of funds for
capital accumulation measured by net foreign investment. Net foreign investment is the difference between domestic saving and domestic investment. Thus,
the impact of economic policies on the trade balance can always be found by
examining their impact on domestic saving and domestic investment. Policies
that increase investment or decrease saving tend to cause a trade deficit, and
policies that decrease investment or increase saving tend to cause a trade surplus.

Our analysis of the open economy has been positive, not normative. That is,
our analysis of how economic policies influence the international flows of capital and goods has not told us whether these policies are desirable. Evaluating
economic policies and their impact on the open economy is a frequent topic of
debate among economists and policymakers.

When a country runs a trade deficit, policymakers must confront the question of whether the trade deficit represents a national problem. Most economists view a trade deficit not as a problem in itself, but perhaps as a symptom of
a problem. Trade deficits typically reflect a low saving rate. A low saving rate
means that we are putting away less for the future. In a closed economy, low
saving leads to low investment and a smaller future capital stock. In an open
economy, low saving leads to a trade deficit and a growing foreign debt, which
eventually must be repaid. In both cases, high current consumption leads to
lower future consumption, implying that future generations bear the burden of
low national saving.

Yet trade deficits are not always a reflection of economic malady. When poor rural economies develop into modern industrial economies, they sometimes finance their high levels of investment with foreign borrowing. In these cases, trade deficits are a sign of economic development. For example, South Korea ran large trade deficits throughout the 1970s, and it became one of the success stories of economic growth. The lesson is that one cannot judge economic performance from the trade balance alone. Instead, one must look at the underlying causes of the international flows.

8-3 | Exchange Rates

Having examined the international flows of capital and of goods and services, we now extend the analysis by considering the prices that apply to these transactions. The *exchange rate* between two countries is the price at which residents of those countries trade with each other. In this section we first examine precisely what the exchange rate measures, and we then discuss how exchange rates are determined.

Nominal and Real Exchange Rates

Economists distinguish between two exchange rates: the nominal exchange rate and the real exchange rate. Let's discuss each in turn and see how they are related.

The Nominal Exchange Rate   The **nominal exchange rate** is the relative price of the currency of two countries. For example, if the exchange rate between the Canadian dollar and the Japanese yen is 90 yen per dollar, then you can exchange 1 dollar for 90 yen in world markets for foreign currency. A Japanese who wants to obtain dollars would pay 90 yen for each dollar she bought. A Canadian who wants to obtain yen would get 90 yen for each dollar he paid. When people refer to "the exchange rate" between two countries, they usually mean the nominal exchange rate.

The Real Exchange Rate   The **real exchange rate** is the relative price of the goods of two countries. That is, the real exchange rate tells us the rate at which we can trade the goods of one country for the goods of another. The real exchange rate is sometimes called the *terms of trade*.

To see the relation between the real and nominal exchange rates, consider a single good produced in many countries: cars. Suppose a Canadian car costs $20,000 and a similar Japanese car costs 2,400,000 yen. To compare the prices of the two cars, we must convert them into a common currency. If a dollar is worth 90 yen, then the Candian car costs 1,800,000 yen. Comparing the price of the Canadian car (1,800,000 yen) and the price of the Japanese car (2,400,000 yen), we conclude that the Canadian car costs three-quarters of

f y i

HOW NEWSPAPERS REPORT THE EXCHANGE RATE

You can find exchange rates reported daily in many newspapers. Here's how they are reported in the Toronto *Globe and Mail*.

Notice in the top line that the Canada—United State exchange rate is reported in two ways. On this Thursday, a Canadian dollar bought $0.6882 U.S., and a U.S. dollar bought $1.45 Canadian currency. We can say the exchange rate is $1.45 Canadian dollars per U.S. dollar, or we can say the exchange rate is 0.6882 U.S. dollars per Canadian dollar. Since 1.45

equals 1/0.6882, these two ways of expressing the exchange rate are equivalent. This book always expresses the exchange rate in units of foreign currency per Canadian dollar—the inverse of most of the entries in the *Globe and Mail* table.

Near the very bottom of the table, it is indicated that the U.S. dollar traded at a slightly higher value compared to the previous day. That means that the Canadian dollar had decreased in value somewhat. Since we are defining the value of the Canadian dollar as our exchange rate, such a fall in the exchange rate is called a *depreciation* of our dollar, and of our exchange rate.

Mid-market rates in Toronto at noon, Dec. 30, 1999. Prepared by the Bank of Montreal Treasury Group.

		$1 U.S. in Cdn. $=	$1 Cdn. in U.S. $=
U.S./Canada spot		1.4530	0.6882
1 month forward		1.4519	0.6888
2 months forward		1.4509	0.6892
3 months forward		1.4498	0.6898
6 months forward		1.4467	0.6912
12 months forward		1.4418	0.6936
3 years forward		1.4265	0.7010
5 years forward		1.4128	0.7078
7 years forward		1.3910	0.7189
10 years forward		1.3630	0.7337
Canadian dollar	High	1.4452	0.6919
in 1999:	Low	1.5475	0.6462
	Average	1.4860	0.6729

Country	Currency	Cdn. $ per unit	U.S. $ per unit
Britain	Pound	2.3430	1.6125
1 month forward		2.3415	1.6127
2 months forward		2.3396	1.6125
3 months forward		2.3378	1.6125
6 months forward		2.3318	1.6118
12 months forward		2.3218	1.6103
Europe	Euro	1.4572	1.0029
1 month forward		1.4591	1.0050
3 months forward		1.4636	1.0095
6 months forward		1.4701	1.0162
12 months forward		1.4830	1.0286
Japan	Yen	0.014200	0.009773
1 month forward		0.014265	0.009825
3 months forward		0.014378	0.009917
6 months forward		0.014563	0.010066
12 months forward		0.014982	0.010391
Algeria	Dinar	0.02213	0.0152
Antigua, Grenada and St. Lucia	E.C. Dollar	0.5401	0.3717
Argentina	Peso	1.45315	1.00010
Australia	Dollar	0.9511	0.6546
Austria	Schill	0.10590	0.07288
Bahamas	Dollar	1.4530	1.0000
Barbados	Dollar	0.7338	0.5051
Belgium	Franc	0.03612	0.02486
Bermuda	Dollar	1.4530	1.0000
Brazil	Real	0.8117	0.5587
Bulgaria	Lev	0.747505	0.5145
Chile	Peso	0.002753	0.001895
China	Renminbi	0.1755	0.1208
Cyprus	Pound	2.5208	1.7349
Czech Rep	Koruna	0.0405	0.0279
Denmark	Krone	0.1958	0.1347
Egypt	Pound	0.4252	0.2927
Fiji	Dollar	0.7265	0.5000

Country	Currency	Cdn. $ per unit	U.S. $ per unit
Finland	Markka	0.2451	0.1687
France	Franc	0.2221	0.1529
Germany	Mark	0.7451	0.5128
Greece	Drachma	0.004416	0.003039
Hong Kong	Dollar	0.1869	0.1286
Hungary	Forint	0.00573	0.00394
Iceland	Krona	0.02002	0.01378
India	Rupee	0.03348	0.02304
Indonesia	Rupiah	0.000208	0.000143
Ireland	Punt	1.8503	1.2734
Isreal	N Shekel	0.3500	0.2409
Italy	Lira	0.000753	0.000518
Jamaica	Dollar	0.03527	0.02427
Jordan	Dinar	2.0523	1.4124
Lebanon	Pound	0.000968	0.000666
Luxembourg	Franc	0.03612	0.02486
Malaysia	Ringgit	0.3824	0.2632
Mexico	N Peso	0.1531	0.1054
Netherlands	Guildr	0.6612	0.4551
New Zealand	Dollar	0.7593	0.5226
Norway	Krone	0.1809	0.1245
Pakistan	Rupee	0.02816	0.01938
Panama	Balboa	1.4530	1.0000
Philippines	Peso	0.03614	0.02488
Poland	Zloty	0.3514	0.2418
Portugal	Escudo	0.00727	0.00500
Romania	Leu	0.000080	0.000055
Russia	Ruble	0.053029	0.036496
Saudi Arabia	Riyal	0.3875	0.2667
Singapore	Dollar	0.8727	0.6006
Slovakia	Koruna	0.0344	0.0237
South Africa	Rand	0.2361	0.1625
South Korea	Won	0.001283	0.000883
Spain	Peseta	0.00876	0.00603
Sudan	Dinar	0.00568	0.0039
Sweden	Krona	0.1702	0.1171
Switzerland	Franc	0.9076	0.6246
Taiwan	Dollar	0.04642	0.0319
Thailand	Baht	0.03880	0.0267
Trinidad, Tobago	Dollar	0.2327	0.1602
Turkey	Lira	0.0000027	0.0000018
Venezuela	Bolivar	0.002241	0.00154
Zambia	Kwacha	0.000526	0.000362
Spec Draw Right S.D.R.		1.9919	1.3709

The U.S. dollar closed at $1.4533 in terms of Canadian funds, up $0.0005 from Wednesday. The pound sterling closed at $2.3481, down $0.0008.

In New York, the Canadian dollar closed down $0.0002 at $0.6881 in terms of U.S. funds. The pound sterling was down $0.0011 to $1.6157.

Source: Globe and Mail, Dec. 31, 1999, B18.

figure 8-10

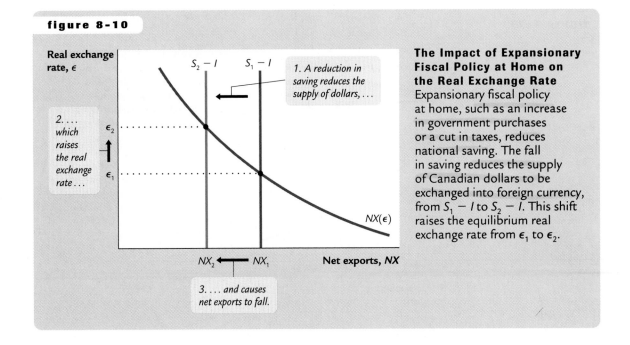

1. A reduction in saving reduces the supply of dollars, ...

2. ... which raises the real exchange rate ...

3. ... and causes net exports to fall.

The Impact of Expansionary Fiscal Policy at Home on the Real Exchange Rate Expansionary fiscal policy at home, such as an increase in government purchases or a cut in taxes, reduces national saving. The fall in saving reduces the supply of Canadian dollars to be exchanged into foreign currency, from $S_1 - I$ to $S_2 - I$. This shift raises the equilibrium real exchange rate from ϵ_1 to ϵ_2.

Fiscal Policy at Home What happens to the real exchange rate if the government reduces national saving by increasing government purchases or cutting taxes? As we discussed earlier, this reduction in saving lowers $S - I$ and thus NX. That is, the reduction in saving causes a trade deficit.

Figure 8-10 shows how the equilibrium real exchange rate adjusts to ensure that NX falls. The change in policy shifts the vertical $S - I$ line to the left, lowering the supply of Canadian dollars to be invested abroad. The lower supply causes the equilibrium real exchange rate to rise from ϵ_1 to ϵ_2—that is, the dollar becomes more valuable. Because of the rise in the value of the dollar, domestic goods become more expensive relative to foreign goods, which causes exports to fall and imports to rise. The change in exports and the change in imports both act to reduce net exports.

Fiscal Policy Abroad What happens to the real exchange rate if foreign governments increase government purchases or cut taxes? This change in fiscal policy reduces world saving and raises the world interest rate. The increase in the world interest rate reduces domestic investment I, which raises $S - I$ and thus NX. That is, the increase in the world interest rate causes a trade surplus.

Figure 8-11 shows that this change in policy shifts the vertical $S - I$ line to the right, raising the supply of Canadian dollars to be invested abroad. The equilibrium real exchange rate falls. That is, the dollar becomes less valuable, and domestic goods become less expensive relative to foreign goods.

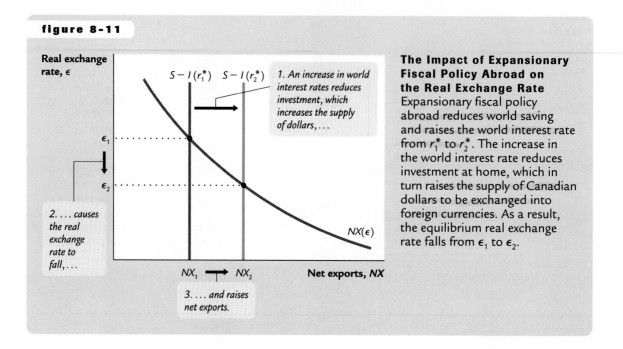

figure 8-11

The Impact of Expansionary Fiscal Policy Abroad on the Real Exchange Rate Expansionary fiscal policy abroad reduces world saving and raises the world interest rate from r_1^* to r_2^*. The increase in the world interest rate reduces investment at home, which in turn raises the supply of Canadian dollars to be exchanged into foreign currencies. As a result, the equilibrium real exchange rate falls from ϵ_1 to ϵ_2.

Shifts in Investment Demand What happens to the real exchange rate if investment demand at home increases, perhaps because the Canadian government introduces an investment tax credit? At the given world interest rate, the increase in investment demand leads to higher investment. A higher value of I means lower values of $S - I$ and NX. That is, the increase in investment demand causes a trade deficit.

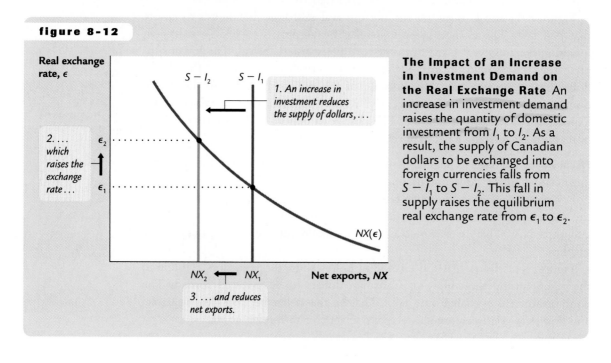

figure 8-12

The Impact of an Increase in Investment Demand on the Real Exchange Rate An increase in investment demand raises the quantity of domestic investment from I_1 to I_2. As a result, the supply of Canadian dollars to be exchanged into foreign currencies falls from $S - I_1$ to $S - I_2$. This fall in supply raises the equilibrium real exchange rate from ϵ_1 to ϵ_2.

Figure 8-12 shows that the increase in investment demand shifts the vertical $S - I$ line to the left, reducing the supply of Canadian dollars to be invested abroad. The equilibrium real exchange rate rises. Hence, when the investment tax credit makes investing in Canada more attractive, it also increases the value of the Canadian dollars necessary to make these investments. When the dollar appreciates, domestic goods become more expensive relative to foreign goods, and net exports fall.

The Effects of Trade Policies

Now that we have a model that explains the trade balance and the real exchange rate, we have the tools to examine the macroeconomic effects of trade policies. Trade policies, broadly defined, are policies designed to influence directly the amount of goods and services exported or imported. Most often, trade policies take the form of protecting domestic industries from foreign competition—either by placing a tax on foreign imports (a tariff) or restricting the amount of goods and services that can be imported (a quota).

As an example of a protectionist trade policy, consider what would happen if the government prohibited the import of foreign cars. For any given real exchange rate, imports would now be lower, implying that net exports (exports minus imports) would be higher. Thus, the net-exports schedule shifts outward, as in Figure 8-13. To see the effects of the policy, we compare the old equilibrium and the new equilibrium. In the new equilibrium, the real

figure 8-13

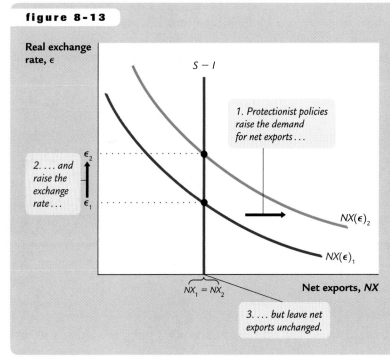

Real exchange rate, ϵ

$S - I$

1. Protectionist policies raise the demand for net exports . . .

ϵ_2

2. . . . and raise the exchange rate . . .

ϵ_1

$NX(\epsilon)_2$

$NX(\epsilon)_1$

$NX_1 = NX_2$

Net exports, NX

3. . . . but leave net exports unchanged.

The Impact of Protectionist Trade Policies on the Real Exchange Rate A protectionist trade policy, such as a ban on imported cars, shifts the net-exports schedule from $NX(\epsilon)_1$ to $NX(\epsilon)_2$, which raises the real exchange rate from ϵ_1 to ϵ_2. Notice that, despite the shift in the net-exports schedule, the equilibrium level of net exports is unchanged.

exchange rate is higher, and net exports are unchanged. Despite the shift in the net-exports schedule, the equilibrium level of net exports remains the same, assuming the protectionist policy does not alter either saving or investment.

This analysis shows that protectionist trade policies do not affect the trade balance. This surprising conclusion is often overlooked in the popular debate over trade policies. Because a trade deficit reflects an excess of imports over exports, one might guess that reducing imports—such as by prohibiting the import of foreign cars—would reduce a trade deficit. Yet our model shows that protectionist policies lead only to an appreciation of the real exchange rate. The increase in the price of domestic goods relative to foreign goods tends to lower net exports by stimulating imports and depressing exports. Thus, the appreciation offsets the increase in net exports that is directly attributable to the trade restriction.

Although protectionist trade policies do not alter the trade balance, they do affect the amount of trade. As we have seen, because the real exchange rate appreciates, the goods and services we produce become more expensive relative to foreign goods and services. We therefore export less in the new equilibrium. Since net exports are unchanged, we must import less as well. (The appreciation of the exchange rate does stimulate imports to some extent, but this only partly offsets the decrease in imports due to the trade restriction.) Thus, protectionist policies reduce both the quantity of imports and the quantity of exports.

This fall in the total amount of trade is the reason economists almost always oppose protectionist policies. International trade benefits all countries by allowing each country to specialize in what it produces best and by providing each country with a greater variety of goods and services. Protectionist policies diminish these gains from trade. Although these policies benefit certain groups within society—for example, a ban on imported cars helps domestic car producers—society on average is worse off when policies reduce the amount of international trade.

CASE STUDY

The Conservative Policy Agenda in the 1980s and 1990s

During the 1984–1993 period, Canada's Conservative government had an economic plan that involved four key elements:

- ➤ Tax reform
- ➤ Deficit reduction
- ➤ Disinflation
- ➤ Free trade

It is instructive to evaluate this package of initiatives using the analysis of this chapter.

The broad principle underlying tax reform was a move toward sales taxes and away from income taxes. This general move took several forms: (1) the introduction of the goods and services tax (GST), (2) the introduction of the capital gains tax exemption, and (3) the increase in the allowed contributions to registered retirement savings plans. All these initiatives were intended to stimulate private saving. Deficit reduction by the government itself is also a direct move toward higher national saving (since overall saving in the country is the excess of private saving over the government budget deficit). The reduction of inflation was also geared to stimulating saving, since (as we noted in Chapter 7) with nominal (not real) interest income subject to tax in Canada, lower inflation is equivalent to a cut in interest-income taxes.

Thus, the first three government initiatives were intended to shift the $S - I$ line to the right, and so to lower the real exchange rate and decrease the trade deficit. By decreasing the rate at which Canadians become more indebted to foreigners, this policy package was intended to increase the standard of living for future generations.

The fourth policy initiative—free trade—has a less obvious effect on the trade balance. The Free Trade Agreement with the United States involved both countries dropping their tariffs by essentially the same amount. Thus, it involved at most a small net shift in the position of the net-exports schedule. But one of the expected outcomes was an increased level of investment spending in Canada. With access to the large U.S. market guaranteed (for firms located in Canada), it was expected that plants in Canada would expand. They no longer had to limit their operations to serve the small Canadian market. Such an increase in investment spending in Canada shifts the $S - I$ line to the left. Thus, free trade involves competing effects on welfare: individuals can consume more goods at lower prices, but the investment effect that may accompany the removal of trade restrictions *in the rest of the world* leads to a larger trade deficit, and so (other things equal) to an increased level of foreign indebtedness in the future. The government was confident that the benefits would exceed the costs in this tradeoff for two reasons. First, the return on the extra capital employed in Canada should generate enough extra Canadian income for Canadians to be able to afford higher interest payments to foreigners. Second, the other three initiatives in the policy package were intended to increase domestic saving more than free trade increased investment. Thus, the net effect of the package was expected to be a reduction in the trade deficit.

While this policy package can be rationalized easily within our analytical framework, it turned out that there were several slips between the design and the execution of these measures. First, the attempt to reduce the government's budget failed; indeed, government deficits increased during this period. Second, changes to the tax system were only partial. The GST turned out to be an administrative headache, and it raised much less revenue than was expected. Also, the capital gains exemption was reduced and then was eliminated in 1994. As a result, disinflation was the only policy (of the first three listed above) that was fully and successfully implemented while the Conservatives were in power. Thus, much of what was to shift the $S - I$ line to the right did not materialize. As a result, the current account deficit (the negative value for Canadian *NX*) did not shrink appreciably. Unfortunately, for future generations of Canadians, the rate of foreign debt accumulation was not decreased.

This fact was not only a concern for future generations. Without the intended increase in national saving, the exchange rate remained higher in the late 1980s and early 1990s than had been the government's intention. The high value of the Canadian dollar removed the competitive advantage that Canadian firms were getting through the reduction of U.S. tariffs. In the end, the fact that the government succeeded with respect to its monetary policy objective (disinflation) but failed with respect to its fiscal policy objective (deficit reduction) meant that the overall outcome for both current and future generations was far less than was possible given the basic consistency of the overall package of intended policies.

When the Liberals took power in the 1990s, they maintained the Conservative policy agenda. They made no further changes to the taxation of interest income and capital gains; they extended the Free Trade Agreement to include Mexico; and they maintained the low inflation policy. Since they contracted fiscal policy sufficiently to eliminate the budget deficit, national saving was increased and the current account deficit shrank as a result.

The Determinants of the Nominal Exchange Rate

Having seen what determines the real exchange rate, we now turn our attention to the nominal exchange rate—the rate at which the currencies of two countries trade. Recall the relationship between the real and the nominal exchange rate:

$$
\begin{matrix}
\text{Real} & & \text{Nominal} & & \text{Ratio of} \\
\text{Exchange} & = & \text{Exchange} & \times & \text{Price} \\
\text{Rate} & & \text{Rate} & & \text{Levels} \\
\epsilon & = & e & & \times (P/P^*).
\end{matrix}
$$

We can write the nominal exchange rate as

$$e = \epsilon \times (P^*/P).$$

This equation shows that the nominal exchange rate depends on the real exchange rate and the price levels in the two countries. Given the value of the real exchange rate, if the domestic price level P rises, then the nominal exchange rate e will fall: because a dollar is worth less, a dollar will buy fewer yen. On the other hand, if the Japanese price level P^* rises, then the nominal exchange rate will increase: because the yen is worth less, a dollar will buy more yen.

It is instructive to consider changes in exchange rates over time. The exchange rate equation can be written

$$\% \text{ Change in } e = \% \text{ Change in } \epsilon + \% \text{ Change in } P^* - \% \text{ Change in } P.$$

The percentage change in ϵ is the change in the real exchange rate. The percentage change in P is the domestic inflation rate π, and the percentage change in P^* is the foreign country's inflation rate π^*. Thus, the percentage change in the nominal exchange rate is

$$\text{\% Change in } e = \text{\% Change in } \epsilon + (\pi^* - \pi)$$

$$\begin{array}{ccc}\text{Percentage Change in} & \text{Percentage Change in} & \text{Difference in} \\ \text{Nominal Exchange Rate} & = \text{Real Exchange Rate} & + \text{Inflation Rates.}\end{array}$$

This equation states that the percentage change in the nominal exchange rate between the currencies of two countries equals the percentage change in the real exchange rate plus the difference in their inflation rates. *If a country has a high rate of inflation relative to Canada, a Canadian dollar will buy an increasing amount of the foreign currency over time. If a country has a low rate of inflation relative to Canada, a Canadian dollar will buy a decreasing amount of the foreign currency over time.*

This analysis shows how monetary policy affects the nominal exchange rate. We know from Chapter 7 that high growth in the money supply leads to high inflation. Here, we have just seen that one consequence of high inflation is a depreciating currency: high π implies falling e. In other words, just as growth in the amount of money raises the price of goods measured in terms of money, it also tends to raise the price of foreign currencies measured in terms of the domestic currency.

CASE STUDY

Inflation and Nominal Exchange Rates

If we look at data on exchange rates and price levels of different countries, we quickly see the importance of inflation for explaining changes in the nominal exchange rate. The most dramatic examples come from periods of very high inflation. For example, the price level in Mexico rose by 2,300 percent from 1983 to 1988. Because of this inflation, the number of pesos a person could buy with a U.S. dollar rose from 144 in 1983 to 2,281 in 1988.

The same relationship holds true for countries with more moderate inflation. Figure 8-14 is a scatterplot showing the relationship between inflation and the exchange rate for 15 countries. On the horizontal axis is the difference between each country's average inflation rate and the average inflation rate of the United States, our base for comparison. This is our measure of $(\pi^* - \pi)$. On the vertical axis is the average percentage change in the exchange rate between each country's currency and the U.S. dollar (% Change in e). The positive relationship between these two variables is clear in this figure. Countries with relatively high inflation tend to have depreciating currencies, and countries with relatively low inflation tend to have appreciating currencies.

As an example, consider the exchange rate between German marks and U.S. dollars. Both Germany and the United States have experienced inflation over the past twenty years, so both the mark and the dollar buy fewer goods than they once did. But, as Figure 8-14 shows, inflation in Germany has been lower

figure 8-14

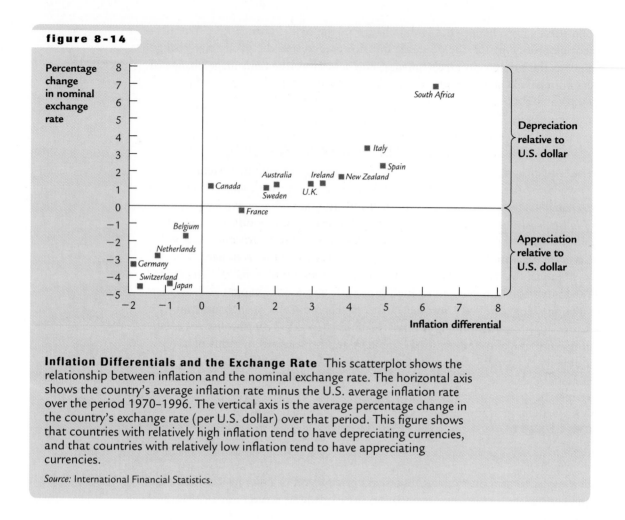

Inflation Differentials and the Exchange Rate This scatterplot shows the relationship between inflation and the nominal exchange rate. The horizontal axis shows the country's average inflation rate minus the U.S. average inflation rate over the period 1970–1996. The vertical axis is the average percentage change in the country's exchange rate (per U.S. dollar) over that period. This figure shows that countries with relatively high inflation tend to have depreciating currencies, and that countries with relatively low inflation tend to have appreciating currencies.

Source: International Financial Statistics.

than inflation in the United States. This means that the value of the mark has fallen less than the value of the dollar. Therefore, the number of German marks one can buy with a U.S. dollar has been falling over time.

The Special Case of Purchasing-Power Parity

A famous hypothesis in economics, called the *law of one price,* states that the same good cannot sell for different prices in different locations at the same time. If a tonne of wheat sold for less in Calgary than in Winnipeg, it would be profitable to buy wheat in Calgary and then sell it in Winnipeg. Astute arbitrageurs would take advantage of such an opportunity and, thereby, would increase the demand for wheat in Calgary and increase the supply in Winnipeg. This would drive the price up in Calgary and down in Winnipeg—thereby ensuring that prices are equalized in the two markets.

The law of one price applied to the international marketplace is called **purchasing-power parity.** It states that if international arbitrage is possible, then a dollar (or any other currency) must have the same purchasing power in every country. The argument goes as follows. If a dollar could buy more wheat domestically than abroad, there would be opportunities to profit by buying wheat domestically and selling it abroad. Profit-seeking arbitrageurs would drive up the domestic price of wheat relative to the foreign price. Similarly, if a dollar could buy more wheat abroad than domestically, the arbitrageurs would buy wheat abroad and sell it domestically, driving down the domestic price relative to the foreign price. Thus, profit-seeking by international arbitrageurs causes wheat prices to be the same in all countries.

We can interpret the doctrine of purchasing-power parity using our model of the real exchange rate. The quick action of these international arbitrageurs implies that net exports are highly sensitive to small movements in the real exchange rate. A small decrease in the price of domestic goods relative to foreign goods—that is, a small decrease in the real exchange rate—causes arbitrageurs to buy goods domestically and sell them abroad. Similarly, a small increase in the relative price of domestic goods causes arbitrageurs to import goods from abroad. Therefore, as in Figure 8-15, the net-exports schedule is very flat at the real exchange rate that equalizes purchasing power among countries: any small movement in the real exchange rate leads to a large change in net exports. This extreme sensitivity of net exports guarantees that the equilibrium real exchange rate is always close to the level ensuring purchasing-power parity.

Purchasing-power parity has two important implications. First, since the net-exports schedule is flat, changes in saving or investment do not influence the real or nominal exchange rate. Second, since the real exchange rate is fixed, all changes in the nominal exchange rate result from changes in price levels.

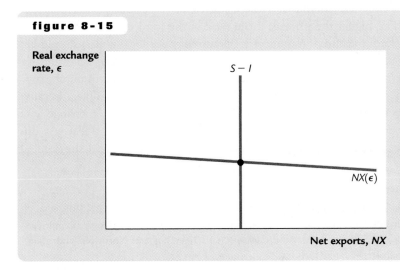

figure 8-15

Real exchange rate, ϵ

$S - I$

$NX(\epsilon)$

Net exports, *NX*

Purchasing-Power Parity
The law of one price applied to the international marketplace suggests that net exports are highly sensitive to small movements in the real exchange rate. This high sensitivity is reflected here with a very flat net-exports schedule.

Is this doctrine of purchasing-power parity realistic? Most economists believe that, despite its appealing logic, purchasing-power parity does not provide a completely accurate description of the world. First, many goods are not easily traded. A haircut can be more expensive in Tokyo than in Toronto, yet there is no room for international arbitrage since it is impossible to transport haircuts. Second, even tradeable goods are not always perfect substitutes. Some consumers prefer Toyotas, and others prefer Fords. Thus, the relative price of Toyotas and Fords can vary to some extent without leaving any profit opportunities. For these reasons, real exchange rates do in fact vary over time.

Although the doctrine of purchasing-power parity does not describe the world perfectly, it does provide a reason why movement in the real exchange rate will be limited. There is much validity to its underlying logic: the farther the real exchange rate drifts from the level predicted by purchasing-power parity, the greater the incentive for individuals to engage in international arbitrage in goods. Although we cannot rely on purchasing-power parity to eliminate all changes in the real exchange rate, this doctrine does provide a reason to expect that a significant number of the changes in the real exchange rate may be temporary.[1]

CASE STUDY

The Big Mac Around the World

The doctrine of purchasing-power parity says that after we adjust for exchange rates, we should find that goods sell for the same price everywhere. Conversely, it says that the exchange rate between two currencies should depend on the price levels in the two countries.

To see how well this doctrine works, *The Economist,* an international newsmagazine, regularly collects data on the price of a good sold in many countries: the McDonald's Big Mac hamburger. According to purchasing-power parity, the price of a Big Mac should be closely related to the country's nominal exchange rate. The higher the price of a Big Mac in the local currency, the higher the exchange rate (measured in units of local currency per U.S. dollar) should be.

Table 8-1 presents the international prices in 1997, when a Big Mac sold for $2.42 in the United States. With these data we can use the doctrine of purchasing-power parity to predict nominal exchange rates. For example, because a Big Mac cost 294 yen in Japan, we would predict that the exchange rate between the dollar and the yen was 294/2.42, or 121, yen per dollar. At this exchange rate, a Big Mac would have cost the same in Japan and the United States.

---

[1] To learn more about purchasing-power parity, see Kenneth A. Froot and Kenneth Rogoff, "Perspectives on PPP and Long-Run Real Exchange Rates," in Gene M. Grossman and Kenneth Rogoff, eds., *Handbook of International Economics,* vol. 3 (Amsterdam: North-Holland, 1995).

b. The citizens of Leverett like to travel abroad. How will this change in the exchange rate affect them?

c. The fiscal policymakers of Leverett want to adjust taxes to maintain the exchange rate at its previous level. What should they do? If they do this, what are the overall effects on saving, investment, net exports, and the interest rate?

4. What will happen to the trade balance and the real exchange rate of a small open economy when government purchases increase, such as during a war? Does your answer depend on whether this is a local war or a world war?

5. In 1995, President Clinton considered placing a 100-percent tariff on the import of Japanese luxury cars. Discuss the economics and politics of such a policy. In particular, how would the policy affect the U.S. trade deficit? How would it affect the exchange rate? Who would be hurt by such a policy? Who would benefit?

6. Suppose that some foreign countries begin to subsidize investment by instituting an investment tax credit.

a. What happens to world investment demand as a function of the world interest rate?

b. What happens to the world interest rate?

c. What happens to investment in our small open economy?

d. What happens to our trade balance?

e. What happens to our real exchange rate?

7. "Travelling in Italy is much cheaper now than it was ten years ago," says a friend. "Ten years ago, a dollar bought 1,000 lire; this year, a dollar buys 1,500 lire."

Is your friend right or wrong? Given that total inflation over this period was about 25 percent in North America and 100 percent in Italy, has it become more or less expensive to travel in Italy? Write your answer using a concrete example—like a cup of Canadian coffee versus a cup of Italian espresso—that will convince your friend.

8. You read in a newspaper that the nominal interest rate is 12 percent per year in Canada and 8 percent per year in the United States. Suppose that the real interest rates are equalized in the two countries and that purchasing-power parity holds.

a. Using the Fisher equation (discussed in Chapter 7), what can you infer about expected inflation in Canada and in the United States?

b. What can you infer about the expected change in the exchange rate between the Canadian dollar and the U.S. dollar?

c. A friend proposes a get-rich-quick scheme: borrow from a U.S. bank at 8 percent, deposit the money in a Canadian bank at 12 percent, and make a 4 percent profit. What's wrong with this scheme?

The Open Economy in the Very Long Run

The main body of this chapter involves the small-open-economy version of the Chapter 3 material. In this appendix, we consider the small-open-economy version of the Chapter 4 and 5 material. The closed-economy analysis focuses on how saving leads to capital accumulation and higher living standards in the future. In the open setting, the assumption of perfect capital mobility makes the quantity of capital employed within the domestic economy independent of national saving. Thus, with both the capital stock and the labour force determined exogenously, real GDP can*not* be increased by national saving. But GNP *is* affected. With higher national saving, the level of foreign indebtedness can be reduced. Higher consumption is possible in the long run as a result of the corresponding reduction in interest payment obligations to foreigners. The purpose of this appendix is to explain this process in detail.

Foreign Debt

In the main part of this chapter, we did not need to distinguish between the trade balance and the current account balance. But now it is helpful to do so. To that end, we divide net exports into two components: the net sale of goods and nonfinancial services to the rest of the world (the trade balance) minus the net interest payments Canadians make each year to foreigners to pay for that year's lending services that were imported. Letting NX stand for the first component, and letting Z and r denote the level of foreign debt and the interest rate involved on that debt, the overall current account balance is $NX - rZ$. As before, net foreign investment, $S - I$, must equal the current account balance, so in this more detailed specification,

$$S - I = NX - rZ.$$

Another way to appreciate this relationship is to note that, when the distinction between GNP and GDP is not ignored for simplicity, national saving is $GNP - T - G$. Since $GNP = GDP - rZ$, and since $GDP = C + I + G + NX$, these two relationships imply $S - I = NX - rZ$.

National wealth is the excess of our assets over our debt, that is, $K - Z$. Since saving is the increase in national wealth ($S = \Delta K - \Delta Z$), and since investment is the change in the capital stock ($I = \Delta K$), the fundamental equation given above can be re-expressed as foreign debt accumulation identity:

$$\Delta Z = rZ - NX.$$

This equation states that our debt to foreigners increases whenever interest payment obligations on the pre-existing debt for that period, rZ, exceed what we earn from our net-export sales from other items that period, NX.

A long-run equilibrium exists when the foreign debt–GDP ratio, Z/Y, is constant. Defining the GDP growth rate as n ($\Delta Y/Y = n$), long-run equilibrium requires $\Delta Z/Z = n$, or $\Delta Z = nZ$. Substituting this balanced growth requirement into the accumulation identity, we have the long-run equilibrium condition

$$(r - n)Z = NX.$$

Before we use these two relationships—the accumulation identity to determine outcomes initially and the equilibrium condition to determine outcomes eventually—we clarify two things. First, this analysis takes both r and n as exogenous variables. The interest rate is determined in the rest of the world via the assumption of perfect capital mobility. The growth rate of the effective labour force is exogenous, as in the Solow model. The second thing to bear in mind is that the interest rate (the marginal product of capital) exceeds the growth rate, so $(r - n)$ is positive. We learned this when we determined which side of the Golden Rule we are on, back in Chapter 4.

Fiscal Policy

We are now in a position to see how our analysis of fiscal policy can be enriched by considering these longer-term relationships. The main initiative of the Canadian government during the 1990s was deficit reduction—accomplished primarily by cuts in government spending. Thus, in Figure 8-16 we explore the effect of a cut in government spending. Initially, the analysis duplicates what we learned when studying Figure 8-10; the only difference here is that spending is decreased, not increased. The graph shows the key implication of fiscal retrenchment—that net exports rise.

We can now appreciate the longer-term implication of this rise in net exports. Consider each term in the foreign debt accumulation identity. Since the preexisting level of Z is determined by whatever history took place *before* this fiscal policy, and since r is exogenous (equal to r^*), higher NX implies lower ΔZ. Thus a higher level of net exports initially makes our foreign debt obligations shrink.

What are the long-term implications of lower debt? This question can be answered by considering the full equilibrium condition. Given that $(r - n)$ is positive and that Z is eventually lower, the left-hand side of the equilibrium condition must be smaller. This means that, eventually, NX must be smaller too. So, as time passes, net exports *must* move in the *opposite* direction from what occurs initially.

To appreciate why this occurs, we must realize that the consumption function requires an amendment to make it applicable in this longer-term setting.

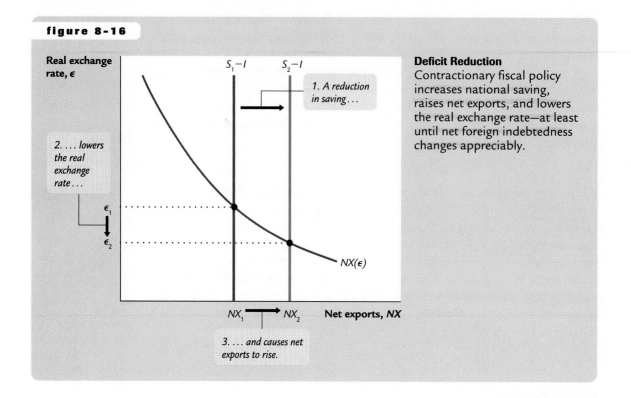

figure 8-16

Real exchange rate, ϵ

$S_1 - I$ $S_2 - I$

1. A reduction in saving...

2. ... lowers the real exchange rate...

ϵ_1

ϵ_2

$NX(\epsilon)$

NX_1 NX_2 Net exports, NX

3. ... and causes net exports to rise.

Deficit Reduction
Contractionary fiscal policy increases national saving, raises net exports, and lowers the real exchange rate—at least until net foreign indebtedness changes appreciably.

In particular, to be both realistic and consistent with the optimization-based theories of consumption, which are introduced in Chapter 16, we must assume that consumption depends on both disposable income and wealth (and therefore foreign indebtedness: $C = C(Y - T, Z)$). Since households cannot afford to consume as much when they are heavily in debt, we know that consumption depends inversely on foreign debt. As a result, since national saving is ($Y - C - G$), S depends positively on Z. Figure 8-17 shows the result of this dependence. While the cut in G shifts the ($S - I$) line to the right initially, the falling level of foreign debt induces a gradual drop in private saving, and the ($S - I$) line drifts back to the left. The algebraic version of the long-run equilibrium condition indicates that this process is not complete until a point like C in Figure 8-17 is reached.

It is instructive to summarize the time path of the real exchange rate following fiscal retrenchment. That response is from point A to B initially, and then from B to C later on. Thus, the analysis predicts that the domestic currency falls in value initially, but that this outcome is reversed and that the exchange rate rises eventually. Many commentators on exchange-rate developments appear to reason in a way that does not reflect this "overshoot" in the real exchange rate. For example, it is usually presumed that tight fiscal policy—since it involves "getting our fiscal house in order"—causes a straightforward appreciation of our currency. The limited success of empirical studies on exchange-rate determination may have a lot to do with the fact that the reversal and

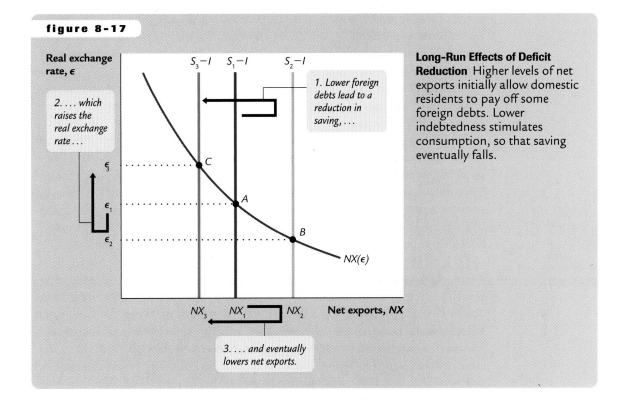

figure 8-17

Real exchange rate, ϵ

2. ... which raises the real exchange rate ...

1. Lower foreign debts lead to a reduction in saving, ...

$S_3 - I$ $S_1 - I$ $S_2 - I$

ϵ_3 C

ϵ_1 A

ϵ_2 B

$NX(\epsilon)$

NX_3 NX_1 NX_2 **Net exports, NX**

3. ... and eventually lowers net exports.

Long-Run Effects of Deficit Reduction Higher levels of net exports initially allow domestic residents to pay off some foreign debts. Lower indebtedness stimulates consumption, so that saving eventually falls.

overshoot features in the theory are often precluded in the way statistical studies are performed.

But we should not be too critical of the empirical work. On balance, our theory suggests that Canada's real exchange rate (vis-à-vis the U.S. dollar) should have fallen during the 1970–2000 time period—both because we had a looser fiscal policy and because we have a more resource-based economy than do the Americans. As a result of our increased dependence on the resource sectors, the demand for our net exports was more affected by the drop in the demand for primary commodities. In addition to these key determinants of the real exchange rate, there was additional downward pressure on our nominal exchange rate, since—until the last few years of the century—we had higher inflation. It has been estimated that of the 30-cent fall in the Canadian dollar over 30 years (from par with the U.S. currency in 1970), roughly 10 cents can be attributed to each of these three factors.

Trickle-Down Economics

As we have seen, anything that raises national saving leads to higher living standards in the longer term. Often the government tries to implement this strategy by offering tax breaks for saving. This policy is criticized on the grounds that only the rich can afford to save, so the poor do not share the benefits. Proponents of this approach answer this criticism by arguing that the benefits "trickle down" indirectly to those on lower incomes, so everyone benefits indirectly after all. Let us assess the validity of this claim—first in a closed-economy setting as a base for comparison, and then in an open setting.

Figure 8-18 shows the diminishing marginal product of capital relationship. Initially, the quantity of capital is given by the position of the supply curve in Figure 8-18. The equilibrium return on capital (the interest rate) is given by the intersection of supply and demand in Figure 8-18: the height of point A. The total earnings of capital (the yield per unit times number of units) is given by the light blue rectangle. Since the area under the marginal product curve is total output, labourers receive the light yellow triangle, and total GDP is the sum of capital's rectangle and labour's triangle. To assess the trickle-down theory, let us assume that capital owners are "rich," while labourers are "poor." We now consider whether an increase in national saving helps labour.

In a closed economy, higher saving means more investment, which leads eventually to a larger capital stock. We show that higher capital stock by moving the supply curve to the right in Figure 8-19. GDP has increased by an amount equal to the trapezoid of dark shaded regions on the right (labour gets the yellow part, capital gets the blue part). Labour's total income has increased by the trapezoid created by the two horizontal dotted lines (both the light and dark yellow regions in Figure 8-19). We can conclude that, even if labour does not benefit in any direct way from the tax cut (or other initiative used to stimulate saving), there appears to be solid support for the trickle-down view. The

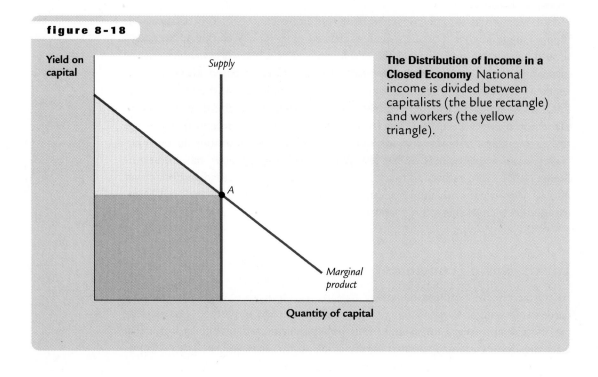

figure 8-18

The Distribution of Income in a Closed Economy National income is divided between capitalists (the blue rectangle) and workers (the yellow triangle).

figure 8-19

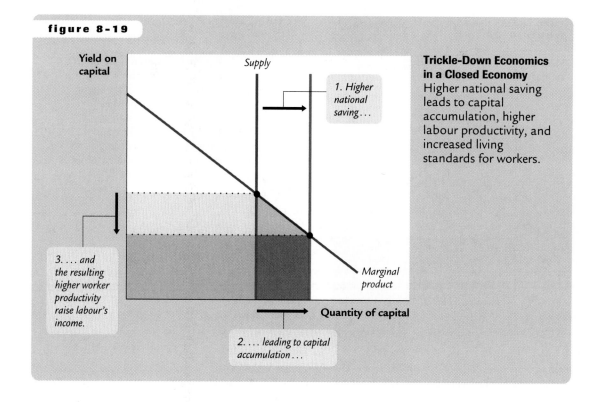

Trickle-Down Economics in a Closed Economy Higher national saving leads to capital accumulation, higher labour productivity, and increased living standards for workers.

Yield on capital

Supply

1. Higher national saving...

3. ... and the resulting higher worker productivity raise labour's income.

Marginal product

Quantity of capital

2. ... leading to capital accumulation...

intuition behind this conclusion is that each worker has more capital with which to work and so receives higher wages.

Does this conclusion carry over to a small open economy? The initial situation in this case is shown in Figure 8-20. With perfect capital mobility, there is a perfectly elastic supply of capital (from the rest of the world) at the prevailing world yield on capital. Supply and demand for capital intersect at point A, so GDP is determined by the trapazoid formed by the perpendicular dropped from point A. Capital owners receive the lower rectangles, while labour receives the upper, yellow triangle. The vertical line in Figure 8-20 indicates what part of the capital is owned by domestic residents. Given the position of this line, we have assumed that domestic residents own the proportion of the capital that is denoted by point B. Thus, domestic capitalists receive the light blue rectangle and foreigners receive the green rectangle. Since GNP is GDP minus income going to foreigners, GNP is the entire coloured area minus this green region.

As in the closed economy, the results of higher saving are shown by shifting the vertical line to the right—as illustrated in Figure 8-21. In this case, the location of point A is unaffected, so GDP is no different. Wealth still increases, because the higher saving allows domestic residents to reduce foreign debt. The smaller interest payment obligation to foreigners is shown by the fact that the green region is smaller in Figure 8-21. Thus GNP increases, even though GDP

figure 8-20

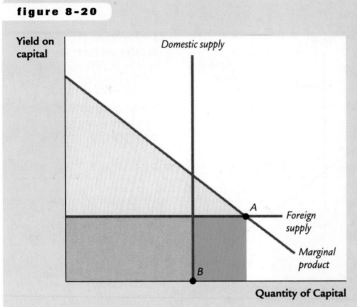

The Distribution of Income in a Small Open Economy National income is divided between capitalists (the shaded rectangles) and labour (the yellow triangle). Foreign capitalists receive the green rectangle; domestic capitalists receive the blue rectangle.

figure 8-21

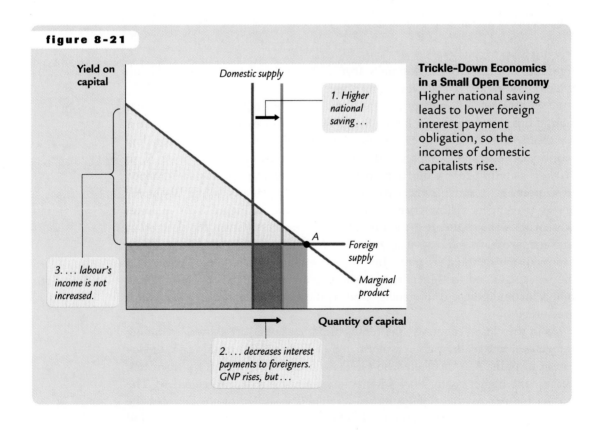

Trickle-Down Economics in a Small Open Economy Higher national saving leads to lower foreign interest payment obligation, so the incomes of domestic capitalists rise.

does not. Since GNP is national income, the aggregate effect is much the same even if the reason for it differs. Domestic residents are better off because they have a smaller mortgage to finance, not because workers have more capital to work with. However, the *distribution* of the benefit is very different. Because workers have no more capital, wages are no higher, and this is why the size of labour's yellow triangle is not affected. We conclude that there is *not* strong support for trickle down in a small open economy setting.

MORE PROBLEMS AND APPLICATIONS |

1. Explain why empirical studies have had difficulty "explaining" changes in the exchange rate.

2. Spokespersons for the labour movement have been highly critical of the "conservative" agenda that has formed the basis of federal government policy in Canada for the last twenty years. Whether the initiative was tax reform, deficit reduction, or disinflation, these individuals criticized the government. Explain whether macroeconomic theory supports this critique.

part THREE

The Economy in the Short Run

In Part Two we developed theories to explain how the economy behaves in the long run. Those theories were based on the classical dichotomy — the premise that real variables such as output and employment are not affected by what happens to nominal variables such as the money supply and the price level. Although classical theories are useful for explaining long-run trends, including the economic growth we observe from decade to decade, most economists believe that the classical dichotomy does not hold in the short run and, therefore, that classical theories cannot explain year-to-year fluctuations in output and employment. Here, in Part Three, we see how economists explain these short-run fluctuations.

Chapter 9 begins our analysis by discussing the key differences between the long run and the short run and by introducing the model of aggregate supply and aggregate demand. With this model we can show how shocks to the economy lead to short-run fluctuations in output and employment. We can also show how policymakers can potentially cause or cure those fluctuations.

The next four chapters develop more fully the model of aggregate supply and aggregate demand. Chapters 10 and 11 present the IS—LM model, which shows how monetary and fiscal policy affect the aggregate demand for goods and services. Chapter 12 presents the Mundell—Fleming model, which describes how aggregate demand is determined in an open economy. Chapter 13 discusses theories of aggregate supply and their implications.

Introduction to Economic Fluctuations

The modern world regards business cycles much as the ancient Egyptians regarded the overflowing of the Nile. The phenomenon recurs at intervals, it is of great importance to everyone, and natural causes of it are not in sight.

—*John Bates Clark, 1898*

Economic fluctuations present a recurring problem for economists and policy-makers. As you can see in Figure 9-1, real GDP does not grow smoothly. Recessions—periods of falling incomes and rising unemployment—are frequent. In 1991, for example, real GDP fell about 2 percent, and the unemployment rate rose from 7.5 percent in 1989 to 11.3 percent in 1992. Recessions are also associated with shorter workweeks: more workers have part-time jobs, and fewer workers work overtime.

Economists call these fluctuations in output and employment the *business cycle.* Although this term suggests that fluctuations in the economy are regular and predictable, neither is the case, as Figure 9-1 makes clear.

In Part Two of this book, we developed models to identify the long-run determinants of national income, unemployment, inflation, and other economic variables. Yet we did not examine why these variables fluctuate so much from year to year. Here in Part Three we develop a model to explain these short-run fluctuations. Because real GDP is the best single measure of economic activity, it is the focus of our model.

Just as Egypt now controls the flooding of the Nile Valley with the Aswan Dam, modern society tries to control the business cycle with appropriate economic policies. The model we develop over the next several chapters shows how monetary and fiscal policies influence the business cycle. We will see that these policies can potentially stabilize the economy or, if poorly conducted, make the problem of economic instability even worse.

figure 9-1

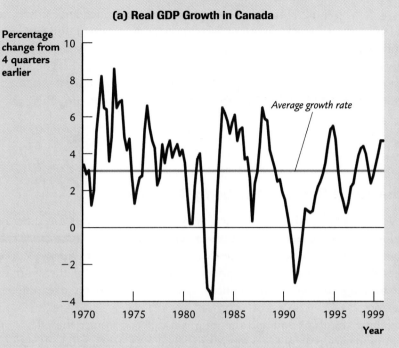

(a) Real GDP Growth in Canada

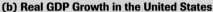

Real GDP Growth in Canada and the United States In Canada the growth rate in real GDP averages around 3.1 percent per year, as indicated by the green line in Panel (a). But there is a wide variation around this average. Recessions are periods during which real GDP falls—that is, during which real GDP growth is negative. U.S. GDP is shown in Panel (b). Clearly business cycles in the two economies are closely connected. But the state of the U.S. economy is not the only important thing for Canada.

Source: Statistics Canada, D14872, and U.S. Department of Commerce.

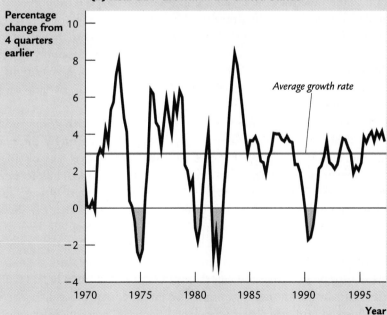

(b) Real GDP Growth in the United States

9-1 | Time Horizons in Macroeconomics

Before we start building a model of short-run economic fluctuations, let's step back and ask a fundamental question: Why do economists need different models for different time horizons? Why can't we stop the course here and be content with the classical models developed in Chapters 3 through 8? The answer, as this book has consistently reminded its reader, is that classical macroeconomic theory applies to the long run but not to the short run. But why is this so?

How the Short Run and the Long Run Differ

Most macroeconomists believe that the key difference between the short run and the long run is the behaviour of prices. *In the long run, prices are flexible and can respond to changes in supply or demand. In the short run, many prices are "sticky" at some predetermined level.* Because prices behave differently in the short run than in the long run, economic policies have different effects over different time horizons.

To see how the short run and the long run differ, consider the effects of a change in monetary policy. Suppose that the Bank of Canada suddenly reduced the money supply by 5 percent. According to the classical model, which almost all economists agree describes the economy in the long run, the money supply affects nominal variables—variables measured in terms of money—but not real variables. As we discussed in Chapter 7, this principle is known as the *classical dichotomy*. In the long run, a 5-percent reduction in the money supply lowers all prices (including nominal wages) by 5 percent while all real variables remain the same. Thus, in the long run, changes in the money supply do not cause fluctuations in output or employment.

In the short run, however, many prices do not respond to changes in monetary policy. A reduction in the money supply does not immediately cause all firms to cut the wages they pay, all stores to change the price tags on their goods, all mail-order firms to issue new catalogues, and all restaurants to print new menus. Instead, there is little immediate change in many prices; that is, many prices are sticky. This short-run price stickiness implies that the short-run impact of a change in the money supply is not the same as the long-run impact.

A model of economic fluctuations must take into account this short-run price stickiness. We will see that the failure of prices to adjust quickly and completely means that, in the short run, output and employment must do some of the adjusting instead. In other words, during the time horizon over which prices are sticky, the classical dichotomy no longer holds: nominal variables can influence real variables, and the economy can deviate from the equilibrium predicted by the classical model.

CASE STUDY

The Puzzle of Sticky Magazine Prices

How sticky are prices? The answer to this question depends on what price we consider. Some commodities, such as wheat, soybeans, and pork bellies, are traded on organized exchanges, and their prices change every minute. No one would call these prices sticky. Yet the prices of most goods and services change much less frequently. One survey found that 39 percent of firms change their prices once a year, and another 10 percent change their prices less than once a year.[1]

The reasons for price stickiness are not always apparent. Consider, for example, the market for magazines. A study has documented that magazines change their newsstand prices very infrequently. The typical magazine allows inflation to erode its real price by about 25 percent before it raises its nominal price. When inflation is 4 percent per year, the typical magazine changes its price about every six years.[2]

Why do magazines leave their prices unchanged for so long? Economists do not have a definitive answer. The question is puzzling because it would seem that for magazines, the cost of a price change is small. To change prices, a mail-order firm must issue a new catalogue and a restaurant must print a new menu, but a magazine publisher can simply print a new price on the cover of the next issue. Perhaps the cost to the publisher of charging the wrong price is also not very great. Or maybe customers would find it inconvenient if the price of their favourite magazine changed every month.

The magazine example shows that explaining at the microeconomic level why prices are sticky can sometimes be difficult. The cause of price stickiness is, therefore, an active area of research, which we discuss more fully in Chapter 19. In this chapter, however, we simply assume that prices are sticky so we can start developing the link between sticky prices and the business cycle. Although not yet fully explained, short-run price stickiness is widely believed to be crucial for understanding short-run economic fluctuations.

The Model of Aggregate Supply and Aggregate Demand

How does introducing sticky prices change our view of how the economy works? We can answer this question by considering economists' two favourite words—supply and demand.

In classical macroeconomic theory, the amount of output depends on the economy's ability to *supply* goods and services, which in turn depends on

[1] Alan S. Blinder, "On Sticky Prices: Academic Theories Meet the Real World," in *Monetary Policy,* N.G. Mankiw, ed. (Chicago: University of Chicago Press, 1994): 117–154. A case study in Chapter 19 discusses this survey in more detail.

[2] Stephen G. Cecchetti, "The Frequency of Price Adjustment: A Study of the Newsstand Prices of Magazines," *Journal of Econometrics* 31 (1986): 255–274.

the supplies of capital and labour and on the available production technology. This is the essence of the models developed in Chapters 3, 4, and 5. Flexible prices are a crucial assumption of classical theory. The theory posits, sometimes implicitly, that prices adjust to ensure that the quantity of output demanded equals the quantity supplied.

The economy works quite differently when prices are sticky. In this case, as we will see, output also depends on the *demand* for goods and services. Demand, in turn, is influenced by monetary policy, fiscal policy, and various other factors. Because monetary and fiscal policy can influence the economy's output over the time horizon when prices are sticky, price stickiness provides a rationale for why these policies may be useful in stabilizing the economy in the short run.

In the rest of this chapter, we develop a model that makes these ideas more precise. The model of supply and demand, which we used in Chapter 1 to discuss the market for pizza, offers some of the most fundamental insights in economics. This model shows how the supply and demand for any good jointly determine the good's price and the quantity sold, and how shifts in supply and

---

f y i

THE SHORT RUN, THE LONG RUN, AND THE VERY LONG RUN

This book discusses many models of the economy, each with its own set of simplifying assumptions. Sometimes it's hard to keep all the models straight. One way to do so is to categorize the models by the time horizon over which they apply. The models fall into three categories:

➤ *The Short Run* This chapter and those that follow present the short-run theory of the economy. This theory assumes that prices are sticky and that, because of this price stickiness, capital and labour are sometimes not fully employed. Price stickiness is widely viewed as being important for explaining the economic fluctuations we observe from month to month or from year to year.

➤ *The Long Run* Chapter 3 presented the basic long-run theory of the economy, called the classical model. Chapter 7 presented the classical theory of money, and Chapter 8 presented the classical theory of the open econ-

omy. These chapters assumed that prices are flexible and, therefore, that capital and labour are fully employed. These chapters also took as fixed the quantities of capital and labour, as well as the technology for turning capital and labour into output. These assumptions are best suited for a time horizon of several years. Over this period, prices can adjust to equilibrium levels, yet capital, labour, and technology are relatively constant.

➤ *The Very Long Run* Chapters 4 and 5 presented the basic theory of economic growth, called the Solow model. This model analyzes the time horizon over which the capital stock, the labour force, and the available technology can change. This model is designed to explain how the economy works over a period of several decades. The appendix to Chapter 8 considered this time span in the open-economy case.

When analyzing economic policies, it is important to keep in mind that they influence the economy over all time horizons. We must, therefore, draw on the insights of all these models.

E as the sum of consumption C, planned investment I, and government purchases G:

$$E = C + I + G.$$

To this equation, we add the consumption function

$$C = C(Y - T).$$

This equation states that consumption depends on disposable income $(Y - T)$, which is total income Y minus taxes T. To keep things simple, for now we take planned investment as exogenously fixed:

$$I = \bar{I}.$$

And as in Chapter 3, we assume that fiscal policy—the levels of government purchases and taxes—is fixed:

$$G = \bar{G},$$
$$T = \bar{T}.$$

Combining these five equations, we obtain

$$E = C(Y - \bar{T}) + \bar{I} + \bar{G}.$$

This equation shows that planned expenditure is a function of income Y, the level of planned investment $\bar{I}$, and the fiscal policy variables $\bar{G}$ and $\bar{T}$.

Figure 10-2 graphs planned expenditure as a function of the level of income. This line slopes upward because higher income leads to higher consumption and thus higher planned expenditure. The slope of this line is the marginal propensity to consume, the MPC: it shows how much planned expenditure increases when income rises by \$1. This planned-expenditure function is the first piece of the model called the Keynesian cross.

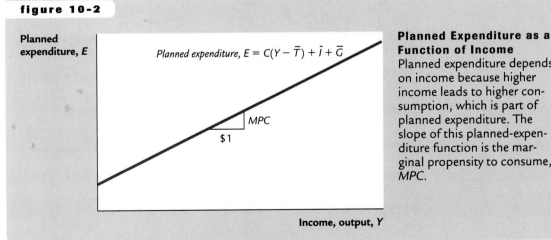

figure 10-2

Planned expenditure, E

Planned expenditure, $E = C(Y - \bar{T}) + \bar{I} + \bar{G}$

MPC

\$1

Income, output, Y

Planned Expenditure as a Function of Income
Planned expenditure depends on income because higher income leads to higher consumption, which is part of planned expenditure. The slope of this planned-expenditure function is the marginal propensity to consume, MPC.

The Economy in Equilibrium The next piece of the Keynesian cross is the assumption that the economy is in equilibrium when actual expenditure equals planned expenditure. This assumption is based on the idea that when people's plans have been realized, they have no reason to change what they are doing. Recalling that Y as GDP equals not only total income but also total actual expenditure on goods and services, we can write this equilibrium condition as

$$\text{Actual Expenditure} = \text{Planned Expenditure}$$
$$Y = E.$$

The 45-degree line in Figure 10-3 plots the points where this condition holds. With the addition of the planned-expenditure function, this diagram becomes the Keynesian cross. The equilibrium of this economy is at point A, where the planned-expenditure function crosses the 45-degree line.

How does the economy get to the equilibrium? In this model, inventories play an important role in the adjustment process. Whenever the economy is not in equilibrium, firms experience unplanned changes in inventories, and this induces them to change production levels. Changes in production in turn influence total income and expenditure, moving the economy toward equilibrium.

For example, suppose the economy were ever to find itself with GDP at a level greater than the equilibrium level, such as the level Y_1 in Figure 10-4. In this case, planned expenditure E_1 is less than production Y_1, so firms are selling less than they are producing. Firms add the unsold goods to their stock of inventories. This unplanned rise in inventories induces firms to lay off workers

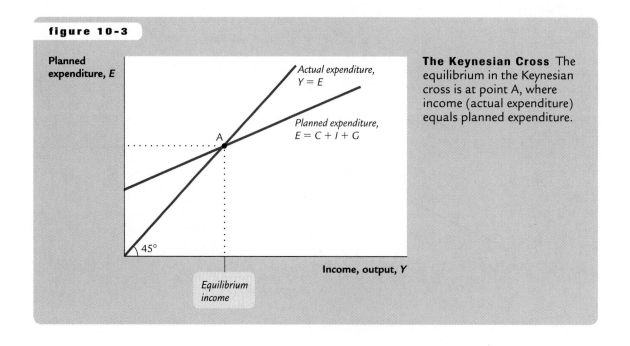

figure 10-3

Planned expenditure, E

Actual expenditure, Y = E

Planned expenditure, E = C + I + G

A

45°

Income, output, Y

Equilibrium income

The Keynesian Cross The equilibrium in the Keynesian cross is at point A, where income (actual expenditure) equals planned expenditure.

and reduce production, and these actions in turn reduce GDP. This process of unintended inventory accumulation and falling income continues until income Y falls to the equilibrium level.

Similarly, suppose GDP were at a level lower than the equilibrium level, such as the level Y_2 in Figure 10-4. In this case, planned expenditure E_2 is greater than production Y_2. Firms meet the high level of sales by drawing down their inventories. But when firms see their stock of inventories dwindle, they hire more workers and increase production. GDP rises, and the economy approaches the equilibrium.

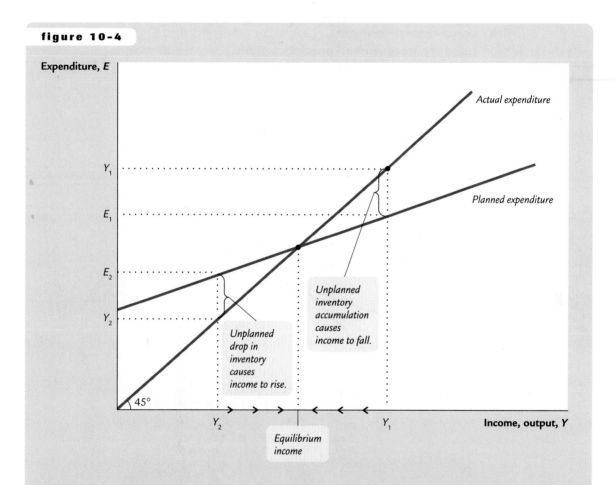

figure 10-4

The Adjustment to Equilibrium in the Keynesian Cross If firms were producing at level Y_1, then planned expenditure E_1 would fall short of production, and firms would accumulate inventories. This inventory accumulation would induce firms to reduce production. Similarly, if firms were producing at level Y_2, then planned expenditure E_2 would exceed production, and firms would run down their inventories. This fall in inventories would induce firms to raise production. In both cases, the firms' decisions drive the economy toward equilibrium.

In summary, the Keynesian cross shows how income Y is determined for given levels of planned investment I and fiscal policy G and T. We can use this model to show how income changes when one of these exogenous variables changes.

Fiscal Policy and the Multiplier: Government Purchases Consider how changes in government purchases affect the economy. Because government purchases are one component of expenditure, higher government purchases result in higher planned expenditure for any given level of income. If government purchases rise by ΔG, then the planned-expenditure schedule shifts upward by ΔG, as in Figure 10-5. The equilibrium of the economy moves from point A to point B.

This graph shows that an increase in government purchases leads to an even greater increase in income. That is, ΔY is larger than ΔG. The ratio $\Delta Y / \Delta G$ is called the **government-purchases multiplier;** it tells us how much income rises in response to a $1 increase in government purchases. An implication of the Keynesian cross is that the government-purchases multiplier is larger than 1.

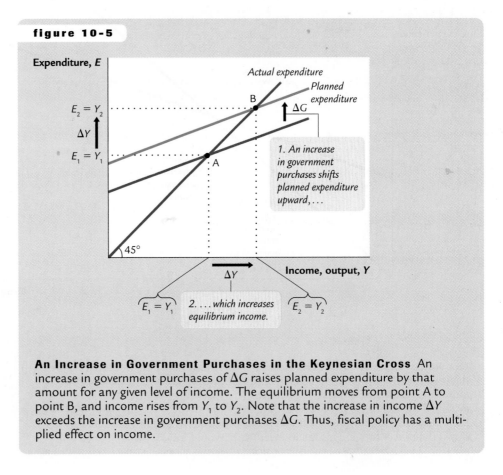

figure 10-5

An Increase in Government Purchases in the Keynesian Cross An increase in government purchases of ΔG raises planned expenditure by that amount for any given level of income. The equilibrium moves from point A to point B, and income rises from Y_1 to Y_2. Note that the increase in income ΔY exceeds the increase in government purchases ΔG. Thus, fiscal policy has a multiplied effect on income.

"Your Majesty, my voyage will not only forge a new route to the spices of the East but also create over three thousand new jobs."

Why does fiscal policy have a multiplied effect on income? The reason is that, according to the consumption function, $C = C(Y - T)$, higher income causes higher consumption. When an increase in government purchases raises income, it also raises consumption, which further raises income, which further raises consumption, and so on. Therefore, in this model, an increase in government purchases causes a greater increase in income.

How big is the multiplier? To answer this question, we trace through each step of the change in income. The process begins when expenditure rises by ΔG, which implies that income rises by ΔG as well. This increase in income in turn raises consumption by $MPC \times \Delta G$, where MPC is the marginal propensity to consume. This increase in consumption raises expenditure and income once again. This second increase in income of $MPC \times \Delta G$ again raises consumption, this time by $MPC \times (MPC \times \Delta G)$, which again raises expenditure and income, and so on. This feedback from consumption to income to consumption continues indefinitely. The total effect on income is

Initial Change in Government Purchases = ΔG

First Change in Consumption $= MPC \times \Delta G$

Second Change in Consumption $= MPC^2 \times \Delta G$

Third Change in Consumption $= MPC^3 \times \Delta G$

$$\Delta Y = (1 + MPC + MPC^2 + MPC^3 + \cdots)\Delta G.$$

The government-purchases multiplier is

$$\Delta Y/\Delta G = 1 + MPC + MPC^2 + MPC^3 + \cdots.$$

This expression for the multiplier is an example of an *infinite geometric series*. A result from algebra allows us to write the multiplier as[2]

$$\Delta Y/\Delta G = 1/(1 - MPC).$$

For example, if the marginal propensity to consume is 0.6, the multiplier is

$$\Delta Y/\Delta G = 1 + 0.6 + 0.6^2 + 0.6^3 + \cdots$$
$$= 1/(1 - 0.6)$$
$$= 2.5.$$

In this case, a \$1.00 increase in government purchases raises equilibrium income by \$2.50.[3]

Fiscal Policy and the Multiplier: Taxes   Consider now how changes in taxes affect equilibrium income. A decrease in taxes of ΔT immediately raises disposable income $Y - T$ by ΔT and, therefore, increases consumption by $MPC \times \Delta T$. For any given level of income Y, planned expenditure is now higher. As Figure 10-6 shows, the planned-expenditure schedule shifts upward by $MPC \times \Delta T$. The equilibrium of the economy moves from point A to point B.

---

[2] *Mathematical note:* We prove this algebraic result as follows. Let

$$z = 1 + x + x^2 + \cdots.$$

Multiply both sides of this equation by x:

$$xz = x + x^2 + x^3 + \cdots.$$

Subtract the second equation from the first:

$$z - xz = 1.$$

Rearrange this last equation to obtain

$$z(1 - x) = 1,$$

which implies

$$z = 1/(1 - x).$$

This completes the proof.

[3] *Mathematical note:* The government-purchases multiplier is most easily derived using a little calculus. Begin with the equation

$$Y = C(Y - T) + I + G.$$

Holding T and I fixed, differentiate to obtain

$$dY = C'dY + dG,$$

and then rearrange to find

$$dY/dG = 1/(1 - C').$$

This is the same as the equation in the text.

figure 10-6

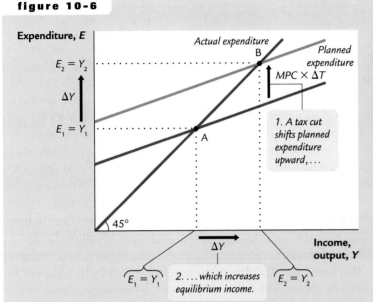

A Decrease in Taxes in the Keynesian Cross A decrease in taxes of ΔT raises planned expenditure by $MPC \times \Delta T$ for any given level of income. The equilibrium moves from point A to point B, and income rises from Y_1 to Y_2. Again, fiscal policy has a multiplied effect on income.

Just as an increase in government purchases has a multiplied effect on income, so does a decrease in taxes. As before, the initial change in expenditure, now $MPC \times \Delta T$, is multiplied by $1/(1 - MPC)$. The overall effect on income of the change in taxes is

$$\Delta Y/\Delta T = -MPC/(1 - MPC).$$

This expression is the **tax multiplier,** the amount income changes in response to a $1 change in taxes. For example, if the marginal propensity to consume is 0.6, then the tax multiplier is

$$\Delta Y/\Delta T = -0.6/(1 - 0.6) = -1.5.$$

In this example, a $1.00 cut in taxes raises equilibrium income by $1.50.[4]

---

[4] *Mathematical note:* As before, the multiplier is most easily derived using a little calculus. Begin with the equation

$$Y = C(Y - T) + I + G.$$

Holding I and G fixed, differentiate to obtain

$$dY = C'(dY - dT),$$

and then rearrange to find

$$dY/dT = -C'/(1 - C').$$

This is the same as the equation in the text.

CASE STUDY

Modest Expectations Concerning Job Creation

Canada's Liberal government was first elected in 1993 on a platform of "jobs, jobs, jobs." Many students, when hearing the term "multiplier," expect that it could be fairly straightforward for governments to fulfull job-creation promises of this sort. But economists now believe that the multiplier terminology may create unrealistic expectations. This trend in thinking will become clearer as our understanding of aggregate demand progresses through this book. For example, we will be considering developments in financial markets—the effects of fiscal policy on interest rates and the exchange rate. We will learn that the size of our fiscal policy multipliers is much reduced by these considerations.

What is a plausible value for the government spending multiplier—given that, at this point, we must limit our attention to the simple formula $1/1 - MPC$)? To answer this question, we must think of taxes, imports, and saving—the main things that keep a new dollar of income earned from being spent on domestically produced goods. The first consideration is the tax system; taxes increase by about $0.25 for each $1 increase in GDP. The second consideration is that the transfer payments people receive from the government decrease as their income increases, and in aggregate this variation means that transfer payments fall by about $0.15 for each $1 increase in GDP. Since "taxes" in our model stand for *net* payments by individuals to government—taxes less transfer receipts—we must take the overall "tax rate" to be 0.25 plus 0.15, or 0.40. Thus the proportion of income not taxed is 0.60. Finally, Canadians tend to import about one-quarter of all goods consumed. With a propensity to spend about 75 percent of each extra dollar of disposable income, we have an overall marginal propensity to consume domestically produced goods (out of each dollar of pretax income, GDP) equal to:

Proportion of Income Not Taxed	$\times$	Proportion of Spending Not Spent on Imports	$\times$	Propensity to Spend	$=$	MPC
(0.60)		(0.75)		(0.75)	$=$	0.34

With the *MPC* estimated at 0.34, the spending multiplier, $1/1 - MPC$), is 1.5.

During the 1994–1999 period, federal budgets involved an average cut in government spending of about $8 billion per year compared to what spending would have been if it had remained a constant fraction of GDP. Thus, we can take $\Delta G = \$8$ billion as representing the magnitude of a typical fiscal policy. The multiplier formula then predicts that ΔY is $12 billion. Since Canada's GDP averaged $835 billion over this period, this typical fiscal policy involves changing output by about 1.4 percent.

How much can this initiative be expected to change unemployment? The answer to this question can be had by relying on Okun's law, which was explained in Chapter 2. Okun's law states that unemployment usually rises by about one-half the percentage fall in GDP. Thus, the effect of this typical fiscal policy is estimated to be a change in the unemployment rate of three-quarters of 1 percentage point. While that represents a little more than 100,000 jobs, with an average unemployment rate over this period of 9 percent, not many would summarize this change as "jobs, jobs, jobs." We must also keep in mind that the simple formula, $1/(1 - MPC)$, *over*estimates the effects of policy.

It is also important to realize that a small multiplier was exactly what the government wanted during this period. Since the government was cutting expendentures to reduce the budget deficit, it did not want to destroy many jobs. A small fiscal multiplier was just what was needed in that case.

The Interest Rate, Investment, and the *IS* Curve

The Keynesian cross is only a steppingstone on our path to the *IS–LM* model. The Keynesian cross is useful because it shows how the spending plans of households, firms, and the government determine the economy's income. Yet it makes the simplifying assumption that the level of planned investment I is fixed. As we discussed in Chapter 3, an important macroeconomic relationship is that planned investment depends on the interest rate r.

To add this relationship between the interest rate and investment to our model, we write the level of planned investment as

$$I = I(r).$$

This investment function is graphed in panel (a) of Figure 10-7. Because the interest rate is the cost of borrowing to finance investment projects, an increase in the interest rate reduces planned investment. As a result, the investment function slopes downward.

To determine how income changes when the interest rate changes, we can combine the investment function with the Keynesian-cross diagram. Because investment is inversely related to the interest rate, an increase in the interest rate from r_1 to r_2 reduces the quantity of investment from $I(r_1)$ to $I(r_2)$. The reduction in planned investment, in turn, shifts the planned-expenditure function downward, as in panel (b) of Figure 10-7. The shift in the planned-expenditure function causes the level of income to fall from Y_1 to Y_2. Hence, an increase in the interest rate lowers income.

The *IS* curve, shown in panel (c) of Figure 10-7, summarizes this relationship between the interest rate and the level of income. In essence, the *IS* curve combines the interaction between r and I expressed by the investment function and the interaction between I and Y demonstrated by the Keynesian cross. Because an increase in the interest rate causes planned investment to fall, which in turn causes income to fall, the *IS* curve slopes downward.

figure 10-7

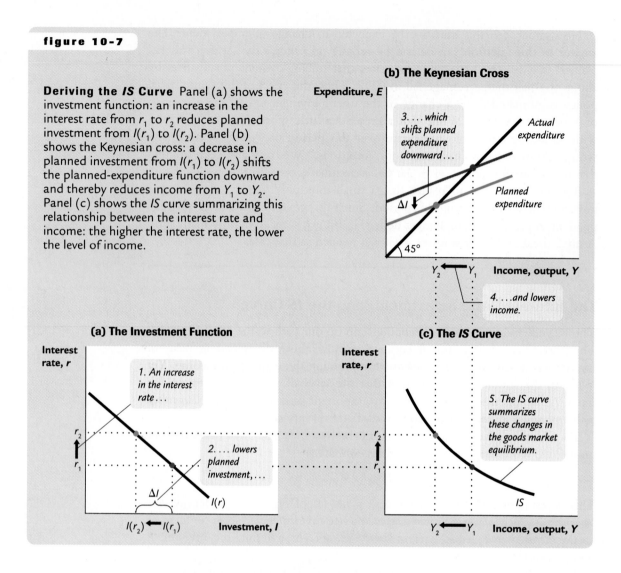

Deriving the *IS* Curve Panel (a) shows the investment function: an increase in the interest rate from r_1 to r_2 reduces planned investment from $I(r_1)$ to $I(r_2)$. Panel (b) shows the Keynesian cross: a decrease in planned investment from $I(r_1)$ to $I(r_2)$ shifts the planned-expenditure function downward and thereby reduces income from Y_1 to Y_2. Panel (c) shows the *IS* curve summarizing this relationship between the interest rate and income: the higher the interest rate, the lower the level of income.

(b) The Keynesian Cross

Expenditure, *E*

3. ...which shifts planned expenditure downward...

Actual expenditure

ΔI

Planned expenditure

45°

Y_2 ← Y_1 Income, output, *Y*

4. ...and lowers income.

(a) The Investment Function

Interest rate, *r*

1. An increase in the interest rate...

r_2

r_1

2. ...lowers planned investment,...

ΔI

$I(r)$

$I(r_2)$ ← $I(r_1)$ Investment, *I*

(c) The *IS* Curve

Interest rate, *r*

r_2

r_1

5. The IS curve summarizes these changes in the goods market equilibrium.

IS

Y_2 ← Y_1 Income, output, *Y*

How Fiscal Policy Shifts the *IS* Curve

The *IS* curve shows us, for any given interest rate, the level of income that brings the goods market into equilibrium. As we learned from the Keynesian cross, the level of income also depends on fiscal policy. The *IS* curve is drawn for a given fiscal policy; that is, when we construct the *IS* curve, we hold *G* and *T* fixed. When fiscal policy changes, the *IS* curve shifts.

Figure 10-8 uses the Keynesian cross to show how an increase in government purchases from G_1 to G_2 shifts the *IS* curve. This figure is drawn for a given interest rate $\bar{r}$ and thus for a given level of planned investment. The Keynesian cross shows that this change in fiscal policy raises planned expenditure and thereby increases equilibrium income from Y_1 to Y_2. Therefore, an increase in government purchases shifts the *IS* curve outward.

figure 10-8

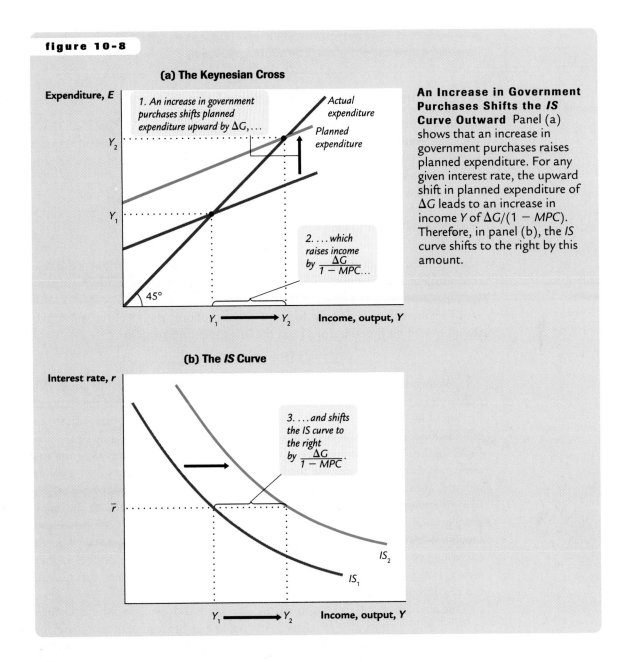

(a) The Keynesian Cross

Expenditure, E

1. An increase in government purchases shifts planned expenditure upward by ΔG,...

Actual expenditure

Planned expenditure

Y_2

Y_1

2. ...which raises income by $\frac{\Delta G}{1 - MPC}$...

$45°$

$Y_1 \longrightarrow Y_2$ Income, output, Y

(b) The *IS* Curve

Interest rate, r

3. ...and shifts the IS curve to the right by $\frac{\Delta G}{1 - MPC}$.

$\bar{r}$

IS_2

IS_1

$Y_1 \longrightarrow Y_2$ Income, output, Y

An Increase in Government Purchases Shifts the *IS* Curve Outward Panel (a) shows that an increase in government purchases raises planned expenditure. For any given interest rate, the upward shift in planned expenditure of ΔG leads to an increase in income Y of $\Delta G/(1 - MPC)$. Therefore, in panel (b), the *IS* curve shifts to the right by this amount.

We can use the Keynesian cross to see how other changes in fiscal policy shift the IS curve. Because a decrease in taxes also expands expenditure and income, it too shifts the IS curve outward. A decrease in government purchases or an increase in taxes reduces income; therefore, such a change in fiscal policy shifts the IS curve inward.

In summary, the IS curve shows the combinations of the interest rate and the level of income that are consistent with equilibrium in the market for goods and services. The IS curve is drawn for a given fiscal policy. Changes in fiscal policy that raise the demand for goods and services shift the IS curve to the right. Changes in fiscal policy that reduce the demand for goods and services shift the IS curve to the left.

A Loanable-Funds Interpretation of the *IS* Curve

When we first studied the market for goods and services in Chapter 3, we noted an equivalence between the supply and demand for goods and services and the supply and demand for loanable funds. This equivalence provides another way to interpret the *IS* curve.

Recall that the national accounts identity can be written as

$$Y - C - G = I$$
$$S = I.$$

The left-hand side of this equation is national saving S, and the right-hand side is investment I. National saving represents the supply of loanable funds, and investment represents the demand for these funds.

To see how the market for loanable funds produces the *IS* curve, substitute the consumption function for C and the investment function for I:

$$Y - C(Y - T) - G = I(r).$$

The left-hand side of this equation shows that the supply of loanable funds depends on income and fiscal policy. The right-hand side shows that the demand for loanable funds depends on the interest rate. The interest rate adjusts to equilibrate the supply and demand for loans.

As Figure 10-9 illustrates, we can interpret the *IS* curve as showing the interest rate that equilibrates the market for loanable funds for any given level of income. When income rises from Y_1 to Y_2, national saving, which equals $Y - C - G$, increases. (Consumption rises by less than income, because the marginal propensity to consume is less than 1.) As panel (a) shows, the increased supply of loanable funds drives down the interest rate from r_1 to r_2. The *IS* curve in panel (b) summarizes this relationship: higher income implies higher saving, which in turn implies a lower equilibrium interest rate. For this reason, the *IS* curve slopes downward.

This alternative interpretation of the *IS* curve also explains why a change in fiscal policy shifts the *IS* curve. An increase in government purchases or a decrease in taxes reduces national saving for any given level of income. The reduced supply of loanable funds raises the interest rate that equilibrates the market. Because the interest rate is now higher for any given level of income, the *IS* curve shifts upward in response to the expansionary change in fiscal policy.

Finally, note that the *IS* curve does not determine either income Y or the interest rate r. Instead, the *IS* curve is a relationship between Y and r arising in the market for goods and services or, equivalently, the market for loanable funds. To determine the equilibrium of the economy, we need another relationship between these two variables, to which we now turn.

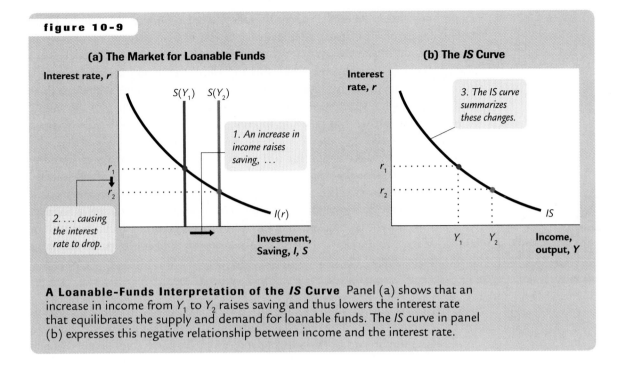

figure 10-9

(a) The Market for Loanable Funds

Interest rate, *r*

$S(Y_1)$ $S(Y_2)$

1. An increase in income raises saving, ...

r_1

r_2

2. . . . causing the interest rate to drop.

$I(r)$

Investment, Saving, *I, S*

(b) The *IS* Curve

Interest rate, *r*

3. The IS curve summarizes these changes.

r_1

r_2

IS

Y_1 Y_2

Income, output, *Y*

A Loanable-Funds Interpretation of the *IS* Curve Panel (a) shows that an increase in income from Y_1 to Y_2 raises saving and thus lowers the interest rate that equilibrates the supply and demand for loanable funds. The *IS* curve in panel (b) expresses this negative relationship between income and the interest rate.

10-2| The Money Market and the *LM* Curve

The *LM* curve plots the relationship between the interest rate and the level of income that arises in the market for money balances. To understand this relationship, we begin by looking at a theory of the interest rate, called the **theory of liquidity preference.**

The Theory of Liquidity Preference

In his classic work *The General Theory,* Keynes offered his view of how the interest rate is determined in the short run. That explanation is called the theory of liquidity preference, because it posits that the interest rate adjusts to balance the supply and demand for the economy's most liquid asset—money. Just as the Keynesian cross is a building block for the *IS* curve, the theory of liquidity preference is a building block for the *LM* curve.

To develop this theory, we begin with the supply of real money balances. If *M* stands for the supply of money and *P* stands for the price level, then *M/P* is the supply of real money balances. The theory of liquidity preference assumes there is a fixed supply of real balances. That is,

$$(M/P)^s = \overline{M}/\overline{P}.$$

The money supply M is an exogenous policy variable chosen by a central bank, such as the Bank of Canada. The price level P is also an exogenous variable in this model. (We take the price level as given because the $IS-LM$ model—our ultimate goal in this chapter—explains the short run when the price level is fixed.) These assumptions imply that the supply of real balances is fixed and, in particular, does not depend on the interest rate. Thus, when we plot the supply of real money balances against the interest rate in Figure 10-10, we obtain a vertical supply curve.

Next, consider the demand for real money balances. The theory of liquidity preference posits that the interest rate is one determinant of how much money people choose to hold. The reason is that the interest rate is the opportunity cost of holding money: it is what you forgo by holding some of your assets as money, which does not bear interest, instead of as interest-bearing bank deposits or bonds. When the interest rate rises, people want to hold less of their wealth in the form of money. Thus, we can write the demand for real money balances as

$$(M/P)^{\mathrm{d}} = L(r),$$

where the function $L(\ )$ shows that the quantity of money demanded depends on the interest rate. Figure 10-11 illustrates this relationship. This demand curve slopes downward because higher interest rates reduce the quantity of real balances demanded.[5]

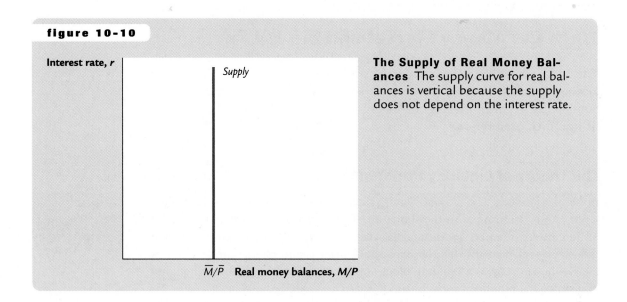

figure 10-10

Interest rate, r

Supply

$\overline{M}/\overline{P}$ Real money balances, M/P

The Supply of Real Money Balances The supply curve for real balances is vertical because the supply does not depend on the interest rate.

---

[5] Note that r is being used to denote the interest rate here, as it was in our discussion of the IS curve. More accurately, it is the nominal interest rate that determines money demand and the real interest rate that determines investment. To keep things simple, we are ignoring expected inflation, which creates the difference between the real and nominal interest rates. The role of expected inflation in the $IS-LM$ model is explored in Chapter 11.

figure 10-11

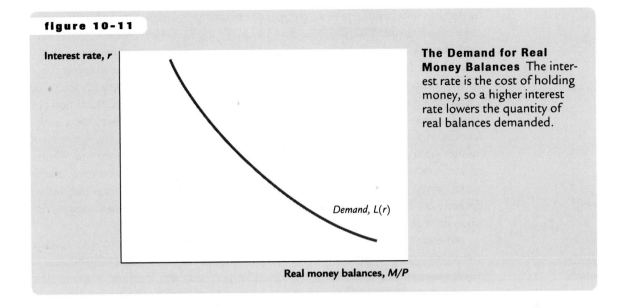

The Demand for Real Money Balances The interest rate is the cost of holding money, so a higher interest rate lowers the quantity of real balances demanded.

To explain what interest rate prevails in the economy, we combine the supply and demand for real money balances in Figure 10-12. According to the theory of liquidity preference, the interest rate adjusts to equilibrate the money market. At the equilibrium interest rate, the quantity of real balances demanded equals the quantity supplied.

How does the interest rate get to this equilibrium of money supply and money demand? The adjustment occurs because whenever the money market

figure 10-12

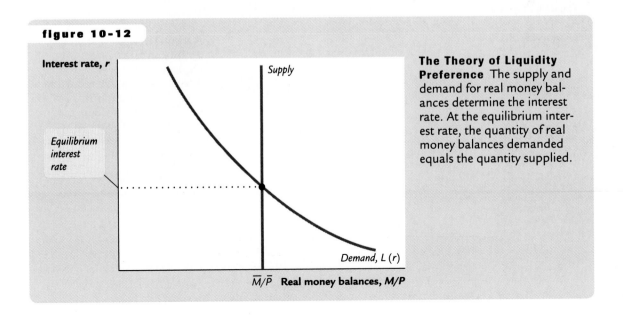

The Theory of Liquidity Preference The supply and demand for real money balances determine the interest rate. At the equilibrium interest rate, the quantity of real money balances demanded equals the quantity supplied.

is not in equilibrium, people try to adjust their portfolios of assets and, in the process, alter the interest rate. For instance, if the interest rate is above the equilibrium level, the quantity of real balances supplied exceeds the quantity demanded. Individuals holding the excess supply of money try to convert some of their non-interest-bearing money into interest-bearing bank deposits or bonds. Banks and bond issuers, who prefer to pay lower interest rates, respond to this excess supply of money by lowering the interest rates they offer. Conversely, if the interest rate is below the equilibrium level, so that the quantity of money demanded exceeds the quantity supplied, individuals try to obtain money by selling bonds or making bank withdrawals. To attract now scarcer funds, banks and bond issuers respond by increasing the interest rates they offer. Eventually, the interest rate reaches the equilibrium level, at which people are content with their portfolios of monetary and nonmonetary assets.

Now that we have seen how the interest rate is determined, we can use the theory of liquidity preference to show how the interest rate responds to changes in the supply of money. Suppose, for instance, that the Bank of Canada suddenly decreases the money supply. A fall in M reduces M/P, because P is fixed in the model. The supply of real balances shifts to the left, as in Figure 10-13. The equilibrium interest rate rises from r_1 to r_2, and the higher interest rate makes people satisfied to hold the smaller quantity of real money balances. The opposite would occur if the Bank of Canada had suddenly increased the money supply. Thus, according to the theory of liquidity preference, a decrease in the money supply raises the interest rate, and an increase in the money supply lowers the interest rate.

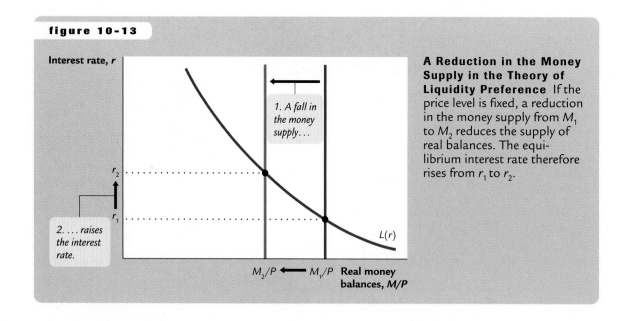

figure 10-13

Interest rate, r

1. A fall in the money supply...

r_2

r_1

2. ... raises the interest rate.

$L(r)$

M_2/P ⟵ M_1/P **Real money balances, M/P**

A Reduction in the Money Supply in the Theory of Liquidity Preference If the price level is fixed, a reduction in the money supply from M_1 to M_2 reduces the supply of real balances. The equilibrium interest rate therefore rises from r_1 to r_2.

CASE STUDY

Tight Money and Rising Interest Rates

The early 1980s saw a large and speedy reduction in North American inflation rates. During the 1980–1982 period, Canada's CPI increased at an average annual rate of 11.2 percent; during the next three years, that rate of increase slowed to just 4.7 percent. This 6.5-percentage-point reduction in inflation was achieved by a dramatic tightening of monetary policy.

During the 1970s, the quantity of real money balances (M1 divided by the CPI) had been growing at an average rate of 2.8 percent per year. Then, during the 1980–1982 period, Canadian real money growth was pushed down to an average of −7.8 percent per year. After that, monetary policy was eased significantly; average growth in real balances was 1.7 percent per year in the 1983–1985 period.

How does such a monetary tightening influence interest rates? The answer depends on the time horizon. Our analysis of the Fisher effect in Chapter 6 suggests that the change in monetary policy would lower inflation, which, in turn, would lead to lower nominal interest rates. Yet the theory of liquidity preference predicts that, in the short run when prices are sluggish, anti-inflationary monetary policy involves a leftward shift of the LM curve and higher nominal interest rates.

Both conclusions are consistent with experience. Nominal interest rates did fall in the 1980s as inflation fell. For example, the three-month treasury bill rate fell from an average of 14.7 percent in the 1980–1982 period to an average of 10 percent in the 1983–1985 period. But it is instructive to consider the year-to-year sequence. The interest rate rose from 12.7 percent in 1980 to 17.8 percent in 1981, and it did not fall below 12.7 percent until 1983.

Income, Money Demand, and the *LM* Curve

Having developed the theory of liquidity preference as an explanation for what determines the interest rate, we can now use the theory to derive the LM curve. We begin by considering the following question: how does a change in the economy's level of income Y affect the market for real money balances? The answer (which should be familiar from Chapter 7) is that the level of income affects the demand for money. When income is high, expenditure is high, so people engage in more transactions that require the use of money. Thus, greater income implies greater money demand. We can express these ideas by writing the money demand function as

$$(M/P)^{\mathrm{d}} = L(r, Y).$$

The quantity of real money balances demanded is negatively related to the interest rate and positively related to income.

Using the theory of liquidity preference, we can figure out what happens to the equilibrium interest rate when the level of income changes. For example, consider what happens in Figure 10-14 when income increases from Y_1 to Y_2. As panel (a) illustrates, this increase in income shifts the money demand curve to the right. With the supply of real money balances unchanged, the interest rate must rise from r_1 to r_2 to equilibrate the money market. Therefore, according to the theory of liquidity preference, higher income leads to a higher interest rate.

The *LM* curve plots this relationship between the level of income and the interest rate. The higher the level of income, the higher the demand for real money balances, and the higher the equilibrium interest rate. For this reason, the *LM* curve slopes upward, as in panel (b) of Figure 10-14.

How Monetary Policy Shifts the *LM* Curve

The *LM* curve tells us the interest rate that equilibrates the money market at any level of income. Yet, as we saw earlier, the equilibrium interest rate also depends on the supply of real balances, M/P. This means that the *LM* curve is drawn for a *given* supply of real money balances. If real balances change—for example, if the Fed alters the money supply—the *LM* curve shifts.

We can use the theory of liquidity preference to understand how monetary policy shifts the *LM* curve. Suppose that the Bank of Canada decreases the

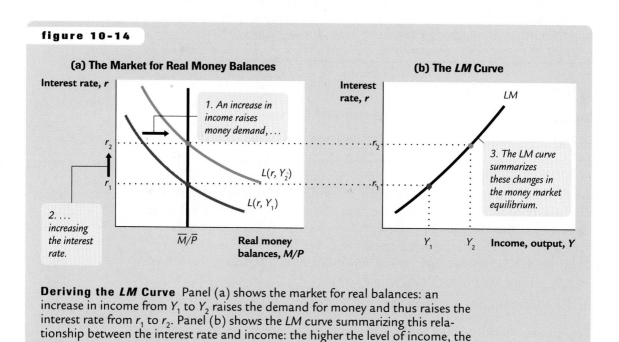

figure 10-14

(a) The Market for Real Money Balances

Interest rate, *r*

1. An increase in income raises money demand, . . .

r_2

r_1

$L(r, Y_2)$

$L(r, Y_1)$

2. . . . increasing the interest rate.

$\overline{M/P}$

Real money balances, M/P

(b) The *LM* Curve

Interest rate, *r*

LM

r_2

r_1

3. The LM curve summarizes these changes in the money market equilibrium.

Y_1 Y_2 **Income, output, Y**

Deriving the *LM* Curve Panel (a) shows the market for real balances: an increase in income from Y_1 to Y_2 raises the demand for money and thus raises the interest rate from r_1 to r_2. Panel (b) shows the *LM* curve summarizing this relationship between the interest rate and income: the higher the level of income, the higher the interest rate.

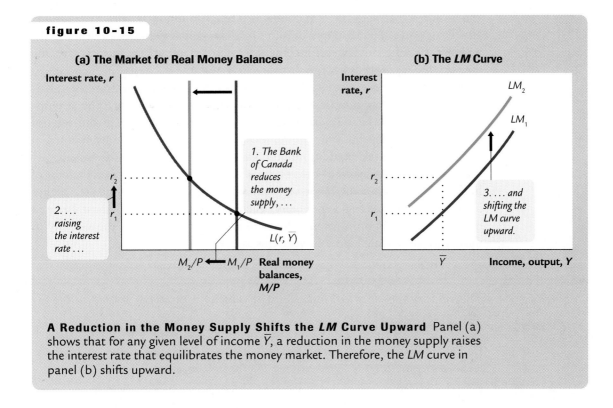

figure 10-15

A Reduction in the Money Supply Shifts the *LM* Curve Upward Panel (a) shows that for any given level of income $\overline{Y}$, a reduction in the money supply raises the interest rate that equilibrates the money market. Therefore, the *LM* curve in panel (b) shifts upward.

money supply from M_1 to M_2, which causes the supply of real balances to fall from M_1/P to M_2/P. Figure 10-15 shows what happens. Holding constant the amount of income and thus the demand curve for real balances, we see that a reduction in the supply of real balances raises the interest rate that equilibrates the money market. Hence, a decrease in real balances shifts the *LM* curve upward.

In summary, the LM curve shows the combinations of the interest rate and the level of income that are consistent with equilibrium in the market for real money balances. The LM curve is drawn for a given supply of real money balances. Decreases in the supply of real money balances shift the LM curve upward. Increases in the supply of real money balances shift the LM curve downward.

A Quantity-Equation Interpretation of the *LM* Curve

When we first discussed aggregate demand and the short-run determination of income in Chapter 9, we derived the aggregate demand curve from the quantity theory of money. We described the money market with the quantity equation,

$$MV = PY,$$

and assumed that velocity V is constant. This assumption implies that, for any given price level P, the supply of money M by itself determines the level of income Y. Because the level of income does not depend on the interest rate, the quantity theory is equivalent to a vertical LM curve.

We can derive the more realistic upward-sloping LM curve from the quantity equation by relaxing the assumption that velocity is constant. The assumption of constant velocity is based on the assumption that the demand for real money balances depends only on the level of income. Yet, as we have noted in our discussion of the liquidity-preference model, the demand for real money balances also depends on the interest rate: a higher interest rate raises the cost of holding money and reduces money demand. When people respond to a higher interest rate by holding less money, each dollar they do hold must be used more often to support a given volume of transactions—that is, the velocity of money must increase. We can write this as

$$MV(r) = PY.$$

The velocity function $V(r)$ indicates that velocity is positively related to the interest rate.

This form of the quantity equation yields an LM curve that slopes upward. Because an increase in the interest rate raises the velocity of money, it raises the level of income for any given money supply and price level. The LM curve expresses this positive relationship between the interest rate and income.

This equation also shows why changes in the money supply shift the LM curve. For any given interest rate and price level, the money supply and the level of income must move together. Thus, increases in the money supply shift the LM curve to the right, and decreases in the money supply shift the LM curve to the left.

Keep in mind that the quantity equation is merely another way to express the theory behind the LM curve. This quantity-theory interpretation of the LM curve is substantively the same as that provided by the theory of liquidity preference. In both cases, the LM curve represents a positive relationship between income and the interest rate that arises from the money market.

Finally, remember that the LM curve by itself does not determine either income Y or the interest rate r that will prevail in the economy. Like the IS curve, the LM curve is only a relationship between these two endogenous variables. The IS and LM curves together determine the economy's equilibrium.

10-3 | Conclusion: The Short-Run Equilibrium

We now have all the pieces of the IS–LM model. The two equations of this model are

$$Y = C(Y - T) + I(r) + G \qquad IS,$$
$$M/P = L(r, Y) \qquad\qquad LM.$$

The model takes fiscal policy, G and T, monetary policy M, and the price level P as exogenous. Given these exogenous variables, the IS curve provides the combinations of r and Y that satisfy the equation representing the goods market, and the LM curve provides the combinations of r and Y that satisfy the equation representing the money market. These two curves are shown together in Figure 10-16.

The equilibrium of the economy is the point at which the IS curve and the LM curve cross. This point gives the interest rate r and the level of income Y that satisfy conditions for equilibrium in both the goods market and the money market. In other words, at this intersection, actual expenditure equals planned expenditure, and the demand for real money balances equals the supply.

figure 10-16

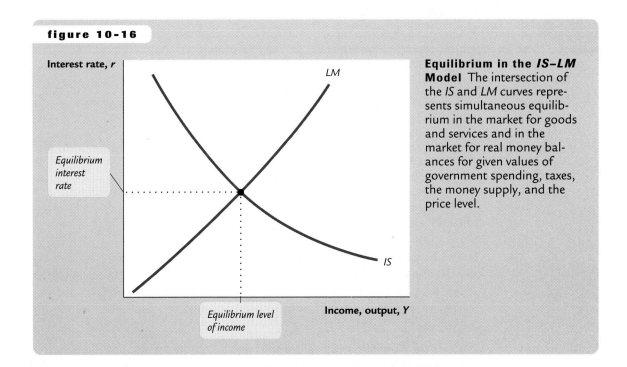

Interest rate, r

Equilibrium interest rate

Equilibrium level of income

Income, output, Y

Equilibrium in the *IS–LM* Model The intersection of the *IS* and *LM* curves represents simultaneous equilibrium in the market for goods and services and in the market for real money balances for given values of government spending, taxes, the money supply, and the price level.

As we conclude this chapter, let's recall that our ultimate goal in developing the $IS-LM$ model is to analyze short-run fluctuations in economic activity. Figure 10-17 illustrates how the different pieces of our theory fit together. In this chapter we developed the Keynesian cross and the theory of liquidity preference as building blocks for the $IS-LM$ model. As we see more fully in the next chapter, the $IS-LM$ model helps explain the position and slope of the aggregate demand curve. The aggregate demand curve, in turn, is a piece of the model of aggregate supply and aggregate demand, which economists use to explain the short-run effects of policy changes and other events on national income.

figure 10-17

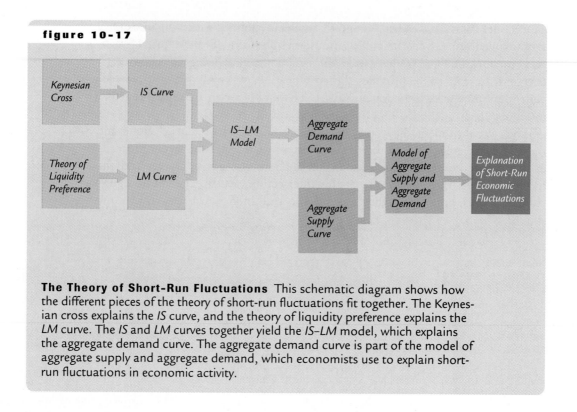

The Theory of Short-Run Fluctuations This schematic diagram shows how the different pieces of the theory of short-run fluctuations fit together. The Keynesian cross explains the *IS* curve, and the theory of liquidity preference explains the *LM* curve. The *IS* and *LM* curves together yield the *IS–LM* model, which explains the aggregate demand curve. The aggregate demand curve is part of the model of aggregate supply and aggregate demand, which economists use to explain short-run fluctuations in economic activity.

Summary

1. The Keynesian cross is a basic model of income determination. It takes fiscal policy and planned investment as exogenous and then shows that there is one level of national income at which actual expenditure equals planned expenditure. It shows that changes in fiscal policy have a multiplied impact on income.

2. Once we allow planned investment to depend on the interest rate, the Keynesian cross yields a relationship between the interest rate and national income. A higher interest rate lowers planned investment, and this in turn lowers national income. The downward-sloping *IS* curve summarizes this negative relationship between the interest rate and income.

3. The theory of liquidity preference is a basic model of the determination of the interest rate. It takes the money supply and the price level as exogenous and assumes that the interest rate adjusts to equilibrate the supply and demand for real money balances. The theory implies that increases in the money supply lower the interest rate.

4. Once we allow the demand for real balances to depend on national income, the theory of liquidity preference yields a relationship between income and the interest rate. A higher level of income raises the demand for real bal-

ances, and this in turn raises the interest rate. The upward-sloping *LM* curve summarizes this positive relationship between income and the interest rate.

5. The *IS–LM* model combines the elements of the Keynesian cross and the elements of the theory of liquidity preference. The *IS* curve shows the points that satisfy equilibrium in the goods market, and the *LM* curve shows the points that satisfy equilibrium in the money market. The intersection of the *IS* and *LM* curves shows the interest rate and income that satisfy equilibrium in both markets.

KEY CONCEPTS

IS–LM model

IS curve

LM curve

Keynesian cross

Government-purchases multiplier

Tax multiplier

Theory of liquidity preference

QUESTIONS FOR REVIEW

1. Use the Keynesian cross to explain why fiscal policy has a multiplied effect on national income.

2. Use the theory of liquidity preference to explain why an increase in the money supply lowers the interest rate. What does this explanation assume about the price level?

3. Why does the *IS* curve slope downward?

4. Why does the *LM* curve slope upward?

PROBLEMS AND APPLICATIONS

1. Use the Keynesian cross to predict the impact of

   a. An increase in government purchases.

   b. An increase in taxes.

   c. An equal increase in government purchases and taxes.

2. In the Keynesian cross, assume that the consumption function is given by

   $$C = 200 + 0.75 (Y - T).$$

   Planned investment is 100; government purchases and taxes are both 100.

   a. Graph planned expenditure as a function of income.

   b. What is the equilibrium level of income?

   c. If government purchases increase to 125, what is the new equilibrium income?

   d. What level of government purchases is needed to achieve an income of 1,600?

3. Although our development of the Keynesian cross in this chapter assumes that taxes are a fixed amount, in many countries taxes depend on income. Let's represent the tax system by writing tax revenue as

   $$T = \overline{T} + tY,$$

   where $\overline{T}$ and t are parameters of the tax code. The parameter t is the marginal tax rate: if income rises by \$1, taxes rise by $t \times \$1$.

a. How does this tax system change the way consumption responds to changes in GDP?

b. In the Keynesian cross, how does this tax system alter the government-purchases multiplier?

c. In the *IS–LM* model, how does this tax system alter the slope of the *IS* curve?

4. Consider the impact of an increase in thriftiness in the Keynesian cross. Suppose the consumption function is

$$C = \overline{C} + c(Y - T),$$

where $\overline{C}$ is a parameter called *autonomous consumption* and c is the marginal propensity to consume.

a. What happens to equilibrium income when the society becomes more thrifty, as represented by a decline in $\overline{C}$?

b. What happens to equilibrium saving?

c. Why do you suppose this result is called the *paradox of thrift*?

d. Does this paradox arise in the classical model of Chapter 3? Why or why not?

5. Suppose that the money demand function is

$$(M/P)^{\mathrm{d}} = 1{,}000 - 100r,$$

where r is the interest rate in percent. The money supply M is 1,000 and the price level P is 2.

a. Graph the supply and demand for real money balances.

b. What is the equilibrium interest rate?

c. Assume that the price level is fixed. What happens to the equilibrium interest rate if the supply of money is raised from 1,000 to 1,200?

d. If the central bank wishes to raise the interest rate to 7 percent, what money supply should it set?

chapter 11

Aggregate Demand II

Science is a parasite: the greater the patient population the better the advance in physiology and pathology; and out of pathology arises therapy. The year 1932 was the trough of the great depression, and from its rotten soil was belatedly begot a new subject that today we call macroeconomics.

— *Paul Samuelson*

In Chapter 10 we assembled the pieces of the $IS-LM$ model. We saw that the IS curve represents the equilibrium in the market for goods and services, that the LM curve represents the equilibrium in the market for real money balances, and that the IS and LM curves together determine the interest rate and national income in the short run when the price level is fixed. Now we turn our attention to applying the $IS-LM$ model to analyze three issues.

First, we examine the potential causes of fluctuations in national income. We use the $IS-LM$ model to see how changes in the exogenous variables (government purchases, taxes, and the money supply) influence the endogenous variables (the interest rate and national income). We also examine how various shocks to the goods markets (the IS curve) and the money market (the LM curve) affect the interest rate and national income in the short run.

Second, we discuss how the $IS-LM$ model fits into the model of aggregate supply and aggregate demand we introduced in Chapter 9. In particular, we examine how the $IS-LM$ model provides a theory of the slope and position of the aggregate demand curve. Here we relax the assumption that the price level is fixed, and we show that the $IS-LM$ model implies a negative relationship between the price level and national income. The model can also tell us what events shift the aggregate demand curve and in what direction.

Third, we examine the Great Depression of the 1930s. As this chapter's opening quotation indicates, this episode gave birth to short-run macroeconomic theory, for it led Keynes and his many followers to think that aggregate demand was the key to understanding fluctuations in national income. With the benefit of hindsight, we can use the $IS-LM$ model to discuss the various explanations of this traumatic economic downturn.

11-1 Explaining Fluctuations With the *IS–LM* Model

The intersection of the *IS* curve and the *LM* curve determines the level of national income. When one of these curves shifts, the short-run equilibrium of the economy changes, and national income fluctuates. In this section we examine how changes in policy and shocks to the economy can cause these curves to shift.

How Fiscal Policy Shifts the *IS* Curve and Changes the Short-Run Equilibrium

We begin by examining how changes in fiscal policy (government purchases and taxes) alter the economy's short-run equilibrium. Recall that changes in fiscal policy influence planned expenditure and thereby shift the *IS* curve. The *IS–LM* model shows how these shifts in the *IS* curve affect income and the interest rate.

Changes in Government Purchases Consider an increase in government purchases of ΔG. The government-purchases multiplier in the Keynesian cross tells us that, at any given interest rate, this change in fiscal policy raises the level of income by $\Delta G/(1 - MPC)$. Therefore, as Figure 11-1 shows, the *IS* curve shifts to the right by this amount. The equilibrium of the economy moves from point A to point B. The increase in government purchases raises both income and the interest rate.

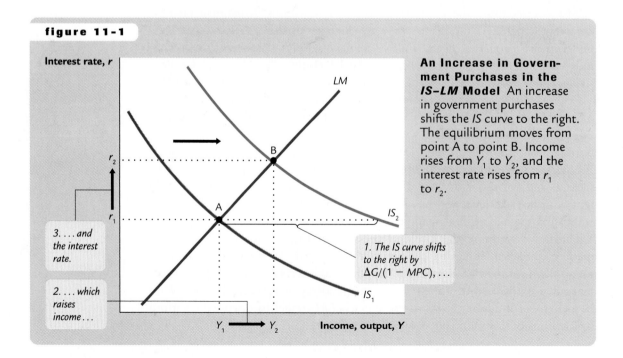

figure 11-1

Interest rate, r

An Increase in Government Purchases in the *IS–LM* Model An increase in government purchases shifts the *IS* curve to the right. The equilibrium moves from point A to point B. Income rises from Y_1 to Y_2, and the interest rate rises from r_1 to r_2.

3. . . . and the interest rate.

2. . . . which raises income . . .

1. The IS curve shifts to the right by $\Delta G/(1 - MPC)$, . . .

LM

IS_2

IS_1

Income, output, Y

spending cut does not cause a recession, but it does cause a large fall in the interest rate. Although the level of income is not changed, the combination of a spending cut and a monetary expansion does change the allocation of the economy's resources. The spending cut shrinks the government sector, while the lower interest rate stimulates investment. Income is not affected because these two effects exactly balance.

From this example we can see that the impact of a change in fiscal policy depends on the policy the Bank of Canada pursues — that is, on whether it holds the money supply, the interest rate, or the level of income constant. More generally, whenever analyzing a change in one policy, we must make an assumption about its effect on the other policy. What assumption is most appropriate depends on the case at hand and the many political considerations that lie behind economic policymaking.

Perhaps the most significant interaction between monetary and fiscal policy occurs in the case of a small open economy. In that case, the fundamental choice for monetary policy is whether to fix the exchange rate or to allow a floating exchange rate. As we shall see in Chapter 12, this choice dramatically affects the power of fiscal policy. With a floating exchange rate (and this has been Canada's policy for years), the effect of fiscal policy on real GDP is very much blunted. This is good news for those who do not want spending cuts to raise unemployment very much, but this is bad news for those who want to use expansionary fiscal policy to create jobs. We will explore these issues more fully in Chapter 12, after we have completed our development of the closed-economy model of aggregate demand.

CASE STUDY

Policy Analysis With Macroeconometric Models

The *IS–LM* model shows how monetary and fiscal policy influence the equilibrium level of income. The predictions of the model, however, are qualitative, not quantitative. The *IS–LM* model shows that increases in government purchases raise GDP and that increases in taxes lower GDP. But when economists analyze specific policy proposals, they need to know not just the direction of the effect but the size as well. For example, if the federal government cuts spending by $5 billion and if monetary policy is not altered, how much will GDP fall? To answer this question, economists need to go beyond the graphical representation of the *IS–LM* model.

Macroeconometric models of the economy provide one way to evaluate policy proposals. A **macroeconometric model** is a model that describes the economy quantitatively, rather than just qualitatively. Many of these models are essentially more complicated and more realistic versions of our *IS–LM* model. The economists who build macroeconometric models use historical data to estimate parameters such as the marginal propensity to consume, the sensitivity of investment to the interest rate, and the sensitivity of money demand to the interest rate. Once a model is built, economists can simulate the effects of alternative policies with the help of a computer.

It is interesting to note that estimates of Canada's one-year government spending multiplier have changed substantially over the years. In the situation in which the Bank of Canada keeps the money supply constant, $\Delta Y/\Delta G$ was estimated to be 1.42 twenty years ago.[1] This estimate meant that an increase in government spending of $1 billion was expected to raise overall GDP by $1.42 billion after one year. By 1986, multiplier estimates had fallen to 0.77.[2] Finally, by the early 1990s, those using macroeconometric models were reporting government spending multipliers in the 0.50–0.67 range.[3] This wide variation in estimates for $\Delta Y/\Delta G$, all involving the same behaviour on the part of the Bank of Canada, implies a great deal of imprecision in the planning of fiscal policy. Why do the estimates of the power of fiscal policy keep shrinking as more research proceeds? Economists believe there are two reasons for this trend.

The first concerns the role of expectations on the part of households and firms. To see the importance of expectations, compare a temporary increase in government spending to a permanent one. The *IS* curve shifts out to the right in both cases, so interest rates rise, and this causes some cutback in the investment component of aggregate demand. But the size of this investment response depends on how permanent firms expect the rise in interest rates to be. If the increase in government spending is temporary, the rise in interest rates should be temporary as well, so firms' investment spending is not curtailed to a very great extent. But if the increase in government spending is expected to be permanent, the rise in interest rates matters much more in firms' long-range planning decisions, and there is a much bigger cutback in investment spending. Thus, the government spending multiplier is smaller when the change in spending is expected to last a long time.

You might think that, since changes in investment spending lag behind interest rate changes, this expectations issue cannot matter much for determining the multiplier value for a time horizon of just one year. But such a view amounts to assuming that individuals cannot see the interest changes coming. Anyone who understands the *IS–LM* model knows that permanently higher government spending raises interest rates. They also know that the value of existing financial assets (stocks and bonds) will fall when newly issued bonds promising higher yields are issued. No one wants to hold an asset with a low yield when better yields are expected. Thus, in an attempt to avoid a capital loss on existing financial assets, owners sell them the moment they expect a capital loss. That moment occurs as soon as they see a reason for interest rate increases—that is, *just* after the government spending increase has been *announced* (even before it is implemented). But if everyone tries to sell financial assets at the same time, the price of those assets drops quickly. As a result, the effective yield that a new purchaser can earn on them—the going rate of inter-

[1] John Helliwell, T. Maxwell, and H.E.L. Waslander, "Comparing the Dynamics of Canadian Macro Models," *Canadian Journal of Economics* 12 (May 1979): 133–138.

[2] John Bossons, "Issues in the Analysis of Government Deficits," in John Sargent, ed., *Fiscal and Monetary Policy,* Research Studies of the Royal Commission on the Economic Union and Development Prospects for Canada 21 (Toronto: University of Toronto Press, 1986): 85–112.

[3] John Helliwell, "What's Left for Macroeconomic and Growth Policies?," *Bell Canada Papers on Economic and Public Policy* 2 (1994): 5–48.

est—rises immediately. The moral of the story is that when individuals react to well-informed expectations, their reactions have the effect of bringing the long-run implications of fiscal policy forward in time.

Over the last twenty years, economists have made major strides in their ability to model and simulate how individuals form expectations. Because of this development, the estimated econometric models have done a much better job of including the short-run implications of future government policies. This is a fundamental reason why the estimates of $\Delta Y/\Delta G$ have shrunk so much over time as research methods have improved.

The second explanation for the decrease in $\Delta Y/\Delta G$ estimates follows from increased globalization. With financial markets becoming ever more integrated throughout the world, there has developed an ever-expanding pool of "hot money." These funds move into or out of a country like Canada the moment that the interest rate rises above or sinks below interest rate levels in other countries. This flow of funds dominates the trading in the foreign exchange markets, and so it results in large changes in exchange rates. We must wait until Chapter 12 to learn how these exchange-rate changes reduce the power of fiscal policy. But it is worth noting now that globalization has increased the size and speed of these exchange-rate effects, and so it is not surprising that estimated fiscal policy multipliers have shrunk over time.

Shocks in the *IS–LM* Model

Because the *IS–LM* model shows how national income is determined in the short run, we can use the model to examine how various economic disturbances affect income. So far we have seen how changes in fiscal policy shift the *IS* curve and how changes in monetary policy shift the *LM* curve. Similarly, we can group other disturbances into two categories: shocks to the *IS* curve and shocks to the *LM* curve.

Shocks to the *IS* curve are exogenous changes in the demand for goods and services. Some economists, including Keynes, have emphasized that such changes in demand can arise from investors' *animal spirits*—exogenous and perhaps self-fulfilling waves of optimism and pessimism. For example, suppose that firms become pessimistic about the future of the economy and that this pessimism causes them to build fewer new factories. This reduction in the demand

for investment goods causes a contractionary shift in the investment function: at every interest rate, firms want to invest less. The fall in investment reduces planned expenditure and shifts the *IS* curve to the left, reducing income and employment. This fall in equilibrium income in part validates the firms' initial pessimism.

Shocks to the *IS* curve may also arise from changes in the demand for consumer goods. Suppose that consumer confidence rises, as people become less worried about losing their jobs. This induces consumers to save less for the future and consume more today. We can interpret this change as an upward shift in the consumption function. This shift in the consumption function increases planned expenditure and shifts the *IS* curve to the right, and this raises income.

Shocks to the *LM* curve arise from exogenous changes in the demand for

---

f y i

WHAT IS THE BANK OF CANADA'S POLICY INSTRUMENT — THE MONEY SUPPLY OR THE INTEREST RATE?

Our analysis of monetary policy has been based on the assumption that the Bank of Canada influences the economy by controlling the money supply. By contrast, when you hear about Bank of Canada policy in the media, the policy instrument mentioned most often is the Bank Rate. It is the rate charged by the Bank of Canada when loaning reserves to the chartered banks, and it affects the overnight rate charged by the chartered banks when making overnight loans to each other. Which is the correct way of discussing policy? The answer is both.

In recent years, the Bank of Canada has used the interest rate as its short-term policy instrument. This means that when the Bank decides on a target for the interest rate, the Bank's bond traders are told to conduct the open-market operations necessary to hit that target. These open-market operations change the money supply and shift the *LM* curve so that the equilibrium interest rate (determined by the intersection of the *IS* and *LM* curves) equals the target interest rate that the Bank's policymaking committee has chosen.

As a result of this operating procedure, Bank of Canada policy is often discussed in terms of changing interest rates. Keep in mind, however, that behind these changes in interest rates are the necessary changes in the money supply. A newspaper might report, for instance, that "the Bank of Canada has lowered interest rates." To be more precise, we can translate this statement as meaning "the Bank has instructed its bond traders to buy bonds in open-market operations so as to increase the money supply, shift the *LM* curve, and reduce the equilibrium interest rate to hit a new lower target."

Why has the Bank of Canada chosen to use an interest rate, rather than the money supply, as its short-term policy instrument? One possible answer is that shocks to the *LM* curve are more prevalent than shocks to the *IS* curve. If so, a policy of targeting the interest rate leads to greater macroeconomic stability than a policy of targeting the money supply. (Problem 7 at the end of this chapter asks you to analyze this issue.) Another possible answer is that interest rates are easier to measure than the money supply. As we saw in Chapter 7, the Bank of Canada has several different measures of money — *M*1, *M*2, and so on — which sometimes move in different directions. Rather than deciding which measure is best, the Bank of Canada avoids the question by using the interest rate as its short-term policy instrument.

money. For example, suppose that the demand for money increases substantially, as it does when people become worried about the security of holding wealth in less liquid forms—a sensible worry if they expect a recession. According to the theory of liquidity preference, when money demand rises, the interest rate necessary to equilibrate the money market is higher (for any given level of income and money supply). Hence, an increase in money demand shifts the *LM* curve upward, which tends to raise the interest rate and depress income—that is, to cause the very recession that individuals had feared.

In summary, several kinds of events can cause economic fluctuations by shifting the *IS* curve or the *LM* curve. Remember, however, that such fluctuations are not inevitable. Policymakers can try to use the tools of monetary and fiscal policy to offset exogenous shocks. If policymakers are sufficiently quick and skillful (admittedly, a big if), shocks to the *IS* or *LM* curves need not lead to fluctuations in income or employment.

11-2| *IS–LM* as a Theory of Aggregate Demand

We have been using the *IS–LM* model to explain national income in the short run when the price level is fixed. To see how the *IS–LM* model fits into the model of aggregate supply and aggregate demand introduced in Chapter 9, we now examine what happens in the *IS–LM* model if the price level is allowed to change. As was promised when we began our study of this model, the *IS–LM* model provides a theory to explain the position and slope of the aggregate demand curve.

From the *IS–LM* Model to the Aggregate Demand Curve

Recall from Chapter 9 that the aggregate demand curve describes a relationship between the price level and the level of national income. In Chapter 9 this relationship was derived from the quantity theory of money. The analysis showed that for a given money supply, a higher price level implies a lower level of income. Increases in the money supply shift the aggregate demand curve to the right, and decreases in the money supply shift the aggregate demand curve to the left.

To understand the determinants of aggregate demand more fully, we now use the *IS–LM* model, rather than the quantity theory, to derive the aggregate demand curve. First, we use the *IS–LM* model to show why national income falls as the price level rises—that is, why the aggregate demand curve is downward sloping. Second, we examine what causes the aggregate demand curve to shift.

To explain why the aggregate demand curve slopes downward, we examine what happens in the *IS–LM* model when the price level changes. This is done in Figure 11-5. For any given money supply *M,* a higher price level *P* reduces the supply of real money balances *M/P*. A lower supply of real money balances shifts the *LM* curve upward, which raises the equilibrium interest rate and lowers the equilibrium level of income, as shown in panel (a). Here the price level

figure 11-5

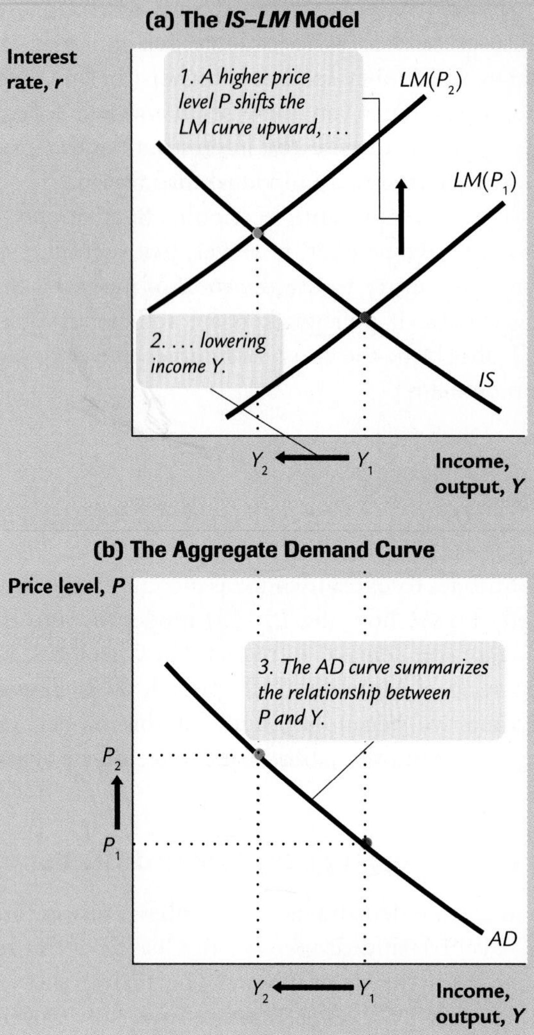

(a) The *IS–LM* Model

Interest rate, r

1. A higher price level P shifts the LM curve upward, …

$LM(P_2)$

$LM(P_1)$

2. … lowering income Y.

IS

Y_2 ← Y_1 Income, output, *Y*

(b) The Aggregate Demand Curve

Price level, *P*

3. The AD curve summarizes the relationship between P and Y.

P_2

P_1

AD

Y_2 ← Y_1 Income, output, *Y*

Deriving the Aggregate Demand Curve With the *IS–LM* Model Panel (a) shows the *IS–LM* model: an increase in the price level from P_1 to P_2 lowers real money balances and thus shifts the *LM* curve upward. The shift in the *LM* curve lowers income from Y_1 to Y_2. Panel (b) shows the aggregate demand curve summarizing this relationship between the price level and income: the higher the price level, the lower the level of income.

rises from P_1 to P_2, and income falls from Y_1 to Y_2. The aggregate demand curve in panel (b) plots this negative relationship between national income and the price level. In other words, the aggregate demand curve shows the set of equilibrium points that arise in the *IS–LM* model as we vary the price level and see what happens to income.

What causes the aggregate demand curve to shift? Because the aggregate demand curve is merely a summary of results from the *IS–LM* model, events that shift the *IS* curve or the *LM* curve (for a given price level) cause the aggregate demand curve to shift. For instance, an increase in the money supply raises income in the *IS–LM* model for any given price level; it thus shifts the aggregate demand curve to the right, as shown in panel (a) of Figure 11-6. Similarly, an increase in government purchases or a decrease in taxes raises income in

figure 11-6

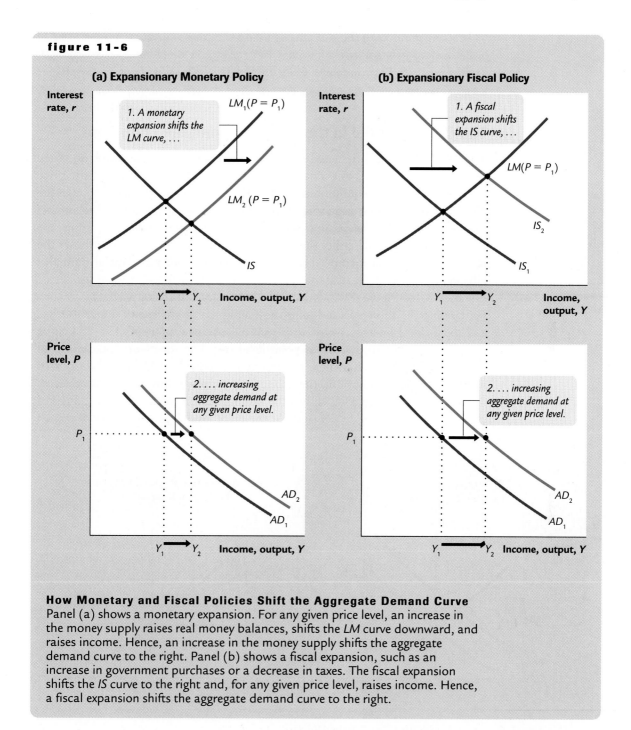

(a) Expansionary Monetary Policy

Interest rate, r

1. A monetary expansion shifts the LM curve, ...

$LM_1(P = P_1)$

$LM_2(P = P_1)$

IS

$Y_1 \rightarrow Y_2$ Income, output, Y

Price level, P

2. ... increasing aggregate demand at any given price level.

P_1

AD_2

AD_1

$Y_1 \rightarrow Y_2$ Income, output, Y

(b) Expansionary Fiscal Policy

Interest rate, r

1. A fiscal expansion shifts the IS curve, ...

$LM(P = P_1)$

IS_2

IS_1

$Y_1 \rightarrow Y_2$ Income, output, Y

Price level, P

2. ... increasing aggregate demand at any given price level.

P_1

AD_2

AD_1

$Y_1 \rightarrow Y_2$ Income, output, Y

How Monetary and Fiscal Policies Shift the Aggregate Demand Curve
Panel (a) shows a monetary expansion. For any given price level, an increase in the money supply raises real money balances, shifts the *LM* curve downward, and raises income. Hence, an increase in the money supply shifts the aggregate demand curve to the right. Panel (b) shows a fiscal expansion, such as an increase in government purchases or a decrease in taxes. The fiscal expansion shifts the *IS* curve to the right and, for any given price level, raises income. Hence, a fiscal expansion shifts the aggregate demand curve to the right.

the *IS–LM* model for a given price level; it also shifts the aggregate demand curve to the right, as shown in panel (b) of Figure 11-6. Conversely, a decrease in the money supply, a decrease in government purchases, or an increase in taxes lowers income in the *IS–LM* model and shifts the aggregate demand curve to the left.

We can summarize these results as follows: *A change in income in the IS–LM model resulting from a change in the price level represents a movement along the aggregate demand curve. A change in income in the IS–LM model for a fixed price level represents a shift in the position of the aggregate demand curve.*

The *IS–LM* Model in the Short Run and the Long Run

The *IS–LM* model is designed to explain the economy in the short run when the price level is fixed. Yet, now that we have seen how a change in the price level influences the equilibrium in the *IS–LM* model, we can also use the model to describe the economy in the long run when the price level adjusts to ensure that the economy produces at its natural rate. By using the *IS–LM* model to describe the long run, we can show clearly how the Keynesian model of income determination differs from the classical model of Chapter 3.

Panel (a) of Figure 11-7 shows the three curves that are necessary for understanding the short-run and long-run equilibria: the *IS* curve, the *LM* curve, and the vertical line representing the natural rate of output $\bar{Y}$. The *LM* curve is, as always, drawn for a fixed price level, P_1. The short-run equilibrium of the economy is point K, where the *IS* curve crosses the *LM* curve. Notice that in this short-run equilibrium, the economy's income is less than its natural rate.

Panel (b) of Figure 11-7 shows the same situation in the diagram of aggregate supply and aggregate demand. At the price level P_1, the quantity of output

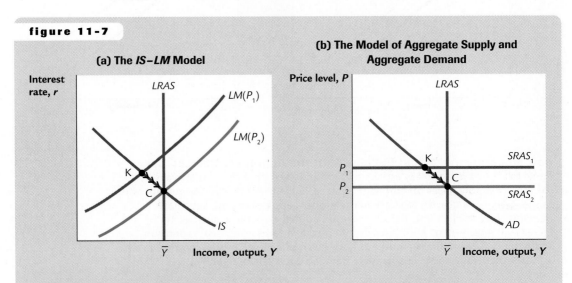

figure 11-7

(a) The *IS–LM* Model

(b) The Model of Aggregate Supply and Aggregate Demand

The Short-Run and Long-Run Equilibria We can compare the short-run and long-run equilibria using either the *IS–LM* diagram in panel (a) or the aggregate supply–aggregate demand diagram in panel (b). In the short run, the price level is stuck at P_1. The short-run equilibrium of the economy is therefore point K. In the long run, the price level adjusts so that the economy is at the natural rate. The long-run equilibrium is therefore point C.

demanded is below the natural rate. In other words, at the existing price level, there is insufficient demand for goods and services to keep the economy producing at its potential.

In these two diagrams we can examine the short-run equilibrium at which the economy finds itself and the long-run equilibrium toward which the economy gravitates. Point K describes the short-run equilibrium, because it assumes that the price level is stuck at P_1. Eventually, the low demand for goods and services causes prices to fall, and the economy moves back toward its natural rate. When the price level reaches P_2, the economy is at point C, the long-run equilibrium. The diagram of aggregate supply and aggregate demand shows that at point C, the quantity of goods and services demanded equals the natural rate of output. This long-run equilibrium is achieved in the *IS*–*LM* diagram by a shift in the *LM* curve: the fall in the price level raises real money balances and therefore shifts the *LM* curve to the right.

Short run = sticky

We can now see the key difference between Keynesian and classical approaches to the determination of national income. The Keynesian assumption (represented by point K) is that the price level is stuck. Depending on monetary policy, fiscal policy, and the other determinants of aggregate demand, output may deviate from the natural rate. The classical assumption (represented by point C) is that the price level is fully flexible. The price level adjusts to ensure that national income is always at the natural rate.

To make the same point somewhat differently, we can think of the economy as being described by three equations. The first two are the *IS* and *LM* equations:

$$Y = C(Y - T) + I(r) + G \qquad IS,$$
$$M/P = L(r, Y) \qquad\qquad LM.$$

The *IS* equation describes the goods market, and the *LM* equation describes the money market. These two equations contain three endogenous variables: *Y, P,* and *r.* The Keynesian approach is to complete the model with the assumption of fixed prices, so the Keynesian third equation is

$$P = P_1.$$

This assumption implies that *r* and *Y* must adjust to satisfy the *IS* and *LM* equations. The classical approach is to complete the model with the assumption that output reaches the natural rate, so the classical third equation is

$$Y = \overline{Y}.$$

This assumption implies that *r* and *P* must adjust to satisfy the *IS* and *LM* equations.

Which assumption is most appropriate? The answer depends on the time horizon. The classical assumption best describes the long run. Hence, our long-run analysis of national income in Chapter 3 and prices in Chapter 7 assumes that output equals the natural rate. The Keynesian assumption best describes the short run. Therefore, our analysis of economic fluctuations relies on the assumption of a fixed price level.

11-3 | The Great Depression

Now that we have developed the model of aggregate demand, let's use it to address the question that originally motivated Keynes: what caused the Great Depression in the United States? For Canada, there is not such a puzzle. Since Canada exports such a large fraction of Canadian GDP to the United States, a depression in that country means a very big decrease in aggregate demand in Canada. Canada had no bank failures, so there is every reason to suspect that the loss in export sales was the dominant event. But what caused the Great Depression in the United States? Even today, more than half a century after the event, economists continue to debate the cause of this major economic downturn in the world's most powerful economy. The Great Depression provides an extended case study to show how economists use the *IS–LM* model to analyze economic fluctuations.[4]

The Spending Hypothesis: Shocks to the *IS* Curve

Since the decline in U.S. income in the early 1930s coincided with falling interest rates, some economists have suggested that the cause of the decline was a contractionary shift in the *IS* curve. This view is sometimes called the *spending hypothesis,* because it places primary blame for the Depression on an exogenous fall in spending on goods and services. Economists have attempted to explain this decline in spending in several ways.

Some argue that a downward shift in the consumption function caused the contractionary shift in the *IS* curve. The stock market crash of 1929 may have been partly responsible for this decline in consumption. By reducing wealth and increasing uncertainty, the crash may have induced consumers to save more of their income.

Others explain the decline in spending by pointing to the large drop in investment in housing. Some economists believe that the residential investment boom of the 1920s was excessive, and that once this "overbuilding" became apparent, the demand for residential investment declined drastically. Another possible explanation for the fall in residential investment is the reduction in immigration in the 1930s: a more slowly growing population demands less new housing.

Once the Depression began, several events occurred that could have reduced spending further. First, the widespread bank failures in the United States (some 9,000 banks failed in the 1930–1933 period) may have reduced investment. Banks play the crucial role of getting the funds available for investment to those investors who can best use them. The closing of many banks in the early 1930s

---

[4] For a flavour of the debate, see Milton Friedman and Anna J. Schwartz, *A Monetary History of the United States, 1867–1960* (Princeton, NJ: Princeton University Press, 1963); Peter Temin, *Did Monetary Forces Cause the Great Depression?* (New York: W. W. Norton, 1976); the essays in Karl Brunner, ed., *The Great Depression Revisited* (Boston: Martinus Nijhoff Publishing, 1981); and the symposium on the Great Depression in the Spring 1993 issue of the *Journal of Economic Perspectives.*

may have prevented some investors from getting the funds they needed and thus may have led to a further contractionary shift in the investment function.[5]

In addition, U.S. fiscal policy of the 1930s caused a contractionary shift in the *IS* curve. Politicians at that time were more concerned with balancing the budget than with using fiscal policy to stimulate the economy. The Revenue Act of 1932 increased various taxes, especially those falling on lower- and middle-income consumers.[6] The Democratic platform of that year expressed concern about the budget deficit and advocated an "immediate and drastic reduction of governmental expenditures." In the midst of historically high unemployment, policymakers searched for ways to raise taxes and reduce government spending.

There are, therefore, several ways to explain a contractionary shift in the *IS* curve. Keep in mind that these different views are not inconsistent with one another. There may be no single explanation for the decline in spending. It is possible that all of these changes coincided, and together they led to a major reduction in spending.

The Money Hypothesis: A Shock to the *LM* Curve

The U.S. money supply fell 25 percent from 1929 to 1933, during which time the unemployment rate rose from 3.2 percent to 25.2 percent. This fact provides the motivation and support for what is called the *money hypothesis,* which places primary blame for the Depression on the Federal Reserve for allowing the money supply to fall by such a large amount.[7] The best known advocates of this interpretation are Milton Friedman and Anna Schwartz, who defend it in their treatise on U.S. monetary history. Friedman and Schwartz argue that contractions in the money supply have caused most economic downturns and that the Great Depression is a particularly vivid example.

Using the *IS–LM* model, we might interpret the money hypothesis as explaining the Depression by a contractionary shift in the *LM* curve. Seen in this way, however, the money hypothesis runs into two problems.

The first problem is the behaviour of *real* money balances. Monetary policy leads to a contractionary shift in the *LM* curve only if real money balances fall. Yet from 1929 to 1931, real money balances rose slightly, since the fall in the money supply was accompanied by an even greater fall in the price level. Although the monetary contraction may be responsible for the rise in unemployment from 1931 to 1933, when real money balances did fall, it probably should not be blamed for the initial downturn from 1929 to 1931.

---

[5] Ben Bernanke, "Non-Monetary Effects of the Financial Crisis in the Propagation of the Great Depression," *American Economic Review* 73 (June 1983): 257–276.

[6] E. Cary Brown, "Fiscal Policy in the 'Thirties: A Reappraisal," *American Economic Review* 46 (December 1956): 857–879.

[7] We discuss the reason for this large decrease in the money supply in Chapter 18, where we examine the money supply process in more detail (case study "Bank Failures and Deposit Insurance.")

The second problem for the money hypothesis is the behaviour of interest rates. If a contractionary shift in the *LM* curve triggered the Depression, we should have observed higher interest rates. Yet nominal interest rates fell continuously from 1929 to 1933.

These two reasons appear sufficient to reject the view that the Depression was instigated by a contractionary shift in the *LM* curve. But was the fall in the money stock irrelevant? Next, we turn to another mechanism through which monetary policy might have been responsible for the severity of the Depression—the deflation of the 1930s.

The Money Hypothesis Again: The Effects of Falling Prices

From 1929 to 1933 the U.S. price level fell 25 percent. Many economists blame this deflation for the severity of the Great Depression. They argue that the deflation may have turned what in 1931 was a typical economic downturn into an unprecedented period of high unemployment and depressed income. If correct, this argument gives new life to the money hypothesis. Since the falling money supply was, plausibly, responsible for the falling price level, it could have been responsible for the severity of the Depression. To evaluate this argument, we must discuss how changes in the price level affect income in the *IS–LM* model.

The Stabilizing Effects of Deflation In the *IS–LM* model we have developed so far, falling prices raise income. For any given supply of money *M,* a lower price level implies higher real money balances *M/P*. An increase in real money balances causes an expansionary shift in the *LM* curve, leading to higher income.

Another channel through which falling prices expand income is called the **Pigou effect.** Arthur Pigou, a prominent classical economist in the 1930s, pointed out that real money balances are part of households' wealth. As prices fall and real money balances rise, consumers should feel wealthier and spend more. This increase in consumer spending should cause an expansionary shift in the *IS* curve, also leading to higher income.

These two reasons led some economists in the 1930s to believe that falling prices would help the economy restore itself to full employment. Yet other economists were less confident in the economy's ability to correct itself. They pointed to other effects of falling prices, to which we now turn.

The Destabilizing Effects of Deflation Economists have proposed two theories to explain how falling prices could depress income rather than raise it. The first, called the **debt-deflation theory,** concerns the effects of unexpected falls in the price level. The second concerns the effects of expected deflation.

The debt-deflation theory begins with an observation that should be familiar from Chapter 7: unanticipated changes in the price level redistribute wealth between debtors and creditors. If a debtor owes a creditor $1,000, then the real amount of this debt is $1,000/P,$ where *P* is the price level. A fall in the price level raises the real amount of this debt—the amount of purchasing power the debtor must repay the creditor. Therefore, an unexpected deflation enriches creditors and impoverishes debtors.

The debt-deflation theory then posits that this redistribution of wealth affects spending on goods and services. In response to the redistribution from debtors to creditors, debtors spend less and creditors spend more. If these two groups have equal spending propensities, there is no aggregate impact. But it seems reasonable to assume that debtors have higher propensities to spend than creditors—perhaps that is why the debtors are in debt in the first place. In this case, debtors reduce their spending by more than creditors raise theirs. The net effect is a reduction in spending, a contractionary shift in the *IS* curve, and lower national income.

To understand how *expected* changes in prices can affect income, we need to add a new variable to the *IS–LM* model. Our discussion of the model so far has not distinguished between the nominal and real interest rates. Yet we know from previous chapters that investment depends on the real interest rate and that money demand depends on the nominal interest rate. If i is the nominal interest rate and π^e is expected inflation, then the *ex ante* real interest rate $r = i - \pi^e$. We can now write the *IS–LM* model as

$$Y = C(Y - T) + I(i - \pi^e) + G \qquad IS,$$
$$M/P = L(i, Y) \qquad\qquad\qquad LM.$$

Expected inflation enters as a variable in the *IS* curve. Thus, changes in expected inflation shift the *IS* curve, when it is drawn with the *nominal* interest rate on the y axis—as in Figure 11-8.

Let's use this extended *IS–LM* model to examine how changes in expected inflation influence the level of income. We begin by assuming that everyone expects the price level to remain the same. In this case, there is no expected inflation ($\pi^e = 0$), and these two equations produce the familiar *IS–LM* model. Now suppose that everyone suddenly expects that the price level will fall in the future, so that π^e becomes negative. Figure 11-8 shows what happens. At any

figure 11-8

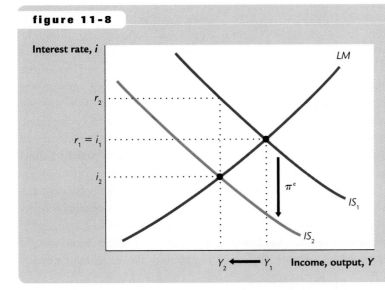

Expected Deflation in the *IS–LM* Model An expected deflation (a negative value of π^e) raises the real interest rate for any given nominal interest rate, and this depresses investment spending. The reduction in investment shifts the *IS* curve downward (measuring vertically, by an amount equal to the expected deflation). The level of income falls from Y_1 to Y_2. The nominal interest rate falls from i_1 to i_2, and the real interest rate rises from r_1 to r_2.

given nominal interest rate, the real interest rate is higher by the amount that π^e has dropped. Thus, the *IS* curve shifts down by this amount, as investment spending is reduced. An expected deflation thus leads to a reduction in national income from Y_1 to Y_2. The nominal interest rate falls from i_1 to i_2, and since this is less than the drop in π^e, the real interest rate rises from r_1 to r_2.

The logic behind this figure is straightforward. When firms come to expect deflation, they become reluctant to borrow to buy investment goods because they believe they will have to repay these loans later in more valuable dollars. The fall in investment depresses planned expenditure, which in turn depresses income. The fall in income reduces the demand for money, and this reduces the nominal interest rate that equilibrates the money market. The nominal interest rate falls by less than the expected deflation, so the real interest rate rises.

Note that there is a common thread in these two stories of destabilizing deflation. In both, falling prices depress national income by causing a contractionary shift in the *IS* curve. Because a deflation of the size observed from 1929 to 1933 is unlikely except in the presence of a major contraction in the money supply, these two explanations give some of the responsibility for the Depression—especially its severity—to the Federal Reserve in the United States. In other words, if falling prices are destabilizing, then a contraction in the money supply can lead to a fall in income, even without a decrease in real money balances or a rise in nominal interest rates.

Could the Depression Happen Again?

Economists study the Depression both because of its intrinsic interest as a major economic event and to provide guidance to policymakers so that it will not happen again. To state with confidence whether this event could recur, we would need to know why it happened. Because there is not yet agreement on the causes of the Great Depression, it is impossible to rule out with certainty another depression of this magnitude.

Yet most economists believe that the mistakes that led to the Great Depression are unlikely to be repeated. Central banks seem unlikely to allow the money supply to fall by one-fourth. Many economists believe that the deflation of the early 1930s was responsible for the depth and length of the Depression. And it seems likely that such a prolonged deflation was possible only in the presence of a falling money supply.

The fiscal-policy mistakes of the Depression are also unlikely to be repeated. Fiscal policy in the 1930s not only failed to help but actually further depressed aggregate demand. Few economists today would advocate such a rigid adherence to a balanced budget in the face of massive unemployment.

In addition, there are many institutions today that would help prevent the events of the 1930s from recurring. The system of deposit insurance (now available in both Canada and the United States, and discussed in Chapter 18) makes widespread bank failures less likely. The income tax causes an automatic reduction in taxes when income falls, which stabilizes the economy. Finally,

Recall that we define the exchange rate e as the amount of foreign currency per unit of domestic currency—for example, e might be \$0.70 (U.S.) per Canadian dollar. For the purposes of the Mundell–Fleming model, we do not need to distinguish between the real and nominal exchange rates. In Chapter 8 we related net exports to the real exchange rate ε, which equals eP/P^*, where P is the domestic price level and P^* is the foreign price level. Because the Mundell–Fleming model assumes that prices are fixed, changes in the real exchange rate are proportional to changes in the nominal exchange rate. That is, when the nominal exchange rate rises, foreign goods become less expensive compared to domestic goods, which depresses exports and stimulates imports.

The second equation describes the money market. It states that the supply of real money balances, M/P, equals the demand, $L(r, Y)$. The demand for real balances depends negatively on the interest rate and positively on overall output. As long as we have a floating exchange rate, the money supply M is an exogenous variable controlled by the central bank. Like the $IS-LM$ model, the Mundell–Fleming model takes the price level P as an exogenous variable, so there is no difference between nominal and real interest rates.

The third equation states that the world interest rate r^* determines the interest rate in this economy. This equation holds because we are examining a small open economy. That is, the economy is sufficiently small relative to the world economy that it can borrow or lend as much as it wants in world financial markets without affecting the world interest rate.

Although the idea of perfect capital mobility is expressed mathematically with a simple equation, it is important not to lose sight of the sophisticated process that this equation represents. Imagine that some event were to occur that would normally raise the interest rate (such as a decline in domestic saving). In a small open economy, the domestic interest rate might rise by a little bit for a short time, but as soon as it did, foreigners would see the higher interest rate and start lending to this country (by, for instance, buying this country's bonds). The capital inflow would drive the domestic interest rate back toward r^*. Similarly, if any event were ever to start driving the domestic interest rate downward, capital would flow out of the country to earn a higher return abroad, and this capital outflow would drive the domestic interest rate back upward toward r^*. Hence, the $r = r^*$ equation represents the assumption that the international flow of capital is sufficiently rapid and large as to keep the domestic interest rate equal to the world interest rate.

It should be recalled from our discussion in Chapter 8 (in particular from Figure 8-2) that there are deviations of the Canadian interest rate from the world interest rate. One form of departure is a risk premium that depends on such factors as international concern about political instability in Canada (for example, Quebec separation). We consider risk premiums later on in this chapter, but initially they are ignored. The second reason for departures from the $r = r^*$ condition is that it takes some time for international lenders to react to yield differentials (and in doing so, to eliminate them). Thus, we view $r = r^*$

as representing full equilibrium, and we can consider temporary deviations from this full equilibrium while discussing the time sequence involved in the Mundell–Fleming model.

These three equations fully describe the Mundell–Fleming model. Our job is to examine the implications of these equations for short-run fluctuations in a small open economy. If you do not understand the equations, you should review Chapters 8 and 10 before continuing.

The Model on a *Y–r* Graph

One way to depict the Mundell–Fleming model is to use a graph in which income *Y* is on the horizontal axis and the interest rate *r* is on the vertical axis. This presentation is comparable to our analysis of the closed economy in the *IS–LM* model. As Figure 12-1 shows, the *IS* curve slopes downward, and the *LM* curve slopes upward. New in this graph is the horizontal line representing the world interest rate.

Two features of this graph deserve special attention. First, because the exchange rate influences the demand for goods, the *IS* curve is drawn for a given value of the exchange rate (say, $0.70 (U.S.) per Canadian dollar). An increase in the exchange rate (say, to $0.90 (U.S.) per Canadian dollar) makes Canadian goods more expensive relative to foreign goods, which reduces net exports. Hence, an increase in the value of our dollar shifts the *IS* curve to the left. To remind us that the position of the *IS* curve depends on the exchange rate, the *IS* curve is labeled *IS(e)*.

Second, the three curves in Figure 12-1 all intersect at the same point. This might seem an unlikely coincidence. But, in fact, the exchange rate adjusts to ensure that all three curves pass through the same point.

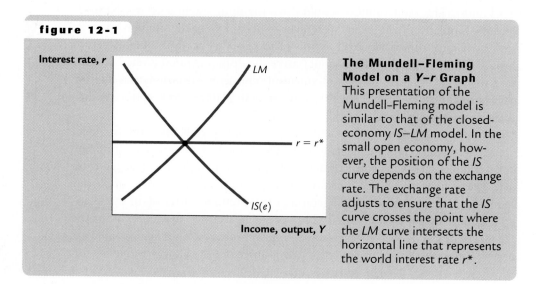

figure 12-1

Interest rate, *r*

LM

r = r*

IS(e)

Income, output, *Y*

The Mundell–Fleming Model on a *Y–r* Graph This presentation of the Mundell-Fleming model is similar to that of the closed-economy *IS–LM* model. In the small open economy, however, the position of the *IS* curve depends on the exchange rate. The exchange rate adjusts to ensure that the *IS* curve crosses the point where the *LM* curve intersects the horizontal line that represents the world interest rate *r**.

To see why all three curves must intersect at a single point, let's imagine a hypothetical situation in which they did not, as in panel (a) of Figure 12-2. Here, the domestic interest rate—the point where the *IS* and *LM* curves intersect—would be higher than the world interest rate. Since Canada would be offering a higher rate of return than is available in world financial markets, investors from around the world would want to buy Canadian financial assets. But first these foreign investors must convert their funds into dollars. In the process, they would bid up the value of the Canadian dollar. This rise in the exchange rate would shift the *IS* curve downward until the domestic interest rate equaled the world interest rate.

Alternatively, imagine that the *IS* and *LM* curves intersect at a point where the domestic interest rate is below the world interest rate, as in panel (b) of Figure 12-2. Since Canada would be offering a lower rate of return, investors would want to invest in world financial markets. But, to be able to buy foreign financial assets, they must convert their Canadian dollars into foreign currency. In the process of doing so, they would depress the value of the Canadian dollar.

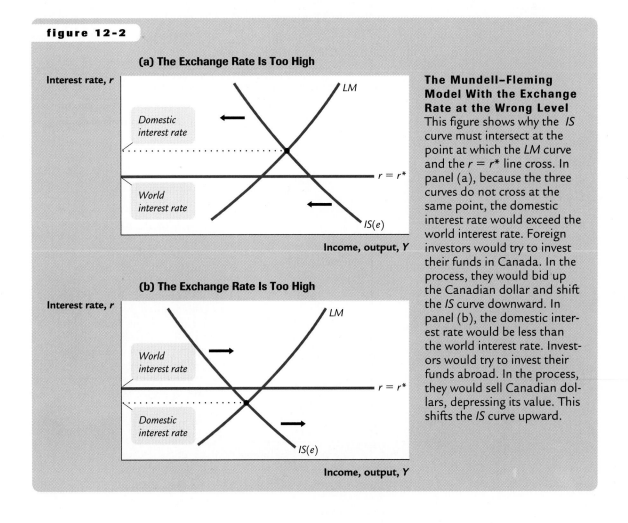

figure 12-2

(a) The Exchange Rate Is Too High

Interest rate, *r*

Domestic interest rate

World interest rate

LM

$r = r^*$

IS(e)

Income, output, *Y*

(b) The Exchange Rate Is Too High

Interest rate, *r*

World interest rate

Domestic interest rate

LM

$r = r^*$

IS(e)

Income, output, *Y*

The Mundell–Fleming Model With the Exchange Rate at the Wrong Level This figure shows why the *IS* curve must intersect at the point at which the *LM* curve and the $r = r^*$ line cross. In panel (a), because the three curves do not cross at the same point, the domestic interest rate would exceed the world interest rate. Foreign investors would try to invest their funds in Canada. In the process, they would bid up the Canadian dollar and shift the *IS* curve downward. In panel (b), the domestic interest rate would be less than the world interest rate. Investors would try to invest their funds abroad. In the process, they would sell Canadian dollars, depressing its value. This shifts the *IS* curve upward.

The fall in the exchange rate would stimulate Canadian export sales and so shift the *IS* curve upward until the domestic interest rate equaled the world interest rate.

To sum up, the equilibrium in this graph is found where the *LM* curve crosses the line representing the world interest rate. The exchange rate then adjusts and shifts the *IS* curve so that the *IS* curve crosses this point as well.

The Model on a *Y–e* Graph

The second way to depict the model is to use a graph in which income is on the horizontal axis and the exchange rate is on the vertical axis, as in Figure 12-3. This graph is drawn holding the interest rate constant at the world interest rate. The two equations in this figure are

$$Y = C(Y - T) + I(r^*) + G + NX(e) \qquad IS^*,$$

$$M/P = L(r^*, Y) \qquad\qquad\qquad LM^*.$$

We label these curves *IS** and *LM** to remind us that we are holding the interest rate constant at the world interest rate r^*. The equilibrium of the economy is found where the *IS** curve and the *LM** curve intersect. This intersection determines the exchange rate and the level of income.

The *IS** curve slopes downward because a higher exchange rate lowers net exports and thus lowers aggregate income. To show how this works, Figure 12-4 combines the net-exports schedule and the Keynesian-cross diagram to derive the *IS** curve. An increase in the Canadian dollar from e_1 to e_2 lowers

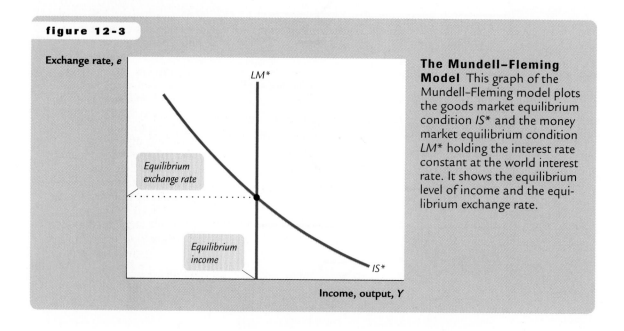

figure 12-3

Exchange rate, *e*

LM*

Equilibrium
exchange rate

Equilibrium
income

IS*

Income, output, *Y*

The Mundell–Fleming Model This graph of the Mundell-Fleming model plots the goods market equilibrium condition *IS** and the money market equilibrium condition *LM** holding the interest rate constant at the world interest rate. It shows the equilibrium level of income and the equilibrium exchange rate.

figure 12-4

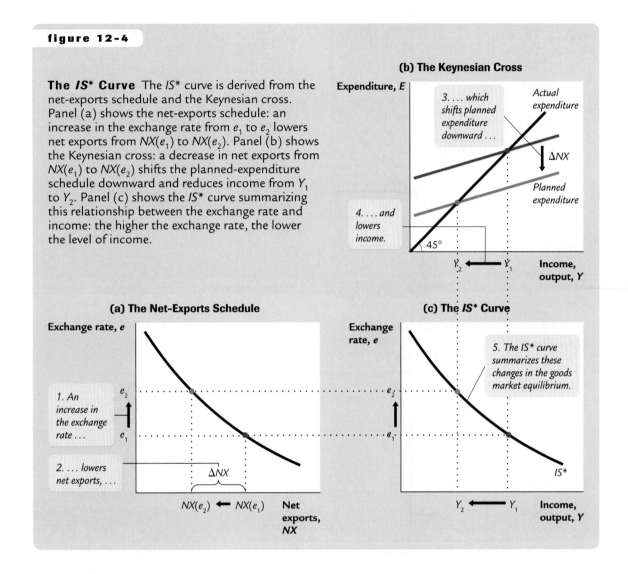

The IS* Curve The IS* curve is derived from the net-exports schedule and the Keynesian cross. Panel (a) shows the net-exports schedule: an increase in the exchange rate from e_1 to e_2 lowers net exports from $NX(e_1)$ to $NX(e_2)$. Panel (b) shows the Keynesian cross: a decrease in net exports from $NX(e_1)$ to $NX(e_2)$ shifts the planned-expenditure schedule downward and reduces income from Y_1 to Y_2. Panel (c) shows the IS* curve summarizing this relationship between the exchange rate and income: the higher the exchange rate, the lower the level of income.

(b) The Keynesian Cross

Expenditure, *E*

3. ... which shifts planned expenditure downward ...

Actual expenditure

ΔNX

Planned expenditure

4. ... and lowers income.

45°

$Y_2 \longleftarrow Y_1$ Income, output, *Y*

(a) The Net-Exports Schedule

Exchange rate, *e*

1. An increase in the exchange rate ...

e_2

e_1

2. ... lowers net exports, ...

ΔNX

$NX(e_2) \longleftarrow NX(e_1)$ Net exports, *NX*

(c) The IS* Curve

Exchange rate, *e*

5. The IS* curve summarizes these changes in the goods market equilibrium.

e_2

e_1

IS*

$Y_2 \longleftarrow Y_1$ Income, output, *Y*

net exports from $NX(e_1)$ to $NX(e_2)$. The reduction in net exports reduces planned expenditure and thus lowers income. Just as the standard *IS* curve combines the investment schedule and the Keynesian cross, the *IS** curve combines the net-exports schedule and the Keynesian cross.

The *LM** curve is vertical because the exchange rate does not enter into the *LM** equation. Given the world interest rate, the *LM** equation determines aggregate income, regardless of the exchange rate. Figure 12-5 shows how the *LM** curve arises from the world interest rate and the *LM* curve, which relates the interest rate and income.

We can now use the *IS*–LM** diagram (Figure 12-3) for the Mundell–Fleming model to show how aggregate income Y and the Canadian dollar *e* respond to changes in policy.

figure 12-5

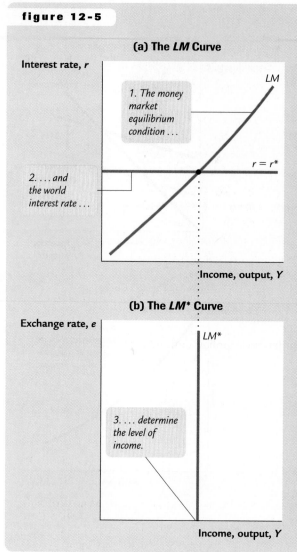

(a) The _LM_ Curve

Interest rate, _r_

1. The money market equilibrium condition . . .

LM

$r = r^*$

2. . . . and the world interest rate . . .

Income, output, _Y_

(b) The _LM*_ Curve

Exchange rate, _e_

LM*

3. . . . determine the level of income.

Income, output, _Y_

The _LM*_ Curve Panel (a) shows the standard _LM_ curve [which graphs the equation $M/P = L(r,Y)$] together with a horizontal line representing the world interest rate r^*. The intersection of these two curves determines the level of income, regardless of the exchange rate. Therefore, as panel (b) shows, the _LM*_ curve is vertical.

12-2 | The Small Open Economy Under Floating Exchange Rates

Before analyzing the impact of policies in an open economy, we must specify the international monetary system in which the country has chosen to operate. We start with the system relevant for most major economies today: **floating exchange rates.** Under floating exchange rates, the exchange rate is allowed to fluctuate freely in response to changing economic conditions.

Fiscal Policy

Suppose that the government stimulates domestic spending by increasing government purchases or by cutting taxes. Because such expansionary fiscal policy increases planned expenditure, it shifts the IS^* curve to the right, as in Figure 12-6. As a result, the exchange rate appreciates, while the level of income remains the same.

Notice that fiscal policy has very different effects in a small open economy than it does in a closed economy. In the closed-economy $IS-LM$ model, a fiscal expansion raises income, whereas in a small open economy with a floating exchange rate, a fiscal expansion leaves income at the same level. Why the difference? In a closed economy, when income rises, the interest rate rises, because higher income increases the demand for money. That is not possible in a small open economy: as soon as the interest rate tries to increase above the world interest rate r^*, capital flows in from abroad. This capital inflow increases the demand for the domestic currency in the market for foreign-currency exchange and, thus, bids up the value of the domestic currency. The appreciation of the exchange rate makes domestic goods expensive relative to foreign goods, and this reduces net exports. The fall in net exports offsets the effects of the expansionary fiscal policy on income.

Why is the fall in net exports so great as to render fiscal policy completely powerless to influence income? To answer this question, consider the equation that describes the money market:

$$M/P = L(r, Y).$$

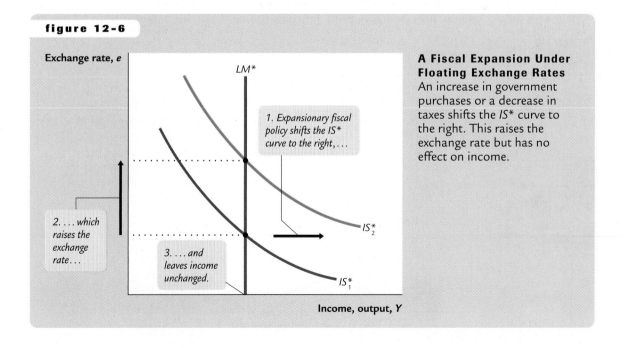

figure 12-6

Exchange rate, e

LM^*

1. Expansionary fiscal policy shifts the IS* curve to the right, ...

IS_2^*

2. ... which raises the exchange rate...

3. ... and leaves income unchanged.

IS_1^*

Income, output, Y

A Fiscal Expansion Under Floating Exchange Rates An increase in government purchases or a decrease in taxes shifts the IS^* curve to the right. This raises the exchange rate but has no effect on income.

In both closed and open economies, the quantity of real money balances supplied M/P is fixed, and the quantity demanded (determined by r and Y) must equal this fixed supply. In a closed economy, a fiscal expansion causes the equilibrium interest rate to rise. This increase in the interest rate (which reduces the quantity of money demanded) allows equilibrium income to rise (which increases the quantity of money demanded). By contrast, in a small open economy, r is fixed at r^*, so there is only one level of income that can satisfy this equation, and this level of income does not change when fiscal policy changes. Thus, when the government increases spending or cuts taxes, the appreciation of the exchange rate and the fall in net exports must be exactly large enough to offset fully the normal expansionary effect of the policy on income.

Monetary Policy

Suppose now that the Bank of Canada increases the money supply. Because the price level is assumed to be fixed, the increase in the money supply means an increase in real balances. The increase in real balances shifts the LM^* curve to the right, as in Figure 12-7. Hence, an increase in the money supply raises income and lowers the exchange rate.

Although monetary policy influences income in an open economy, as it does in a closed economy, the monetary transmission mechanism is different. Recall that in a closed economy an increase in the money supply increases spending because it lowers the interest rate and stimulates investment. In a small open economy, the interest rate is fixed by the world interest rate. As soon as an increase in the money supply puts downward pressure on the domestic interest rate, capital flows out of the economy, as investors seek a higher return elsewhere. This capital outflow prevents the domestic interest rate from falling. In

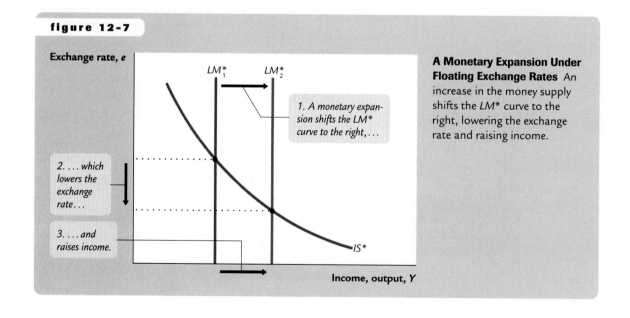

figure 12-7

Exchange rate, e

LM^*_1 LM^*_2

1. A monetary expansion shifts the LM^* curve to the right, . . .

2. . . . which lowers the exchange rate . . .

3. . . . and raises income.

IS^*

Income, output, Y

A Monetary Expansion Under Floating Exchange Rates An increase in the money supply shifts the LM^* curve to the right, lowering the exchange rate and raising income.

addition, because the capital outflow increases the supply of the domestic currency in the market for foreign-currency exchange, the exchange rate depreciates. The fall in the exchange rate makes domestic goods inexpensive relative to foreign goods and, thereby, stimulates net exports. Hence, in a small open economy, monetary policy influences income by altering the exchange rate rather than the interest rate.

CASE STUDY

Tight Monetary Policy Combined With Loose Fiscal Policy

During the late 1980s, Canada experienced a combination of tight monetary policy and loose fiscal policy. The Governor of the Bank of Canada, John Crow, was committed to bringing inflation down to zero, and his success earned him quite a reputation among the world central bankers. But both the federal and provincial governments were following an expansionary fiscal policy; their expenditures were far in excess of their tax revenues. Government deficits were increasing at record rates.

The Mundell–Fleming model predicts that both policies would raise the value of the Canadian dollar, and, indeed, Canadian currency did rise. In 1985 1 Canadian dollar could be purchased for $0.71 (U.S.), and by 1991 its price had risen to $0.89 (U.S.). This rise in the Canadian dollar made imported goods less expensive, and it made Canadian industries that compete against these foreign sellers less competitive. It is no wonder that this period witnessed a dramatic increase in "cross-border shopping."

Many analysts have noted that it was unfortunate that Canada's monetary-fiscal policy mix during this period was so counterproductive for Canadian firms' gaining a foothold in the U.S. markets following the signing of the Free Trade Agreement in January 1989. At the very time Canadian producers were becoming more competitive in the United States, because of the removal of U.S. tariffs on Canadian exports, these firms were becoming less competitive because of the dramatic rise in the value of the Canadian dollar.

Canada witnessed a similar mix of tight money and loose fiscal policy some 30 years earlier. John Diefenbaker, Canada's prime minister at the time, was trying to reduce unemployment during the worst postwar recession up to that point by raising government spending and cutting taxes. But James Coyne, the Governor of the Bank of Canada, was focused exclusively on keeping the inflation rate close to zero. Thus, Coyne refused to print any new currency to help finance the government's deficit. The result was just what our model predicts. Funds flowed into Canada, and the value of the Canadian dollar increased dramatically. This put a further profit squeeze on Canadian exporting firms, so that as rapidly as the government was creating jobs in the government sector, the rising Canadian dollar was destroying jobs in the exporting and import-competing sectors.

The dispute between the government and the Bank of Canada Governor became so bitter during the Coyne affair that the Bank of Canada Act was changed following this incident. Now the Governor must resign immediately if he or she is issued a written directive from the Minister of Finance that directs monetary policy to be other than what the Governor thinks is appropriate. Many analysts speculated that a directive might be issued in late 1993, when the Liberal government of Jean Chrétien came to power. The Liberals had campaigned on a platform of expansionary fiscal policy to create jobs, and they had been critical of John Crow's tight monetary policy. But as it turned out, a directive was not necessary, because Crow's seven-year appointment ended in February 1994. The Liberals simply waited out John Crow's tenure and then appointed Gordon Thiesson, Crow's senior deputy governor. This appointment signalled that the Liberals supported the Bank of Canada's low-inflation policy after all.

Trade Policy

Suppose that the government reduces the demand for imported goods by imposing an import quota or a tariff. What happens to aggregate income and the exchange rate?

Because net exports equal exports minus imports, a reduction in imports means an increase in net exports. That is, the net-exports schedule shifts to the right, as in Figure 12-8. This shift in the net-exports schedule increases planned expenditure and thus moves the IS^* curve to the right. Because the LM^* curve is vertical, the trade restriction raises the exchange rate but does not affect income.

Often a stated goal of policies to restrict trade is to alter the trade balance NX. Yet, as we first saw in Chapter 8, such policies do not necessarily have that effect. The same conclusion holds in the Mundell–Fleming model under floating exchange rates. Recall that

$$NX(e) = Y - C(Y - T) - I(r^*) - G.$$

Because a trade restriction does not affect income, consumption, investment, or government purchases, it does not affect the trade balance. Although the shift in the net-exports schedule tends to raise NX, the increase in the exchange rate reduces NX by the same amount.

World Interest Rate Changes

Consider an increase in the general level of world interest rates. In the Mundell–Fleming model, this means that Canadian interest rates must rise (as the law of one price operates in the world bond markets). But will this cause a rise or fall in the level of aggregate demand in Canada? Clearly, the higher borrowing cost will depress the investment spending component of aggregate demand, but can the exchange-rate change insulate aggregate demand from this depressing effect of higher interest rates? We now use the model to answer this question.

figure 12-8

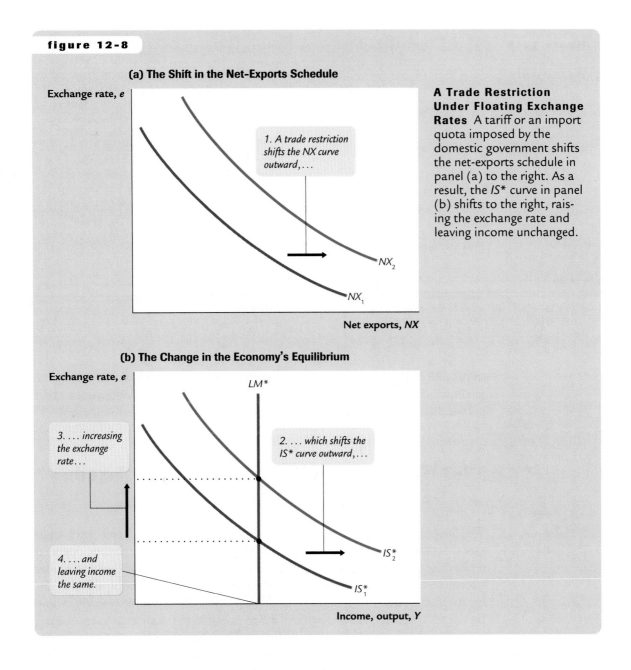

(a) The Shift in the Net-Exports Schedule

Exchange rate, *e*

1. A trade restriction shifts the NX curve outward,...

NX_2

NX_1

Net exports, *NX*

A Trade Restriction Under Floating Exchange Rates A tariff or an import quota imposed by the domestic government shifts the net-exports schedule in panel (a) to the right. As a result, the *IS** curve in panel (b) shifts to the right, raising the exchange rate and leaving income unchanged.

(b) The Change in the Economy's Equilibrium

Exchange rate, *e*

LM*

3. ... increasing the exchange rate...

2. ... which shifts the IS curve outward,...*

4. ... and leaving income the same.

IS_2^*

IS_1^*

Income, output, *Y*

From Figure 12-5 we know that higher world interest rates cause *LM** to shift to the right. Also, since higher interest rates depress firms' investment spending on new plant and equipment, *IS** shifts back to the left. These shifts are shown in Figure 12-9, where equilibrium moves from point A to point B. With funds initially leaving the country in pursuit of the high yields available in other parts of the world, the domestic currency depreciates, as shown in Figure 12-9. The model shows that this depreciation in the Canadian dollar must be of such a magnitude that aggregate demand rises. New exports are

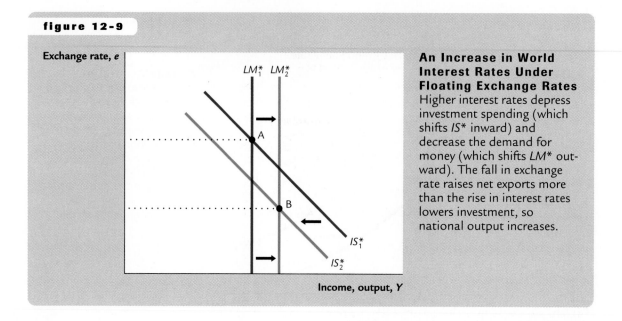

figure 12-9

An Increase in World Interest Rates Under Floating Exchange Rates Higher interest rates depress investment spending (which shifts *IS** inward) and decrease the demand for money (which shifts *LM** outward). The fall in exchange rate raises net exports more than the rise in interest rates lowers investment, so national output increases.

stimulated more than investment expenditure is reduced.[2] Thus, one advantage of allowing a floating exchange rate is that we do not have to suffer a recession just because there are increases in either world tariffs or world interest rates.

12-3 The Small Open Economy Under Fixed Exchange Rates

We now turn to the second type of exchange-rate system: **fixed exchange rates.** In the 1950s and 1960s, most of the world's major economies operated within the Bretton Woods system—an international monetary system under which most governments agreed to fix exchange rates. The world abandoned this system in the early 1970s, and exchange rates were allowed to float freely. Some European countries later reinstated a system of fixed exchange rates among themselves (as a common currency, the euro, was introduced in 1999), and some economists have advocated a return to a worldwide system of fixed exchange rates. In this section we discuss how such a system works, and we examine the impact of economic policies on an economy with a fixed exchange rate.

How a Fixed-Exchange-Rate System Works

Under a system of fixed exchange rates, a central bank stands ready to buy or sell the domestic currency for foreign currencies at a predetermined price. Sup-

---

[2] This strong prediction is not maintained as the Mundell–Fleming model is made more general—as we explain in the appendix to this chapter.

pose, for example, that the Bank of Canada announced that it was going to fix the exchange rate at $0.70 (U.S.) per dollar. It would then stand ready to give $1 (Canadian) in exchange for $0.70 (U.S.) or to give $0.70 (U.S.) in exchange for $1 (Canadian). To carry out this policy, the Bank of Canada would need a reserve of Canadian dollars (which it can print) and a reserve of U.S. dollars (which it must have accumulated in past transactions).

A fixed exchange rate dedicates a country's monetary policy to the single goal of keeping the exchange rate at the announced level. In other words, the essence of a fixed-exchange-rate system is the commitment of the central bank to allow the money supply to adjust to whatever level will ensure that the equilibrium exchange rate equals the announced exchange rate. Moreover, as long as the central bank stands ready to buy or sell foreign currency at the fixed exchange rate, the money supply adjusts automatically to the necessary level.

To see how fixing the exchange rate determines the money supply, consider the following example. Suppose that the Bank of Canada announces that it will fix the exchange rate at $0.70 (U.S.) per dollar, but, in the current equilibrium with the current money supply, the exchange rate is $0.75 (U.S.) per dollar. This situation is illustrated in panel (a) of Figure 12-10. Notice that there is a profit opportunity: an arbitrageur could buy $75 (U.S.) in the marketplace for $100 (Canadian), and then sell the U.S. dollars to the Bank of Canada for $107 ($75/$0.70), making a profit of $7.00. When the Bank of Canada buys these U.S. dollars from the arbitrageur, the Canadian dollars it pays for them automatically increase the domestic money supply. The rise in the money supply shifts the LM^* curve to the right, lowering the equilibrium exchange rate. In this way, the money supply continues to rise until the equilibrium exchange rate falls to the announced level.

Conversely, suppose that the Bank of Canada announces that it will fix the exchange rate at $0.70 (U.S.) per dollar, when the equilibrium is $0.65 (U.S.) per dollar. Panel (b) of Figure 12-10 shows this situation. In this case, an arbitrageur could make a profit by buying $70 (U.S.) from the Bank of Canada for $100 and then selling the U.S. dollars in the marketplace for $108 Canadian ($70/$0.65). When the Bank of Canada sells these U.S. dollars, the Canadian dollars it receives are no longer circulating among private transactors, so this policy automatically reduces the money supply. The fall in the money supply shifts the LM^* curve to the left, raising the equilibrium exchange rate. The money supply continues to fall until the equilibrium exchange rate rises to the announced level.

These examples make clear that fixing the exchange rate requires a commitment on the part of the Bank of Canada to either buy or sell whatever amount of foreign exchange is demanded by private participants in foreign-currency markets. Fixing a Canadian dollar price below the free-market equilibrium can be done indefinitely, because all the Bank of Canada needs is an unlimited supply of Canadian dollars (which it can print). Nevertheless, this policy is limited by the willingness of Canadians to tolerate the inflation that eventually accompanies rapid growth in the domestic money supply.

Fixing the Canadian dollar at a price above the free-market equilibrium, on the other hand, cannot be done indefinitely. This follows from the basic fact that the Bank of Canada cannot print foreign exchange. Private traders know

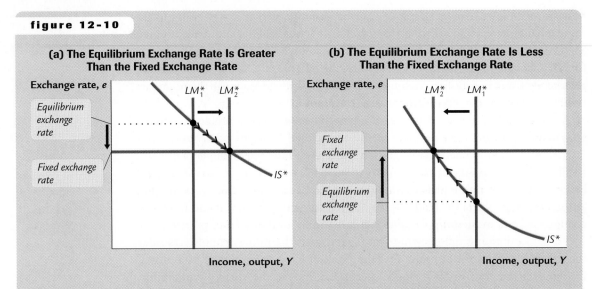

figure 12-10

(a) The Equilibrium Exchange Rate Is Greater Than the Fixed Exchange Rate

Exchange rate, e

Equilibrium exchange rate

Fixed exchange rate

LM_1^* LM_2^*

IS^*

Income, output, Y

(b) The Equilibrium Exchange Rate Is Less Than the Fixed Exchange Rate

Exchange rate, e

Fixed exchange rate

Equilibrium exchange rate

LM_2^* LM_1^*

IS^*

Income, output, Y

How a Fixed Exchange Rate Governs the Money Supply In panel (a), the equilibrium exchange rate initially exceeds the fixed level. Arbitrageurs will buy foreign currency in foreign-exchange markets and sell it to the Bank of Canada for a profit. This process automatically increases the money supply, shifting the LM^* curve to the right and lowering the exchange rate. In panel (b), the equilibrium exchange rate is below the fixed level. Arbitrageurs will buy dollars in foreign-exchange markets and use them to buy foreign currency from the Bank of Canada. This process automatically reduces the money supply, shifting the LM^* curve to the left and raising the exchange rate.

this, and they can easily determine how rapidly the Bank of Canada's reserves of foreign exhange are running out. Canada's balance of payments data record precisely this—the amount by which the country's foreign exchange reserves have been depleted each period. Armed with this information, private traders can readily guess when the Bank of Canada will have to give up fixing the exchange rate at such a high value. It is in this situation that we hear about a "speculative run against the currency" in the media. Once private traders see that a country's currency is about to fall in value, they sell off that currency to avoid the almost certain capital loss. This very action hastens the exchange-rate change and verifies the speculator's expectations.

It is important to understand that this exchange-rate system fixes the nominal exchange rate. Whether it also fixes the real exchange rate depends on the time horizon under consideration. If prices are flexible, as they are in the long run, then the real exchange rate can change even while the nominal exchange rate is fixed. Therefore, in the long run described in Chapter 8, a policy to fix the nominal exchange rate would not influence any real variable, including the real exchange rate. A fixed nominal exchange rate would influence only the money supply and the price level. Yet in the short run described by the Mundell–Fleming model, prices are fixed, so a fixed nominal exchange rate implies a fixed real exchange rate as well.

CASE STUDY

The International Gold Standard

During the late nineteenth and early twentieth centuries, most of the world's major economies operated under a gold standard. Each country maintained a reserve of gold and agreed to exchange one unit of its currency for a specified amount of gold. Through the gold standard, the world's economies maintained a system of fixed exchange rates.

To see how an international gold standard fixes exchange rates, suppose that the U.S. Treasury stands ready to buy or sell 1 ounce of gold for $100, and the Bank of England stands ready to buy or sell 1 ounce of gold for 100 pounds. Together, these policies fix the rate of exchange between dollars and pounds: $1 must trade for 1 pound. Otherwise, the law of one price would be violated, and it would be profitable to buy gold in one country and sell it in the other.

Suppose, for example, that the exchange rate were 2 pounds per dollar. In this case, an arbitrageur could buy 200 pounds for $100, use the pounds to buy 2 ounces of gold from the Bank of England, bring the gold to the United States, and sell it to the Treasury for $200—making a $100 profit. Moreover, by bringing the gold to the United States from England, the arbitrageur would increase the money supply in the United States and decrease the money supply in England.

Thus, during the era of the gold standard, the international transport of gold by arbitrageurs was an automatic mechanism adjusting the money supply and stabilizing exchange rates. This system did not completely fix exchange rates, because shipping gold across the Atlantic was costly. Yet the international gold standard did keep the exchange rate within a range dictated by transportation costs. It thereby prevented large and persistent movements in exchange rates.[3]

Fiscal Policy

Let's now examine how economic policies affect a small open economy with a fixed exchange rate. Suppose that the government stimulates domestic spending by increasing government purchases or by cutting taxes. This policy shifts the IS^* curve to the right, as in Figure 12-11, putting upward pressure on the exchange rate. But because the central bank stands ready to trade foreign and domestic currency at the fixed exchange rate, arbitrageurs quickly respond to the rising exchange rate by selling foreign currency to the central bank, leading to an automatic monetary expansion. The rise in the money supply shifts the LM^* curve to the right. Thus, in contrast to the situation under floating exchange rates, a fiscal expansion under fixed exchange rates raises aggregate income.

---

[3] For more on how the gold standard worked, see the essays in Barry Eichengreen, ed., *The Gold Standard in Theory and History* (New York: Methuen, 1985).

figure 12-11

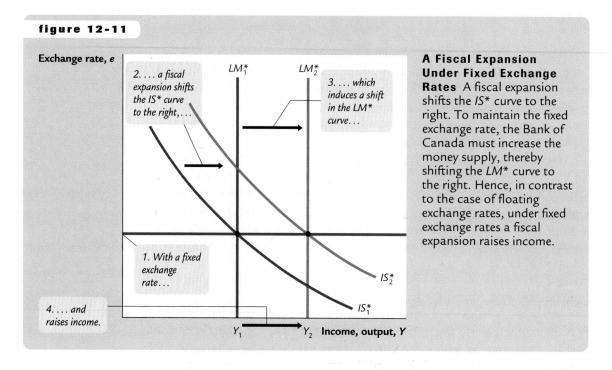

figure 12-11

A Fiscal Expansion Under Fixed Exchange Rates A fiscal expansion shifts the *IS** curve to the right. To maintain the fixed exchange rate, the Bank of Canada must increase the money supply, thereby shifting the *LM** curve to the right. Hence, in contrast to the case of floating exchange rates, under fixed exchange rates a fiscal expansion raises income.

Monetary Policy

Imagine that a central bank operating with a fixed exchange rate were to try to increase the money supply—for example, by buying bonds from the public. What would happen? The initial impact of this policy is to shift the *LM** curve to the right, lowering the exchange rate, as in Figure 12-12. But, because the central bank is committed to trading foreign and domestic currency at a fixed

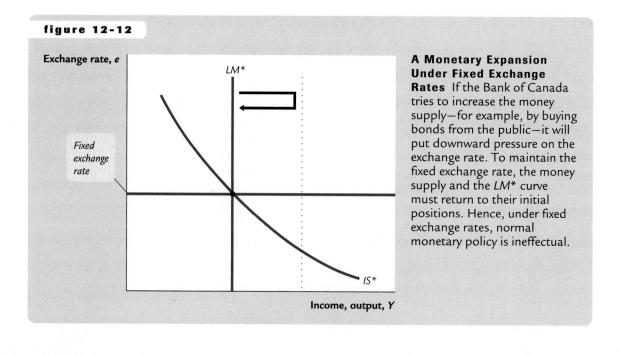

figure 12-12

A Monetary Expansion Under Fixed Exchange Rates If the Bank of Canada tries to increase the money supply—for example, by buying bonds from the public—it will put downward pressure on the exchange rate. To maintain the fixed exchange rate, the money supply and the *LM** curve must return to their initial positions. Hence, under fixed exchange rates, normal monetary policy is ineffectual.

exchange rate, arbitrageurs quickly respond to the falling exchange rate by selling the domestic currency to the central bank, causing the money supply and the LM^* curve to return to their initial positions. Hence, monetary policy as usually conducted is ineffectual under a fixed exchange rate. By agreeing to fix the exchange rate, the central bank gives up its control over the money supply.

A country with a fixed exchange rate can, however, conduct a type of monetary policy: it can decide to change the level at which the exchange rate is fixed. A reduction in the value of the currency is called a **devaluation,** and an increase in its value is called a **revaluation.** In the Mundell–Fleming model, a devaluation shifts the LM^* curve to the right; it acts like an increase in the money supply under a floating exchange rate. A devaluation thus expands net exports and raises aggregate income. Conversely, a revaluation shifts the LM^* curve to the left, reduces net exports, and lowers aggregate income.

CASE STUDY

Devaluation and the Recovery From the Great Depression

The Great Depression of the 1930s was a global problem. Although events in the United States may have precipitated the downturn for many other Western countries like Canada, all of the world's major economies experienced huge declines in production and employment. Yet not all governments responded to this calamity in the same way.

One key difference among governments was how committed they were to the fixed exchange rate set by the international gold standard. Some countries, such as France, Germany, Italy, and the Netherlands, maintained the old rate of exchange between gold and currency. Other countries, such as Denmark, Finland, Norway, Sweden, and the United Kingdom, reduced the amount of gold they would pay for each unit of currency by about 50 percent. By reducing the gold content of their currencies, these governments devalued their currencies relative to those of other countries.

The subsequent experience of these two groups of countries conforms to the prediction of the Mundell–Fleming model. Those countries that pursued a policy of devaluation recovered quickly from the Depression. The lower value of the currency stimulated exports and expanded production. By contrast, those countries that maintained the old exchange rate suffered longer with a depressed level of economic activity.[4]

Trade Policy

Suppose that the government reduces imports by imposing an import quota or a tariff. This policy shifts the net-exports schedule to the right and thus shifts the IS^* curve to the right, as in Figure 12-13. The shift in the IS^* curve tends

[4] Barry Eichengreen and Jeffrey Sachs, "Exchange Rates and Economic Recovery in the 1930s," *Journal of Economic History* 45 (December 1985): 925–946.

to raise the exchange rate. To keep the exchange rate at the fixed level, the money supply must rise, shifting the LM^* curve to the right.

The result of a trade restriction under a fixed exchange rate is very different from that under a floating exchange rate. In both cases, a trade restriction shifts the net-exports schedule to the right, but only under a fixed exchange rate does a trade restriction increase net exports NX. The reason is that a trade restriction under a fixed exchange rate induces monetary expansion rather than an appreciation of the exchange rate. The monetary expansion, in turn, raises aggregate income. Recall the accounting identity

$$NX = S - I.$$

When income rises, saving also rises, and this implies an increase in net exports.

This analysis can be used to consider tariffs levied by foreigners as well. In that case, our net exports are reduced so the shifts in IS^* and LM^* are to the left, instead of to the right (as they are in Figure 12-13). In contrast to the floating-exchange-rate case, then, Canada must suffer a recession following the imposition of foreign trade restrictions, if the exchange rate is fixed.

Similarly, if we have a fixed exchange rate, we must suffer a recession if world commodity prices change—as they did in the 1990s during the Asian crisis—to reduce Canadian net exports. At the time of the Asian crisis, Canada had a floating exchange rate. While the dip in the Canadian dollar (down to $0.63 (U.S.) in mid-1998) caused concern, it did provide Canada some insulation from this major event. While our exports of primary commodities suffered during the Asian crisis, at least our manufacturing exports were stimulated by the lower domestic currency. Many analysts concluded that it was fortunate that Canada had not opted for a fixed exchange rate at this time.

figure 12-13

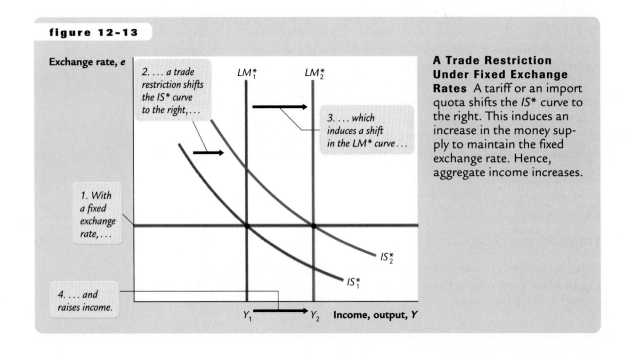

2. . . . a trade restriction shifts the IS* curve to the right, . . .

3. . . . which induces a shift in the LM* curve . . .

1. With a fixed exchange rate, . . .

4. . . . and raises income.

A Trade Restriction Under Fixed Exchange Rates A tariff or an import quota shifts the IS* curve to the right. This induces an increase in the money supply to maintain the fixed exchange rate. Hence, aggregate income increases.

World Interest-Rate Changes

The analysis of foreign interest-rate increases under fixed exchange rates is similar to that for trade restrictions imposed by other countries. Higher interest rates lower investment spending by firms, so IS^* shifts to the left for this reason, rather than because of a reduction in net exports. However, whatever causes the IS^* curve to shift is insignificant; LM^* must still shift to the left to keep the exchange rate fixed. (Just picture Figure 12-13 running in reverse.) Thus, Canada must suffer a recession following an increase in world interest rates if the exchange rate is fixed.

This same analysis applies to small open economies in Europe that have maintained fixed exchange rates with one another. In the early 1990s, German reunification meant a big increase in government spending to improve conditions in the former East Germany. Given the commitment to low inflation on the part of the German central bank, this spending led to higher German interest rates. Our model shows that the only way that the other European countries could avoid a recession—that would otherwise accompany this increase in interest rates caused by the changes happening in Germany—was to shift away from fixed exchange rates. This is exactly what happened in 1992.

Policy in the Mundell–Fleming Model: A Summary

The Mundell–Fleming model shows that the effect of almost any economic policy on a small open economy depends on whether the exchange rate is floating or fixed. Table 12-1 summarizes our analysis of the short-run effects of fiscal, monetary, and trade policies, and world interest rate changes, on income,

table 12-1

The Mundell-Fleming Model: Summary of Policy Effects and the Impact of Events in the Rest of the World

	EXCHANGE-RATE REGIME					
	FLOATING			FIXED		
	IMPACT ON:					
Policy/World Event	Y	e	NX	Y	e	NX
Fiscal expansion	0	↑	↓	↑	0	0
Monetary expansion	↑	↓	↑	0	0	0
Import restriction	0	↑	0	↑	0	↑
Export restriction	0	↓	0	↓	0	↓
Higher interest rates	↑	↓	↑	↓	0	0

Note: This table shows the direction of impact of various economic policies on income Y, the exchange rate e, and the trade balance NX. A " ↑ " indicates that the variable increases; a " ↓ " indicates that it decreases; a "0" indicates no effect. Remember that the exchange rate is defined as the amount of foreign currency per unit of domestic currency (for example, $0.70 (U.S.)/Canadian dollar).

the exchange rate, and the trade balance. What is most striking is that all of the results are different under floating and fixed exchange rates.

To be more specific, the Mundell–Fleming model shows that the power of monetary and fiscal policy to influence aggregate income depends on the exchange-rate regime. Under floating exchange rates, only monetary policy can affect income. The usual expansionary impact of fiscal policy is offset by a rise in the value of the currency. Under fixed exchange rates, only fiscal policy can affect income. The normal potency of monetary policy is lost because the money supply is dedicated to maintaining the exchange rate at the announced level.

CASE STUDY

Regional Tensions Within Canada

The Mundell–Fleming model can be used to help explain why regional tensions increased in Canada during the late 1980s. At that time, the Ontario government was running an expansionary fiscal policy. We now know that the overall impact of such a policy (throughout the country) has no effect on aggregate demand. Instead it creates a higher Canadian dollar, which forces net exports to be reduced by the same amount as government spending is increased. But consider the distribution of these two effects within the country.

The increase in the government spending component of aggregate demand is concentrated entirely within Ontario, whereas the crowding out of preexisting net export demand is felt in all provinces. The result is that demand in Ontario is increased, while that in the rest of the country is decreased. The two effects add up to zero as far as overall demand in the entire country is concerned. Thus, fiscal policy *does* work under floating exchange rates after all, but only from one province's point of view. Ontario can reduce its unemployment problem, but *only* by worsening the same problem for the other regions!

12-4| Interest-Rate Differentials

So far, our analysis in this chapter has assumed that the interest rate in a small open economy is equal to the world interest rate: $r = r^*$. To some extent, however, as we noted in Chapter 8, interest rates differ around the world. We now extend our analysis by considering the causes and effects of international interest-rate differentials.

Country Risk and Exchange-Rate Expectations

When we assumed earlier that the interest rate in our small open economy is determined by the world interest rate, we were applying the law of one price. We reasoned that if the domestic interest rate were above the world interest rate, people from abroad would lend to that country, driving the domestic interest rate down. And if the domestic interest rate were below the world interest rate, domestic residents would lend abroad to earn a higher return, driving the domestic interest rate up. In the end, the domestic interest rate would equal the world interest rate.

Why doesn't this logic always apply? There are two reasons.

One reason is country risk. When investors buy Canadian government bonds or make loans to Canadian corporations, they are fairly confident that they will be repaid with interest. By contrast, in some less-developed countries, it is plausible to fear that a revolution or other political upheaval might lead to a default on loan repayments. Borrowers in such countries often have to pay higher interest rates to compensate lenders for this risk.

Another reason interest rates differ across countries is expected changes in the exchange rate. For example, suppose that people expect the French franc to fall in value relative to the U.S. dollar. Then loans made in francs will be repaid in a less valuable currency than loans made in dollars. To compensate for this expected fall in the French currency, the interest rate in France will be higher than the interest rate in the United States.

Thus, because of both country risk and expectations of exchange-rate changes, the interest rate of a small open economy can differ from interest rates in other economies around the world. Let's now see how this fact affects our analysis.

Differentials in the Mundell–Fleming Model

As outlined in Chapter 8, to incorporate interest-rate differentials into the Mundell–Fleming model, we assume that the interest rate in our small open economy is determined by the world interest rate plus a risk premium θ:

$$r = r^* + \theta.$$

The risk premium is determined by the perceived political risk of making loans in a country and the expected change in the real exchange rate. For our purposes here, we can take the risk premium as exogenous in order to examine how changes in the risk premium affect the economy.

The model is largely the same as before. The two equations are

$$Y = C(Y - T) + I(r^* + \theta) + G + NX(e) \qquad IS^*,$$
$$M/P = L(r^* + \theta, Y) \qquad\qquad\qquad LM^*.$$

For any given fiscal policy, monetary policy, price level, and risk premium, these two equations determine the level of income and exchange rate that equilibrate the goods market and the money market. Holding constant the risk premium, monetary policy, fiscal policy, and trade policy work as we have already seen.

Now suppose that political turmoil causes the country's risk premium θ to rise. The effects are just like the increase in foreign interest rates that we considered earlier. The most direct effect is that the domestic interest rate r rises, so the analysis is just like our earlier discussion of world interest-rate increases. The higher interest rate has two effects. First, the IS^* curve shifts to the left, because the higher interest rate reduces investment. Second, the LM^* curve shifts to the right, because the higher interest rate reduces the demand for money, and this allows a higher level of income for any given money supply. [Recall that Y must satisfy the equation $M/P = L(r^* + \theta, Y)$.] As Figure 12-14 shows, these two shifts cause income to rise and the currency to depreciate.

This analysis has an important implication: expectations of the exchange rate are partially self-fulfilling. For example, suppose that people come to believe that the French franc will not be valuable in the future. Investors will place a larger risk premium on French assets: θ will rise in France. This expectation will drive up French interest rates and, as we have just seen, will drive down the value of the French currency. *Thus, the expectation that a currency will lose value in the future causes it to lose value today.*

One surprising—and perhaps inaccurate—prediction of this analysis is that an increase in country risk as measured by θ will cause the economy's income to increase. This occurs in Figure 12-14 because of the rightward shift in the LM^* curve. Although higher interest rates depress investment, the depreciation of the currency stimulates net exports by an even greater amount. As a result, aggregate income rises.

There are three reasons why, in practice, such a boom in income does not occur. First, the central bank might want to avoid the large depreciation of the domestic currency and, therefore, may respond by decreasing the money supply M. Second, the depreciation of the domestic currency increases the price of imported goods, causing an increase in the price level P (which shrinks the real money supply). We pursue this possibility in the appendix to this chapter. Third, when some event increases the country risk premium θ, residents of the

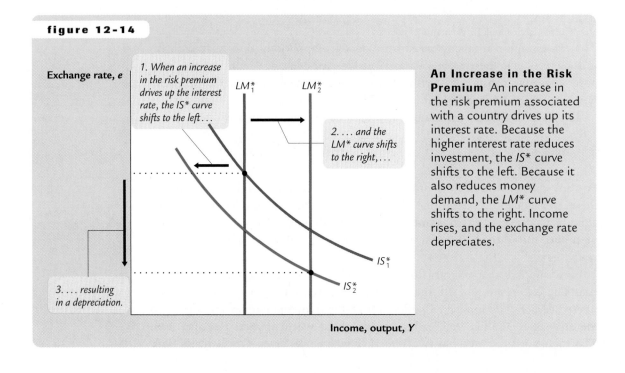

figure 12-14

Exchange rate, e

1. When an increase in the risk premium drives up the interest rate, the IS* curve shifts to the left...

LM^*_1 LM^*_2

2. ... and the LM* curve shifts to the right, ...

IS^*_1

IS^*_2

3. ... resulting in a depreciation.

Income, output, Y

An Increase in the Risk Premium An increase in the risk premium associated with a country drives up its interest rate. Because the higher interest rate reduces investment, the IS* curve shifts to the left. Because it also reduces money demand, the LM* curve shifts to the right. Income rises, and the exchange rate depreciates.

country might respond to the same event by increasing their demand for money (for any given income and interest rate), because money is often the safest asset available. All three of these changes would tend to shift the LM^* curve toward the left, which mitigates the fall in the exchange rate but also tends to depress income.

Thus, increases in country risk are not desirable. In the short run, they typically lead to a depreciating currency and, through the three channels just described, falling aggregate income. In addition, because a higher interest rate reduces investment, the long-run implication is reduced capital accumulation and lower economic growth.

CASE STUDY

International Financial Crisis: Mexico 1994–1995

In August 1994, a Mexican peso was worth 30 U.S. cents. A year later, it was worth only 16 cents. What explains this massive fall in the value of the Mexican currency? Country risk is a large part of the story.

At the beginning of 1994, Mexico was a country on the rise. The recent passage of the North American Free Trade Agreement (NAFTA), which reduced trade barriers among the United States, Canada, and Mexico, made many confident about the future of the Mexican economy. Investors around the world were eager to make loans to the Mexican government and to Mexican corporations.

Political developments soon changed that perception. A violent uprising in the Chiapas region of Mexico made the political situation in Mexico seem precarious. Then Luis Donaldo Colosio, the leading presidential candidate, was assassinated. The political future looked less certain, and many investors started placing a larger risk premium on Mexican assets.

At first, the rising risk premium did not affect the value of the peso, for Mexico was operating with a fixed exchange rate. As we have seen, under a fixed exchange rate, the central bank agrees to trade the domestic currency (pesos) for a foreign currency (U.S. dollars) at a predetermined rate. Thus, when an increase in the country risk premium put downward pressure on the value of the peso, the Mexican central bank had to accept pesos and pay out U.S. dollars. This automatic exchange-market intervention contracted the Mexican money supply (shifting the LM^* curve to the left) when the currency might otherwise have depreciated.

Yet Mexico's reserves of foreign currency were too small to maintain its fixed exchange rate. When Mexico ran out of dollars at the end of 1994, the Mexican government announced a devaluation of the peso. This choice had repercussions, however, because the government had repeatedly promised that it would not devalue. Investors became even more distrustful of Mexican policymakers and feared further Mexican devaluations.

Investors around the world (including those in Mexico) avoided buying Mexican assets. The country risk premium rose once again, adding to the upward pressure on interest rates and the downward pressure on the peso. The

Mexican stock market plummeted. When the Mexican government needed to roll over some of its debt that was coming due, investors were unwilling to buy the new debt. Default appeared to be the government's only option. In just a few months, Mexico had gone from being a promising emerging economy to being a risky economy with a government on the verge of bankruptcy.

Then the United States stepped in. The U.S. government had three motives: to help its neighbour to the south, to prevent the massive illegal immigration that might follow government default and economic collapse, and to prevent the investor pessimism regarding Mexico from spreading to other developing countries. The U.S. government, together with the International Monetary Fund (IMF), led an international effort to bail out the Mexican government. In particular, the United States provided loan guarantees for Mexican government debt, which allowed the Mexican government to refinance the debt that was coming due. These loan guarantees helped restore confidence in the Mexican economy, thereby reducing to some extent the country risk premium.

Although the U.S. loan guarantees may well have stopped a bad situation from getting worse, they did not prevent the Mexican meltdown of 1994–1995 from being a painful experience for the Mexican people. Not only did the Mexican currency lose much of its value, but Mexico also went through a deep recession. Fortunately, by the late 1990s, aggregate income was growing again, and the worst appeared to be over. But the lesson from this experience is clear and could well apply again in the future: changes in perceived country risk, often attributable to political instability, are an important determinant of interest rates and exchange rates in small open economies.

CASE STUDY

International Financial Crisis: Asia 1997–1998

Toward the end of 1997, as the Mexican economy was recovering from its financial crisis, a similar story started to unfold in several Asian economies, including Thailand, South Korea, and especially Indonesia. The symptoms were familiar: high interest rates, falling asset values, and a depreciating currency. In Indonesia, for instance, short-term nominal interest rates rose above 50 percent, the stock market lost about 90 percent of its value (measured in U.S. dollars), and the rupiah fell against the U.S. dollar by more than 80 percent. The crisis led to rising inflation in these countries (as the depreciating currency made imports more expensive) and to falling GDP (as high interest rates and reduced confidence depressed spending). Real GDP in Indonesia fell about 15 percent in 1998, making the downturn larger than any recession in North America since the Great Depression of the 1930s.

What sparked this firestorm? The problem began in the Asian banking systems. For many years, the governments in the Asian nations had been more involved in managing the allocation of resources—in particular, financial resources—than is true in Canada and other developed countries. Some commentators had applauded this "partnership" between government and private enterprise and had even suggested that Canada should follow the example. Over time, however, it became clear that many Asian banks had been extending loans to those with the most political clout rather than to those with the most profitable investment projects. Once rising default rates started to expose this "crony capitalism," as it was then called, international investors started to lose confidence in the future of these economies. The risk premiums for Asian assets rose, causing interest rates to skyrocket and currencies to collapse.

International crises of confidence often involve a vicious circle that can amplify the problem. Here is one theory about what happened in Asia:

1. Problems in the banking system eroded international confidence in these economies.

2. Loss of confidence raised risk premiums and interest rates.

3. Rising interest rates, together with the loss of confidence, depressed the prices of stock and other assets.

4. Falling asset prices reduced the value of collateral being used for bank loans.

5. Reduced collateral increased default rates on bank loans.

6. Greater defaults exacerbated problems in the banking system. Now return to step 1 to complete and continue the circle.

Some economists have used this vicious-circle argument to suggest that the Asian crisis was a self-fulfilling prophecy: bad things happened merely because people expected bad things to happen. Most economists, however, thought the political corruption of the banking system was a real problem, which was then compounded by this vicious circle of reduced confidence.

As the Asian crisis developed, the IMF and the United States tried to restore confidence, much as they had with Mexico a few years earlier. In particular, the IMF made loans to the Asian countries to help them over the crisis; in exchange for these loans, it exacted promises that the governments would reform their banking systems and eliminate crony capitalism. The IMF's hope was that the short-term loans and longer-term reforms would restore confidence, lower the risk premium, and turn the vicious circle into a virtuous circle.

12-5| Should Exchange Rates Be Floating or Fixed?

Having analyzed how an economy works under floating and fixed exchange rates, we turn to the question of which exchange-rate regime is preferable. The international monetary system is often a topic of heated debate among international economists and policy-makers. Historically, most economists have favoured a system of floating exchange rates. Yet, in recent years, some have advocated a return to fixed exchange rates.

The primary argument for a floating exchange rate is that it allows monetary policy to be used for other purposes. Under fixed rates, monetary policy is committed to the single goal of maintaining the exchange rate at its announced level. Yet the exchange rate is only one of many macroeconomic variables that monetary policy can influence. A system of floating exchange rates leaves monetary policymakers free to pursue other goals, such as stabilizing employment or prices.

"Then it's agreed. Until the dollar firms up, we let the clamshell float."

Advocates of fixed exchange rates argue that exchange-rate uncertainty makes international trade more difficult. After the world abandoned the Bretton Woods system of fixed exchange rates in the early 1970s, both real and nominal exchange rates became (and remained) much more volatile than anyone had expected. Some economists attribute this volatility to irrational and destabilizing speculation by international investors. Business executives often claim that this volatility is harmful because it increases the uncertainty that accompanies international business transactions. Yet, despite this exchange-rate volatility, the amount of world trade has continued to rise under floating exchange rates.

Advocates of fixed exchange rates sometimes argue that a commitment to a fixed exchange rate is one way to discipline a nation's monetary authority and prevent excessive growth in the money supply. Yet there are many other policy rules to which the central bank could be committed. In Chapter 14, for instance, we discuss policy rules such as targets for nominal GDP or the inflation rate. Fixing the exchange rate has the advantage of being simpler to implement than these other policy rules, because the money supply adjusts automatically, but this policy may lead to greater volatility in income and employment. Indeed, in the Mundell–Fleming model, shocks to the IS^* curve *must* affect real GDP more under fixed exchange rates. In the appendix to this chapter, we explore the generality of this strong prediction. We extend the Mundell–Fleming model to allow for a direct effect of the exchange rate on the cost of living index, and for the interest rate differential to depend on the expected change in the exchange rate. In this more general setting, the shock-absorber feature of a floating rate is weakened.

In the end, the choice between floating and fixed rates is not as stark as it may seem at first. During periods of fixed exchange rates, countries can change the value of their currency if maintaining the exchange rate conflicts too severely with other goals. During periods of floating exchange rates, countries often use informal targets for the exchange rate when deciding whether to expand or contract the money supply. We rarely observe exchange rates that are completely fixed or completely floating. Instead, under both systems, stability of the exchange rate is usually one among many of the central bank's objectives.

CASE STUDY

Monetary Union

If you have ever driven the 6,000 kilometres from Halifax to Vancouver, you will recall that you never needed to change your money from one form of currency to another. In all provinces, local residents are happy to accept the Canadian dollar for the items you might buy. Such a *monetary union* is the most extreme form of a fixed exchange rate. The exchange rate between Nova Scotia dollars and British Columbia dollars is irrevocably fixed.

If you have ever made a similar 6,000-kilometre trip across Europe, however, your experience was probably very different. You didn't have to travel far before needing to exchange your French francs for German marks, Dutch guilders, Spanish pesetas, or Italian lira. The large number of currencies in Europe made traveling less convenient and more expensive. Every time you crossed a border, you had to wait in line at a bank to get the local money, and you had to pay the bank a fee for the service.

Recently, however, this has started to change. Many countries in Europe have decided to form their own monetary union and use a common currency called the euro, which was introduced in January 1999. The adoption of the euro is an extension of the *European Monetary System (EMS)*, which during the previous two decades had attempted to limit exchange-rate fluctuations among participating countries. When the euro is fully adopted, this goal will be achieved: the exchange rate between France and Germany will be as fixed as the exchange rate between Nova Scotia and British Columbia.

The introduction of a common currency has its costs. The most important is that the nations of Europe will no longer be able to conduct their own monetary policies. Instead, a European central bank, with participation of all member countries, will set a single monetary policy for all of Europe. The central banks of the individual countries will monitor local conditions but they will have no control over the money supply or interest rates. Critics of the move toward a common currency argue that the cost of losing national monetary policy is large. If a recession hits one country but not others in Europe, that country may wish it had the tool of monetary policy to combat the downturn.

Why, according to these economists, is monetary union a bad idea for Europe if it works so well in Canada and the United States? These economists argue that the North American economies are different from Europe in two important ways. First, labour is more mobile among Canadian provinces and among U.S. states than among European countries. This is in part because much of Canada and the United States has a common language and in part because many North Americans are descended from immigrants, who have shown a willingness to move. Therefore, when a regional recession occurs, North American workers are more likely to move from high-unemployment areas to low-unemployment ones. Second, Canada and the United States have strong central governments that can use fiscal policy to redistribute resources among regions. Because Europe does not have these two advantages, it will suffer more when it restricts itself to a single monetary policy.

Advocates of a common currency believe that the loss of national monetary policy is more than offset by other gains. With a single currency in all of Europe, travelers and businesses will no longer need to worry about exchange rates, and this should encourage more international trade. In addition, a common currency may have the political advantage of making Europeans feel more connected to one another. The twentieth century was marked by two world wars, both of which were sparked by European discord. If a common currency makes the nations of Europe more harmonious, it will benefit the entire world.

12-6 The Mundell–Fleming Model With a Changing Price Level

So far we have been using the Mundell–Fleming model to study the small open economy in the short run when the price level is fixed. To see how this model relates to models we have examined previously, let's consider what happens when the price level changes.

To examine price adjustment in an open economy, we must distinguish between the nominal exchange rate e and the real exchange rate ϵ, which equals eP/P^*. We can write the Mundell–Fleming model as

$$Y = C(Y - T) + I(r^*) + G + NX(\epsilon) \qquad IS^*,$$
$$M/P = L(r^*, Y) \qquad LM^*.$$

These equations should be familiar by now. The first equation describes the IS^* curve, and the second equation describes the LM^* curve. Note that net exports depend on the real exchange rate.

Figure 12-15 shows what happens when the price level falls. Because a lower price level raises the level of real money balances, the LM^* curve shifts to the right, as in panel (a) of Figure 12-15. The real exchange rate depreciates, and the equilibrium level of income rises. The aggregate demand curve summarizes this negative relationship between the price level and the level of income, as shown in panel (b) of Figure 12-15.

figure 12-15

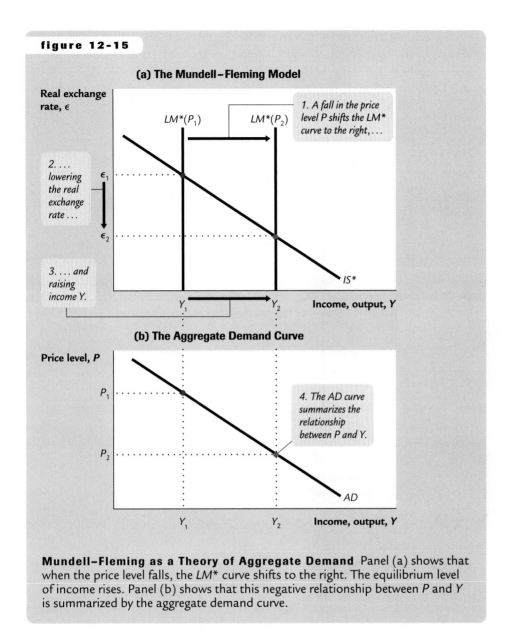

(a) The Mundell–Fleming Model

Real exchange rate, ϵ

$LM^*(P_1)$ $LM^*(P_2)$

1. A fall in the price level P shifts the LM* curve to the right, . . .

2. . . . lowering the real exchange rate . . .

ϵ_1

ϵ_2

3. . . . and raising income Y.

IS^*

Y_1 Y_2 Income, output, Y

(b) The Aggregate Demand Curve

Price level, **P**

P_1

4. The AD curve summarizes the relationship between P and Y.

P_2

AD

Y_1 Y_2 Income, output, Y

Mundell–Fleming as a Theory of Aggregate Demand Panel (a) shows that when the price level falls, the *LM** curve shifts to the right. The equilibrium level of income rises. Panel (b) shows that this negative relationship between *P* and *Y* is summarized by the aggregate demand curve.

Thus, just as the *IS–LM* model explains the aggregate demand curve in a closed economy, the Mundell–Fleming model explains the aggregate demand curve for a small open economy. In both cases, the aggregate demand curve shows the set of equilibria that arise as the price level varies. And in both cases, anything that changes the equilibrium for a given price level shifts the aggregate demand curve. Policies that raise income shift the aggregate demand curve to the right; policies that lower income shift the aggregate demand curve to the left.

We can use this diagram to show how the short-run model in this chapter is related to the long-run model in Chapter 8. Figure 12-16 shows the short-run and long-run equilibria. In both panels of the figure, point K describes the short-run equilibrium, because it assumes a fixed price level. At this equilib-

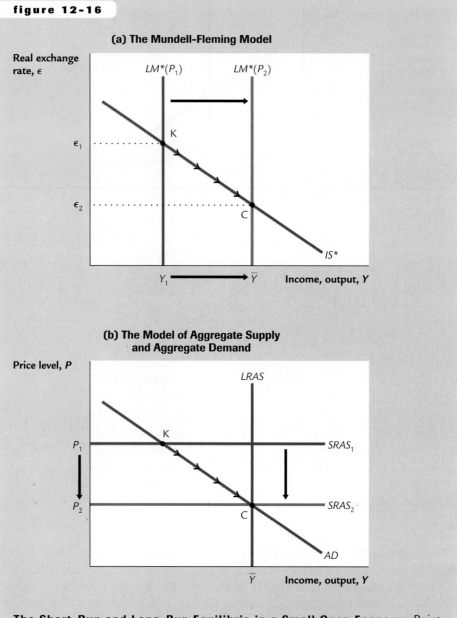

figure 12-16

(a) The Mundell-Fleming Model

Real exchange rate, ϵ

$LM^*(P_1)$ $LM^*(P_2)$

K

ϵ_1

ϵ_2

C

IS^*

Y_1 $\overline{Y}$ Income, output, Y

(b) The Model of Aggregate Supply and Aggregate Demand

Price level, **P**

LRAS

K

P_1 $SRAS_1$

P_2 $SRAS_2$

C

AD

$\overline{Y}$ Income, output, Y

The Short-Run and Long-Run Equilibria in a Small Open Economy Point K in both panels shows the equilibrium under the Keynesian assumption that the price level is fixed at P_1. Point C in both panels shows the equilibrium under the classical assumption that the price level adjusts to maintain income at its natural rate $\overline{Y}$.

Extensions to the Mundell–Fleming Model

One of the most important properties of the Mundell–Fleming model is the insulation a flexible exchange rate provides in the face of demand shocks. As we discovered in the main text of this chapter, a reduction in demand leads to a lower domestic currency, which stimulates net exports. With new jobs created in the export- and import-competing sectors—to replace those lost due to the initial drop in demand—a floating exchange rate provides the economy with an automatic stabilizer. Why is it that a number of countries are prepared to give up this automatic stabilizer? Perhaps policymakers in these countries feel that the Mundell–Fleming model is too simplified. We explore this question in this appendix by examining whether the property of insulation from demand shocks remains as the model is extended.

Three extensions are considered. First, since the exchange rate is an important determinant of the domestic price of imports, we allow the exchange rate to have a direct effect on the consumer price index (CPI). Second, we allow domestic prices and wages to be endogenous. Third, we consider endogenous exchange-rate expectations.

The Exchange Rate and the CPI

Households buy both domestically produced goods and imports. If we use P^d, P^f, and λ to denote the price of domestically produced goods, the price of foreign goods (denominated in foreign currency), and the proportion of each household budget that is devoted to domestically produced goods, the consumer price index can be written as

$$P = \lambda P^d + (1 - \lambda)P^f/e.$$

(P^f/e) is the price of imports in domestic currency units.

With respect to prices, two simplifications are involved in the Mundell–Fleming model. First, fixed prices—both at home and abroad—are assumed. This simplification involves setting $P^d = P^f = 1$. Second, the price of domestically produced goods, P^d, and the overall consumer price index, P, are assumed to be the same thing. By focusing on the formal definition of the CPI, we can see that this second simplification is inappropriate. Even with $P^d = P^f = 1$, the consumer price index is not constant. Indeed, it must change whenever the exchange rate does:

$$P = \lambda + (1 - \lambda)/e.$$

The revised model becomes

$$Y = C(Y-T) + I(r^*) + G + NX(e),$$
$$M/P = L(Y, r^*),$$
$$P = \lambda + (1 - \lambda)/e.$$

Compared to the basic Mundell–Fleming model, this extension involves the exchange rate affecting the money market. (Once the third equation is used to replace P in the LM^* equation, we can see that e becomes an important part of that relationship.) Given this complication, we must re-derive the LM^* locus. This is accomplished in Figure 12-17. There we see that, because a lower domestic currency makes imports more expensive, the CPI is higher when e is lower. As a result, the real money supply is smaller when the domestic currency falls in value, and the LM curve in panel (a) shifts to the left. The positive slope of the LM^* locus in panel (b) summarizes this outcome.

figure 12-17

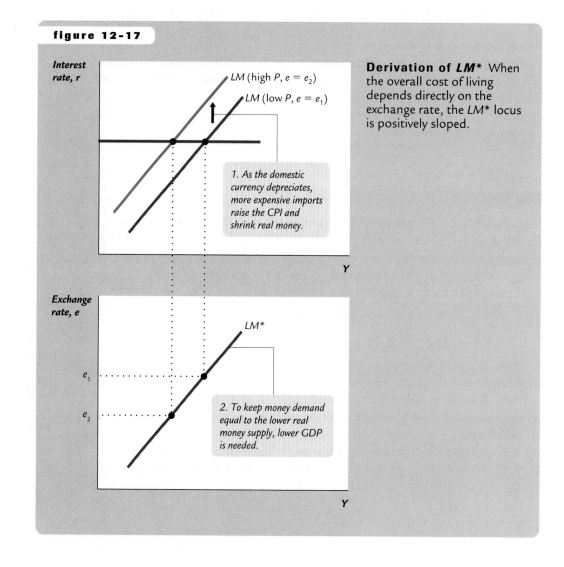

Interest rate, r

LM (high P, $e = e_2$)

LM (low P, $e = e_1$)

1. As the domestic currency depreciates, more expensive imports raise the CPI and shrink real money.

Y

Exchange rate, e

LM^*

e_1

e_2

2. To keep money demand equal to the lower real money supply, lower GDP is needed.

Y

Derivation of LM^* When the overall cost of living depends directly on the exchange rate, the LM^* locus is positively sloped.

We are now in a position to reassess the insulation property. A drop in demand—perhaps caused by lower government spending—shifts IS^* to the left as usual. The revised result is shown in Figure 12-18. With a floating exchange rate, the economy moves from A to B; with a fixed exchange rate, the central bank must move LM^* to the left and the economy moves from A to C. (Only the final outcome, not the shift in LM^*, is shown in Figure 12-18.) Since output falls in both scenarios, a floating exchange rate no longer provides complete insulation from demand shocks. Nevertheless, since the fall in output is less with a floating rate, some insulation still remains. It is important to note a second difference between the fixed- and flexible-exchange-rate cases. The CPI is not affected under fixed rates, while the CPI must rise under floating rates. This is one reason why some countries have opted for fixed exchange rates. A floating rate provides some (but reduced) insulation for real output, but that insulation is "purchased" at the expense of having to accept an increase in the general cost of living. In short, under floating rates, a decrease in spending is like an oil shock—it is *stagflationary*.

Flexible Domestic Prices

Let us continue extending the Mundell–Fleming model by letting P^d become an endogenous variable. Just to illustrate how this extension can affect the

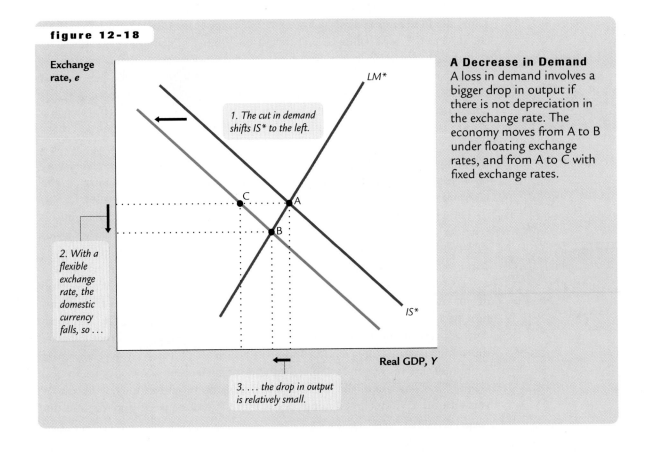

figure 12-18

Exchange rate, *e*

1. The cut in demand shifts IS^* to the left.

2. With a flexible exchange rate, the domestic currency falls, so . . .

3. . . . the drop in output is relatively small.

LM^*

IS^*

Real GDP, *Y*

A Decrease in Demand
A loss in demand involves a bigger drop in output if there is not depreciation in the exchange rate. The economy moves from A to B under floating exchange rates, and from A to C with fixed exchange rates.

model's properties, we focus on one special case. We assume that the price of domestically produced goods adjusts one-for-one with changes in wages,

$$\Delta P^d / P^d = \Delta W / W,$$

and we assume that wages adjust one-for-one with changes in the overall cost of living,

$$\Delta W / W = \Delta P / P.$$

Together, these relationships imply $\Delta P^d / P^d = \Delta P / P$. When this condition is substituted into the percentage-change version of the consumer price index,

$$(\Delta P / P) = \lambda(\Delta P^d / P^d) + (1 - \lambda)((\Delta P^f / P^f) - (\Delta e / e)),$$

we have

$$\Delta P^d / P^d = \Delta P / P = (\Delta P^f / P^f - \Delta e / e),$$

which implies that the *real* exchange rate, $e P^d / P^f$, is *constant*.

The revised *IS* relationship is

$$Y = C(Y - T) + I(r^*) + G + NX(e P^d / P^f).$$

Since the real exchange rate is fixed, the *IS** locus that follows from this relationship is *vertical,* and the effect of a drop in government spending is shown in Figure 12-19. The economy moves from point A to B under flexible exchange rates, and from A to C with a fixed rate. Since the effect on real output is the same, the insulation feature of a floating exchange rate is lost completely. While the direct effect of a falling domestic currency remains favourable (it stimulates demand for domestically produced goods), the model now contains an indirect effect that is unfavourable (the falling domestic currency raises the general cost of living, and therefore wages). Higher domestic costs make the economy less competitive. In this specific model, the direct and indirect effects of the falling dollar just cancel.

This version of the model gives even more support for those who choose a fixed exchange rate. In this case, a fixed exchange rate does not involve giving up any built-in stability, and we avoid the increase in the cost of living (which accompanies a drop in spending only in the flexible-exchange-rate case).

The choice with respect to the exchange-rate regime seems to depend on whether a country's labour-market institutions lead to sticky nominal wages or sticky real wages in the short run. In many European countries there is a synchronized annual adjustment in most nominal wage rates (and this adjustment reflects the previous year's increase in the CPI). As a result, the present version of our model seems particularly suited to European countries, and their adoption of a common currency is therefore supported by the analysis. In North America, on the other hand, many workers have wage contracts that stipulate the nominal wage for a considerable time into the future. As a result, most economists are more comfortable assuming sticky *nominal* wages, not sticky real wages, for Canada and the United States. This presumption makes the earlier version of the Mundell–Fleming model more appropriate for Canada; and this

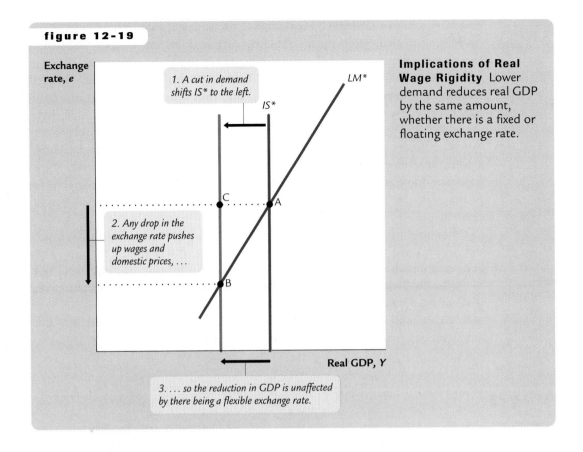

figure 12-19

Implications of Real Wage Rigidity Lower demand reduces real GDP by the same amount, whether there is a fixed or floating exchange rate.

analysis supports our decision to reject currency union with the United States (fixed exchange rates).

Exchange-Rate Expectations

To keep things relatively straightforward, let us revert to the $P^d = P^f = 1$ simplification, and concentrate instead on exchange-rate expectations. In the main text of this chapter we noted that perfect capital mobility forces the domestic interest rate to equal the foreign rate plus the risk premium:

$$r = r^* + \theta.$$

Thus far, we have limited our attention to exogenous changes in θ. The purpose of this part of the appendix is to consider θ as an endogenous variable.

We know that θ must rise whenever asset holders expect the domestic currency to fall. Since our currency does fall (under flexible exchange rates) when there is a drop in government spending, let us now add this expectation effect to our analysis of fiscal retrenchment.

We saw the outcome of a reduction in G in Figure 12-18—when there was no risk-premium effect. At least as far as avoiding part of an undesirable drop in real output is concerned, a floating exchange rate is appealing; it allows the economy to move to point B, not point C. But since well-informed individuals understand that this drop in the domestic currency will occur, they will adjust their expectations, and θ will rise accordingly. In the main text of this chapter, we learned that such a rise in θ must shift the IS^* locus to the left (since higher interest rates lower investment spending) and shift the LM^* locus to the right (since higher interest rates reduce money demand). Once these additional shifts are added (in Figure 12-20), we see that the more complete comparison of the outcomes under alternative exchange-rate regimes is a move from A to C with a fixed exchange rate, and a move from A to D under flexible rates. As is shown in the figure, point D may be just as far to the left as point C. If so, a floating rate does not operate as a built-in stabilizer with respect to real output outcomes.

Of course, these additional shifts in the IS^* and LM^* loci are only temporary, since once the exchange rate stops changing, θ will return to zero. This consideration leads many policymakers to opt for a floating exchange rate but to intervene in an ongoing fashion to smooth out the short-run variations in the exchange rate. (This is called managed floating.) But it is easy to see that such an attempt to smooth the exchange rate may backfire. To appreciate this fact, consider rewriting the interest arbitrage condition, $r = r^* + \theta$.

figure 12-20

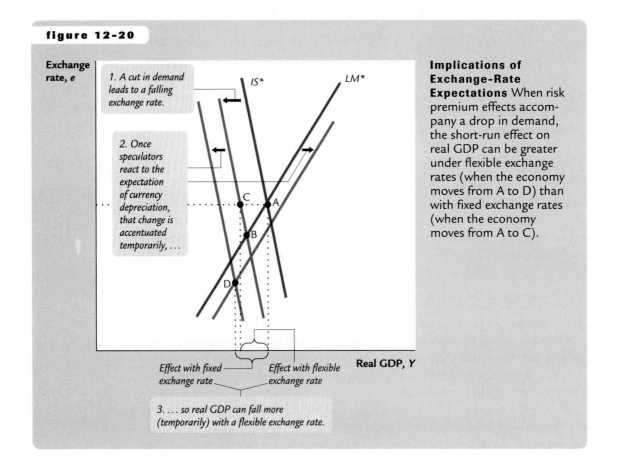

Exchange rate, e

1. A cut in demand leads to a falling exchange rate.

2. Once speculators react to the expectation of currency depreciation, that change is accentuated temporarily, ...

IS^* LM^*

Effect with fixed exchange rate   Effect with flexible exchange rate   **Real GDP, Y**

3. ... so real GDP can fall more (temporarily) with a flexible exchange rate.

Implications of Exchange-Rate Expectations When risk premium effects accompany a drop in demand, the short-run effect on real GDP can be greater under flexible exchange rates (when the economy moves from A to D) than with fixed exchange rates (when the economy moves from A to C).

Let θ be represented by the expected depreciation in the domestic currency, minus $(e - e^{\text{exp}})$, where e^{exp} stands for the expected exchange rate. Also, let the interest-rate deviation $(r^* - r)$ be represented by the random variable v. The interest-arbitrage relationship then becomes:

$$e_t = e_t^{\text{exp}} + v_t.$$

The t subscripts denote the current time period. In forming expectations about the exchange rate, it is reasonable to assume that individuals will put some weight on where they expect the exchange rate to be going (its full equilibrium value, e^*) and some weight on where the exchange rate has been (its value in the previous time period, e_{t-1}). Letting those weights be $(1 - \gamma)$ and γ, expectation formation is given by

$$e_t^{\text{exp}} = (1 - \gamma)e^* + \gamma e_{t-1}.$$

Substituting this expression into the interest arbitrage condition, we have

$$e_t = (1 - \gamma)e^* + \gamma e_{t-1} + v_t.$$

Simple examination of this relationship indicates that exchange-rate volatility is smallest when γ is zero. Suppose that the random disturbance term, v_t, is nonzero for just one period. If γ is zero, the exchange rate will be affected for just that one period. But if γ is positive, the effect of that one disturbance will last for many periods. For example, if γ is one-half, the exchange rate will still be affected by one-half of the original amount one period later, and by one-quarter of the original amount two periods later, and so on.

So low volatility in the exchange rate requires a low value of γ. But if individuals know that the central bank is smoothing the exchange rate, they have every reason to put a large weight on the previous period's value when forming expectations. Thus, the more the central bank tries to smooth the exchange rate, the more rational it is for individuals to choose a high value for γ, and the more volatile is the exchange rate after all.

This conclusion is an example of the Lucas critique (discussed in Chapter 14). Exchange-rate smoothing makes sense if the direct effect of policy on expectation formation is ignored, but not otherwise. Partly because of this ambiguity, many central banks have opted for stabilizing the rate of inflation, not the exchange rate.

An Attempt at Perspective

In a world of capital mobility, with speculators constantly on the lookout for fixed-exchange-rate promises to "test," the most credible form of fixed exchange rates is currency union. In Canada's case, this means eliminating the Canadian dollar and using the U.S. dollar as our currency. This choice was hotly debated in the media in 1999.

The main advantage of currency union is the possibility that a lower risk premium could bring lower interest rates and a higher capital/labour ratio. With the U.S. Fed pursuing roughly the same inflation rate as the Bank of

Canada, there is little basis for choice on this criterion. Without negotiation, however, Canadians would relinquish seigniorage revenue (a small consideration) and lender-of-last-resort facilities for financial crises (a significant consideration) by choosing currency union. The final issue concerns whether a separate currency imparts built-in stability to the economy. The basic answer to this question, which follows from our series of extensions to the Mundell–Fleming model, is that a floating rate does act as a buffer. This shock-absorber property is often exaggerated to a significant degree, but as long as Canada approximates what Mundell has called an "optimum currency area," it is likely that *some* of this property of flexible exchange rates will remain.

To appreciate what is meant by an optimum currency area, it is instructive to think of North America divided in two ways—first between north and south, and second between west and east. First, assume that the north produces wheat and the south produces cars. A shift in tastes (higher demand for cars and lower demand for wheat) results in inflation in the south and unemployment in the north. If there is a separate currency for the north and a floating exchange rate, a depreciating northern currency can reduce the inflation and unemployment problems. Now assume that the west produces wheat and the east produces cars. The same shift in tastes causes inflation in the east and unemployment in the west. As before, if there is a separate currency for the west, a flexible exchange rate is a substitute for factor mobility, so it can decrease the costs of adjusting to the shock.

In the first scenario, north and south are the areas for which it would be helpful to have separate currencies; in the second scenario, it is the east and west that represent optimum currency areas. The problem in North America is that—over time—the second scenario is becoming the more relevant one, while currencies are still based on our national border (north versus south). The greater this mismatch is, the less sense it makes (on short-run macroeconomic stability grounds) to maintain a separate Canadian currency. As a result, we can expect the debate on Canada's exchange-rate policy to continue. It is interesting to note that, as Mundell has contributed to the development of open-economy macroeconomics following his original model, he has argued for a return to fixed exchange rates.

MORE PROBLEMS AND APPLICATIONS

1. Explain how the imposition of a tariff by foreign governments (on our exports) affects real GDP and the overall price level (under flexible exchange rates) in each of the extended versions of the Mundell–Fleming model.

2. Explain how the imposition of a tariff by the domestic government (on our imports) affects real GDP and the overall price level (under flexible exchange rates) in each of the extended versions of the Mundell–Fleming model.

3. Explain how an increase in world interest rates affects real GDP and the overall price level (under flexible exchange rates) in each of the extended versions of the Mundell–Fleming model.

Aggregate Supply

There is always a temporary tradeoff between inflation and unemployment; there is no permanent tradeoff. The temporary tradeoff comes not from inflation per se, but from unanticipated inflation, which generally means, from a rising rate of inflation.

— *Milton Friedman*

Most economists analyze short-run fluctuations in aggregate income and the price level using the model of aggregate demand and aggregate supply. In the previous three chapters, we examined aggregate demand in some detail. The *IS–LM* model—along with its open-economy cousin the Mundell–Fleming model—shows how changes in monetary and fiscal policy and shocks to the money and goods markets shift the aggregate demand curve. In this chapter, we turn our attention to aggregate supply and develop theories that explain the position and slope of the aggregate supply curve.

When we introduced the aggregate supply curve in Chapter 9, we established that aggregate supply behaves very differently in the short run than in the long run. In the long run, prices are flexible, and the aggregate supply curve is vertical. When the aggregate supply curve is vertical, shifts in the aggregate demand curve affect the price level, but the output of the economy remains at its natural rate. By contrast, in the short run, prices are sticky, and the aggregate supply curve is not vertical. In this case, shifts in aggregate demand do cause fluctuations in output. In Chapter 9 we took a simplified view of price stickiness by drawing the short-run aggregate supply curve as a horizontal line, representing the extreme situation in which all prices are fixed. Our task now is to refine this understanding of short-run aggregate supply.

Unfortunately, one fact makes this task more difficult: economists disagree about how best to explain aggregate supply. As a result, this chapter begins by presenting four prominent models of the short-run aggregate supply curve. Among economists, each of these models has some prominent adherents (as well as some prominent critics), and you can decide for yourself which you find most plausible. Although these models differ in some significant details, they are also related in an important way: they share a common theme about what makes the short-run and long-run aggregate supply curves differ and a common conclusion that the short-run aggregate supply curve is upward sloping.

After examining the models, we investigate an implication of the short-run aggregate supply curve. We show that this curve implies a tradeoff between two measures of economic performance—inflation and unemployment. According to this tradeoff, to reduce the rate of inflation policymakers must temporarily raise unemployment, and to reduce unemployment they must accept higher inflation. As the quotation at the beginning of the chapter suggests, the tradeoff between inflation and unemployment is only temporary. One goal of this chapter is to explain why policymakers face such a tradeoff in the short run and, just as important, why they do not face it in the long run.

13-1 | Four Models of Aggregate Supply

Classes in physics often begin by assuming away the existence of friction, but no good engineer would ever take this assumption as a literal description of how the world works. Similarly, this book began with classical macroeconomic theory, but it would be a mistake to assume that this model is true in all circumstances. Our job now is to look more deeply into the "frictions" of macroeconomics.

We do this by examining four prominent models of aggregate supply, roughly in the order of their development. In all the models, some market imperfection (that is, some type of friction) causes the output of the economy to deviate from the classical benchmark. As a result, the short-run aggregate supply curve is upward sloping, rather than vertical, and shifts in the aggregate demand curve cause the level of output to deviate temporarily from the natural rate. These temporary deviations represent the booms and busts of the business cycle.

Although each of the four models takes us down a different theoretical route, each route ends up in the same place. That final destination is a short-run aggregate supply equation of the form

$$Y = \overline{Y} + \alpha(P - P^e), \qquad \alpha > 0,$$

where Y is output, $\overline{Y}$ is the natural rate of output, P is the price level, and P^e is the expected price level. This equation states that output deviates from its natural rate when the price level deviates from the expected price level. The parameter α indicates how much output responds to unexpected changes in the price level; $1/\alpha$ is the slope of the aggregate supply curve.

Each of the four models tells a different story about what lies behind this short-run aggregate supply equation. In other words, each highlights a particular reason why unexpected movements in the price level are associated with fluctuations in aggregate output.

The Sticky-Wage Model

To explain why the short-run aggregate supply curve is upward sloping, many economists stress the sluggish adjustment of nominal wages. In many industries,

figure 13-3

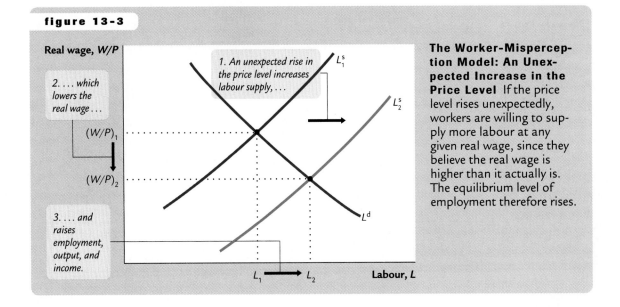

Real wage, W/P

2. ... which lowers the real wage ...

$(W/P)_1$

$(W/P)_2$

3. ... and raises employment, output, and income.

1. An unexpected rise in the price level increases labour supply, ...

L_1^s

L_2^s

L^d

$L_1 \longrightarrow L_2$ Labour, L

The Worker-Misperception Model: An Unexpected Increase in the Price Level If the price level rises unexpectedly, workers are willing to supply more labour at any given real wage, since they believe the real wage is higher than it actually is. The equilibrium level of employment therefore rises.

CASE STUDY

The Cyclical Behaviour of the Real Wage

In any model with an unchanging labour demand curve, such as the two models we have just discussed, employment rises when the real wage falls. In the sticky-wage and worker-misperception models, an unexpected rise in the price level lowers the real wage and thereby raises the quantity of labour hired and the amount of output produced. Thus, the real wage should be *countercyclical*: it should fluctuate in the opposite direction from employment and output. Keynes himself wrote in *The General Theory* that "an increase in employment can only occur to the accompaniment of a decline in the rate of real wages."

The earliest attacks on *The General Theory* came from economists challenging Keynes's prediction. Figure 13-4 is a scatterplot of the percentage change in average weekly earnings (measured in real terms) and the percentage change in real GDP using annual data for Canada. If Keynes's prediction were correct, this figure would show a clear negative relationship. Yet it shows only a weak correlation between the real wage and output. Indeed, almost as often as not, the year-to-year changes in the observations in this scatterplot show both variables moving up and down together—implying that the real wage is often *procyclical*. In many periods, then, abnormally high labour costs cannot explain the low employment and output observed in recessions.

How should we interpret this evidence? Most economists conclude that the sticky-wage and worker-misperception models cannot, by themselves, fully explain aggregate supply. They advocate models in which the labour demand curve shifts over the business cycle. These shifts may arise because firms have sticky prices and cannot sell all they want at those prices; we discuss this

figure 13-4

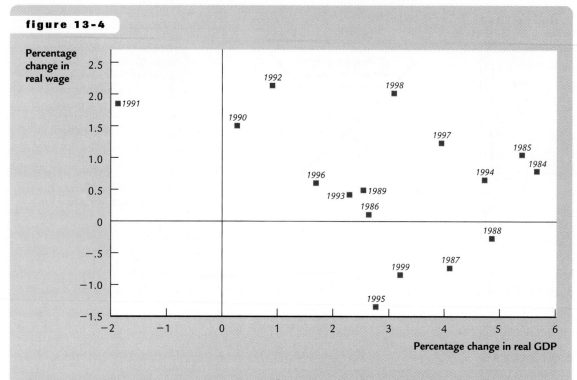

The Cyclical Behavior of the Real Wage This scatterplot shows the percentage change in real GDP and the percentage change in the real wage (measured here as average weekly earnings—industrial aggregate—deflated by the GDP deflator). As output fluctuates, the real wage often moves in the same direction. That is, the real wage is somewhat procyclical. This observation is inconsistent with the sticky-wage and worker-misperception models. CANSIM Series L57711, D15612, D20463.

possibility below. Alternatively, the labour demand curve may shift because of shocks to technology, which alter labour productivity. The theory we discuss in Chapter 19, called the theory of real business cycles, gives a prominent role to technology shocks as a source of economic fluctuations.[3]

The Imperfect-Information Model

The third explanation for the upward slope of the short-run aggregate supply curve, the **imperfect-information model,** again assumes that markets clear

[3] For some of the recent work on the cyclical behavior of the real wage, see Mark J. Bils, "Real Wages Over the Business Cycle: Evidence From Panel Data," *Journal of Political Economy* 93 (1985): 666–689; Scott Sumner and Stephen Silver, "Real Wages, Employment, and the Phillips Curve," *Journal of Political Economy* 97 (June 1989): 706–720; and Gary Solon, Robert Barsky, and Jonathan A. Parker, "Measuring the Cyclicality of Real Wages: How Important Is Composition Bias?" *Quarterly Journal of Economics* 109 (February 1994): 1–25.

figure 13-7

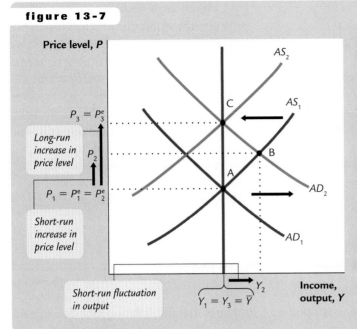

How Shifts in Aggregate Demand Lead to Short-Run Fluctuations Here the economy begins in a long-run equilibrium, point A. When aggregate demand increases unexpectedly, the price level rises from P_1 to P_2. Because the price level P_2 is above the expected price level P_2^e, output rises temporarily above the natural rate, as the economy moves along the short-run aggregate supply curve from point A to point B. In the long run, the expected price level rises to P_3^e, causing the short-run aggregate supply curve to shift upward. The economy returns to a new long-run equilibrium, point C, where output is back at its natural rate.

of the economy moves from point B to point C. The actual price level rises from P_2 to P_3, and output falls from Y_2 to Y_3. In other words, the economy returns to the natural level of output in the long run, but at a much higher price level.

This analysis shows an important principle, which holds for each of the four models of aggregate supply: long-run monetary neutrality and short-run monetary *nonneutrality* are perfectly compatible. Short-run nonneutrality is represented here by the movement from point A to point B, and long-run monetary neutrality is represented by the movement from point A to point C. We reconcile the short-run and long-run effects of money by emphasizing the adjustment of expectations about the price level.

13-2 | Inflation, Unemployment, and the Phillips Curve

Two goals of economic policymakers are low inflation and low unemployment, but often these goals conflict. Suppose, for instance, that policymakers were to use monetary or fiscal policy to expand aggregate demand. This policy would move the economy along the short-run aggregate supply curve to a point of higher output and a higher price level. (Figure 13-7 shows this as the change from point A to point B.) Higher output means lower unemployment, because firms need more workers when they produce more. A higher price level, given the previous year's price level, means higher inflation. Thus, when policymakers move the economy up along the short-run aggregate supply curve, they reduce the unemployment rate and raise the inflation rate. Conversely, when they contract aggregate demand and move the economy down the short-run aggregate supply curve, unemployment rises and inflation falls.

This tradeoff between inflation and unemployment, called the *Phillips curve,* is our topic in this section. As we have just seen (and will derive more formally in a moment), the Phillips curve is a reflection of the short-run aggregate supply curve: as policymakers move the economy along the short-run aggregate supply curve, unemployment and inflation move in opposite directions. The Phillips curve is a useful way to express aggregate supply because inflation and unemployment are such important measures of economic performance.

Deriving the Phillips Curve From the Aggregate Supply Curve

The **Phillips curve** in its modern form states that the inflation rate depends on three forces:

➤ Expected inflation

➤ The deviation of unemployment from the natural rate, called cyclical unemployment

➤ Supply shocks.

These three forces are expressed in the following equation:

$$\pi = \pi^e - \beta(u - u^n) + v$$

$$\text{Inflation} = \frac{\text{Expected}}{\text{Inflation}} - \left(\beta \times \frac{\text{Cyclical}}{\text{Unemployment}}\right) + \frac{\text{Supply}}{\text{Shock,}}$$

where β is a parameter measuring the response of inflation to cyclical unemployment. Notice that there is a minus sign before the cyclical unemployment term: high unemployment tends to reduce inflation. This equation summarizes the relationship between inflation and unemployment.

Where does this equation for the Phillips curve come from? Although it may not seem familiar, we can derive it from our equation for aggregate supply. To see how, write the aggregate supply equation as

$$P = P^e + (1/\alpha)(Y - \overline{Y}).$$

With one addition, one subtraction, and one substitution, we can manipulate this equation to yield a relationship between inflation and unemployment.

Here are the three steps. First, add to the right-hand side of the equation a supply shock v to represent exogenous events (such as a change in world oil prices) that alter the price level and shift the short-run aggregate supply curve:

$$P = P^e + (1/\alpha)(Y - \overline{Y}) + v.$$

Next, to go from the price level to inflation rates, subtract last year's price level P_{-1} from both sides of the equation to obtain

$$(P - P_{-1}) = (P^e - P_{-1}) + (1/\alpha)(Y - \overline{Y}) + \nu.$$

The term on the left-hand side, $P - P_{-1}$, is the difference between the current price level and last year's price level, which is inflation π.[9] The term on the right-hand side, $P^e - P_{-1}$, is the difference between the expected price level and last year's price level, which is expected inflation π^e. Therefore, we can replace $P - P_{-1}$ with π and $P^e - P_{-1}$ with π^e:

$$\pi = \pi^e + (1/\alpha)(Y - \overline{Y}) + \nu.$$

Third, to go from output to unemployment, recall from Chapter 2 that Okun's law gives a relationship between these two variables. One version of Okun's law states that the deviation of output from its natural rate is inversely related to the deviation of unemployment from its natural rate; that is, when output is higher than the natural rate of output, unemployment is lower than the natural rate of unemployment. We can write this as

$$(1/\alpha)(Y - \overline{Y}) = -\beta(u - u^n).$$

---

f y i

THE HISTORY OF THE MODERN PHILLIPS CURVE

The Phillips curve is named after New Zealand-born economist A. W. Phillips. In 1958 Phillips observed a negative relationship between the unemployment rate and the rate of wage inflation in data for the United Kingdom.[10] The Phillips curve that economists use today differs in three ways from the relationship Phillips examined.

First, the modern Phillips curve substitutes price inflation for wage inflation. This difference is not crucial, because price inflation and wage inflation are closely related. In periods when wages are rising quickly, prices are rising quickly as well.

Second, the modern Phillips curve includes expected inflation. This addition is due to the work of Milton Friedman and Edmund Phelps. In developing the worker-misperception model in the 1960s, these two economists emphasized the importance of expectations for aggregate supply.

Third, the modern Phillips curve includes supply shocks. Credit for this addition goes to OPEC, the Organization of Petroleum Exporting Countries. In the 1970s OPEC caused large increases in the world price of oil, which made economists more aware of the importance of shocks to aggregate supply.

---

[9] *Mathematical note:* This statement is not precise, because inflation is really the *percentage* change in the price level. To make the statement more precise, interpret P as the logarithm of the price level. By the properties of logarithms, the change in P is roughly the inflation rate. The reason is that $dP = d(\log \text{price level}) = d(\text{price level})/\text{price level}$.

[10] A. W. Phillips, "The Relationship Between Unemployment and the Rate of Change of Money Wages in the United Kingdom, 1861–1957," *Economica* 25 (November 1958): 283–299.

Using this Okun's law relationship, we can substitute $-\beta(u - u^n)$ for $(1/\alpha)$ $(Y - \bar{Y})$ in the previous equation to obtain:

$$\pi = \pi^e - \beta(u - u^n) + \nu.$$

Thus, we can derive the Phillips curve equation from the aggregate supply equation.

All this algebra is meant to show one thing: the Phillips curve equation and the short-run aggregate supply equation represent essentially the same macroeconomic ideas. In particular, both equations show a link between real and nominal variables that causes the classical dichotomy (the theoretical separation of real and nominal variables) to break down in the short run. According to the short-run aggregate supply equation, output is related to unexpected movements in the price level. According to the Phillips curve equation, unemployment is related to unexpected movements in the inflation rate. The aggregate supply curve is more convenient when we are studying output and the price level, whereas the Phillips curve is more convenient when we are studying unemployment and inflation. But we should not lose sight of the fact that the Phillips curve and the aggregate supply curve are merely two sides of the same coin.

Adaptive Expectations and Inflation Inertia

To make the Phillips curve useful for analyzing the choices facing policymakers, we need to say what determines expected inflation. A simple and often plausible assumption is that people form their expectations of inflation based on recently observed inflation. This assumption is called **adaptive expectations.** For example, suppose that people expect prices to rise this year at the same rate as they did last year. Then expected inflation π^e equals last year's inflation π_{-1}:

$$\pi^e = \pi_{-1}.$$

In this case, we can write the Phillips curve as

$$\pi = \pi_{-1} - \beta(u - u^n) + \nu,$$

which states that inflation depends on past inflation, cyclical unemployment, and a supply shock.

The first term in this form of the Phillips curve, π_{-1}, implies that inflation has inertia. That is, like an object moving through space, inflation keeps going unless something acts to stop it. In particular, if unemployment is at its natural rate and if there are no supply shocks, the price level will continue to rise at the rate it has been rising. This inertia arises because past inflation influences expectations of future inflation and because these expectations influence the wages and prices that people set. Robert Solow captured the concept of inflation inertia well when, during the high inflation of the 1970s, he wrote, "Why is our money ever less valuable? Perhaps it is simply that we have inflation because we expect inflation, and we expect inflation because we've had it."

In the model of aggregate supply and aggregate demand, inflation inertia is interpreted as persistent upward shifts in both the aggregate supply curve and the aggregate demand curve. Consider first aggregate supply. If prices have been rising quickly, people will expect them to continue to rise quickly. Because the position of the short-run aggregate supply curve depends on the expected price level, the short-run aggregate supply curve will shift upward over time. It will continue to shift upward until some event, such as a recession or a supply shock, changes inflation and thereby changes expectations of inflation.

The aggregate demand curve must also shift upward to confirm the expectations of inflation. Most often, the continued rise in aggregate demand is due to persistent growth in the money supply. If the Bank of Canada suddenly halted money growth, aggregate demand would stabilize, and the upward shift in aggregate supply would cause a recession. The high unemployment in the recession would reduce inflation and expected inflation, causing inflation inertia to subside.

Two Causes of Rising and Falling Inflation

The second and third terms in the Phillips curve equation show the two forces that can change the rate of inflation.

The second term, $\beta(u - u^n)$, shows that cyclical unemployment—the deviation of unemployment from its natural rate—exerts upward or downward pressure on inflation. Low unemployment pulls the inflation rate up. This is called **demand-pull inflation** because high aggregate demand is responsible for this type of inflation. High unemployment pulls the inflation rate down. The parameter β measures how responsive inflation is to cyclical unemployment.

The third term, ν, shows that inflation also rises and falls because of supply shocks. An adverse supply shock, such as the rise in world oil prices in the 1970s, implies a positive value of ν and causes inflation to rise. This is called **cost-push inflation** because adverse supply shocks are typically events that push up the costs of production. A beneficial supply shock, such as the oil glut that led to a fall in oil prices in the 1980s, makes ν negative and causes inflation to fall.

The Short-Run Tradeoff Between Inflation and Unemployment

Consider the options the Phillips curve gives to a policymaker who can influence aggregate demand with monetary or fiscal policy. At any moment, expected inflation and supply shocks are beyond the policymaker's immediate control. Yet, by changing aggregate demand, the policymaker can alter output, unemployment, and inflation. The policymaker can expand aggregate demand to lower unemployment and raise inflation. Or the policymaker can depress aggregate demand to raise unemployment and lower inflation.

Figure 13-8 plots the Phillips curve equation and shows the short-run tradeoff between inflation and unemployment. The policymaker can manipulate aggregate demand to choose a combination of inflation and unemployment on this curve, called the *short-run Phillips curve*.

figure 13-8

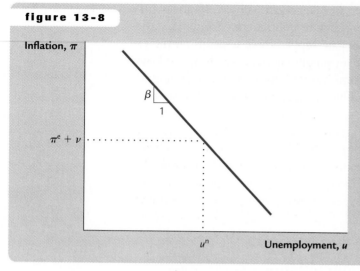

The Short-Run Tradeoff Between Inflation and Unemployment In the short run, there is a negative relationship between inflation and unemployment. At any point in time, a policymaker who controls aggregate demand can choose a combination of inflation and unemployment on this short-run Phillips curve.

Notice that the position of the short-run Phillips curve depends on the expected rate of inflation. If expected inflation rises, the curve shifts upward, and the policymaker's tradeoff becomes less favourable: inflation is higher for any level of unemployment. Figure 13-9 shows how the tradeoff depends on expected inflation.

Because people adjust their expectations of inflation over time, the tradeoff between inflation and unemployment holds only in the short run. The policymaker cannot keep inflation above expected inflation (and thus unemployment below its natural rate) forever. Eventually, expectations adapt to whatever inflation rate the policymaker has chosen. In the long run, the classical dichotomy

figure 13-9

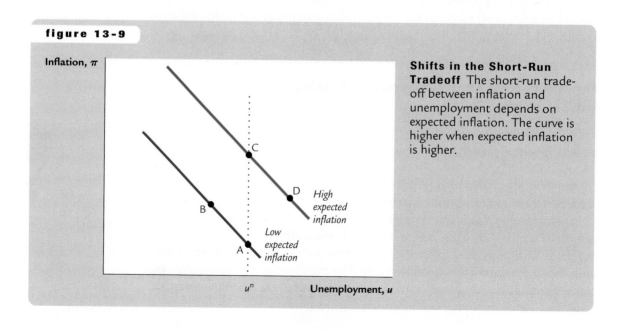

Shifts in the Short-Run Tradeoff The short-run tradeoff between inflation and unemployment depends on expected inflation. The curve is higher when expected inflation is higher.

holds, unemployment returns to its natural rate, and there is no tradeoff between inflation and unemployment.

To follow this process explicitly, assume that the economy is initially at point A in Figure 13-9—a point at which actual and expected inflation coincide. Then, assume that expansionary monetary or fiscal policy is used to move the economy from point A to point B. The short-run tradeoff is operating; there are lower unemployment and higher inflation. But the economy cannot stay at point B since it involves actual inflation being greater than peoples' expectations of inflation. As individuals revise their expectations upward, there is a tendency for the point showing the economy's outcome to move up in Figure 13-9. Often, in this situation, the government begins to contract aggregate demand—now that it realizes that the inflationary consequences of its previous policy are larger than first assumed. This reaction creates a tendency for the point showing the economy's outcome to move back to the right in Figure 13-9. The net effect of these two tendencies—the upward revision in inflationary expectations and the backing off of aggregate demand policy—is an upward-sloping move from point B to point C. At this stage, there is not a tradeoff; both unemployment and inflation are rising.

Point C is sustainable in the long run. Unemployment has returned to the natural rate and actual and expected inflation are consistent (they are both high). When the government wants to fight inflation, contractionary monetary and fiscal policy move the outcome from point C to point D. Again we see a short-run tradeoff—inflation falling but unemployment rising. But because actual inflation is less than expected inflation at point D, expectations are revised down. The economy spends a long time at point D if people are slow to adjust expectations, and there will be a significant sacrifice involved in fighting inflation—a prolonged period of high unemployment.

CASE STUDY

Inflation and Unemployment in Canada

Figure 13-10 depicts the history of inflation and unemployment in Canada since 1956. We see that the pre-1970 observations (all squares without a date label) are well summarized by the negatively sloped Phillips curve. During this period, there were few large supply shocks, and the government never allowed aggregate demand to expand so much that a sustained inflation developed. As a result, inflationary expectations played little role.

Then, in the 1970s, things changed. The large supply shock of the OPEC oil-price increases and the government's shift to more expansionary monetary and fiscal policy caused inflation to shoot up with little reduction in unemployment. The time path for the early 1970s is shown by the upward-pointing arrows in Figure 13-10. In the later 1970s, aggregate demand policy was tightened somewhat, and wage and price controls were imposed for the 1975–1978 period. As a result, the economy slid down its short-run Phillips curve; but with inflationary expectations much higher by then, that short-run Phillips curve was farther out from the origin than the earlier one.

figure 13-10

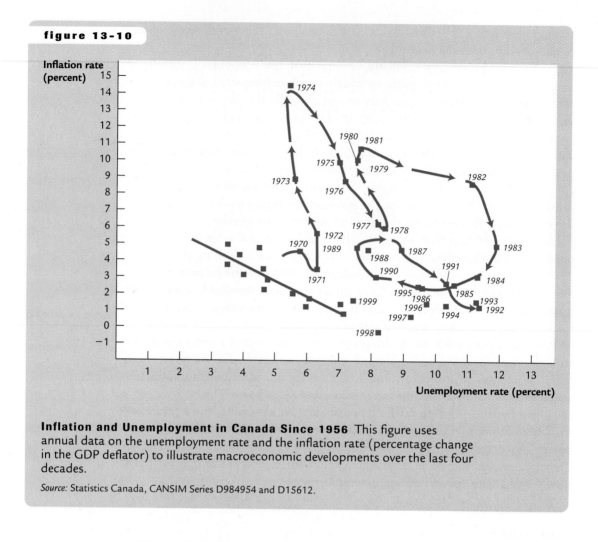

Inflation and Unemployment in Canada Since 1956 This figure uses annual data on the unemployment rate and the inflation rate (percentage change in the GDP deflator) to illustrate macroeconomic developments over the last four decades.

Source: Statistics Canada, CANSIM Series D984954 and D15612.

The second OPEC shock occurred in 1979. Again, given that demand policy was used to try to insulate unemployment from this event, inflation shot up (see the second set of arrows pointing up in Figure 13-10). By 1981, concern about high inflation peaked, and the Bank of Canada embarked on an enthusiastic disinflation. The contractionary monetary policy pushed the economy down its short-run Phillips curve once again (see the arrows that are farthest to the right in Figure 13-10). But, after two bouts of high inflation, inflationary expectations had ratcheted up to very high levels. As a result the short-run Phillips curve was even farther out from the origin.

Both actual and expected inflation came down during the 1981–1985 period. Perhaps because the inflation problem had become less severe, there was a partial reverse of policy in the 1986–1990 period, so unemployment fell and inflation started rising again. The arrows for this period in Figure 13-10 indicate that Canada's short-run Phillips curve had returned part of the way back toward the origin by then (and this is consistent with the fact that lower inflationary expectations had become widespread by then).

Finally, beginning in 1990, the second contractionary monetary policy was initiated. Again, inflation dropped quite dramatically, while unemployment was pushed higher again. By 1993, the battle against inflation had been won, but it took the remainder of the decade for unemployment to come down significantly. The modern Phillips curve (augmented by supply shocks and inflationary expectations) is a very useful vehicle for interpreting Canada's unemployment and inflation experience of the last 45 years.

Disinflation and the Sacrifice Ratio

Imagine an economy in which unemployment is at its natural rate and inflation is running at 6 percent. What would happen to unemployment and output if the central bank pursued a policy to reduce inflation from 6 to 2 percent?

The Phillips curve shows that in the absence of a beneficial supply shock, lowering inflation requires a period of high unemployment and reduced output. But by how much and for how long would unemployment need to rise above the natural rate? Before deciding whether to reduce inflation, policymakers must know how much output would be lost during the transition to lower inflation. This cost can then be compared with the benefits of lower inflation.

Much research has used the available data to examine the Phillips curve quantitatively. The results of these studies are often summarized in a number called the **sacrifice ratio,** the percentage of a year's real GDP that must be forgone to reduce inflation by 1 percentage point. Estimates of the sacrifice ratio vary substantially—between 2 percent and 5 percent. These estimates mean that, for every percentage point that inflation is to fall, something between 2 percent and 5 percent of one year's GDP must be sacrificed.[11]

We can also express the sacrifice ratio in terms of unemployment. Okun's law says that a change of 1 percentage point in the unemployment rate translates into a change of 2 percentage points in GDP. Therefore, reducing inflation by 1 percentage point requires between 1 percentage point and 2.5 percentage points of cyclical unemployment.

We can use the midrange values for the sacrifice ratio to estimate by how much and for how long unemployment must rise to reduce inflation. If reducing inflation by 1 percentage point requires a sacrifice of 3.5 percent of a year's GDP, reducing inflation by 4 percentage points requires a sacrifice of 14 percent of a year's GDP. Equivalently, this reduction in inflation requires a sacrifice of 7 percentage points of cyclical unemployment.

This disinflation could take various forms, each totaling the same sacrifice of 14 percent of a year's GDP. For example, a rapid disinflation would lower out-

---

[11] Barry Cozier and G. Wilkinson, *Some Evidence on Hysteresis and the Costs of Disinflation in Canada,* Technical Report No. 55 (Ottawa: Bank of Canada, 1991); William M. Scarth, "Fighting Inflation: Are the Costs of Getting to Zero Too High?," in Robert C. York, ed., *Taking Aim: The Debate on Zero Inflation,* Study No. 10 (Toronto: C.D. Howe Institute, 1990): 81–103.

put by 7 percent for 2 years: this is sometimes called the *cold-turkey* solution to inflation. A gradual disinflation would depress output by 2 percent for 7 years.

Rational Expectations and the Possibility of Painless Disinflation

Because the expectation of inflation influences the short-run tradeoff between inflation and unemployment, it is crucial to understand how people form expectations. So far, we have been assuming that expected inflation depends on recently observed inflation. Although this assumption of adaptive expectations is plausible, it is probably too simple to apply in all circumstances.

An alternative approach is to assume that people have **rational expectations.** That is, we might assume that people optimally use all the available information, including information about current government policies, to forecast the future. Because monetary and fiscal policies influence inflation, expected inflation should also depend on the monetary and fiscal policies in effect. According to the theory of rational expectations, a change in monetary or fiscal policy will change expectations, and an evaluation of any policy change must incorporate this effect on expectations. If people do form their expectations rationally, then inflation may have less inertia than it first appears.

Here is how Thomas Sargent, a prominent advocate of rational expectations, describes its implications for the Phillips curve:

An alternative "rational expectations" view denies that there is any inherent momentum to the present process of inflation. This view maintains that firms and workers have now come to expect high rates of inflation in the future and that they strike inflationary bargains in light of these expectations. However, it is held that people expect high rates of inflation in the future precisely because the government's current and prospective monetary and fiscal policies warrant those expectations. . . . Thus inflation only seems to have a momentum of its own; it is actually the long-term government policy of persistently running large deficits and creating money at high rates which imparts the momentum to the inflation rate. An implication of this view is that inflation can be stopped much more quickly than advocates of the "momentum" view have indicated and that their estimates of the length of time and the costs of stopping inflation in terms of foregone output are erroneous. . . . [Stopping inflation] would require a change in the policy regime: there must be an abrupt change in the continuing government policy, or strategy, for setting deficits now and in the future that is sufficiently binding as to be widely believed. . . . How costly such a move would be in terms of foregone output and how long it would be in taking effect would depend partly on how resolute and evident the government's commitment was.[12]

Thus, advocates of rational expectations argue that the short-run Phillips curve does not accurately represent the options that policymakers have available. They believe that if policymakers are credibly committed to reducing inflation, rational people will understand the commitment and will quickly lower

---

[12] Thomas J. Sargent, "The Ends of Four Big Inflations," in Robert E. Hall, ed., *Inflation: Causes and Effects* (Chicago: University of Chicago Press, 1982).

their expectations of inflation. Inflation can then come down without a rise in unemployment and fall in output. According to the theory of rational expectations, traditional estimates of the sacrifice ratio are not useful for evaluating the impact of alternative policies. Under a credible policy, the costs of reducing inflation may be much lower than estimates of the sacrifice ratio suggest.

In the most extreme case, one can imagine reducing the rate of inflation without causing any recession at all. A painless disinflation has two requirements. First, the plan to reduce inflation must be announced before the workers and firms who set wages and prices have formed their expectations. Second, the workers and firms must believe the announcement; otherwise, they will not reduce their expectations of inflation. If both requirements are met, the announcement will immediately shift the short-run tradeoff between inflation and unemployment downward, permitting a lower rate of inflation without higher unemployment.

Although the rational-expectations approach remains controversial, almost all economists agree that expectations of inflation influence the short-run tradeoff between inflation and unemployment. The credibility of a policy to reduce inflation is therefore one determinant of how costly the policy will be. Unfortunately, it is often difficult to predict whether the public will view the announcement of a new policy as credible. The central role of expectations makes forecasting the results of alternative policies far more difficult.

CASE STUDY

The Sacrifice Ratio in Practice

The Phillips curve with adaptive expectations implies that reducing inflation requires a period of high unemployment and low output. By contrast, the rational-expectations approach suggests that reducing inflation can be much less costly. What happens during actual disinflations?

Consider the Canadian disinflation in the 1980s. This decade began with inflation over 10 percent. Yet because of the tight monetary policies pursued by the Bank of Canada, the rate of inflation fell substantially in the first few years of the decade. This episode provides a natural experiment with which to estimate how much output is lost during the process of disinflation.

The first question is, how much did inflation fall? As measured by the GDP deflator, inflation reached a peak of 10.8 percent in 1981 and then hit a low of 2.5 percent by the end of 1985. Thus, we can estimate that the Bank of Canada engineered a reduction in inflation of 8.3 points over four years.

The second question is, how much output was lost during this period? Table 13-1 shows the unemployment rate from 1982 to 1985. Assuming that the natural rate of unemployment was 8.5 percent (see Figure 6-1), we can compute the amount of cyclical unemployment in each year. In total over this period, there were 11.5 point-years of cyclical unemployment. Okun's law says that 1 percentage point of unemployment implies 2 percentage points of GDP. Therefore, 22 percentage points of annual GDP were lost during the disinflation.

table 13-1

Unemployment During the Disinflation of the 1980s

Year	Unemployment Rate	Natural Rate	Cyclical Unemployment
1982	11.0%	8.5%	2.5%
1983	11.8	8.5	3.3
1984	11.2	8.5	3.7
1985	10.5	8.5	2.0
		Total	11.5%

Now we can compute the sacrifice ratio for this episode. We know that 22 percentage points of GDP were lost, and that inflation fell by 8.3 percentage points. Hence, 22/8.3, or 2.7, percentage points of GDP were lost for each percentage-point reduction in inflation. The estimate of the sacrifice ratio from the disinflation of the 1980s is 2.7.

This estimate of the sacrifice ratio is at the low end of the estimates made before this episode. Why is it that inflation was reduced at a smaller cost than many economists had predicted? One explanation is that the contractionary monetary policy of the early 1980s was far more dramatic than the earlier less-concerted attempts to reduce inflation. Perhaps the Bank of Canada's tough stand was credible enough to influence expectations of inflation directly. Yet the change in expectations was not large enough to make the disinflation painless: in 1983 unemployment reached its highest level since the Great Depression.

Another interpretation of our estimate of the sacrifice ratio is that it is a miscalculation. In the three years previous to the disinflation policy, the unemployment rate was 7.5 percent, and this value was what most Canadian economists (including those working at the Bank of Canada) had been estimating the natural unemployment rate to be back then. If we change the third column of Table 13-1 to a series of 7.5 percent entries, instead of a column of 8.5 percent entries, the total point-years of cyclical unemployment over this period rises from 11.5 percent to 15.5 percent. The estimated sacrifice ratio jumps to 3.7 percent, not 2.7 percent. Furthermore, since unemployment did not return to 7.5 percent until 1989, it can be argued that the cyclical unemployment in the 1986–1988 period should also be attributed to the disinflation policy. During the 1986–1988 years there was an additional 3.6 point-years of cyclical unemployment, and counting this additional excess capacity boosts the overall sacrifice ratio to 4.6. Thus, disinflation is seen as much more costly if a lower estimate of the natural unemployment rate is used in the calculations.

Which estimate of the natural rate is more credible? A glance back at Figure 6-1 suggests that the natural rate *did* rise form 7.5 percent to 8.5 percent over this period. But the important issue is *why*. If this rise is due to such things as increased generosity of the employment-insurance system, as some believe, then our first estimate of the sacrifice ratio using the 8.5 percent natural rate is the better one. But if the natural unemployment rate rose *only because* the actual unemployment rate did, then our second estimate of the sacrifice ratio is more accurate.

The possibility that the natural rate could depend on the actual rate is discussed more fully in the next section of this chapter. It remains a controversial topic of current research. At this point, economists must simply admit that their estimates of the sacrifice ratio are not pinned down with a great degree of accuracy.

Another controversy concerning estimates of the sacrifice ratio stems from the fact that the contractionary monetary policy in the early 1980s forced the federal government's debt–GDP ratio to rise dramatically in the latter half of the 1980s. By raising interest rates, the Bank of Canada magnified the government's debt service payment obligations, and by slowing economic growth the Bank cut government revenues. Both these developments increased the budget deficit. Since unemployment then had to be pushed up during the 1990s, as contractionary fiscal policy was used to eliminate the deficit, it can be argued that some of this excess unemployment should be attributed to the disinflation. Allowing for this, the estimated sacrifice ratio is very large.

Although the Canadian disinflation of the 1980s is only one historical episode, this kind of analysis can be applied to other disinflations. A recent study documented the results of 65 disinflations in 19 countries. In almost all these episodes, the reduction in inflation came at the cost of temporarily lower output. Yet the size of the output loss varied from episode to episode. Rapid disinflations usually had smaller sacrifice ratios than slower ones. That is, in contrast to what the Phillips curve with adaptive expectations suggests, a cold-turkey approach appears less costly than a gradual one. Moreover, countries with more flexible wage-setting institutions, such as shorter labour contracts, had smaller sacrifice ratios. These findings indicate that reducing inflation always has some cost, but that policies and institutions can affect its magnitude.[13]

Challenges to the Natural-Rate Hypothesis

Our discussion of the cost of disinflation—and indeed our entire discussion of economic fluctuations in the past four chapters—has been based on an assumption called the **natural-rate hypothesis.** This hypothesis is summarized in the following statement:

> *Fluctuations in aggregate demand affect output and employment only in the short run. In the long run, the economy returns to the levels of output, employment, and unemployment described by the classical model.*

The natural-rate hypothesis allows macroeconomists to study separately short-run and long-run developments in the economy. It is one expression of the classical dichotomy.

Recently, three challenges have been posed for the natural-rate hypothesis. First, it has been pointed out that the observations on inflation and unemploy-

---

[13] Laurence Ball, "What Determines the Sacrifice Ratio?" in N. Gregory Mankiw, ed., *Monetary Policy* (Chicago: University of Chicago Press, 1994).

ment in the 1990s are, at first blush, puzzling when interpreted within this model. In Canada, for example, by 1993, inflation was essentially a constant at about 1.5–2.0 percent. Surely, argue the critics, in such a situation, expectations of inflation must have settled at about this same number without too much of a time lag. If so, the natural-rate model implies that the observed unemployment rate must be the natural rate. But since Canada's unemployment rate remained above 9 percent until 1998, this reasoning means that Canada's natural rate was this very high number for much of the decade. Since few economists can think of structural reasons why this should be so, the natural-rate hypothesis seems to be threatened.

We should not be too quick to jump to this conclusion, however. After all, for simplicity's sake, our derivation of the expectations-augmented Phillips curve has abstracted from open-economy considerations. Let us briefly indicate how things change when this simplification is not involved. In a closed-economy model, with labour as the only variable factor in the short run, markup pricing involves prices rising by the same amount as wages: $\Delta P/P = \Delta W/W$. In an open economy, with both labour and imported intermediate products as variable factors in the short run, markup pricing involves

$$(\Delta P/P) = (\Delta W/W) + \gamma (\Delta R/R),$$

where R denotes the raw material price that must be paid for these imported inputs and γ stands for the importance of intermediate imports in the production of final goods. Combining this markup pricing relationship with a Phillips curve determining wage changes,

$$(\Delta W/W) = (\Delta P/P)^e - \beta (u - u^n),$$

we have

$$(\Delta P/P) = (\Delta P/P)^e - \beta (u - u^n) + \gamma (\Delta R/R).$$

Even when expectations are fully realized, this relationship does not imply that the actual unemployment rate equals the natural rate. Instead, unemployment is given by

$$u = u^n + (\gamma/\beta) (\Delta R/R).$$

Since the price Canadian firms must pay for intermediate imports rises whenever our real exchange rate falls, and since Canada's real exchange rate was falling significantly through the 1990s, the last term in this equation was positive throughout this period. Thus, the open-economy version of the natural-rate hypothesis implies that Canada's actual unemployment rate exceeded our natural rate during this period after all.

This reasoning helps makes sense of the American experience in the 1990s as well. Given the closed-economy version of the natural-rate hypothesis, analysts were puzzled as to why U.S. inflation did not accelerate in the late 1990s when the U.S. unemployment rate fell below 4 percent. Many thought that the natural rate was not this low and, with actual and expected inflation likely coinciding at the time, the model predicts rising inflation. But, once again, the last equation directs our attention to the real exchange rate. The Americans' real exchange rate was rising through the 1990s, and the equation indicates that—with no inflation surprises—the actual unemployment rate must fall below the natural rate. So exchange-rate considerations can go a long way toward answering this challenge to the natural-rate hypothesis.

The second challenge stems from the proposition that the family of short-run Phillips curves may be *curves,* not straight lines as shown in earlier figures in this chapter. The reason why this might be the case is that wages tend to be less sticky in the upward direction than they are when market pressures are pushing wages down. Statistical studies lend some support to this concern, and Figure 13-11 indicates why this can be important. Figure 13-11 shows two short-run Phillips curves that embody this relative downward rigidity hypothesis in a dramatic way; each Phillips curve is steep when positive inflation is involved and quite flat when negative inflation is involved. One short-run Phillips curve corresponds to underlying expectations of inflation equal to 5 percent, and the other is relevant for zero inflationary expectations.

We compare two long-run situations. First, suppose that the economy has average inflation of 5 percent, but shocks push the economy back and forth between points A and B. Half the time inflation is 6 percent, and the other half of the time inflation is 4 percent. Because the average is 5 percent, it is reasonable to assume inflationary expectations of 5 percent. What are the implications of this volatility for unemployment? Again, because the economy bounces back and forth between points A and B, the average outcome is point C, which corresponds to the natural unemployment rate. Now let us see how things differ when the volatility shifts the outcome between the steep and the flatter regions of a short-run Phillips curve. This occurs in Figure 13-11 if the average inflation rate is zero. In this case, if inflation fluctuates between plus and minus 1 percent, the economy moves between points D and E. Average inflation is zero, but average unemployment is given by the intersection of the straight line

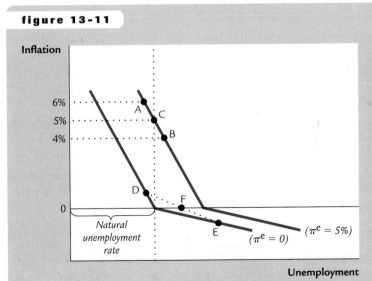

figure 13-11

Inflation

Unemployment

Implications of a Non-Linear Short-Run Phillips Curve Shocks push the economy between points A and B (with an average outcome given by C) if a high inflation target is adopted. Shocks push the economy between points D and E (with an average outcome of F) if a low inflation target is chosen. The low target makes higher average unemployment possible.

joining points D and E and the horizontal axis—that is, by point F. The average unemployment rate exceeds the natural rate.

Thus, as long as the Phillips curve is flatter at low inflation rates and the economy is subject to ongoing shocks, then there is a long-run tradeoff after all—in an average outcomes sense. It appears that we can have lower average unemployment if we choose a small positive inflation rate—enough to make what the evidence shows is a small degree of nonlinearity in the short-run Phillips curves not matter. This is one of the reasons why policymakers often target a low but positive inflation rate instead of zero.

There is one other argument that some economists have stressed to explain why aggregate demand may affect output and employment even in the long run. They have pointed out a number of mechanisms through which recessions might leave permanent scars on the economy by altering the natural rate of unemployment. **Hysteresis** is the term used to describe the long-lasting influence of history on the natural rate.

A recession can have permanent effects if it changes the people who become unemployed. For instance, workers might lose valuable job skills when unemployed, lowering their ability to find a job even after the recession ends. Alternatively, a long period of unemployment may change an individual's attitude toward work and reduce his desire to find employment. In either case, the recession permanently inhibits the process of job search and raises the amount of frictional unemployment.

Another way in which a recession can permanently affect the economy is by changing the process that determines wages. Those who become unemployed may lose their influence on the wage-setting process. Unemployed workers may lose their status as union members, for example. More generally, some of the *insiders* in the wage-setting process become *outsiders*. If the smaller group of insiders cares more about high real wages and less about high employment, then the recession may permanently push real wages further above the equilibrium level and raise the amount of wait unemployment.

Hysteresis remains a controversial theory. Some economists believe the theory helps explain persistently high unemployment in Europe, for the rise in European unemployment starting in the early 1980s coincided with disinflation but continued after inflation stabilized. Moreover, the increase in unemployment tended to be larger for those countries that experienced the greatest reductions in inflations, such as Ireland, Italy, and Spain. Yet there is still no consensus whether the hysteresis phenomenon is significant, or why it might be more pronounced in some countries than in others. (Other explanations of high European unemployment, discussed in Chapter 6, give little role to the disinflation.) If true, however, the theory is important, because hysteresis greatly increases the cost of recessions. Put another way, hysteresis raises the sacrifice ratio, because output is lost even after the period of disinflation is over.[14]

---

[14] Olivier J. Blanchard and Lawrence H. Summers, "Beyond the Natural Rate Hypothesis," *American Economic Review* 78 (May 1988): 182–187; Laurence Ball, "Disinflation and the NAIRU," in Christina D. Romer and David H. Romer, eds., *Reducing Inflation: Motivation and Strategy* (Chicago: University of Chicago Press, 1997): 167–185.

13-3| Conclusion

We began this chapter by discussing four models of aggregate supply, each of which focuses on a different reason why the short-run aggregate supply curve is upward sloping. The four models have similar predictions for the aggregate economy, and all of them yield a short-run tradeoff between inflation and unemployment. A convenient way to express and analyze that tradeoff is with the Phillips-curve equation, according to which inflation depends on expected inflation, cyclical unemployment, and supply shocks.

Keep in mind that not all economists endorse all the ideas discussed here. There is widespread disagreement, for instance, about the practical importance of rational expectations and the relevance of hysteresis. If you find it difficult to fit all the pieces together, you are not alone. The study of aggregate supply remains one of the most unsettled—and therefore one of the most exciting—research areas in macroeconomics.

Summary

1. The four theories of aggregate supply—the sticky-wage, worker-misperception, imperfect-information, and sticky-price models—attribute deviations of output and employment from the natural rate to various market imperfections. According to all four theories, output rises above the natural rate when the price level exceeds the expected price level, and output falls below the natural rate when the price level is less than the expected price level.

2. Economists often express aggregate supply in a relationship called the Phillips curve. The Phillips curve says that inflation depends on expected inflation, the deviation of unemployment from its natural rate, and supply shocks. According to the Phillips curve, policymakers who control aggregate demand face a short-run tradeoff between inflation and unemployment.

3. If expected inflation depends on recently observed inflation, then inflation has inertia, which means that reducing inflation requires either a beneficial supply shock or a period of high unemployment and reduced output. If people have rational expectations, however, then a credible announcement of a change in policy might be able to influence expectations directly and, therefore, reduce inflation without causing a recession.

4. Most economists accept the natural-rate hypothesis, according to which fluctuations in aggregate demand have only short-run effects on output and unemployment. Yet some economists have suggested ways in which recessions can leave permanent scars on the economy by raising the natural rate of unemployment.

KEY CONCEPTS

Sticky-wage model

Worker-misperception model

Imperfect-information model

Sticky-price model

Phillips curve

Adaptive expectations

Demand-pull inflation

Cost-push inflation

Sacrifice ratio

Rational expectations

Natural-rate hypothesis

Hysteresis

QUESTIONS FOR REVIEW

1. Explain the four theories of aggregate supply. On what market imperfection does each theory rely? What do the theories have in common?

2. How is the Phillips curve related to aggregate supply?

3. Why might inflation be inertial?

4. Explain the differences between demand-pull inflation and cost-push inflation.

5. Under what circumstances might it be possible to reduce inflation without causing a recession?

6. Explain two ways in which a recession might raise the natural rate of unemployment.

PROBLEMS AND APPLICATIONS

1. Consider the following changes in the sticky-wage model.

   a. Suppose that labour contracts specify that the nominal wage be fully indexed for inflation. That is, the nominal wage is to be adjusted to fully compensate for changes in the consumer price index. How does full indexation alter the aggregate supply curve in this model?

   b. Suppose now that indexation is only partial. That is, for every increase in the CPI, the nominal wage rises, but by a smaller percentage. How does partial indexation alter the aggregate supply curve in this model?

2. In the sticky-price model, describe the aggregate supply curve in the following special cases. How do these cases compare to the short-run aggregate supply curve we discussed in Chapter 9?

   a. No firms have flexible prices ($s = 1$).

   b. The desired price does not depend on aggregate output ($a = 0$).

3. Suppose that an economy has the Phillips curve

$$\pi = \pi_{-1} - 0.5(u - 0.06).$$

   a. What is the natural rate of unemployment?

   b. Graph the short-run and long-run relationships between inflation and unemployment.

   c. How much cyclical unemployment is necessary to reduce inflation by 5 percentage points? Using Okun's law, compute the sacrifice ratio.

   d. Inflation is running at 10 percent. The Fed wants to reduce it to 5 percent. Give two scenarios that will achieve that goal.

4. According to the rational-expectations approach, if everyone believes that policymakers are committed to reducing inflation, the cost of reducing inflation—the sacrifice ratio—will be lower than if the public is skeptical about the policymakers' intentions. Why might this be true? How might credibility be achieved?

5. Assume that people have rational expectations and that the economy is described by the sticky-wage or sticky-price model. Explain why each of the following propositions is true:

   a. Only unanticipated changes in the money supply affect real GDP. Changes in the money supply that were anticipated when wages and prices were set do not have any real effects.

b. If the Bank of Canada chooses the money supply at the same time as people are setting wages and prices, so that everyone has the same information about the state of the economy, then monetary policy cannot be used systematically to stabilize output. Hence, a policy of keeping the money supply constant will have the same real effects as a policy of adjusting the money supply in response to the state of the economy. (This is called the *policy irrelevance proposition*.)

c. If the Bank of Canada sets the money supply well after people have set wages and prices, so the Bank of Canada has collected more information about the state of the economy, then monetary policy can be used systematically to stabilize output.

6. Suppose that an economy has the Phillips curve

$$\pi = \pi_{-1} - 0.5(u - u^n),$$

and that the natural rate of unemployment is given by an average of the past two years' unemployment:

$$u^n = 0.5(u_{-1} + u_{-2}).$$

a. Why might the natural rate of unemployment depend on recent unemployment (as is assumed in the above equation)?

b. Suppose that the Bank of Canada follows a policy to reduce permanently the inflation rate by 1 percentage point. What effect will that policy have on the unemployment rate over time?

c. What is the sacrifice ratio in this economy? Explain.

d. What do these equations imply about the short-run and long-run tradeoffs between inflation and unemployment?

7. Some economists believe that taxes have an important effect on labour supply. They argue that higher taxes cause people to want to work less and that lower taxes cause them to want to work more. Consider how this effect alters the macroeconomic analysis of tax changes.

a. If this view is correct, how does a tax cut affect the natural rate of output?

b. How does a tax cut affect the aggregate demand curve? The long-run aggregate supply curve? The short-run aggregate supply curve?

c. What is the short-run impact of a tax cut on output and the price level? How does your answer differ from the case without the labour-supply effect?

d. What is the long-run impact of a tax cut on output and the price level? How does your answer differ from the case without the labour-supply effect?

8. Princeton economist Alan Blinder, who has served as Vice Chairman of the U.S. Federal Reserve, once wrote the following:

> The costs that attend the low and moderate inflation rates experienced in the United States and in other industrial countries appear to be quite modest—more like a bad cold than a cancer on society. . . . As rational individuals, we do not volunteer for a lobotomy to cure a head cold. Yet, as a collectivity, we routinely prescribe the economic equivalent of lobotomy (high unemployment) as a cure for the inflationary cold.[15]

What do you think Blinder meant by this? What are the policy implications of the viewpoint Blinder is advocating? Do you agree? Why or why not?

---

[15] Alan Blinder, *Hard Heads, Soft Hearts: Tough-Minded Economics for a Just Society* (Reading, MA: Addison-Wesley, 1987): 51.

part FOUR

Macroeconomic Policy Debates

Discussions among economists are most heated — and most fun — when the topic turns to economic policy. So far in this book we have developed the theories that economists use to study the long-run and short-run behaviour of key macroeconomic variables. We can now apply these tools to some of the debates over macroeconomic policy.

Chapter 14 examines the debate over how policymakers should respond to short-run fluctuations by considering two questions. Should monetary and fiscal policy take an active role in taming the business cycle, or should it remain passive? Should policy be conducted by discretion, or should it be governed by a rule set out in advance? As we will see, there are good arguments on both sides of these questions.

Chapter 15 considers the debate over government debt and budget deficits. From 1970 to 1995, the debt of the Canadian federal government rose from 23 percent to 73 percent of GDP. Although some economists view this fact as relatively insignificant, others see it as one of the most troubling aspects of recent Canadian policy. This chapter discusses the wide range of views about how government debt affects the economy.

14

Stabilization Policy

The Federal Reserve's job is to take away the punch bowl just as the party gets going.

— *William McChesney Martin*

What we need is not a skilled monetary driver of the economic vehicle continuously turning the steering wheel to adjust to the unexpected irregularities of the route, but some means of keeping the monetary passenger who is in the back seat as ballast from occasionally leaning over and giving the steering wheel a jerk that threatens to send the car off the road.

— *Milton Friedman*

How should government policymakers respond to the business cycle? The two quotations above—the first from a former chairman of the Federal Reserve (the U.S. central bank), the second from a prominent critic of central banks—show the diversity of opinion over how this question is best answered.

Some economists, such as William McChesney Martin, view the economy as inherently unstable. They argue that the economy experiences frequent shocks to aggregate demand and aggregate supply. Unless policymakers use monetary and fiscal policy to stabilize the economy, these shocks will lead to unnecessary and inefficient fluctuations in output, unemployment, and inflation. According to the popular saying, macroeconomic policy should "lean against the wind," stimulating the economy when it is depressed and slowing the economy when it is overheated.

Other economists, such as Milton Friedman, view the economy as naturally stable. They blame bad economic policies for the large and inefficient fluctuations we have sometimes experienced. They argue that economic policy should not try to "fine-tune" the economy. Instead, economic policymakers should admit their limited abilities and be satisfied if they do no harm.

This debate has persisted for decades with numerous protagonists advancing various arguments for their positions. The fundamental issue is how policymakers should use the theory of short-run economic fluctuations developed in the preceding chapters. In this chapter we ask two questions that arise in this debate. First, should monetary and fiscal policy take an active role in trying to stabilize the economy, or should policy remain passive? Second, should policymakers be free to use their discretion in responding to changing economic conditions, or should they be committed to following a fixed policy rule?

14-1 | Should Policy Be Active or Passive?

Policymakers in the federal government view economic stabilization as one of their primary responsibilities. The analysis of macroeconomic policy is a regular duty of the Department of Finance and the Bank of Canada. When the government is considering a major change in either fiscal or monetary policy, foremost in the discussion are how the change will influence inflation and unemployment and whether aggregate demand needs to be stimulated or restrained.

Although the government has long conducted monetary and fiscal policy, the view that it should use these policy instruments to try to stabilize the economy is more recent. The federal *White Paper* of 1945 was the key document in which the government first held itself accountable for macroeconomic performance. The *White Paper* states that the "government will be prepared, in periods when unemployment is threatening, to incur deficits and increases in the national debt resulting from its employment and income policy." This policy commitment was written when the memory of the Great Depression was still fresh. The lawmakers who wrote it believed, as many economists do, that in the absence of an active government role in the economy, events like the Great Depression could occur regularly.

To many economists the case for active government policy is clear and simple. Recessions are periods of high unemployment, low incomes, and increased economic hardship. The model of aggregate demand and aggregate supply shows how shocks to the economy can cause recessions. It also shows how monetary and fiscal policy can prevent recessions by responding to these shocks. These economists consider it wasteful not to use these policy instruments to stabilize the economy.

Other economists are critical of the government's attempts to stabilize the economy. These critics argue that the government should take a hands-off approach to macroeconomic policy. At first, this view might seem surprising. If our model shows how to prevent or reduce the severity of recessions, why do these critics want the government to refrain from using monetary and fiscal policy for economic stabilization? To find out, let's consider some of their arguments.

Lags in the Implementation and Effects of Policies

Economic stabilization would be easy if the effects of policy were immediate. Making policy would be like driving a car: policymakers would simply adjust their instruments to keep the economy on the desired path.

Making economic policy, however, is less like driving a car than it is like piloting a large ship. A car changes direction almost immediately after the steering wheel is turned. By contrast, a ship changes course long after the pilot adjusts the rudder, and once the ship starts to turn, it continues turning long after the rudder is set back to normal. A novice pilot is likely to oversteer and, after noticing the mistake, overreact by steering too much in the opposite direction. The ship's path could become unstable, as the novice responds to previous mistakes by making larger and larger corrections.

Like a ship's pilot, economic policymakers face the problem of long lags. Indeed, the problem for policymakers is even more difficult, because the lengths of the lags are hard to predict. These long and variable lags greatly complicate the conduct of monetary and fiscal policy.

Economists distinguish between two lags in the conduct of stabilization policy: the inside lag and the outside lag. The **inside lag** is the time between a shock to the economy and the policy action responding to that shock. This lag arises because it takes time for policymakers first to recognize that a shock has occurred and then to put appropriate policies into effect. The **outside lag** is the time between a policy action and its influence on the economy. This lag arises because policies do not immediately influence spending, income, and employment.

Fiscal policy can have a long inside lag, since changes in spending or taxes must be voted through both the House of Commons and the Senate. The process of parliamentary committee hearings can be slow and cumbersome. An additional problem concerning fiscal policy is that provincial governments sometimes want to push the economy in the opposite direction from what is intended by the federal government. (This coordination problem was discussed more fully in Chapter 12.)

Monetary policy has a much shorter inside lag than fiscal policy, for a central bank can decide on and implement a policy change in less than a day, but monetary policy has a substantial outside lag. Monetary policy works by changing the money supply and thereby interest rates and the exchange rate, which in turn influence investment and net exports. But many firms make investment, import, and export plans far in advance. Therefore, a change in monetary policy is thought not to affect economic activity until about six months after it is made.

The long and variable lags associated with monetary and fiscal policy certainly make stabilizing the economy more difficult. Advocates of passive policy argue that, because of these lags, successful stabilization policy is almost impossible. Indeed, attempts to stabilize the economy can be destabilizing. Suppose that the economy's condition changes between the beginning of a policy action and its impact on the economy. In this case, active policy may end up stimulating the economy when it is overheated or depressing the economy when it is cooling off. Advocates of active policy admit that such lags do require policy-makers to be cautious. But, they argue, these lags do not necessarily mean that policy should be completely passive, especially in the face of a severe and pro-tracted economic downturn.

Some policies, called **automatic stabilizers,** are designed to reduce the lags associated with stabilization policy. Automatic stabilizers are policies that stimulate or depress the economy when necessary without any deliberate policy change. For example, the system of income taxes automatically reduces taxes when the economy goes into a recession, without any change in the tax laws, because individuals and corporations pay less tax when their incomes fall. Similarly, the employment-insurance and welfare systems automatically raise transfer payments when the economy moves into a recession, because more people apply for benefits. One can view these automatic stabilizers as a type of fiscal policy without any inside lag.

CASE STUDY

Profit Sharing as an Automatic Stabilizer

Economists often propose policies to improve the automatic-stabilizing powers of the economy. The economist Martin Weitzman has made one of the most intriguing suggestions: profit sharing. Today, most labour contracts specify a fixed wage. For example, General Motors might pay assembly-line workers $20 an hour. Weitzman recommends that the workers' total pay should depend on their firm's profits. A profit-sharing contract for General Motors might pay workers $10 for each hour of work, but in addition the workers would divide among themselves a share of the firm's profit.

Weitzman argues that profit sharing would act as an automatic stabilizer. Under the current wage system, a fall in demand for a firm's product causes the firm to lay off workers: it is no longer profitable to employ them at the old wage. The firm will rehire these workers only if the wage falls or if demand recovers. Under a profit-sharing system, Weitzman argues, firms would be more likely to maintain employment after a fall in demand. Under our hypothetical profit-sharing contract for General Motors, for example, each additional hour of work would cost the firm only $10; the rest of the compensation for additional workers would come from the workers' share of profits. Because the marginal cost of labour would be so much lower under profit sharing, a fall in demand would not normally cause a firm to lay off workers.

To provide evidence for the advantages of profit sharing, Weitzman points to Japan. Most Japanese workers receive a large fraction of their compensation in the form of year-end bonuses. Weitzman argues that, because of these bonuses, Japanese workers "think of themselves more as permanently employed partners than as hired hands." And, as Weitzman's theory predicts, employment in Japan is much more stable than in countries without any form of profit sharing.

The *New York Times* dubbed Weitzman's proposal "the best idea since Keynes." Advocates of his theory want the government to provide tax incentives to encourage firms to adopt profit-sharing plans. Others, however, have expressed skepticism. They wonder why, if profit sharing is such a good idea, firms and workers don't sign such contracts without prodding from the government. Whether profit sharing would help stabilize the economy, as Weitzman suggests, remains an open question.[1]

The Difficult Job of Economic Forecasting

Because policy influences the economy only after a substantial lag, successful stabilization policy requires the ability to predict accurately future economic conditions. If we cannot predict whether the economy will be in a boom or a recession in six months or a year, we cannot evaluate whether monetary and fiscal policy should now be trying to expand or contract aggregate demand. Unfortunately, economic developments are often unpredictable, at least given our current understanding of the economy.

One way forecasters try to look ahead is with the **index of leading indicators.** This index, called the composite index, is composed of 10 data series—such as stock prices, the number of housing starts, the U.S. leading indicator, the value of orders for new plants and equipment, and the money supply—that often fluctuate in advance of the economy. A large fall in a leading indicator signals that a recession is more likely.

Another way forecasters look ahead is with macroeconometric models, which have been developed both by government agencies and by private firms for forecasting and policy analysis. As we discussed in Chapter 11, these large-scale computer models are made up of many equations, each representing a part of the economy. After making assumptions about the path of the exogenous variables, such as monetary policy, fiscal policy, and foreign variables such as oil prices and trade restrictions, these models yield predictions about unemployment, inflation, and other endogenous variables. Keep in mind, however, that the validity of these predictions is only as good as the model and the forecasters' assumptions about the exogenous variables.

"It's true, Caesar. Rome is declining, but I expect it to pick up in the next quarter."

Drawing by Dana Fradon; © 1988 The New Yorker Magazine, Inc.

[1] Martin L. Weitzman, *The Share Economy* (Cambridge, MA: Harvard University Press, 1984).

CASE STUDY

Two Episodes in Economic Forecasting

"Light showers, bright intervals, and moderate winds." This was the forecast offered by the renowned British national weather service on October 14, 1987. The next day Britain was hit by the worst storm in over two centuries.

Like weather forecasts, economic forecasts are a crucial input to private and public decisionmaking. Business executives rely on economic forecasts when deciding how much to produce and how much to invest in plant and equipment. Government policymakers also rely on them when developing economic policies. Yet also like weather forecasts, economic forecasts are far from precise.

Even the most severe economic downturn, the Great Depression of the 1930s, caught economic forecasters completely by surprise. Even after the stock market crash of 1929, they remained confident that the economy would not suffer a substantial setback. In late 1931, when the economy was clearly in bad shape, the eminent economist Irving Fisher predicted that it would recover quickly. Subsequent events showed that these forecasts were much too optimistic.[2]

Forecasting success is still an elusive goal, as the recession of the early 1990s illustrates. On average, during the first three years of the decade, Canada's real GDP fell by 0.4 percentage points each year. Throughout this period, the federal government surveyed private forecasters to ensure that their own projections of GDP growth agreed with the existing consensus. One of the reasons the government's budget deficit increased so much during the 1990–1992 period is that Finance Department officials (and other forecasters) overestimated GDP growth by over 3 percentage points per year! (With lower levels of income being earned, the existing set of tax rates did not generate the amount of revenue that the government expected.)

This low level of forecasting accuracy is discouraging for those who favour an active stabilization policy. Furthermore, there is significant disparity among the various forecasters' estimates. For example, in the federal budget of 1994 (delivered in February of that year), it was noted that the private forecasts for real GDP growth in that year ranged from 2.9 percent to 4.3 percent. More important, Statistics Canada (one of the most respected statistical agencies in the world) finds that it must revise its estimates of real GDP *several* times—even *after* the period in question has become a matter of history. Journalist Bruce Little used the graph shown in Figure 14-1 to indicate how much data revision goes on. For example, in just the nine months between June 1992 and March 1993, the estimate for GDP growth during the first quarter of 1992 was revised downward *four* times, with the final estimate's being a growth rate that is only

---

[2] Kathryn M. Dominguez, Ray C. Fair, and Matthew D. Shapiro, "Forecasting the Depression: Harvard Versus Yale," *American Economic Review* 78 (September 1988): 595–612. This article shows how badly economic forecasters did during the Great Depression, and it argues that they could not have done any better with the modern forecasting techniques available today.

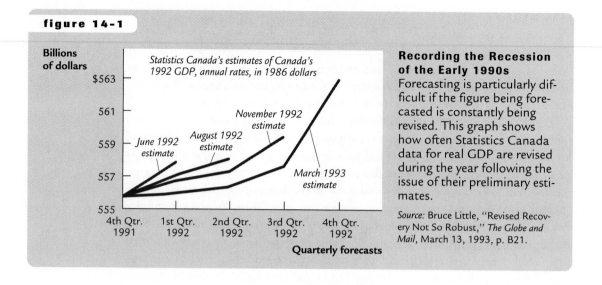

figure 14-1

Statistics Canada's estimates of Canada's 1992 GDP, annual rates, in 1986 dollars

Billions of dollars

Recording the Recession of the Early 1990s
Forecasting is particularly difficult if the figure being forecasted is constantly being revised. This graph shows how often Statistics Canada data for real GDP are revised during the year following the issue of their preliminary estimates.

Source: Bruce Little, "Revised Recovery Not So Robust," *The Globe and Mail*, March 13, 1993, p. B21.

one-sixth of the initial measurement. And this is just getting recorded history straight—this is not forecasting at all. Although economic forecasts are an essential input to private and public decisionmaking, they are very uncertain.

Ignorance, Expectations, and the Lucas Critique

The prominent economist Robert Lucas once wrote, "As an advice-giving profession we are in way over our heads." Even many of those who advise policymakers would agree with this assessment. Economics is a young science, and there is still much that we do not know. Economists cannot be completely confident when they assess the effects of alternative policies. This ignorance suggests that economists should be cautious when offering policy advice.

Although there are many topics about which economists' knowledge is limited, Lucas has emphasized the issue of how people form expectations of the future. Expectations play a crucial role in the economy because they influence all sorts of economic behaviour. For instance, households decide how much to consume based on expectations of future income, and firms decide how much to invest based on expectations of future profitability. These expectations depend on many things, including the economic policies being pursued by the government. Thus, when policymakers estimate the effect of any policy change, they need to know how people's expectations will respond to the policy change. Lucas has argued that traditional methods of policy evaluation—such as those that rely on standard macroeconometric models—do not adequately take into account this impact of policy on expectations. This criticism of traditional policy evaluation is known as the **Lucas critique**.[3]

[3] Robert E. Lucas, Jr., "Econometric Policy Evaluation: A Critique," *Carnegie Rochester Conference on Public Policy* 1 (Amsterdam: North-Holland, 1976), 19–46.

An important example of the Lucas critique arises in the analysis of disinflation. As you may recall from Chapter 13, the cost of reducing inflation is often measured by the sacrifice ratio, which is the number of percentage points of GDP that must be forgone to reduce inflation by 1 percentage point. Because these estimates of the sacrifice ratio are often large, they have led some economists to argue that policymakers should learn to live with inflation, rather than incurring the large cost of reducing it.

According to advocates of the rational-expectations approach, however, these estimates of the sacrifice ratio are unreliable because they are subject to the Lucas critique. Traditional estimates of the sacrifice ratio are based on adaptive expectations, that is, on the assumption that expected inflation depends on past inflation. Adaptive expectations may be a reasonable premise in some circumstances, but if the policymakers make a credible change in policy, workers and firms setting wages and prices will rationally respond by adjusting their expectations of inflation appropriately. This change in inflation expectations will quickly alter the short-run tradeoff between inflation and unemployment. As a result, reducing inflation can potentially be much less costly than is suggested by traditional estimates of the sacrifice ratio.

We encounter two other examples of the Lucas critique in this book. First, in the appendix to Chapter 12, we examine whether the central bank should smooth the exchange rate or not. We find that the answer to this question depends fundamentally on whether individuals adjust their forecasts of the exchange rate to reflect this intervention by the authorities. Second, in Chapter 16, we study the household consumption function. We learn that economists have sometimes made very inaccurate predictions concerning how consumers respond to changes in personal-income tax rates. This is because analysts have ignored the effect of the government's policies on consumers' expectations. In Chapter 16, we see how economists have learned to respect the Lucas critique by modifying their theory of consumer behaviour.

The Lucas critique leaves us with two lessons. The more narrow lesson is that economists evaluating alternative policies need to consider how policy affects expectations and, thereby, behaviour. The broader lesson is that policy evaluation is hard, so economists engaged in this task should be sure to show the requisite humility.

The Historical Record

In judging whether government policy should play an active or passive role in the economy, we must give some weight to the historical record. If the economy has experienced many large shocks to aggregate supply and aggregate demand, and if policy has successfully insulated the economy from these shocks, then the case for active policy should be clear. Conversely, if the economy has experienced few large shocks, and if the fluctuations we have observed can be traced to inept economic policy, then the case for passive policy should be clear. In other words, our view of stabilization policy should be influenced by whether policy has historically been stabilizing or destabilizing. For this reason, the debate over macroeconomic policy frequently turns into a debate over macroeconomic history.

Yet history does not settle the debate over stabilization policy. Disagreements over history arise because it is not easy to identify the sources of economic fluctuations. The historical record often permits more than one interpretation.

The Great Depression is a case in point. Economists' views on macroeconomic policy are often related to their views on the cause of the Depression. Some economists believe that a large contractionary shock to private spending caused the Depression. They assert that policymakers should have responded by stimulating aggregate demand. Other economists believe that the large fall in the money supply in the United States caused the Depression. They assert that the Depression would have been avoided if the U.S. central bank, the Fed, had been pursuing a passive monetary policy of increasing the money supply at a steady rate. Hence, depending on one's beliefs about its cause, the Great Depression can be viewed either as an example of why active monetary and fiscal policy is necessary or as an example of why it is dangerous.

CASE STUDY

Is the Stabilization of the Economy a Figment of the Data?

Keynes wrote *The General Theory* in the 1930s, and in the wake of the Keynesian revolution, governments around the world began to view economic stabilization as a primary responsibility. Some economists believe that the development of Keynesian theory has had a profound influence on the behaviour of the economy. Comparing data from before World War I and after World War II, they find that real GDP and unemployment have become much more stable. This, some Keynesians claim, is the best argument for active stabilization policy: it has worked.

In a series of provocative and influential papers, economist Christina Romer has challenged this assessment of the historical record. She argues that the measured reduction in volatility reflects not an improvement in economic policy and performance but rather an improvement in the economic data. The older data are much less accurate than the newer data. Romer claims that the higher volatility of unemployment and real GDP reported for the period before World War I is largely a figment of the data.

Romer uses various techniques to make her case. One is to construct more accurate data for the earlier period. This task is difficult because data sources are not readily available. A second way is to construct *less* accurate data for the recent period—that is, data that are comparable to the older data and thus suffer from the same imperfections. After constructing new "bad" data, Romer finds that the recent period appears almost as volatile as the early period, suggesting that the volatility of the early period may be largely an artifact of data construction.

Romer's work is an important part of the continuing debate over whether macroeconomic policy has improved the performance of the economy. Although her work remains controversial, most economists now believe that the economy is only slightly more stable than it was in the past.[4]

14-2 | Should Policy Be Conducted by Rule or by Discretion?

A second topic of debate among economists is whether economic policy should be conducted by rule or by discretion. Policy is conducted by rule if policymakers announce in advance how policy will respond to various situations and commit themselves to following through on this announcement. Policy is conducted by discretion if policymakers are free to size up events as they occur and choose whatever policy seems appropriate at the time.

The debate over rules versus discretion is distinct from the debate over passive versus active policy. Policy can be conducted by rule and yet be either passive or active. For example, a passive policy rule might specify steady growth in the money supply of 2 percent per year. An active policy rule might specify that

$$\text{Money Growth} = 2\% + (\text{Unemployment Rate} - 7\%).$$

Under this rule, the money supply grows at 2 percent if the unemployment rate is 7 percent, but for every percentage point by which the unemployment rate exceeds 7 percent, money growth increases by an extra percentage point. This rule tries to stabilize the economy by raising money growth when the economy is in a recession.

We begin this section by discussing why policy might be improved by a commitment to a policy rule. We then examine several possible policy rules.

Distrust of Policymakers and the Political Process

Some economists believe that economic policy is too important to be left to the discretion of policymakers. Although this view is more political than economic, evaluating it is central to how we judge the role of economic policy. If politicians are incompetent or opportunistic, then we may not want to give them the discretion to use the powerful tools of monetary and fiscal policy.

Incompetence in economic policy arises for several reasons. Some economists view the political process as erratic, perhaps because it reflects the shifting

[4] Christina D. Romer, "Spurious Volatility in Historical Unemployment Data," *Journal of Political Economy* 94 (February 1986): 1–37; Christina D. Romer, "Is the Stabilization of the Postwar Economy a Figment of the Data?" *American Economic Review* 76 (June 1986): 314–334.

power of special interest groups. In addition, macroeconomics is complicated, and politicians often do not have sufficient knowledge of it to make informed judgments. This ignorance allows charlatans to propose incorrect but superficially appealing solutions to complex problems. The political process often cannot weed out the advice of charlatans from that of competent economists.

Opportunism in economic policy arises when the objectives of policymakers conflict with the well-being of the public. Some economists fear that politicians use macroeconomic policy to further their own electoral ends. If citizens vote on the basis of economic conditions prevailing at the time of the election, then politicians have an incentive to pursue policies that will make the economy look good during election years. A new government might cause a recession soon after coming into office to lower inflation and then stimulate the economy as the next election approaches to lower unemployment; this would ensure that both inflation and unemployment are low on election day. Manipulation of the economy for electoral gain, called the **political business cycle,** has been the subject of extensive research by economists and political scientists.[5]

Politicians have not fully abided by the principles set out in the 1945 *White Paper* on income and employment. We noted earlier that this statement of government intent involved the government's increasing the national debt during recessions, by having spending exceed taxes when the economy might benefit from stimulation. Most politicians like this message—it excuses budget deficits. Indeed, it is based on the proposition that running a deficit *is* the responsible policy in some instances. But many politicians seem to have ignored a later section of the *White Paper*, in which it is clearly stated that "in periods of buoyant employment and income, budget plans will call for surpluses." If this part of the *White Paper*'s advice had been heeded, than Canadians would have witnessed budget surpluses as often as budget deficits. The result would have been no long-run increase in the national debt.

Distrust of the political process leads some economists to advocate placing economic policy outside the realm of politics. Some have proposed constitutional amendments, such as a balanced-budget amendment, that would tie the hands of legislators and insulate the economy from both incompetence and opportunism.

The Time Inconsistency of Discretionary Policy

If we assume that we can trust our policymakers, discretion at first glance appears superior to a fixed policy rule. Discretionary policy is, by its nature, flexible. As long as policymakers are intelligent and benevolent, there might appear to be little reason to deny them flexibility in responding to changing conditions.

---

[5] William Nordhaus, "The Political Business Cycle," *Review of Economic Studies* 42 (1975): 169–190; Edward Tufte, *Political Control of the Economy* (Princeton, NJ: Princeton University Press, 1978).

ing, central banks are left are with a fair amount of discretion. Inflation targets are usually set as a range—for example, an inflation rate of 1 to 3 percent in Canada's case—rather than a particular number. Thus, the central bank can choose where in the range it wants to be. In addition, the central banks are sometimes allowed to adjust their targets for inflation, at least temporarily, if some exogenous event (such as an easily identified supply shock such as the introduction of the GST) pushes inflation outside of the range that was previously announced.

In light of this flexibility, what is the purpose of inflation targeting? Although inflation targeting does leave the central bank with some discretion, the policy does constrain how this discretion is used. When a central bank is told to "do the right thing," it is hard to hold the central bank accountable, for people can argue forever about what the right thing is in any specific circumstance. By contrast, when a central bank has announced an inflation target, the public can more easily judge whether the central bank is meeting that target. Thus, although inflation targeting does not tie the hands of the central bank, it does increase the transparency of monetary policy and, by doing so, makes central bankers more accountable for their actions.[6]

CASE STUDY

Central-Bank Independence

Suppose you were put in charge of writing the constitution and laws for a country. Would you give the political leader of the country authority over the policies of the central bank? Or would you allow the central bank to make decisions free from such political influence? In other words, assuming that monetary policy is made by discretion rather than by rule, who should exercise that discretion?

Countries vary greatly in how they choose to answer this question. In some countries, the central bank is a branch of the government; in others, the central bank is largely independent. In Canada, the Governor of the Bank of Canada is appointed for a 7-year term. The Governor must resign if he or she does not wish to implement the monetary policy of the government. But the government must put its detailed instructions in writing and on public record, so the Governor has significant power if there is a disagreement. In the United States, Fed governors are appointed by the president for 14-year terms, and they cannot be recalled if the president is unhappy with their decisions. This institutional structure gives the Fed a degree of independence similar to that of the Supreme Court.

---

[6] See Ben S. Bernanke and Frederic S. Mishkin, "Inflation Targeting: A New Framework for Monetary Policy?" *Journal of Economic Perspectives* 11 (Spring 1997): 97–116.

Many researchers have investigated the effects of constitutional design on monetary policy. They have examined the laws of different countries to construct an index of central-bank independence. This index is based on various characteristics, such as the length of bankers' terms, the role of government officials on the bank board, and the frequency of contact between the government and the central bank. The researchers have then examined the correlation between central-bank independence and macroeconomic performance.

The results of these studies are striking: more independent central banks are strongly associated with lower and more stable inflation. Figure 14-2 shows a scatterplot of central-bank independence and average inflation for the period 1955 to 1988. Countries that had an independent central bank, such as Germany, Switzerland, and the United States, tended to have low average inflation. Countries that had central banks with less independence, such as New Zealand and Spain, tended to have higher average inflation.

Researchers have also found there is no relationship between central-bank independence and real economic activity. In particular, central-bank independence is not correlated with average unemployment, the volatility of unemployment, the average growth of real GDP, or the volatility of real GDP.

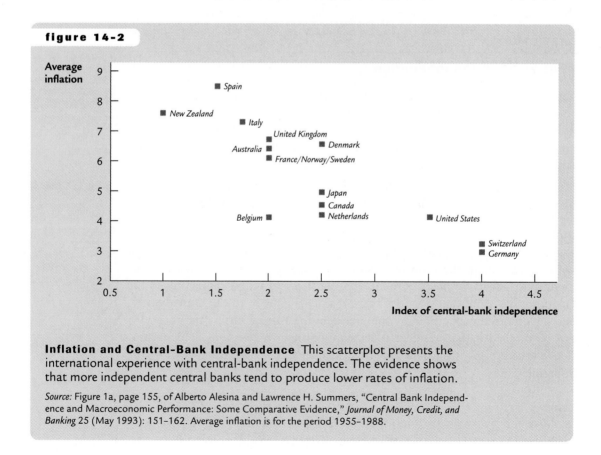

figure 14-2

Inflation and Central-Bank Independence This scatterplot presents the international experience with central-bank independence. The evidence shows that more independent central banks tend to produce lower rates of inflation.

Source: Figure 1a, page 155, of Alberto Alesina and Lawrence H. Summers, "Central Bank Independence and Macroeconomic Performance: Some Comparative Evidence," *Journal of Money, Credit, and Banking* 25 (May 1993): 151–162. Average inflation is for the period 1955–1988.

Summary

1. Advocates of active policy view the economy as subject to frequent shocks that will lead to unnecessary fluctuations in output and employment unless monetary or fiscal policy responds. Many believe that economic policy has been successful in stabilizing the economy.

2. Advocates of passive policy argue that because monetary and fiscal policies work with long and variable lags, attempts to stabilize the economy are likely to end up being destabilizing. In addition, they believe that our present understanding of the economy is too limited to be useful in formulating successful stabilization policy and that inept policy is a frequent source of economic fluctuations.

3. Advocates of discretionary policy argue that discretion gives more flexibility to policymakers in responding to various unforeseen situations.

4. Advocates of policy rules argue that the political process cannot be trusted. They believe that politicians make frequent mistakes in conducting economic policy and sometimes use economic policy for their own political ends. In addition, advocates of policy rules argue that a commitment to a fixed policy rule is necessary to solve the problem of time inconsistency.

KEY CONCEPTS

Inside and outside lags
Automatic stabilizers
Index of leading indicators

Lucas critique
Political business cycle

Time inconsistency
Monetarists

QUESTIONS FOR REVIEW

1. What are the inside lag and the outside lag? Which has the longer inside lag—monetary or fiscal policy? Which has the longer outside lag? Why?

2. Why would more accurate economic forecasting make it easier for policymakers to stabilize the economy? Describe two ways economists try to forecast developments in the economy.

3. Describe the Lucas critique.

4. How does a person's interpretation of macroeconomic history affect his view of macroeconomic policy?

5. What is meant by the "time inconsistency" of economic policy? Why might policymakers be tempted to renege on an announcement they made earlier? In this situation, what is the advantage of a policy rule?

6. List three policy rules that the Bank of Canada might follow. Which of these would you advocate? Why?

7. Give three reasons why requiring a balanced budget might be too restrictive a rule for fiscal policy.

PROBLEMS AND APPLICATIONS

1. Suppose that the tradeoff between unemployment and inflation is determined by the Phillips curve:

$$u = u^n - \alpha(\pi - \pi^e),$$

where u denotes the unemployment rate, u^n the natural rate of unemployment, π the rate of inflation, and π^e the expected rate of inflation. In addition, suppose that the country involves two political parties, the Left and the Right. Suppose that the Left party always follows a policy of high money growth and the Right party always follows a policy of low money growth. What "political business cycle" pattern of inflation and unemployment would you predict under the following conditions?

   a. Every four years, one of the parties takes control based on a random flip of a coin. [*Hint:* What will expected inflation be prior to the election?]

   b. The two parties take turns.

2. When cities pass laws limiting the rent landlords can charge on apartments, the laws usually apply to existing buildings and exempt any buildings not yet built. Advocates of rent control argue that this exemption ensures that rent control does not discourage the construction of new housing. Evaluate this argument in light of the time-inconsistency problem.

3. The *cyclically adjusted budget deficit* is the budget deficit corrected for the effects of the business cycle. In other words, it is the budget deficit that the government would be running if unemployment were at the natural rate. (It is also called the *full-employment budget deficit*.) Some economists have proposed the rule that the cyclically adjusted budget deficit always be balanced. Compare this proposal to a strict balanced-budget rule. Which is preferable? What problems do you see with the rule requiring a balanced cyclically adjusted budget?

Time Inconsistency and the Tradeoff Between Inflation and Unemployment

In this appendix, we examine more analytically the time-inconsistency argument for rules rather than discretion. This material is relegated to an appendix because we will need to use some calculus.[8]

Suppose that the Phillips curve describes the relationship between inflation and unemployment. Letting u denote the unemployment rate, u^n the natural rate of unemployment, π the rate of inflation, and π^e the expected rate of inflation, unemployment is determined by

$$u = u^n - \alpha(\pi - \pi^e).$$

Unemployment is low when inflation exceeds expected inflation and high when inflation falls below expected inflation.

For simplicity, suppose also that the Bank of Canada chooses the rate of inflation. Of course, more realistically, the Bank of Canada controls inflation only imperfectly through its control of the money supply. But for the purposes of illustration, it is useful to assume that the Bank of Canada can control inflation perfectly.

The Bank of Canada likes low unemployment and low inflation. Suppose that the cost of unemployment and inflation, as perceived by the Bank of Canada, can be represented as

$$L(u, \pi) = u + \gamma\pi^2,$$

where the parameter γ represents how much the Bank of Canada dislikes inflation relative to unemployment. $L(u, \pi)$ is called the *loss function*. The Bank of Canada's objective is to make the loss as small as possible.

Having specified how the economy works and the Bank of Canada's objective, let's compare monetary policy made under a fixed rule and under discretion.

First, consider policy under a fixed rule. A rule commits the Bank of Canada to a particular level of inflation. As long as private agents understand that the Bank of Canada is committed to this rule, the expected level of inflation will be the level the Bank of Canada is committed to produce. Since expected

---

[8] The material in this appendix is derived from Finn E. Kydland and Edward C. Prescott, "Rules Rather Than Discretion: The Inconsistency of Optimal Plans," *Journal of Political Economy* 85 (June 1977): 473–492; and Robert J. Barro and David Gordon, "A Positive Theory of Monetary Policy in a Natural Rate Model," *Journal of Political Economy* 91 (August 1983): 589–610.

inflation equals actual inflation ($\pi^e = \pi$), unemployment will be at its natural rate ($u = u^n$).

What is the optimal rule? Since unemployment is at its natural rate regardless of the level of inflation legislated by the rule, there is no benefit to having any inflation at all. Therefore, the optimal fixed rule requires that the Bank of Canada produce zero inflation.

Second, consider discretionary monetary policy. Under discretion, the economy works as follows:

1. Private agents form their expectations of inflation π^e.

2. The Bank of Canada chooses the actual level of inflation π.

3. Based on expected and actual inflation, unemployment is determined.

Under this arrangement, the Bank of Canada minimizes its loss $L(u, \pi)$ subject to the constraint that the Phillips curve imposes. When making its decision about the rate of inflation, the Bank of Canada takes expected inflation as already determined.

To find what outcome we would obtain under discretionary policy, we must examine what level of inflation the Bank of Canada would choose. By substituting the Phillips curve into the Bank of Canada's loss function, we obtain

$$L(u, \pi) = u^n - \alpha(\pi - \pi^e) + \gamma\pi^2.$$

Notice that the Bank of Canada's loss is negatively related to unexpected inflation (the second term in the equation) and positively related to actual inflation (the third term). To find the level of inflation that minimizes this loss, differentiate with respect to π to obtain

$$dL/d\pi = -\alpha + 2\gamma\pi.$$

The loss is minimized when this derivative equals zero. Solving for π, we get

$$\pi = \alpha/(2\gamma).$$

Whatever level of inflation private agents expected, this is the "optimal" level of inflation for the Bank of Canada to choose. Of course, rational private agents understand the objective of the Bank of Canada and the constraint that the Phillips curve imposes. They therefore expect that the Bank of Canada will choose this level of inflation. Expected inflation equals actual inflation [$\pi^e = \pi = \alpha/(2\gamma)$], and unemployment equals its natural rate ($u = u^n$).

Now compare the outcome under optimal discretion to the outcome under the optimal rule. In both cases, unemployment is at its natural rate. Yet discretionary policy produces more inflation than does policy under the rule. *Thus, optimal discretion is worse than the optimal rule.* This is true even though the Bank of Canada under discretion was attempting to minimize its loss, $L(u, \pi)$.

At first it may seem bizarre that the Bank of Canada can achieve a better outcome by being committed to a fixed rule. Why can't the Bank of Canada with discretion mimic the Bank of Canada committed to a zero-inflation rule?

The answer is that the Bank of Canada is playing a game against private decisionmakers who have rational expectations. Unless it is committed to a fixed rule of zero inflation, the Bank of Canada cannot get private agents to expect zero inflation.

Suppose, for example, that the Bank of Canada simply announces that it will follow a zero-inflation policy. Such an announcement by itself cannot be credible. After private agents have formed their expectations of inflation, the Bank of Canada has the incentive to renege on its announcement in order to decrease unemployment. (As we have just seen, once expectations are given, the Bank of Canada's optimal policy is to set inflation at $\pi = \alpha/(2\gamma)$, regardless of π^e.) Private agents understand the incentive to renege and therefore do not believe the announcement in the first place.

This theory of monetary policy has an important corollary. Under one circumstance, the Bank of Canada with discretion achieves the same outcome as the Bank of Canada committed to a fixed rule of zero inflation. If the Bank of Canada dislikes inflation much more than it dislikes unemployment (so that γ is very large), inflation under discretion is near zero, since the Bank of Canada has little incentive to inflate. This finding provides some guidance to those who have the job of appointing central bankers. An alternative to imposing a fixed rule is to appoint an individual with a fervent distaste for inflation. Perhaps this is why even liberal politicians who are more concerned about unemployment than inflation sometimes appoint conservative central bankers who are more concerned about inflation.

MORE PROBLEMS AND APPLICATIONS

1. In the 1970s in Canada, the inflation rate and the natural rate of unemployment both rose. Let's use this model of time inconsistency to examine this phenomenon. Assume that policy is discretionary.

   a. In the model as developed so far, what happens to the inflation rate when the natural rate of unemployment rises?

   b. Let's now change the model slightly by supposing that the Bank of Canada's loss function is quadratic in both inflation and unemployment. That is,

   $$L(u, \pi) = u^2 + \gamma\pi^2.$$

   Follow steps similar to those in the text to solve for the inflation rate under discretionary policy.

   c. Now what happens to the inflation rate when the natural rate of unemployment rises?

   d. In 1987, Prime Minister Brian Mulroney's government appointed the conservative central banker John Crow to head the Bank of Canada. According to this model, what should have happened to inflation and unemployment?

chapter 15

Government Debt and Budget Deficits

All decent people live beyond their incomes nowadays and those who aren't respectable live beyond other people's. A few gifted individuals manage to do both.

— *Saki*

When a government spends more than it collects in taxes, it borrows from the private sector to finance the budget deficit. The accumulation of past borrowing is the government debt. Although attention to the national debt has waxed and waned over the years, it has been especially intense during the past quarter-century. Expressed as a percentage of GDP, the debt doubled from 1975 to 1985, and then almost doubled again from 1985 to 1995. By the late 1990s, the budget deficit had come under control and had even turned into a budget surplus, but the level of debt remained high.

This large increase in government debt during a period of peace and prosperity is unprecedented in Canadian history. Not surprisingly, it sparked a renewed interest among economists and policymakers in the economic effects of government debt. Some view the large budget deficits during the 1975–1995 period as the worst mistake of economic policy since the Great Depression, while others think that the deficits matter very little. This chapter considers various facets of this debate.

We begin simply by looking at the numbers. Section 15-1 examines the size of the Canadian government debt, comparing it to the debt of other countries and to the debt that Canada has had during its own past. It also takes a brief look at what the future may hold. Section 15-2 discusses why measuring changes in government indebtedness is not as straightforward as it might seem. Indeed, some economists have argued that traditional measures are so misleading that they should be ignored completely.

We then look at how government debt affects the economy. Section 15-3 describes the traditional view of government debt, according to which government borrowing reduces national saving, crowds out capital accumulation, and increases interest payment obligations to foreigners. This view is held by most economists and has been implicit in the discussion of fiscal policy throughout this book. Section 15-4 discusses an alternative view, called *Ricardian equivalence,* which is held by a small but influential minority of economists. According to the Ricardian view, government debt does not influence national saving and capital accumulation. As we will see, the debate between the traditional and Ricardian views of government debt arises from disagreements over how consumers respond to the government's debt policy. Section 15-5 then looks at various other possible effects of government debt, including effects on monetary policy, the political process, and the role of a country in the world economy.

15-1 | The Size of the Government Debt

Let's begin by putting the government debt in perspective. At the turn of the century, the debt of the Canadian federal government was about $575 billion. If we divide this number by 30.3 million, roughly the number of people in Canada, we find that each person's share of the government debt was about $19,000. Obviously, this is not a trivial number—few people sneeze at $19,000. Yet if we compare this debt to the roughly $1 million a typical person will earn over his or her working life, the government debt does not look like the catastrophe it is sometimes made out to be.

One way to judge the size of a government's debt is to compare it to the amount of debt other countries have accumulated. Table 15-1 shows the amount of government debt for 19 major countries expressed as a percentage of each country's GDP. On the top of the list are the heavily indebted countries of Belgium and Italy, which have accumulated a debt that exceeds annual GDP. At the bottom are Norway and Australia, which have accumulated relatively small debts. Canada is near the top of the pack. By international standards, then, Canada has been fairly profligate.

Over the course of Canadian history, the indebtedness of the federal government has varied substantially. Figure 15-1 shows the ratio of the federal debt to GDP since 1925. What explains this variation?

Focusing on just the Canadian federal government, national debt is the sum total of all the annual budget deficits incurred since confederation in 1867. That debt reached the $600 billion mark at the turn of the century. Most of this debt accumulated in recent years—only just over 5 percent can be attributed to the country's first 100 years of existence! The federal debt shot up during the Great Depression of the 1930s and ballooned during World War II, as Figure 15–1 shows. These developments have not been interpreted as government mismanagement, however, because people have reasoned that the government had no choice but to get involved in these crises. Most people think that because future generations have benefited from the freedom that the war ensured, it is only fair that they shoulder some of the burden. Issuing debt during the war, therefore, was the government's way of spreading some of the costs to future generations.

table 15-1

How Indebted Are the World's Governments?

Country	Government Debt as a Percentage of GDP
Belgium	125%
Italy	123
Greece	103
Canada	94
Japan	93
Sweden	76
Spain	74
Netherlands	73
Austria	73
Ireland	67
Denmark	67
Germany	66
Portugal	65
France	65
United States	65
United Kingdom	60
Finland	59
Australia	40
Norway	34

Source: OECD Economic Outlook. Figures are based on estimates of gross government debt, including the provinces, and GDP for 1998.

Following the war, the federal government's debt–GDP ratio was 110 percent. By 1970, it was less than 20 percent. The debt ratio was brought under control in three main ways. First, the government ran budget surpluses for a number of years in the 1945–1970 period, and in each of those years the debt was decreased by the amount of the surplus. Second, Canada enjoyed a long period of rapid economic growth. With real GDP growing briskly, the ratio of the outstanding debt to GDP shrank at a rapid rate. Finally, during the Korean War period in the early 1950s, and during the 1965–1980 period, Canada's inflation rate reduced the real value of the debt by a significant amount. Unexpected inflation is simply a gradual (some would say "civilized") way for a country to default on some of its debt.

By 1994, the federal debt ratio had climbed back up to almost 74 percent. There were two main reasons for this dramatic reversal of the postwar trend. First, Canada's average growth rate for real GDP had been lower since the mid-1970s, when most Western countries began suffering from a slowdown in productivity growth. Second, the government simply overspent. The federal government ran a deficit *every* year between 1971 and 1998.

figure 15-1

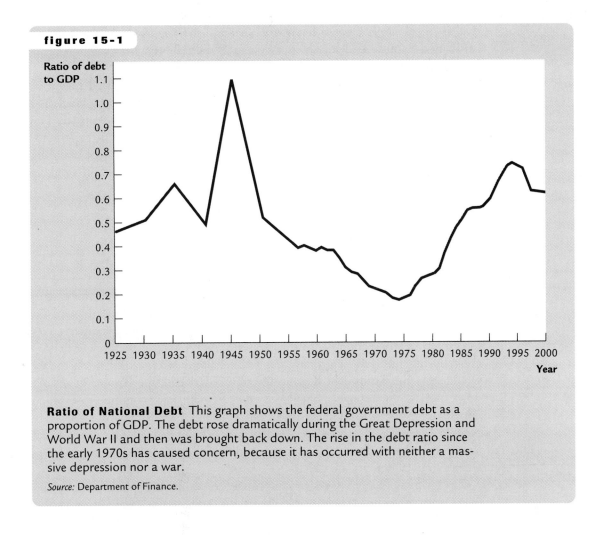

Ratio of National Debt This graph shows the federal government debt as a proportion of GDP. The debt rose dramatically during the Great Depression and World War II and then was brought back down. The rise in the debt ratio since the early 1970s has caused concern, because it has occurred with neither a massive depression nor a war.

Source: Department of Finance.

Broadly speaking, there are three reasons why many were concerned about the resulting increase in debt. First, Canadians were more indebted to foreigners. As a proportion of GDP, Canada's net foreign debt (including all forms, not just government debt) was almost 50 percent in 1994. This put Canada in *first* place among G7 countries in foreign debt standings. (The second- and third-place finishers were Italy at 12 percent and the United States at 10 percent.) Just to pay the interest on that debt, Canadians had to give up 4.5 percent of GDP in 1994. On average, it is unrealistic to expect Canada's economy to grow at that rate in real terms, so the prospects for an improvement in the Canadian standard of living were bleak. Second, many regard debt as worrisome because it may lead to further tax increases in order to pay for the interest. The tax–GDP ratio in Canada increased from 31.5 percent in 1980 to 37.5 percent in 1993, and despite higher taxes, federal debt service costs rose from 20 percent of tax revenue to 32 percent of revenue over this same period. Finally, the existence of the debt raises issues of equity. Some regard it as immoral that one generation "spends beyond its means," thereby lowering the standard of living for future generations through such mechanisms as reduced government programs.

During the middle of the 1990s, the federal government started to get its budget deficit under control. A combination of spending cuts, rising taxes, and rapid economic growth caused the ratio of debt to GDP to stabilize and decline by about 10 percentage points by the end of the century. Recent experience has tempted some observers to think that exploding government debt is a thing of the past. But as the following case study suggests, the problem is likely to reappear.

CASE STUDY

Canadian Deficits and Debt: Past, Present, and Future

As noted earlier, between 1973 and 1993 our federal government debt ratio rose dramatically—by 50 percentage points. The Trudeau Liberals were in power for the first 10 years of this period, and the Mulroney Conservatives took over for the second half of this episode. As the size of the budget deficits grew during the Trudeau years, the Conservatives were adamant that they would stop the rise in debt if given the chance. Indeed, the Conservatives did run a more contractionary policy. Why did the debt ratio continue to explode nonetheless? When the Liberals took office again in 1993, why did they succeed in reversing the trend in the debt ratio—when the Conservatives had failed? To answer these questions, we need to understand the basic accounting relationships of deficits and debt.

The primary deficit is the excess of the government's program spending over its tax revenue. Program spending is all government expenditure except interest payments. The overall deficit is the primary deficit plus the government's interest payment obligations on its outstanding debt. To reduce the outstanding debt, the government must run an overall surplus, and this, in turn, requires a primary surplus that exceeds the existing interest payment obligations. As a first step, then, the government must eliminate its primary deficit. While this first step is not sufficient to reduce Canada's national debt, you might think that it would be enough to eliminate the explosive growth in the *ratio* of the debt to GDP. History suggests that this is not the case. Brian Mulroney's Conservative government maintained an average primary balance of zero, and was therefore much more prudent than the Trudeau Liberals, who averaged a sizable primary deficit. Despite this effort by the Conservatives, the deficit and debt problem worsened during their term of office. To appreciate why, let's carefully distinguish the primary deficit, the overall deficit, the debt, and the debt ratio.

Letting D and B stand for the government's deficit and the stock of outstanding bonds, respectively, we can summarize the key relationships as follows. The deficit is the excess of government spending over tax revenue (the primary deficit, $G - T$) plus interest payments on the outstanding bonds, rB:

$$D = G - T + rB.$$

The national debt increases by the size of the current deficit:

$$\Delta B = D.$$

Using lowercase letters to stand for the ratio of each item to GDP (i.e., $g = G/Y$, $t = T/Y$, $d = D/Y$, and $b = B/Y$), then the deficit ratio is

$$d = g - t + rb,$$

and the increase in the debt ratio is

$$\Delta b = d - nb,$$

where n stands for the long-run average growth rate in output (which takes place because of productivity increases and population growth). This last relationship may require further explanation. Since $b = B/Y$, b rises whenever its numerator grows more than its denominator does. Thus,

$$\Delta b/b = \Delta B/B - \Delta Y/Y.$$

If Y grows at rate n ($\Delta Y/Y = n$) and the bond stock grows by the size of the deficit ($\Delta B = D$), this relationship can be rewritten as

$$\Delta b/b = D/B - n,$$

or

$$\Delta b = d - nb.$$

If the government sets the primary deficit ratio at some target value, it is setting ($g - t$) as an exogenous constant. The implications for the debt ratio can then be seen by eliminating d from our two key relationships:

$$\Delta b = (g - t) + (r - n)b.$$

Consider the Conservatives' policy of setting ($g - t$) at zero. This relationship says that the debt ratio must *forever* rise—Δb is forever positive—if r exceeds n. That is, the debt ratio rises without bound if the interest rate the government pays on government bonds (the growth rate for the numerator of the debt ratio) exceeds the economy's underlying average growth rate (the growth rate for the denominator of the debt ratio).

Since r exceeded n throughout the 1970s and 1980s, it is not surprising that Canada's debt ratio rose *inexorably,* despite the Conservatives' success in keeping ($g - t$) at zero.

The economy's average growth rate exceeded interest rates during the 1950s and 1960s in Canada, when such factors as the postwar reconstruction of industry, the shift of population to the cities, and the development of Canada's natural resources made growth particularly high. Given this temporary excess of n over r and the fact that the federal government often ran budget surpluses, it is not surprising that the debt ratio fell during these years (as shown in Figure 15-1). But considering long-run average values, we must realize that r exceeds

n, so it is impossible to grow out of the debt problem by keeping the primary deficit at zero.[1]

When the Liberals took over in 1993, they switched to targeting the overall deficit ratio instead of targeting just the primary deficit ratio. Could we have expected this policy to have greater success in controlling the debt ratio?

The Liberal policy involves switching the exogenous and endogenous variables. Under the previous regime, $(g - t)$ was exogenous and d was endogenous. The Liberals' plan made d exogenous, and to accomplish this, they allowed g or t to become endogenous. Since the plan accomplished most of the deficit reduction through expenditure cuts, not tax increases, we take g as the endogenous variable in the following illustration.

Using a subscript of -1 to stand for previous period's values, the debt-ratio growth equation can be rewritten as

$$b = (1 - n)b_{-1} + d$$

This debt-ratio growth equation says that the value of this period's debt ratio is equal to the value of last period's debt ratio plus the adjustments that indicate how both the numerator and the denominator of the debt ratio have grown over the period. The numerator has grown by the size of the deficit, and the denominator has grown by the economy's rate of growth. The debt-ratio growth equation involves both these adjustments in ratio terms.

If d is an exogenous constant, the debt-ratio growth equation states that b *cannot* keep growing forever. Except for the constant d, this year's debt ratio is just a *fraction*, $(1 - n)$, of last period's value. So the Liberal plan had to work. It involved the government's "making room" in its budget by cutting programs by whatever was necessary to meet both the interest payment obligations *and* the overall deficit target. This policy succeeded, but it involved more pain in terms of lost programs.

To illustrate the magnitude of these cutbacks, Table 15-2 presents a simulation of the Liberal policy. The simulation starts with values for the deficit ratio ($d = 0.06$), the tax ratio ($t = 0.17$), the debt ratio ($b = 0.72$), the program spending ratio ($g = 0.176$), and the interest rate ($r = 0.075$), which represent what the Liberals inherited in 1993. These values satisfy the budget identity

$$d = g - t + rb.$$

From this starting position, the simulation involves an annual growth rate for GDP of 5 percent ($n = 0.05$). While actual history involved year-to-year variation in GDP growth, we simplify by taking just the average trend (3.5 percent real growth plus 1.5 percent inflation). The simulation also involves assumed time paths that—in broad terms—reflect history for the interest rate and the tax rate. In the former case, the 7.5 percent value is involved for the first four

---

[1] When evaluating whether Canada was above or below the Golden Rule level of saving (described in Chapter 4), we noted that the net marginal product of capital, $MPK - \delta$, exceeded the growth rate, here denoted simply by n, by a wide margin. In Chapter 17, we will see that $MPK = r + \delta$ in full equilibrium. In terms of long-run averages, then, we conclude that r exceeds n.

table 15-2			
A Simulation of Federal Fiscal Policy			
Fiscal Year	**Deficit/GDP (*d*)**	**Debt/GDP (*b*)**	**Spending/GDP (*g*)**
1993–1994	0.06	0.74	0.176
1994–1995	0.05	0.76	0.164
1995–1996	0.04	0.76	0.153
1996–1997	0.03	0.75	0.140
1997–1998	0	0.71	0.121
1998–1999	0	0.68	0.129
1999–2000	−0.01	0.63	0.124
2000–2001	−0.01	0.59	0.127
2001–2002	−0.01	0.55	0.129
2002–2003	−0.01	0.51	0.132
2003–2004	−0.01	0.48	0.134

years in the table; then values of 7.0 and 6.5 percent are assumed for one year each, followed by 6 percent for each year thereafter. For the tax ratio, the 17 percent figure is assumed until the end of the 1996–1997 fiscal year; a slightly higher value, 17.5 percent, is assumed after that to reflect the fact that the government did adjust policy by approximately this amount.

The second column in the table indicates the deficit ratio that the government imposed during each fiscal year that followed. We used the $b_{+1} = (1 - n)b + d$ equation to generate the third-column entry (the next year's debt ratio), and we used the $g = d + t - rb$ equation to calculate the fourth-column entry (what had to happen to program spending to meet the deficit-ratio target). Since this book went to press in early 2000, the first seven lines in the table describe history, and the last four lines illustrate what were regarded as future possibilities at the time.

Despite our simplifications, we see that the basic accounting identities do an excellent job of simulating history. They show the debt ratio falling to 63 percent, and just over a 5 percentage point drop in the program spending ratio by the end of 1999–2000 fiscal year. These figures match the true outcomes almost exactly. We see that the Liberals did get control of the debt ratio, but there was pain involved since such a large drop in program spending occurred during such a short period of time.

Because the simulation is so accurate in interpreting the past, it is tempting to extend it to illustrate future possibilities. This is done in the last four lines of the table, where it is assumed that the government runs a surplus of 1 percent of GDP for four years. This is roughly consistent with the government's plan at the time, indicated in the November 1999 *Fiscal and Economic Update*. Also consistent with the government's projections, we have assumed a constant tax-to-GDP ratio. The implications for the debt ratio and program spending are as indicated. The debt ratio can be expected to fall further—down to almost 50 percent—and the program spending ratio will recover by about 1 percentage point. This last outcome is widely referred to as the "fiscal dividend."

A fiscal dividend exists during a period of debt reduction because new room is created in the budget as the debt ratio falls. Lower debt means that the government has lower interest payment obligations, and the government can then use these funds to raise program spending, reduce taxes, or pay down debt. In the table, just to have an explicit simulation, we have assumed that the government chooses a combination of increased spending and debt reduction (budget surpluses). When the increases in the spending ratio (over the lowest value of 0.124 in 1999–2000) are multiplied by the projected values for nominal GDP for these four "future" years (using the 5 percent nominal growth rate), the sum of the increases in program spending is $30 billion. The sum of the four surpluses is $45 billion. In dollar terms then, instead of percentages of GDP, this simulation suggests that the government will have new room in its budget over this four-year period of about $75 billion—of which $30 billion can be "spent" on more generously funded programs (or tax decreases). For comparison, we have calculated how much could be spent if the government devoted none of the new room to debt reduction. In this case, the budget would be balanced in the last four lines. While not reported in the table, the debt ratio comes down less in this case, while the program spending ratio rises more. In cumulated dollar terms over four years, the new room in the budget totals $70 billion in this case, and all of this is spent.

This comparison shows that there is *much* more scope for "good news" budgets in the short run if the debt pay-down option is rejected. But when we consider the long run, we can appreciate that it will be painful for Canadians if a significant part of the "fiscal dividend" is not reserved for debt reduction. Consider the budgetary implications of reducing the debt ratio by 50 percentage points—that is, back to the level of the early 1970s. The interest payments term in the budget identity, rb, would fall by $r\Delta b$, and for a 6 percent interest rate, that's $(.06)(.5) = 0.03$. Thus, there would be 3 percentage points of GDP new room in the budget. Further, it is important to consider the full-equilibrium version of the $\Delta b = d - nb$ equation. In full equilibrium, $\Delta b = 0$, so $d = nb$. If we settle on a full equilibrium with a 20 percent debt ratio, this relationship and a 5 percent growth rate imply that $d = (0.5)(.2) = 0.01$. Thus, moving from a balanced budget (which characterized the Canadian situation when the fiscal dividend debate began) to a full equilibrium involving a 20 percent debt ratio *requires* an *increase* in the deficit ratio of 1 percentage point. (d increases from 0 to 0.01.) Thus, the overall fiscal dividend in the long run is 4 percentage points of GDP.

To put this in perspective, it is worth noting that the entire federal personal income tax system raises just 8 percent of GDP. Thus, as long as debt reduction is part of our fiscal plan, the fiscal dividend will be enough to cut income taxes in half! (We are not suggesting that tax cuts are better than spending increases; this illustration is intended just to show the magnitude of what can accompany debt reduction.)

Of course, the debt ratio can gradually approach any target number, like 20 percent, whether we balance the budget or run surpluses in the short run. The choice between these two options concerns the distribution of costs and benefits over time. Relative to balanced budgets, surpluses involve short-term pain for long-term gain. We postpone spending the fiscal dividend, but we reach the full magnitude of the benefits faster. Why should we be concerned about how long this takes?

To answer this question, many people focus on the aging of the population. With the oldest group within the large baby-boom generation starting retirement in 2011, and with increases in life expectancy generally, the proportion of the Canadian population that is over 65 years of age will double by 2030. This fact will put a strain on our public pension and health-care systems (since most health-care expenses occur in older age). The Auditor General has estimated that the government will need at least 4 percentage points of GDP—beyond what is now spent—to maintain these programs. And surely the government will face other challenges. To mention just two, there are widespread demands (and government promises) for significant tax relief, and there is the growing problem of rising income inequality and seemingly permanent unemployment for the less skilled (see the appendix to Chapter 6). Even ignoring these and all other demands on the public purse, the fiscal dividend is not big enough to cover the aging problem. After all, the government pays over 4 percent of GDP as interest on the debt now, so even if the debt were totally *eliminated,* we would not have enough to meet the challenge posed by the Auditor General.

These facts indicate that we will almost certainly have to return to a series of years involving budget deficits in the longer-term future. To keep this development from pushing debt levels to new heights, many feel that we have a limited number of years to get the debt ratio down if we are to make room for the future rise that will occur when the demographic shock hits.

15-2 | Problems in Measurement

The government budget deficit equals government spending minus government revenue, which in turn equals the amount of new debt the government needs to issue to finance its operations. This definition may sound simple enough, but in fact debates over fiscal policy sometimes arise over how the budget deficit should be measured. Some economists believe that the deficit as currently measured is not a good indicator of the stance of fiscal policy. That is, they believe that the budget deficit does not accurately gauge either the impact of fiscal policy on today's economy or the burden being placed on future generations of taxpayers. In this section we discuss four problems with the usual measure of the budget deficit.

Measurement Problem 1: Inflation

The least controversial of the measurement issues is the correction for inflation. Almost all economists agree that the government's indebtedness should be measured in real terms, not in nominal terms. The measured deficit should equal the change in the government's real debt, not the change in its nominal debt.

The budget deficit as commonly measured, however, does not correct for inflation. To see how large an error this induces, consider the following example. Suppose that the real government debt is not changing; in other words, in real terms, the budget is balanced. In this case, the nominal debt must be rising at the rate of inflation. That is,

$$\Delta B/B = \pi,$$

where π is the inflation rate and B is the stock of government bonds. This implies

$$\Delta B = \pi B.$$

The government would look at the change in the nominal debt ΔB and would report a budget deficit of πB. Hence, most economists believe that the reported budget deficit is overstated by the amount πB.

We can make the same argument in another way. The deficit is government expenditure minus government revenue. Part of expenditure is the interest paid on the government debt. Expenditure should include only the real interest paid on the debt rB, not the nominal interest paid iB. Because the difference between the nominal interest rate i and the real interest rate r is the inflation rate π, the budget deficit is overstated by πB.

This correction for inflation can be large, especially when inflation is high, and it can often change our evaluation of fiscal policy. For example, in 1981, the federal government reported a budget deficit of over $7 billion. But inflation was over 12 percent, and after correction for inflation, the deficit turned into a small surplus.

Measurement Problem 2: Capital Assets

Many economists believe that an accurate assessment of the government's budget deficit requires accounting for the government's assets as well as its liabilities. In particular, when measuring the government's overall indebtedness, we should subtract government assets from government debt. Therefore, the budget deficit should be measured as the change in debt minus the change in assets.

Certainly, individuals and firms treat assets and liabilities symmetrically. When a person borrows to buy a house, we do not say that he is running a budget deficit. Instead, we offset the increase in assets (the house) against the increase in debt (the mortgage) and record no change in net wealth. Perhaps we should treat the government's finances the same way.

A budget procedure that accounts for assets as well as liabilities is called **capital budgeting,** because it takes into account changes in capital. For example, suppose that the government sells one of its office buildings or some of its land and uses the proceeds to reduce the government debt. Under current budget procedures, the reported deficit would be lower. Under capital budgeting, the revenue received from the sale would not lower the deficit, because the reduction in debt would be offset by a reduction in assets. Similarly, under capital budgeting, government borrowing to finance the purchase of a capital good would not raise the deficit.

The major difficulty with capital budgeting is that it is hard to decide which government expenditures should count as capital expenditures. For example, should the highway system be counted as an asset of the government? If so, what is its value? Should spending on education be treated as expenditure on human capital? These difficult questions must be answered if the government is to adopt a capital budget.

Economists and policymakers disagree about whether the federal government should use capital budgeting. Opponents of capital budgeting argue that, although the system is superior in principle to the current system, it is too difficult to implement in practice. Proponents of capital budgeting argue that even an imperfect treatment of capital assets would be better than ignoring them altogether.

Measurement Problem 3: Uncounted Liabilities

Some economists argue that the measured budget deficit is misleading because it excludes some important government liabilities. For example, consider the Canada and Quebec Pension Plans. People pay some of their income into the system when young and expect to receive benefits when old. Perhaps accumulated future public pension benefits should be included in the government's liabilities.

One might argue that pension liabilities are different from government debt because the government can change the laws determining pension benefits. Yet, in principle, the government could always choose not to repay all of its debt: the government honours its debt only because it chooses to do so. Promises to pay the holders of government debt may not be fundamentally different from promises to pay the future recipients the public pension system. In the mid-1990s, the unfunded debt of the Canada Pension Plan was just about the same size as the entire federal government debt that is usually reported, so this measurement issue is important.

A particularly difficult form of government liability to measure is the *contingent liability*—the liability that is due only if a specified event occurs. For example, the government guarantees many forms of private credit, such as student loans, mortgages for low- and moderate-income families, and deposits in banks and trust companies. If the borrower repays the loan, the government pays nothing; if the borrower defaults, the government makes the repayment. When the government provides this guarantee, it undertakes a liability contingent on the borrower's default. Yet this contingent liability is not reflected in the budget deficit, in part because it is not clear what dollar value to attach to it.

Measurement Problem 4: The Business Cycle

Many changes in the government's budget deficit occur automatically in response to a fluctuating economy. For example, when the economy goes into a recession, incomes fall, so people pay less in personal income taxes. Profits fall, so corporations pay less in corporate profit taxes. More people become eligible for government assistance, such as welfare and employment insurance, so government spending rises. Even without any change in the laws governing taxation and spending, the budget deficit increases.

These automatic changes in the deficit are not errors in measurement, for the government truly borrows more when a recession depresses tax revenue and boosts government spending. But these changes do make it more difficult to use the deficit to monitor changes in fiscal policy. That is, the deficit can rise or fall either because the government has changed policy or because the economy has changed direction. For some purposes, it would be good to know which is occurring.

Many economists believe that government spending and tax rates should be set so that the budget *would* be balanced *if* real GDP was at the natural rate. If this were accomplished, we would observe deficits during recessions (when unemployment is high and the government is making more transfer payments and collecting fewer tax dollars), and we would observe surpluses during booms (when employment and tax revenue are high and employment insurance and welfare payments are low). To assess fiscal policy, then, we need to know what the deficit would be if we were not undergoing a business cycle.

To solve this problem, the Department of Finance calculates what it calls the **cyclically adjusted budget deficit**—what the excess of spending over revenue would be if Canadian GDP were at it natural-rate value. We can now clarify how these data are used. For example, in 1994, just after the Liberal government took office, the actual federal deficit was about $40 billion, while the cyclically adjusted deficit was estimated to be approximately $25 billion. According to these calculations, about $15 billion of the $40 billion total resulted from the fact that unemployment was so high in 1994. According to this approach, any attempt to push the deficit below $15 billion is regarded as inappropriate, since that part of the deficit was simply due to the state of the economy. It would vanish automatically when the economy returned to the natural rate. Efforts to eliminate it any earlier just prolong and deepen the recession. It is true that the national debt increases while we wait for this automatic elimination of that fraction of the deficit to take place. However, since there should be budget surpluses in the boom years, there should be no tendency for debt to grow over the longer run.

As the 1994 example makes clear, the cyclically adjusted deficit is a useful measure because it reflects policy changes but not the current stage of the business cycle.

Summing Up

Economists differ in the importance they place on these measurement problems. Some believe that the problems are so severe that the measured budget deficit is almost meaningless. Most take these measurement problems seriously but still view the measured budget deficit as a useful indicator of fiscal policy.

The undisputed lesson is that to evaluate fully what fiscal policy is doing, economists and policymakers must look at more than just the measured budget deficit. And, in fact, they do. No economic statistic is perfect. Whenever we see a number reported in the media, we need to know what it is measuring and what it is leaving out. This is especially true for data on government debt and budget deficits.

15-3| The Traditional View of Government Debt

Imagine that you are an economist working for the Department of Finance in Ottawa. You receive a letter from a member of Parliament (MP):

> Dear Finance Canada Economist:
>
>   Parliament is about to consider the govenment's proposal to cut all taxes by 20 percent. Before deciding whether to endorse the policy, I would like your analysis. I see little hope of reducing government spending any further, so the tax cut would mean an increase in the budget deficit. How would the tax cut and budget deficit affect the economy and the economic well-being of the country?
>
> Sincerely,
> Member of Parliament

Before responding to the MP, you open your favourite economics textbook—this one, of course—to see what the models predict for such a change in fiscal policy.

To analyze the long-run effects of this policy change, you turn to the models in Chapters 3, 4, and 5. The model in Chapter 3 shows that a tax cut stimulates consumer spending and reduces national saving. The reduction in saving raises the interest rate, which crowds out investment. The Solow growth model introduced in Chapter 4 shows that lower investment eventually leads to a lower steady-state capital stock and a lower level of output. Because we concluded in Chapter 5 that the Canadian economy has less capital than in the Golden Rule steady state (the steady state with maximum consumption), the fall in steady-state capital means lower consumption and reduced economic well-being.

To analyze the short-run effects of the policy change, you use the *IS–LM* model in Chapters 10 and 11. This model shows that a tax cut stimulates consumer spending, which implies an expansionary shift in the *IS* curve. If there is no change in monetary policy, the shift in the *IS* curve leads to an expansionary shift in the aggregate demand curve. In the short run, when prices are sticky, the expansion in aggregate demand leads to higher output and lower unemployment. Over time, as prices adjust, the economy returns to the natural rate of output, and the higher aggregate demand results in a higher price level.

To see how international trade affects your analysis, you turn to the open-economy models in Chapters 8 and 12. The model in Chapter 8 shows that when national saving falls, people start financing investment by borrowing from abroad, causing a trade deficit. Although the inflow of capital from abroad lessens the effect of the fiscal-policy change on capital accumulation, it leads to Canada becoming more indebted to foreign countries. The fiscal-policy change also causes the Canadian dollar to appreciate, which makes foreign goods cheaper in Canada and domestic goods more expensive abroad. The Mundell–Fleming model in Chapter 12 shows that the appreciation of the dollar and the resulting fall in net exports reduce the short-run expansionary impact of the fiscal change on output and employment.

With all these models in mind, you draft a response:

Dear MP:

A tax cut financed by government borrowing would have many effects on the economy. The immediate impact of the tax cut would be to stimulate consumer spending. Higher consumer spending affects the economy in both the short run and the long run.

In the short run, higher consumer spending would raise the demand for goods and services and thus raise output and employment. Interest rates would also rise, however, as investors competed for a smaller flow of saving. Higher interest rates would discourage investment and would encourage capital to flow in from abroad. The dollar would rise in value against foreign currencies, and Canadian firms would become less competitive in world markets.

In the long run, the smaller national saving caused by the tax cut would mean a smaller capital stock and a greater foreign debt. Therefore, the output of the nation would be smaller, and a greater share of that output would be owed to foreigners.

The overall effect of the tax cut on economic well-being is hard to judge. Current generations would benefit from higher consumption and higher employment, although inflation would likely be higher as well. Future generations would bear much of the burden of today's budget deficits: they would be born into a nation with a smaller capital stock and a larger foreign debt.

Your faithful servant,
Finance Canada Economist

The MP replies:

Dear Finance Canada Economist:

Thank you for your letter. It made sense to me. But yesterday my committee heard testimony from a prominent economist who called herself a "Ricardian" and who reached quite a different conclusion. She said that a tax cut by itself would not stimulate consumer spending. She concluded that the budget deficit would therefore not have all the effects you listed. What's going on here?

Sincerely,

MP

After studying the next section, you write back to the MP, explaining in detail the debate over Ricardian equivalence.

15-4 The Ricardian View of Government Debt

The traditional view of government debt presumes that when the government cuts taxes and runs a budget deficit, consumers respond to their higher after-tax income by spending more. An alternative view, called **Ricardian equivalence,** questions this presumption. According to the Ricardian view, consumers are forward-looking and, therefore, base their spending not only on their current income but also on their expected future income. As we explore more fully in Chapter 16, the forward-looking consumer is at the heart of many modern theories of consumption. The Ricardian view of government debt applies the logic of the forward-looking consumer to analyze the effects of fiscal policy.

The Basic Logic of Ricardian Equivalence

Consider the response of a forward-looking consumer to the tax cut that Parliament is debating. The consumer might reason as follows:

> The government is cutting taxes without any plans to reduce government spending. Does this policy alter my set of opportunities? Am I richer because of this tax cut? Should I consume more?
>
> Maybe not. The government is financing the tax cut by running a budget deficit. At some point in the future, the government will have to raise taxes to pay off the debt and accumulated interest. So the policy really represents a tax cut today coupled with a tax hike in the future. The tax cut merely gives me transitory income that eventually will be taken back. I am not any better off, so I will leave my consumption unchanged.

The forward-looking consumer understands that government borrowing today means higher taxes in the future. A tax cut financed by government debt does not reduce the tax burden; it merely reschedules it. It therefore should not encourage the consumer to spend more.

One can view this argument another way. Suppose that the government borrows $1,000 from the typical citizen to give that citizen a $1,000 tax cut. In essence, this policy is the same as giving the citizen a $1,000 government bond as a gift. One side of the bond says, "The government owes you, the bondholder, $1,000 plus interest." The other side says, "You, the taxpayer, owe the government $1,000 plus interest." Overall, the gift of a bond from the government to the typical citizen does not make the citizen richer or poorer, because the value of the bond is offset by the value of the future tax liability.

The general principle is that government debt is equivalent to future taxes, and if consumers are sufficiently forward-looking, future taxes are equivalent to current taxes. Hence, financing the government by debt is equivalent to financing it by taxes. This view is called *Ricardian equivalence* after the famous nineteenth-century economist David Ricardo, because he first noted the theoretical argument.

The implication of Ricardian equivalence is that a debt-financed tax cut leaves consumption unaffected. Households save the extra disposable income to pay the future tax liability that the tax cut implies. This increase in private saving just offsets the decrease in public saving. National saving—the sum of private and public saving—remains the same. The tax cut therefore has none of the effects that the traditional analysis predicts.

The logic of Ricardian equivalence does not mean that all changes in fiscal policy are irrelevant. Changes in fiscal policy do influence consumer spending if they influence present or future government purchases. For example, suppose that the government cuts taxes today because it plans to reduce government purchases in the future. If the consumer understands that this tax cut does not require an increase in future taxes, he feels richer and raises his consumption. But note that it is the reduction in government purchases, rather than the reduction in taxes, that stimulates consumption: the announcement of a future reduction in government purchases would raise consumption today even if current taxes were unchanged, because it would imply lower taxes at some time in the future.

Consumers and Future Taxes

The essence of the Ricardian view is that when people choose their consumption, they rationally look ahead to the future taxes implied by government debt. But how forward-looking are consumers? Defenders of the traditional view of government debt believe that the prospect of future taxes does not have as large an influence on current consumption as the Ricardian view assumes. Here are some of their arguments.[2]

Myopia Proponents of the Ricardian view of fiscal policy assume that people are rational when making decisions such as choosing how much of their income to consume and how much to save. When the government borrows to pay for current spending, rational consumers look ahead to the future taxes required to support this debt. Thus, the Ricardian view presumes that people have substantial knowledge and foresight.

[2] For a survey of the debate over Ricardian equivalence, see Douglas Bernheim, "Ricardian Equivalence: An Evaluation of Theory and Evidence," *NBER Macroeconomics Annual* (1987): 263–303. See also the symposium on budget deficits in the Spring 1989 issue of the *Journal of Economic Perspectives*.

---

f y i

RICARDO ON RICARDIAN EQUIVALENCE

David Ricardo was a millionaire stockbroker and one of the great economists of all time. His most important contribution was his 1817 book *Principles of Political Economy and Taxation*, in which he developed the theory of comparative advantage, which economists still use to explain the gains from international trade. Ricardo was also a member of the British Parliament, where he put his own theories to work and opposed the corn laws, which restricted international trade in grain.

Ricardo was interested in the alternative ways in which a government might pay for its expenditure. In an 1820 article called "Essay on the Funding System," he considered an example of a war that cost 20 million pounds. He noted that if the interest rate were 5 percent, this expense could be financed with a one-time tax of 20 million pounds, a perpetual tax of 1 million pounds, or a tax of 1.2 million pounds for 45 years. He wrote:

> In point of economy, there is no real difference in either of the modes; for twenty million in one payment, one million per annum for ever, or 1,200,0000 pounds for 45 years, are precisely of the same value.

Ricardo was aware that the issue involved the linkages among generations:

> It would be difficult to convince a man possessed of 20,000 pounds, or any other sum, that a perpetual payment of 50 pounds per annum was equally burdensome with a single tax of 1000 pounds. He would have some vague notion that the 50 pounds per annum would be paid by posterity, and would not be paid by him; but if he leaves his fortune to his son, and leaves it charged with this perpetual tax, where is the difference whether he leaves him 20,000 pounds with the tax, or 19,000 pounds without it?

Although Ricardo viewed these alternative methods of government finance as equivalent, he did not think other people would view them as such:

> The people who pay taxes . . . do not manage their private affairs accordingly. We are apt to think that the war is burdensome only in proportion to what we are at the moment called to pay for it in taxes, without reflecting on the probable duration of such taxes.

Thus, Ricardo doubted that people were rational and farsighted enough to look ahead fully to their future tax liabilities.

As a policymaker, Ricardo took seriously the government debt. Before the British Parliament, he once declared,

> This would be the happiest country in the world, and its progress in prosperity would go beyond the powers of imagination to conceive, if we got rid of two great evils—the national debt and the corn laws.

It is one of the great ironies in the history of economic thought that Ricardo rejected the theory that now bears his name!

---

cisively to support the traditional view. The large budget deficits coincided with low national saving, high real interest rates, and large trade deficits. Indeed, advocates of the traditional view of government debt often claim that the experience of the 1980s confirms their position.

Yet those who hold the Ricardian view of government debt interpret these events differently. Perhaps saving was low in the 1980s because people were optimistic about future economic growth—an optimism that was also reflected in a booming stock market. Or perhaps saving was low because people expected that the tax cut would eventually lead not to higher taxes but to lower

government spending instead. Because it is hard to rule out any of these interpretations, both views of government debt survive.

15-5| Other Perspectives on Government Debt

The policy debates over government debt have many facets. So far we have
considered the traditional and Ricardian views of government debt. According
to the traditional view, a government budget deficit expands aggregate demand
and stimulates output in the short run but crowds out capital and depresses
economic growth in the long run. According to the Ricardian view, a government budget deficit has none of these effects, because consumers understand
that a budget deficit represents merely postponement of a tax burden. Here we
consider several other perspectives on government debt, which could be used
to modify either the traditional or the Ricardian viewpoint.

Effects on Monetary Policy

It is often argued that a large budget deficit leads to high expectations of inflation. We first discussed such a possibility in Chapter 7. As we saw, one way for
a government to finance a budget deficit is simply to print money—a policy
that leads to higher inflation. Indeed, when countries experience hyperinflation, the typical reason is that fiscal policymakers are relying on the inflation tax
to pay for some of their spending. The ends of hyperinflations almost always
coincide with fiscal reforms that include large cuts in government spending
and, therefore, a reduced need for seigniorage.

In addition to this link between the budget deficit and inflation, some economists have suggested that a high level of debt might also encourage the government to create inflation. Because most government debt is specified in
nominal terms, the real value of the debt falls when the price level rises. This is
the usual redistribution between creditors and debtors caused by unexpected
inflation—here the debtor is the government and the creditor is the private
sector. But this debtor, unlike others, has access to the monetary printing press.
A high level of debt might encourage the government to print money, thereby
raising the price level and reducing the real value of its debts.

Despite these concerns about a possible link between government debt and
monetary policy, there is little evidence that this link is important in most
developed countries. In North America, for instance, inflation was high in the
1970s, even though government debt was low relative to GDP (at least by the
standards of the years to follow). Monetary policymakers got inflation under
control in the early 1980s, just as fiscal policymakers presided over a large increase in the debt ratio. Thus, although monetary policy might be driven by
fiscal policy in some situations, such as during the classic hyperinflations, this
situation appears not to be the norm in most countries today. There are several
reasons for this. First, most governments can finance deficits by selling debt and

don't need to rely on seigniorage. Second, central banks often have enough independence to resist political pressure for more expansionary monetary policy. Third, and most important, policymakers in all parts of government know that inflation is a poor solution to fiscal problems.

Debt and the Political Process

Fiscal policy is made not by angels but by an imperfect political process. Some economists worry that the possibility of financing government spending by issuing debt makes that political process all the worse.

This idea has a long history. Nineteenth-century economist Knut Wicksell claimed that if the benefit of some type of government spending exceeded its cost, it should be possible to finance that spending in a way that would receive unanimous support from the voters. He concluded that government spending should be undertaken only when support was, in fact, nearly unanimous. In the case of debt finance, however, Wicksell was concerned that "the interests [of future taxpayers] are not represented at all or are represented inadequately in the tax-approving assembly."

Many economists have echoed this theme more recently. In their 1977 book *Democracy in Deficit,* James Buchanan and Richard Wagner argued for a balanced-budget rule for fiscal policy on the grounds that it "will have the effect of bringing the real costs of public outlays to the awareness of decision makers; it will tend to dispel the illusory 'something for nothing' aspects of fiscal choice." Similarly, Martin Feldstein, president of the National Bureau of Economic Research in the United States, argues that "only the 'hard budget constraint' of having to balance the budget" can force politicians to judge whether spending's "benefits really justify its costs."

These arguments have led some economists to favour a constitutional amendment that would require a balanced budget on an annual basis. Often these proposals have escape clauses for times of national emergency, such as wars and depressions, when a budget deficit is a reasonable policy response. Some critics of these proposals argue that, even with the escape clauses, such a constitutional amendment would tie the hands of policymakers too severely. Others claim that a balanced-budget requirement can be evaded easily with accounting tricks. Despite these concerns, several Canadian provinces have introduced legislation that restricts the size of their deficits (New Brunswick in 1993, and Alberta, Saskatchewan, and Manitoba in 1995). As this discussion makes clear, the debate over the desirability of a balanced-budget amendment is as much political as economic.

International Dimensions

Government debt may affect a nation's role in the world economy. As we first saw in Chapter 8, when a government budget deficit reduces national saving, it often leads to a trade deficit, which in turn is financed by borrowing from abroad. For instance, many observers have blamed U.S. fiscal policy for the recent switch of the United States from a major creditor in the world economy to a major debtor. This link between the budget deficit and the trade deficit leads to two further effects of government debt.

First, high levels of government debt may increase the risk that an economy will experience capital flight—an abrupt decline in the demand for a country's assets in world financial markets. International investors are aware that a government can always deal with its debt simply by defaulting. This approach was used as far back as 1335, when England's King Edward III defaulted on his debt to Italian bankers. More recently, several Latin American countries defaulted on their debts in the 1980s, and Russia did the same in 1998. The higher the level of the government debt, the greater the temptation of default. Thus, as government debt increases, international investors may come to fear default and curtail their lending. If this loss of confidence occurs suddenly, the result could be the classic symptoms of capital flight: a collapse in the value of the currency and an increase in interest rates. As we discussed in Chapter 12, this is precisely what happened to Mexico in the early 1990s when default appeared likely.

Second, high levels of government debt financed by foreign borrowing may reduce a nation's political clout in world affairs. This fear was emphasized by economist Ben Friedman in his 1988 book *Day of Reckoning*. He wrote, "World power and influence have historically accrued to creditor countries. It is not coincidental that America emerged as a world power simultaneously with our transition from a debtor nation . . . to a creditor supplying investment capital to the rest of the world." Friedman suggests that if the United States continues to run large trade deficits, it will eventually lose some of its international influence. So far, the record has not been kind to this hypothesis: since Friedman wrote, the United States has run another decade of trade deficits and remains a leading superpower. But perhaps other events—such as the collapse of the Soviet Union—offset the fall in political clout that the United States would have experienced from its increased indebtedness.

CASE STUDY

The Benefits of Indexed Bonds

Several years ago, the federal government started to issue bonds that pay a return based on the consumer price index. These bonds are long-term. They have a 20- to 25-year maturity period, and they pay a low interest rate of about 4 percent, so a $1,000 bond pays only $40 per year in interest. But that interest payment grows with the overall price level as measured by the CPI. In addition, when the $1,000 of principal is repaid, that amount is also adjusted for changes in the CPI. The 4 percent, therefore, is a real interest rate. No longer do professors of macroeconomics need to define the real interest rate as an abstract construct. They can open up the daily newspaper, point to the bond-yields table, and say, "Look here, this is a nominal interest rate, and this is a real interest rate." (Professors in the United Kingdom and several other countries have long enjoyed this luxury because indexed bonds have been trading in other countries for years.)

Of course, making macroeconomics easier to teach was not the reason that the government chose to index some of the government debt. That was just a positive externality. Its goal was to introduce a new type of government bond that should benefit bondholder and taxpayer alike. These bonds are a win–win proposition because they insulate both sides of the transaction from inflation risk. Bondholders should care about the real interest rate they earn, and taxpayers should care about the real interest rate they pay. When government bonds are specified in nominal terms, both sides take on risk that is neither productive nor necessary. The new indexed bonds eliminate this inflation risk.

In addition, the new bonds have three other benefits:

First, the bonds may encourage the private sector to begin issuing its own indexed securities. Financial innovation is, to some extent, a public good. Once an innovation has been introduced into the market, the idea is nonexcludable (people cannot be prevented from using it) and nonrival (one person's use of the idea does not diminish other people's use of it). Just as a free market will not adequately supply the public goods of national defense and basic research, it will not adequately supply financial innovation. The government's new bonds can be viewed as a remedy for that market failure.

Second, the bonds reduce the government's incentive to produce surprise inflation. After many years of large budget deficits, the government is now a substantial debtor, and its debts are specified almost entirely in dollar terms. What is unique about the federal government, in contrast to most debtors, is that it can just print the money it needs. The greater the government's nominal debts, the more incentive the government has to inflate away its debt. The government's small switch toward indexed debt reduces this potentially problematic incentive very slightly.

Third, if the bonds were issued for much shorter maturity periods, they could provide data that might be useful for monetary policy. Many macroeconomic theories point to expected inflation as a key variable to explain the relationship between inflation and unemployment. But what is expected inflation? One way to measure it is to survey private forecasters. Another way is to look at the difference between the yield on nominal bonds and the yield on real bonds. As this book goes to press, these yields were 6.5 percent and 4 percent, respectively, so at the time, Canadians were expecting inflation of 2.5 percent per year over the coming 20 to 25 years.

In the past, economists have proposed a variety of rules that could be used to conduct monetary policy, as we discussed in the preceding chapter. Indexed bonds expand the number of possible rules. Here is one idea: The Bank of Canada announces a target for the inflation rate. Then, every day, the Bank measures expected inflation as the spread between the yield on nominal debt and the yield on indexed debt. If expected inflation is above the target, the Bank contracts the money supply. If expected inflation is below the target, the

Bank expands the money supply. In this way, the Bank can use the bond market's inflation forecast to ensure that the money supply is growing at the rate needed to keep inflation close to its target.

The new indexed bonds could, therefore, if made available for shorter terms, produce many benefits: less inflation risk, more financial innovation, better government incentives, more informed monetary policy, and easier lives for students and teachers of macroeconomics.[6]

15-6 | Conclusion

Fiscal policy and government debt have been central in the Canadian political debate over the past decade. When Paul Martin became Minister of Finance in 1993, he made reducing the budget deficit a high priority of the Liberal government. Some members of the Liberal party worried that they might lose popular support since deficit reduction was perceived as a priority more suited to the Reform and Conservative parties.

This chapter has discussed the parallel debate among economists over government debt and budget deficits. Economists disagree about how fiscal policy is best measured and how fiscal policy affects the economy. To be sure, these are among the most important and controversial questions facing policymakers today. Given the growing fiscal dividend in the short term, and the aging of the baby boomers in the longer term, there seems little doubt that these debates will continue in the years to come.

Summary

1. Taken together, the current size of the federal and provincial government debts is large by international standards. Nevertheless, after a 20-year rise in the federal debt–GDP ratio of 50 percentage points, this trend ended and the debt ratio began to fall in 1994. Questions concerning the extent to which the government should gear current fiscal policy to reinforce this turnaround will dominate debate in the coming years.

2. Standard measures of the budget deficit are imperfect measures of fiscal policy because they do not correct for the effects of inflation, do not offset changes in government liabilities with changes in government assets, omit some liabilities altogether, and do not correct for the effects of the business cycle.

---

[6] To read more about indexed bonds, see John Y. Campbell and Robert J. Shiller, "A Scorecard for Indexed Government Debt," *NBER Macroeconomics Annual,* (1996): 155–197; and David W. Wilcox, "Policy Watch: The Introduction of Indexed Government Debt in the United States," *The Journal of Economic Perspectives* 12 (Winter 1998): 219–227.

3. According to the traditional view of government debt, a debt-financed tax cut stimulates consumer spending and lowers national saving. This increase in consumer spending leads to greater aggregate demand and higher income in the short run, but it leads to a lower capital stock and higher foreign indebtedness, and so to lower income in the long run.

4. According to the Ricardian view of government debt, a debt-financed tax cut does not stimulate consumer spending because it does not raise consumers' overall resources—it merely reschedules taxes from the present to the future. The debate between the traditional and Ricardian views of government debt is ultimately a debate over how consumers behave. Are consumers rational or shortsighted? Do they face binding borrowing constraints? Are they economically linked to future generations through altruistic bequests? Economists' views of government debt hinge on their answers to these questions.

5. Government debt can potentially have various additional effects. Large government debt or budget deficits may encourage excessively expansionary monetary policy and, therefore, lead to greater inflation. The possibility of running budget deficits may encourage politicians to unduly burden future generations when setting government spending and taxes. A high level of government debt may risk capital flight and diminish a nation's influence around the world. Economists differ in which of these effects they consider most important.

KEY CONCEPTS

Capital budgeting
Cyclically adjusted budget deficit
Ricardian equivalence

QUESTIONS FOR REVIEW

1. What is unusual about Canadian fiscal policy between the mid-1970s and the mid-1990s?

2. Why do many economists project falling, and then increasing, budget deficits and government debt over the next several decades?

3. Describe four problems affecting measurement of the government budget deficit.

4. According to the traditional view of government debt, how does a debt-financed tax cut affect public saving, private saving, and national saving?

5. According to the Ricardian view of government debt, how does a debt-financed tax cut affect public saving, private saving, and national saving?

6. Do you believe the traditional or the Ricardian view of government debt? Why?

7. Why might the level of government debt affect the government's incentives regarding money creation?

PROBLEMS AND APPLICATIONS

1. On April 1, 1996, Taco Bell, the fast-food chain, ran a full-page ad in the *New York Times* with this news: "In an effort to help the national debt, Taco Bell is pleased to announce that we have agreed to purchase the Liberty Bell, one of our country's most historic treasures. It will now be called the *Taco Liberty Bell* and will still be accessible to the American public for viewing. We hope our move will prompt other corporations to take similar action to do their part to reduce the country's debt." Would such actions by corporations actually reduce the national debt as it is now measured? How would your answer change if the government adopted capital budgeting? Do you think these actions represent a true reduction in the government's indebtedness? Do you think Taco Bell was serious about this plan? (*Hint:* Note the date.)

2. Draft a letter to the member of Parliament described in Section 15-3, explaining and evaluating the Ricardian view of government debt.

3. The Canada and Quebec pension system levies a tax on workers and pays benefits to the elderly. Suppose that government increases both the tax and the benefits. For simplicity, assume that the government announces that the increases will last for one year only.

   a. How do you suppose this change would affect the economy? (*Hint:* Think about the marginal propensities to consume of the young and the old.)

   b. Does your answer depend on whether generations are altruistically linked?

Estimating the Benefits of Deficit and Debt Reduction

As noted in this chapter, deficit and debt reduction is motivated by a desire to increase living standards for future generations. No specific answer can be given, concerning how much to pursue this policy, because many people have different views concerning what amount of redistribution across generations is appropriate. But debate on this topic can be more constructive if all persons involved have some feel for the *magnitude* of the effect on future living standards.

We can provide an answer to this question by recalling a key relationship from our analysis of a small open economy in Chapter 8. We learned there that a country's net exports equal the excess of the country's output over total spending. That is,

$$\left(\begin{matrix} \text{Net} \\ \text{Exports} \end{matrix}\right) = NX = Y - C - I - G.$$

Now let us note how each of the terms in this equation is determined. First, long-run equilibrium implies that the level of a country's international indebtedness be a constant proportion of its GDP. If we define Z as the quantity of bonds sold to foreigners, then the foreign debt–GDP ratio is Z/Y. This ratio is constant if $\Delta Z/Z = \Delta Y/Y$. Denoting the output growth rate by n, this constant-ratio requirement is satisfied when

$$\Delta Z = nZ.$$

The country's debt increases each period by ΔZ, and this debt must rise whenever the trade surplus, NX, earns less foreign exchange than is necessary to cover the existing interest obligations to foreigners, rZ. That is,

$$\Delta Z = rZ - NX.$$

Combining this definition of debt growth with long-run equilibrium requirement that the debt–GDP ratio be constant yields

$$NX = (r - n)Z.$$

This expression for net exports can be substituted into the left side of the GDP identity above. Now we present expressions for the terms on the right side of that identity.

We take consumption to be proportional to disposable income:

$$C = a(Y + rB - T - rZ),$$

where B is the outstanding stock of government bonds. Disposable income is pre-tax factor earnings plus interest payment receipts from the domestic government debt minus taxes and interest payment obligations to foreigners.

The government budget deficit, D, is

$$D = G + rB - T.$$

Using this equation to replace the transfer payments less taxes term, $rB - T$, in the consumption function, we have

$$C = a(Y + D - G - rZ).$$

Finally, investment is a function of the interest rate:

$$\text{Investment} = I(r).$$

All these relationships can be combined to yield

$$(r - n)Z = Y - a(Y + D - G - rZ) - I(r) - G$$

or

$$Z = \left(\frac{1}{r(1 - a) - n}\right)\left(Y - a(Y + D - G - rZ) - I(r) - G\right).$$

This expression for foreign debt obligations can be used to estimate the effects of deficit reduction on domestic living standards. For simplicity, and to ensure that our calculation underestimates the full benefits of deficit reduction, we assume that lower debt does not decrease the risk premium demanded by foreign lenders.[7] With no change in the interest rate premium, the interest rate is exogenous for a small open economy. This fact means that investment spending is not affected by deficit reduction. Also, since the marginal product of capital equals the interest rate in long-run equilibrium, the quantity of capital and overall real GDP must be independent of deficit reduction as well.

But even though GDP for a small open economy is unaffected by deficit reduction in the long run, GNP *is* affected. GNP equals GDP minus interest payments to foreigners, so we can estimate the benefits of deficit reduction by calculating how much a lower deficit reduces our debt to foreigners.

As just noted, GNP represents the level of domestic income, $Y - rZ$. We substitute the expression for Z into this definition. We divide the resulting equation and the consumption function through by Y and use lowercase letters to denote ratios to GDP: $d = D/Y$, $g = G/Y$, $v = I/Y$, and $c = C/Y$. The result is

$$c = a\left[1 - \left(\frac{r}{r(1 - c) - n}\right)\left(1 - c(1 + d - g) - v - g\right) + d - g\right]$$

We assume that deficit reduction is accomplished through variations in taxes and transfer payments, so that, as a proportion of the economy, the size of government is constant ($\Delta g = 0$). Given this assumption, and the fact that the interest rate is exogenous for a small open economy (so that $\Delta v = 0$), this equa-

---

[7] For an estimate of the benefits of lower interest rates, see the first case study in Chapter 17.

tion implies the following relationship when written in change form:

$$\Delta c = \left(1 + \frac{rc}{r(1 - c) - n}\right)\Delta d.$$

Representative parameter values for the marginal propensity to consume, the average growth rate, and the yield earned by foreigners on stocks and bonds in Canada are $a = 0.9$, $n = 0.05$, and $r = 0.10$. Given recent fiscal policy, an interesting reduction in the deficit ratio is 5 percentage points so $\Delta d = -.05$ is representative. Substituting these values into the last equation indicates that consumption can be expected to rise by 5.6 percentage points of GDP. The fact that this is such a large increase in living standards is the reason why some individuals have been so passionate about deficit and debt reduction.[8]

---

[8] Estimates of this same order of magnitude emerge when a more sophisticated consumption function involving only a slight departure from pure Ricardian equivalence is involved in the calculations. See W.M. Scarth, *Deficit Reduction: Costs and Benefits,* Commentary No. 61 (Toronto: C.D. Howe Institute, 1994).

part FIVE

More on the Microeconomics Behind Macroeconomics

To understand the economy as a whole, we must understand the households and firms that make up the economy. In the next four chapters we look more closely at the behaviour of households and firms. These chapters present microeconomic models that help refine our macroeconomic analysis.

Chapter 16 looks at how consumers behave. It begins with the simple consumption function that we have used throughout much of this book and then discusses more sophisticated models of consumer behaviour.

Chapter 17 examines the determinants of the three types of investment spending—business fixed investment, residential investment, and inventory investment. It discusses why investment depends on the interest rate, what might cause the investment function to shift, and why investment fluctuates so much over the business cycle.

Chapter 18 studies the supply and demand for money. It discusses the role of the banking system in determining the money supply, as well as the various theories of the money demand function. This discussion offers new insights into the instruments and problems of monetary policy.

Chapter 19 presents some recent developments in the theory of short-run economic fluctuations. It discusses the avenues of research that economists are now exploring to improve our understanding of the business cycle, and it highlights the disagreements about which avenues are likely to prove most fruitful.

16

Consumption

Consumption is the sole end and purpose of all production.

— *Adam Smith*

How do households decide how much of their income to consume today and how much to save for the future? This is a microeconomic question because it addresses the behaviour of individual decisionmakers. Yet its answer has macroeconomic consequences. As we have seen in previous chapters, households' consumption decisions affect the way the economy as a whole behaves both in the long run and in the short run.

The consumption decision is crucial for long-run analysis because of its role in economic growth. The Solow growth model of Chapters 4 and 5 shows that the saving rate is a key determinant of the steady-state capital stock and thus of the level of economic well-being. The saving rate measures how much of its income the present generation is putting aside for its own future and for future generations.

The consumption decision is crucial for short-run analysis because of its role in determining aggregate demand. Consumption is six-tenths of GDP, so fluctuations in consumption are a key element of booms and recessions. The *IS–LM* model of Chapters 10 and 11 shows that changes in consumers' spending plans can be a source of shocks to the economy, and that the marginal propensity to consume is a determinant of the fiscal-policy multipliers.

In previous chapters we explained consumption with a function that relates consumption to disposable income: $C = C(Y - T)$. This approximation allowed us to develop simple models for long-run and short-run analysis. But it is too simple to provide a complete explanation of consumer behaviour. In this chapter we examine the consumption function in greater detail and develop a more thorough explanation of what determines aggregate consumption.

Since macroeconomics began as a field of study, many economists have written about the theory of consumer behaviour and suggested alternative ways of interpreting the data on consumption and income. This chapter presents the views of four prominent economists, roughly in historical order. By examining the theories of consumer behaviour developed by John Maynard Keynes,

Irving Fisher, Franco Modigliani, and Milton Friedman, this chapter provides an overview of the diverse approaches to explaining consumption.

16-1 | John Maynard Keynes and the Consumption Function

We begin our study of consumption with John Maynard Keynes's *General Theory,* which was published in 1936. Keynes made the consumption function central to his theory of economic fluctuations, and it has played a key role in macroeconomic analysis ever since. Let's consider what Keynes thought about the consumption function, and then see what puzzles arose when his ideas were confronted with the data.

Keynes's Conjectures

Today, economists who study consumption rely on sophisticated techniques of data analysis. With the help of computers, they analyze aggregate data on the behaviour of the overall economy from the national accounts and detailed data on the behaviour of individual households from surveys. Because Keynes wrote in the 1930s, however, he had neither the advantage of these data nor the computers necessary to analyze such large data sets. Instead of relying on statistical analysis, Keynes made conjectures about the consumption function based on introspection and casual observation.

First and most important, Keynes conjectured that the **marginal propensity to consume**—the amount consumed out of an additional dollar of income—is between zero and one. He wrote that the "fundamental psychological law, upon which we are entitled to depend with great confidence, . . . is that men are disposed, as a rule and on the average, to increase their consumption as their income increases, but not by as much as the increase in their income." That is, when a person earns an extra dollar, he typically spends some of it and saves some of it. As we saw in Chapter 10 when we developed the Keynesian cross, the marginal propensity to consume was crucial to Keynes's policy recommendations for how to reduce widespread unemployment. The power of fiscal policy to influence the economy—as expressed by the fiscal-policy multipliers—arises from the feedback between income and consumption.

Second, Keynes posited that the ratio of consumption to income, called the **average propensity to consume,** falls as income rises. He believed that saving was a luxury, so he expected the rich to save a higher proportion of their income than the poor. Although not essential for Keynes's own analysis, the postulate that the average propensity to consume falls as income rises became a central part of early Keynesian economics.

Third, Keynes thought that income is the primary determinant of consumption and that the interest rate does not have an important role. This conjecture stood in stark contrast to the beliefs of the classical economists who preceded him. The classical economists held that a higher interest rate encourages saving and discourages consumption. Keynes admitted that the interest rate could influence consumption as a matter of theory. Yet he wrote that "the main conclusion suggested by experience, I think, is that the short-period influence of the rate of interest on individual spending out of a given income is secondary and relatively unimportant."

On the basis of these three conjectures, the Keynesian consumption function is often written as

$$C = \overline{C} + cY, \qquad \overline{C} > 0, \quad 0 < c < 1,$$

where C is consumption, Y is disposable income, $\overline{C}$ is a constant, and c is the marginal propensity to consume. This consumption function, shown in Figure 16-1, is graphed as a straight line.

Notice that this consumption function exhibits the three properties that Keynes posited. It satisfies Keynes's first property because the marginal propensity to consume c is between zero and one, so that higher income leads to higher consumption and also to higher saving. This consumption function satisfies Keynes's second property because the average propensity to consume APC is

$$APC = C/Y = \overline{C}/Y + c.$$

As Y rises, $\overline{C}/Y$ falls, and so the average propensity to consume C/Y falls. And finally, this consumption function satisfies Keynes's third property because the interest rate is not included in this equation as a determinant of consumption.

figure 16-1

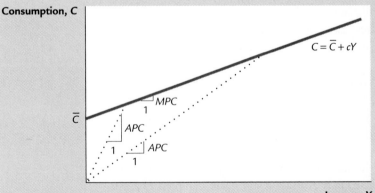

The Keynesian Consumption Function This figure graphs a consumption function with the three properties that Keynes conjectured. First, the marginal propensity to consume c is between zero and one. Second, the average propensity to consume falls as income rises. Third, consumption is determined by current income.

Note: The marginal propensity to consume, *MPC*, is the slope of the consumption function. The average propensity to consume, *APC* = *C*/*Y*, equals the slope of a line drawn from the origin to a point on the consumption function.

The Early Empirical Successes

Soon after Keynes proposed the consumption function, economists began collecting and examining data to test his conjectures. The earliest studies indicated that the Keynesian consumption function is a good approximation of how consumers behave.

In some of these studies, researchers surveyed households and collected data on consumption and income. They found that households with higher income consumed more, which confirms that the marginal propensity to consume is greater than zero. They also found that households with higher income saved more, which confirms that the marginal propensity to consume is less than one. In addition, these researchers found that higher-income households saved a larger fraction of their income, which confirms that the average propensity to consume falls as income rises. Thus, these data verified Keynes's conjectures about the marginal and average propensities to consume.

In other studies, researchers examined aggregate data on consumption and income for the period between the two world wars. These data also supported the Keynesian consumption function. In years when income was unusually low, such as during the depths of the Great Depression, both consumption and saving were low, indicating that the marginal propensity to consume is between zero and one. In addition, during those years of low income, the ratio of consumption to income was high, confirming Keynes's second conjecture. Finally, because the correlation between income and consumption was so strong, no other variable appeared to be important for explaining consumption. Thus, the data also confirmed Keynes's third conjecture that income is the primary determinant of how much people choose to consume.

Secular Stagnation, Simon Kuznets, and the Consumption Puzzle

Although the Keynesian consumption function met with early successes, two anomalies soon arose. Both concern Keynes's conjecture that the average propensity to consume falls as income rises.

The first anomaly became apparent after some economists made a dire—and, it turned out, erroneous—prediction during World War II. On the basis of the Keynesian consumption function, these economists reasoned that as incomes in the economy grew over time, households would consume a smaller and smaller fraction of their incomes. They feared that there might not be enough profitable investment projects to absorb all this saving. If so, the low consumption would lead to an inadequate demand for goods and services, resulting in a depression once the wartime demand from the government ceased. In other words, on the basis of the Keynesian consumption function, these economists predicted that the economy would experience what they called *secular stagnation*—a long depression of indefinite duration—unless fiscal policy was used to expand aggregate demand.

Fortunately for the economy, but unfortunately for the Keynesian consumption function, the end of World War II did not throw Western economies into another depression. Although incomes were much higher after the war than before, these higher incomes did not lead to large increases in the rate of saving. Keynes's conjecture that the average propensity to consume would fall as income rose appeared not to hold.

The second anomaly arose when economist Simon Kuznets constructed new aggregate data on consumption and income for the United States dating back to 1869. Kuznets assembled these data in the 1940s and would later receive the Nobel Prize for this work. He discovered that the ratio of consumption to income was remarkably stable from decade to decade, despite large increases in income over the period he studied. Again, Keynes's conjecture that the average propensity to consume would fall as income rose appeared not to hold.

The failure of the secular-stagnation hypothesis and the findings of Kuznets both indicated that the average propensity to consume is fairly constant over long periods of time. This fact presented a puzzle that motivated much of the subsequent work on consumption. Economists wanted to know why some studies confirmed Keynes's conjectures and others refuted them. That is, why did Keynes's conjectures hold up well in the studies of household data and in the studies of short time-series, but fail when long time-series were examined?

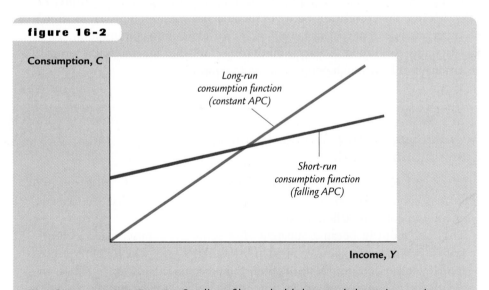

figure 16-2

The Consumption Puzzle Studies of household data and short time-series found a relationship between consumption and income similar to the one Keynes conjectured. In the figure, this relationship is called the short-run consumption function. But studies of long time-series found that the average propensity to consume did not vary systematically with income. This relationship is called the long-run consumption function. Notice that the short-run consumption function has a falling average propensity to consume, whereas the long-run consumption function has a constant average propensity to consume.

Figure 16-2 illustrates the puzzle. The evidence suggested that there were two consumption functions. For the household data or for the short time-series, the Keynesian consumption function appeared to work well. Yet for the long time-series, the consumption function appeared to have a constant average propensity to consume. In Figure 16-2, these two relationships between consumption and income are called the short-run and long-run consumption functions. Economists needed to explain how these two consumption functions could be consistent with each other.

In the 1950s, Franco Modigliani and Milton Friedman each proposed explanations of these seemingly contradictory findings. Both economists later won Nobel Prizes, in part because of their work on consumption. But before we see how Modigliani and Friedman tried to solve the consumption puzzle, we must discuss Irving Fisher's contribution to consumption theory. Both Modigliani's life-cycle hypothesis and Friedman's permanent-income hypothesis rely on the theory of consumer behaviour proposed much earlier by Irving Fisher.

16-2 | Irving Fisher and Intertemporal Choice

The consumption function introduced by Keynes relates current consumption to current income. This relationship, however, is incomplete at best. When people decide how much to consume and how much to save, they consider both the present and the future. The more consumption they enjoy today, the less they will be able to enjoy tomorrow. In making this tradeoff, households must look ahead to the income they expect to receive in the future and to the consumption of goods and services they hope to be able to afford.

The economist Irving Fisher developed the model with which economists analyze how rational, forward-looking consumers make intertemporal choices—that is, choices involving different periods of time. Fisher's model illuminates the constraints consumers face, the preferences they have, and how these constraints and preferences together determine their choices about consumption and saving.

The Intertemporal Budget Constraint

Most people would prefer to increase the quantity or quality of the goods and services they consume—to wear nicer clothes, eat at better restaurants, or see more movies. The reason people consume less than they desire is that their consumption is constrained by their income. In other words, consumers face a limit on how much they can spend, called a *budget constraint*. When they are deciding how much to consume today versus how much to save for the future, they face an **intertemporal budget constraint,** which measures the total resources available for consumption today and in the future. Our first step in developing Fisher's model is to examine this constraint in some detail.

To keep things simple, we examine the decision facing a consumer who lives for two periods. Period one represents the consumer's youth, and period two represents the consumer's old age. The consumer earns income Y_1 and consumes C_1 in period one, and earns income Y_2 and consumes C_2 in period two. (All variables are real—that is, adjusted for inflation.) Because the consumer has the opportunity to borrow and save, consumption in any single period can be either greater or less than income in that period.

Consider how the consumer's income in the two periods constrains consumption in the two periods. In the first period, saving equals income minus consumption. That is,

$$S = Y_1 - C_1,$$

where S is saving. In the second period, consumption equals the accumulated saving, including the interest earned on that saving, plus second-period income. That is,

$$C_2 = (1 + r)S + Y_2,$$

where r is the real interest rate. For example, if the interest rate is 5 percent, then for every \$1 of saving in period one, the consumer enjoys an extra \$1.05 of consumption in period two. Because there is no third period, the consumer does not save in the second period.

Note that the variable S can represent either saving or borrowing and that these equations hold in both cases. If first-period consumption is less than first-period income, the consumer is saving, and S is greater than zero. If first-period consumption exceeds first-period income, the consumer is borrowing, and S is less than zero. For simplicity, we assume that the interest rate for borrowing is the same as the interest rate for saving.

To derive the consumer's budget constraint, combine the two equations above. Substitute the first equation for S into the second equation to obtain

$$C_2 = (1 + r)(Y_1 - C_1) + Y_2.$$

To make the equation easier to interpret, we must rearrange terms. To place all the consumption terms together, bring $(1 + r)C_1$ from the right-hand side to the left-hand side of the equation to obtain

$$(1 + r)C_1 + C_2 = (1 + r)Y_1 + Y_2.$$

Now divide both sides by $(1 + r)$ to obtain

$$C_1 + \frac{C_2}{1 + r} = Y_1 + \frac{Y_2}{1 + r}.$$

This equation relates consumption in the two periods to income in the two periods. It is the standard way of expressing the consumer's intertemporal budget constraint.

The consumer's budget constraint is easily interpreted. If the interest rate is zero, the budget constraint shows that total consumption in the two periods equals total income in the two periods. In the usual case in which the interest

figure 16-3

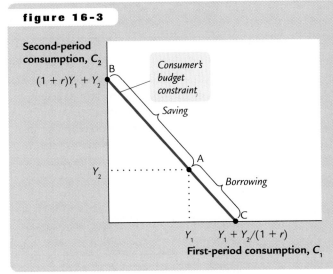

The Consumer's Budget Constraint
This figure shows the combinations of first-period and second-period consumption the consumer can choose. If he chooses points between A and B, he consumes less than his income in the first period and saves the rest for the second period. If he chooses points between A and C, he consumes more than his income in the first period and borrows to make up the difference.

rate is greater than zero, future consumption and future income are discounted by a factor $1 + r$. This **discounting** arises from the interest earned on savings. In essence, because the consumer earns interest on current income that is saved, future income is worth less than current income. Similarly, because future consumption is paid for out of savings that have earned interest, future consumption costs less than current consumption. The factor $1/(1 + r)$ is the price of second-period consumption measured in terms of first-period consumption: it is the amount of first-period consumption that the consumer must forgo to obtain 1 unit of second-period consumption.

Figure 16-3 graphs the consumer's budget constraint. Three points are marked on this figure. At point A, the consumer consumes exactly his income in each period ($C_1 = Y_1$ and $C_2 = Y_2$), so there is neither saving nor borrowing between the two periods. At point B, the consumer consumes nothing in the first period ($C_1 = 0$) and saves all income, so second-period consumption C_2 is $(1 + r)Y_1 + Y_2$. At point C, the consumer plans to consume nothing in the second period ($C_2 = 0$) and borrows as much as possible against second-period income, so first-period consumption C_1 is $Y_1 + Y_2/(1 + r)$. Of course, these are only three of the many combinations of first- and second-period consumption that the consumer can afford: all the points on the line from B to C are available to the consumer.

Consumer Preferences

The consumer's preferences regarding consumption in the two periods can be represented by **indifference curves.** An indifference curve shows the combinations of first-period and second-period consumption that make the consumer equally happy.

---

f y i

PRESENT VALUE, OR WHY A $1,000,000 PRIZE IS WORTH ONLY $623,000

The use of discounting in the consumer's budget constraint illustrates an important fact of economic life: a dollar in the future is less valuable than a dollar today. This is true because a dollar today can be deposited in an interest-bearing bank account and produce more than one dollar in the future. If the interest rate is 5 percent, for instance, then a dollar today can be turned to $1.05 dollars next year, $1.1025 in two years, $1.1576 in three years, . . . , or $2.65 in 20 years.

Economists use a concept called *present value* to compare dollar amounts from different times. The present value of any amount in the future is the amount that would be needed today, given available interest rates, to produce that future amount. Thus, if you are going to be paid X dollars in T years and the interest rate is r, then the present value of that payment is

Present Value $= X/(1+r)^T$.

In light of this definition, we can see a new interpretation of the consumer's budget constraint in our two-period consumption problem. The intertemporal budget constraint states that the present value of consumption must equal the present value of income.

The concept of present value has many applications. Suppose, for instance, that you won a million-dollar lottery. Such prizes are usually paid out over time—say, $50,000 a year for 20 years. What is the present value of such a delayed prize? By applying the above formula for each of the 20 payments and adding up the result, we learn that the million-dollar prize, discounted at an interest rate of 5 percent, has a present value of only $623,000. (If the prize were paid out as a dollar a year for a million years, the present value would be a mere $20!) Sometimes a million dollars isn't all it's cracked up to be.

Figure 16-4 shows two of the consumer's many indifference curves. The consumer is indifferent among combinations W, X, and Y, because they are all on the same curve. Not surprisingly, if the consumer's first-period consumption is reduced, say from point W to point X, second-period consumption must increase to keep him equally happy. If first-period consumption is reduced again, from point X to point Y, the amount of extra second-period consumption he requires for compensation is greater.

The slope at any point on the indifference curve shows how much second-period consumption the consumer requires in order to be compensated for a 1-unit reduction in first-period consumption. This slope is the **marginal rate of substitution** between first-period consumption and second-period consumption. It tells us the rate at which the consumer is willing to substitute second-period consumption for first-period consumption.

Notice that the indifference curves in Figure 16-4 are not straight lines and, as a result, the marginal rate of substitution depends on the levels of consumption in the two periods. When first-period consumption is high and second-period consumption is low, as at point W, the marginal rate of substitution is low: the consumer requires only a little extra second-period consumption to

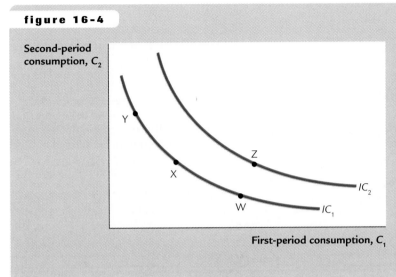

Second-period consumption, C_2

First-period consumption, C_1

The Consumer's Preferences Indifference curves represent the consumer's preferences over first-period and second-period consumption. An indifference curve gives the combinations of consumption in the two periods that make the consumer equally happy. This figure shows two of many indifference curves. Higher indifference curves such as IC_2 are preferred to lower curves such as IC_1. The consumer is equally happy at points W, X, and Y, but prefers point Z to points W, X, or Y.

give up 1 unit of first-period consumption. When first-period consumption is low and second-period consumption is high, as at point Y, the marginal rate of substitution is high: the consumer requires much additional second-period consumption to give up 1 unit of first-period consumption.

The consumer is equally happy at all points on a given indifference curve, but he prefers some indifference curves to others. Because he prefers more consumption to less, he prefers higher indifference curves to lower ones. In Figure 16-4, the consumer prefers the points on curve IC_2 to the points on curve IC_1.

The set of indifference curves gives a complete ranking of the consumer's preferences. It tells us that the consumer prefers point Z to point W, but that may be obvious because point Z has more consumption in both periods. Yet compare point Z and point Y: point Z has more consumption in period one and less in period two. Which is preferred, Z or Y? Because Z is on a higher indifference curve than Y, we know that the consumer prefers point Z to point Y. Hence, we can use the set of indifference curves to rank any combinations of first-period and second-period consumption.

Optimization

Having discussed the consumer's budget constraint and preferences, we can consider the decision about how much to consume. The consumer would like to end up with the best possible combination of consumption in the two periods—that is, on the highest possible indifference curve. But the budget constraint requires that the consumer also end up on or below the budget line, because the budget line measures the total resources available to him.

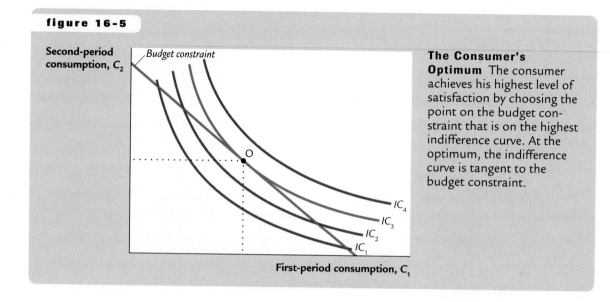

figure 16-5

Second-period consumption, C_2

Budget constraint

IC_4
IC_3
IC_2
IC_1

O

First-period consumption, C_1

The Consumer's Optimum The consumer achieves his highest level of satisfaction by choosing the point on the budget constraint that is on the highest indifference curve. At the optimum, the indifference curve is tangent to the budget constraint.

Figure 16-5 shows that many indifference curves cross the budget line. The highest indifference curve that the consumer can obtain without violating the budget constraint is the indifference curve that just barely touches the budget line, which is curve IC_3 in the figure. The point at which the curve and line touch—point O for "optimum"—is the best combination of consumption in the two periods that the consumer can afford.

Notice that, at the optimum, the slope of the indifference curve equals the slope of the budget line. The indifference curve is *tangent* to the budget line. The slope of the indifference curve is the marginal rate of substitution *MRS,* and the slope of the budget line is 1 plus the real interest rate. We conclude that at point O,

$$MRS = 1 + r.$$

The consumer chooses consumption in the two periods so that the marginal rate of substitution equals 1 plus the real interest rate.

How Changes in Income Affect Consumption

Now that we have seen how the consumer makes the consumption decision, let's examine how consumption responds to an increase in income. An increase in either Y_1 or Y_2 shifts the budget constraint outward, as in Figure 16-6. The higher budget constraint allows the consumer to choose a better combination of first- and second-period consumption—that is, the consumer can now reach a higher indifference curve.

In Figure 16-6, the consumer responds to the shift in his budget constraint by choosing more consumption in both periods. Although not implied by the logic of the model alone, this situation is the most usual. If a consumer wants more of a good when his or her income rises, economists call it a **normal**

figure 16-6

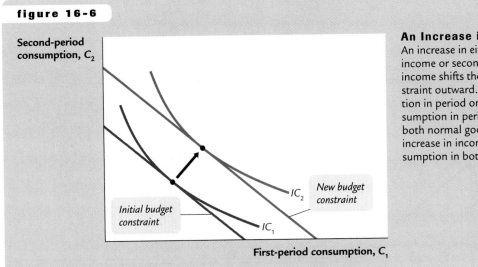

Second-period
consumption, C_2

An Increase in Income
An increase in either first-period
income or second-period
income shifts the budget constraint outward. If consumption in period one and consumption in period two are
both normal goods, this
increase in income raises consumption in both periods.

IC_2 *New budget
constraint*

*Initial budget
constraint*

IC_1

First-period consumption, C_1

good. The indifference curves in Figure 16-6 are drawn under the assumption
that consumption in period one and consumption in period two are both normal goods.

The key conclusion from Figure 16-6 is that regardless of whether the increase in income occurs in the first period or the second period, the consumer
spreads it over consumption in both periods. This behaviour is sometimes
called *consumption smoothing*. Because the consumer can borrow and lend between periods, the timing of the income is irrelevant to how much is consumed today (except, of course, that future income is discounted by the interest
rate). The lesson of this analysis is that consumption depends on the present
value of current and future income—that is, on

$$\text{Present Value of Income} = Y_1 + \frac{Y_2}{1 + r}.$$

Notice that this conclusion is quite different from that reached by Keynes.
*Keynes posited that a person's current consumption depends largely on his current in-
come. Fisher's model says, instead, that consumption is based on the resources the consumer expects over his lifetime.*

How Changes in the Real Interest Rate Affect Consumption

Let's now use Fisher's model to consider how a change in the real interest rate
alters the consumer's choices. There are two cases to consider: the case in
which the consumer is initially saving and the case in which he is initially borrowing. Here we discuss the saving case, and Problem 1 at the end of the chapter asks you to analyze the borrowing case.

Figure 16-7 shows that an increase in the real interest rate rotates the consumer's budget line around the point (Y_1, Y_2) and, thereby, alters the amount

figure 16-7

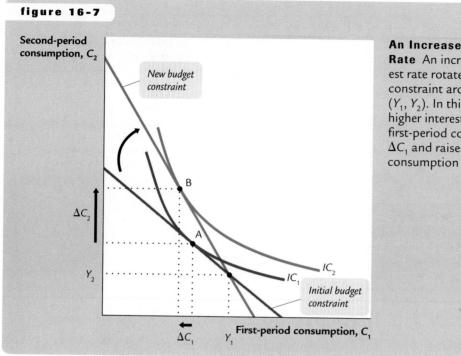

An Increase in the Interest Rate An increase in the interest rate rotates the budget constraint around the point (Y_1, Y_2). In this figure, the higher interest rate reduces first-period consumption by ΔC_1 and raises second-period consumption by ΔC_2.

of consumption he chooses in both periods. Here, the consumer moves from point A to point B. You can see that for the indifference curves drawn in this figure first-period consumption falls and second-period consumption rises.

Economists decompose the impact of an increase in the real interest rate on consumption into two effects: an **income effect** and a **substitution effect.** Textbooks in microeconomics discuss these effects in detail. We summarize them briefly here.

The income effect is the change in consumption that results from the movement to a higher indifference curve. Because the consumer is a saver rather than a borrower (as indicated by the fact that first-period consumption is less than first-period income), the increase in the interest rate makes him better off (as reflected by the movement to a higher indifference curve). If consumption in period one and consumption in period two are both normal goods, the consumer will want to spread this improvement in his welfare over both periods. This income effect tends to make the consumer want more consumption in both periods.

The substitution effect is the change in consumption that results from the change in the relative price of consumption in the two periods. In particular, consumption in period two becomes less expensive relative to consumption in period one when the interest rate rises. That is, because the real interest rate earned on saving is higher, the consumer must now give up less first-period consumption to obtain an extra unit of second-period consumption. This substitution effect tends to make the consumer choose more consumption in period two and less consumption in period one.

The consumer's choice depends on both the income effect and the substitution effect. Both effects act to increase the amount of second-period consumption; hence, we can confidently conclude that an increase in the real interest rate raises second-period consumption. But the two effects have opposite impacts on first-period consumption. Hence, the increase in the interest rate could either lower or raise first-period consumption.

CASE STUDY

Consumption and the Real Interest Rate

Irving Fisher's model shows that, depending on the consumer's preferences, changes in the real interest rate could either raise or lower consumption. In other words, economic theory alone cannot predict how the interest rate influences consumption. Therefore, economists have devoted much energy to examining empirically how the interest rate affects consumption and saving.

Figure 16-8 presents a scatterplot of the personal saving rate and the real interest rate for Canada. This figure shows that there is no apparent relationship

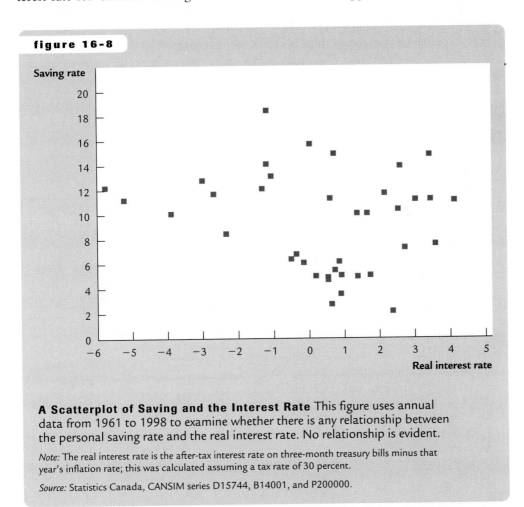

figure 16-8

A Scatterplot of Saving and the Interest Rate This figure uses annual data from 1961 to 1998 to examine whether there is any relationship between the personal saving rate and the real interest rate. No relationship is evident.

Note: The real interest rate is the after-tax interest rate on three-month treasury bills minus that year's inflation rate; this was calculated assuming a tax rate of 30 percent.

Source: Statistics Canada, CANSIM series D15744, B14001, and P200000.

between the two variables. Some economists interpret these data as showing that saving does not depend on the interest rate. They explain this result by claiming that the income and substitution effects of higher interest rates approximately cancel each other.

This sort of evidence, however, is not completely persuasive. The task of estimating the sensitivity of saving to the interest rate is complicated by the identification problem discussed in Chapter 3. That is, when variables are related in more than one way, as these two variables are, it is tricky to separate one relationship from another. Nonetheless, more sophisticated examinations of the data usually find that the real interest rate has little effect on consumption and saving. Keynes's third conjecture—that consumption does not depend much on the interest rate—has held up well in the face of much empirical testing.[1]

Constraints on Borrowing

Fisher's model assumes that the consumer can borrow as well as save. The ability to borrow allows current consumption to exceed current income. In essence, when the consumer borrows, he consumes some of his future income today. Yet for many people such borrowing is impossible. For example, an unemployed individual wishing to go skiing at Whistler or to relax in Florida would probably be unable to finance these vacations with a bank loan. Let's examine how Fisher's analysis changes if the consumer cannot borrow.

The inability to borrow prevents current consumption from exceeding current income. A constraint on borrowing can therefore be expressed as

$$C_1 \leq Y_1.$$

This inequality states that consumption in period one must be less than or equal to income in period one. This additional constraint on the consumer is called a **borrowing constraint** or, sometimes, a *liquidity constraint*.

Figure 16-9 shows how this borrowing constraint restricts the consumer's set of choices. The consumer's choice must satisfy both the intertemporal budget constraint and the borrowing constraint. The

Drawing by Handelsman; © 1985 The New Yorker Magazine, Inc.

"What I'd like, basically, is a temporary line of credit just to tide me over the rest of my life."

---

[1] For some of the recent research on the relationship between consumption and the real interest rate, see Robert E. Hall, "Intertemporal Substitution and Consumption," *Journal of Political Economy* 96 (April 1988): 339–357; and John Y. Campbell and N. Gregory Mankiw, "Consumption, Income, and Interest Rates: Reinterpreting the Time-Series Evidence," *NBER Macroeconomics Annual* (1989): 185–216.

figure 16-9

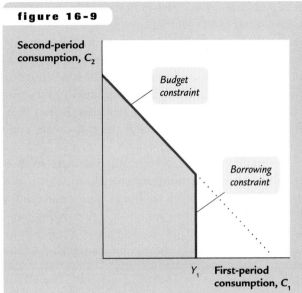

Second-period consumption, C_2

Budget constraint

Borrowing constraint

Y_1 **First-period consumption, C_1**

A Borrowing Constraint If the consumer cannot borrow, he faces the additional constraint that first-period consumption cannot exceed first-period income. The shaded area represents the combination of first-period and second-period consumption the consumer can choose.

figure 16-10

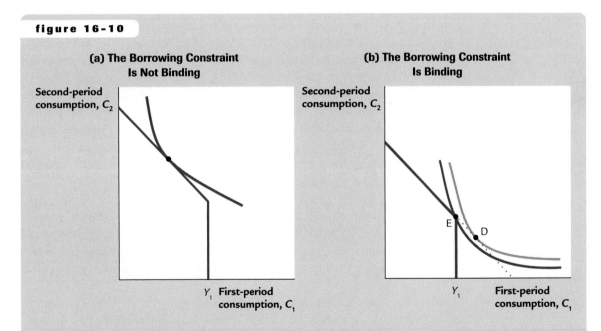

(a) The Borrowing Constraint Is Not Binding

Second-period consumption, C_2

Y_1 **First-period consumption, C_1**

(b) The Borrowing Constraint Is Binding

Second-period consumption, C_2

E   D

Y_1 **First-period consumption, C_1**

The Consumer's Optimum With a Borrowing Constraint When the consumer faces a borrowing constraint, there are two possible situations. In panel (a), the consumer chooses first-period consumption to be less than first-period income, so the borrowing constraint is not binding and does not affect consumption in either period. In panel (b), the borrowing constraint is binding. The consumer would like to borrow and choose point D. But because borrowing is not allowed, the best available choice is point E. When the borrowing constraint is binding, first-period consumption equals first-period income.

shaded area represents the combinations of first-period consumption and second-period consumption that satisfy both constraints.

Figure 16-10 shows how this borrowing constraint affects the consumption decision. There are two possibilities. In panel (a), the consumer wishes to consume less in period one than he earns. The borrowing constraint is not binding in this case and, therefore, does not affect consumption. In panel (b), the consumer would like to consume more in period one than he earns. In this case, the consumer consumes all his first-period income, and the borrowing constraint prevents him from consuming more.

The analysis of borrowing constraints leads us to conclude that there are two consumption functions. For some consumers, the borrowing constraint is not binding, and consumption in both periods depends on the present value of lifetime income, $Y_1 + [Y_2/(1 + r)]$. For other consumers, the borrowing constraint binds, and the consumption function is $C_1 = Y_1$ and $C_2 = Y_2$. *Hence, for those consumers who would like to borrow but cannot, consumption depends only on current income.*

CASE STUDY

The High Japanese Saving Rate

Japan has one of the world's highest saving rates, and this fact is important for understanding both the long-run and short-run performance of its economy. On the one hand, many economists believe that the high Japanese saving rate is a key to the rapid growth Japan experienced in the decades after World War II. Indeed, the Solow growth model developed in Chapters 4 and 5 shows that the saving rate is a primary determinant of a country's steady-state level of income. On the other hand, some economists have argued that the high Japanese saving rate contributed to Japan's slump during the 1990s. High saving means low consumer spending, which according to the *IS–LM* model of Chapters 10 and 11 translates into low aggregate demand and reduced income.

Why do the Japanese consume a much smaller fraction of their income than do North Americans? One reason is that it is harder for households to borrow in Japan. As Fisher's model shows, a household facing a binding borrowing constraint consumes less than it would without the borrowing constraint. Hence, societies in which borrowing constraints are common will tend to have higher rates of saving.

One reason that households often wish to borrow is to buy a home. In Canada, a person can usually buy a home with a down payment of 10 percent. A home buyer in Japan cannot borrow nearly this much: down payments of 40 percent are common. Moreover, housing prices are very high in Japan, primarily because land prices are high. A Japanese family must save a great deal if it is ever to afford its own home.

Although constraints on borrowing are part of the explanation of high Japanese saving, there are many other differences between Japan and Canada that contribute to the difference in the saving rates. For example, cultural differences may lead to differences in consumer preferences regarding present and future consumption. One prominent Japanese economist writes, "The Japanese are simply *different*. They are more risk averse and more patient. If this is true, the long-run implication is that Japan will absorb all the wealth in the world. I refuse to comment on this explanation."[2]

Many economists believe that a low saving rate is one of Canada's biggest economic problems. As we discussed in Chapter 4, increasing national saving is often a stated goal of economic policy. Keep in mind, however, that policies designed to raise saving have their costs. Home buyers in Canada would not be happy if they faced the borrowing constraints that are so common in Japan.

16-3 | Franco Modigliani and the Life-Cycle Hypothesis

In a series of papers written in the 1950s, Franco Modigliani and his collaborators Albert Ando and Richard Brumberg used Fisher's model of consumer behaviour to study the consumption function. One of their goals was to solve the consumption puzzle—that is, to explain the apparently conflicting pieces of evidence that came to light when Keynes's consumption function was brought to the data. According to Fisher's model, consumption depends on a person's lifetime income. Modigliani emphasized that income varies systematically over people's lives and that saving allows consumers to move income from those times in life when income is high to those times when it is low. This interpretation of consumer behaviour formed the basis for his **life-cycle hypothesis**.[3]

The Hypothesis

One important reason that income varies over a person's life is retirement. Most people plan to stop working at about age 65, and they expect their incomes to fall when they retire. Yet they do not want a large drop in their standard of living, as measured by their consumption. To maintain consumption after retirement, people must save during their working years. Let's see what this motive for saving implies for the consumption function.

Consider a consumer who expects to live another T years, has wealth of W, and expects to earn income Y until she retires R years from now. What level of

[2] Fumio Hayashi, "Why Is Japan's Saving Rate So Apparently High?" *NBER Macroeconomics Annual* (1986): 147–210.

[3] For references to the large body of work on the life-cycle hypothesis, a good place to start is the lecture Modigliani gave when he won the Nobel Prize. Franco Modigliani, "Life Cycle, Individual Thrift, and the Wealth of Nations," *American Economic Review* 76 (June 1986): 297–313.

consumption will the consumer choose if she wishes to maintain a smooth level of consumption over her life?

The consumer's lifetime resources are composed of initial wealth W and lifetime earnings of $R \times Y$. (For simplicity, we are assuming an interest rate of zero; if the interest rate were greater than zero, we would need to take account of interest earned on savings as well.) The consumer can divide up her lifetime resources among her T remaining years of life. We assume that she wishes to achieve the smoothest possible path of consumption over her lifetime. Therefore, she divides this total of $W + RY$ equally among the T years and each year consumes

$$C = (W + RY)/T.$$

We can write this person's consumption function as

$$C = (1/T)W + (R/T)Y.$$

For example, if the consumer expects to live for 50 more years and work for 30 of them, then $T = 50$ and $R = 30$, so her consumption function is

$$C = 0.02W + 0.6Y.$$

This equation says that consumption depends on both income and wealth. An extra \$1 of income per year raises consumption by \$0.60 per year, and an extra \$1 of wealth raises consumption by \$0.02 per year.

If every individual in the economy plans consumption like this, then the aggregate consumption function is much the same as the individual one. In particular, aggregate consumption depends on both wealth and income. That is, the economy's consumption function is

$$C = \alpha W + \beta Y,$$

where the parameter α is the marginal propensity to consume out of wealth, and the parameter β is the marginal propensity to consume out of income.

Implications

Figure 16-11 graphs the relationship between consumption and income predicted by the life-cycle model. For any given level of wealth $W,$ the model yields a conventional consumption function similar to the one shown in Figure 16-1. Notice, however, that the intercept of the consumption function, which shows what would happen to consumption if income ever fell to zero, is not a fixed value, as it is in Figure 16-1. Instead, the intercept here is αW and, thus, depends on the level of wealth.

This life-cycle model of consumer behaviour can solve the consumption puzzle. According to the life-cycle consumption function, the average propensity to consume is

$$C/Y = \alpha(W/Y) + \beta.$$

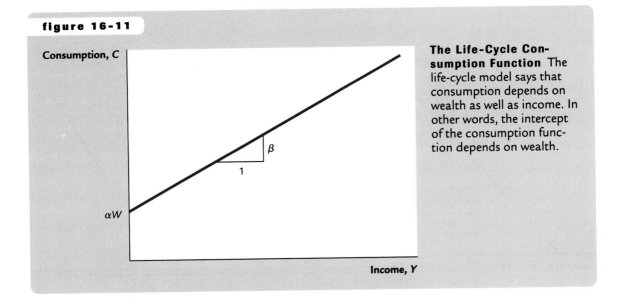

figure 16-11

The Life-Cycle Consumption Function The life-cycle model says that consumption depends on wealth as well as income. In other words, the intercept of the consumption function depends on wealth.

Because wealth does not vary proportionately with income from person to person or from year to year, we should find that high income corresponds to a low average propensity to consume when looking at data across individuals or over short periods of time. But, over long periods of time, wealth and income grow together, resulting in a constant ratio W/Y and thus a constant average propensity to consume.

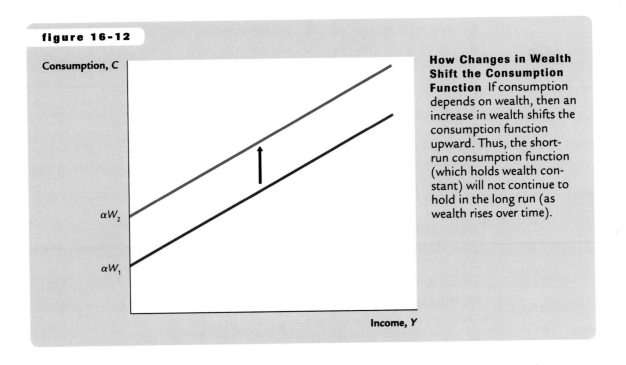

figure 16-12

How Changes in Wealth Shift the Consumption Function If consumption depends on wealth, then an increase in wealth shifts the consumption function upward. Thus, the short-run consumption function (which holds wealth constant) will not continue to hold in the long run (as wealth rises over time).

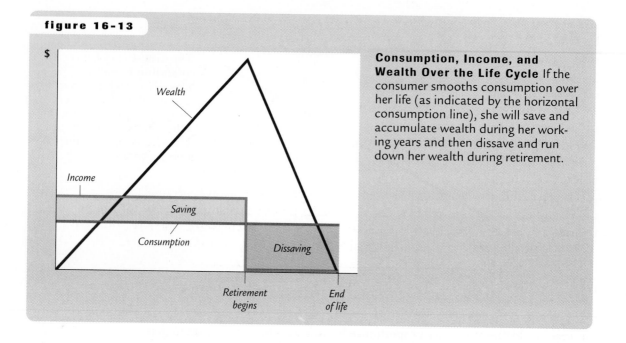

figure 16-13

Consumption, Income, and Wealth Over the Life Cycle If the consumer smooths consumption over her life (as indicated by the horizontal consumption line), she will save and accumulate wealth during her working years and then dissave and run down her wealth during retirement.

To make the same point somewhat differently, consider how the consumption function changes over time. As Figure 16-11 shows, for any given level of wealth, the life-cycle consumption function looks like the one Keynes suggested. But this function holds only in the short run when wealth is constant. In the long run, as wealth increases, the consumption function shifts upward, as in Figure 16-12. This upward shift prevents the average propensity to consume from falling as income increases. In this way, Modigliani resolved the consumption puzzle posed by Simon Kuznets's data.

The life-cycle model makes many other predictions as well. Most important, it predicts that saving varies over a person's lifetime. If a person begins adulthood with no wealth, she will accumulate wealth during her working years and then run down her wealth during her retirement years. Figure 16-13 illustrates the consumer's income, consumption, and wealth over her adult life. According to the life-cycle hypothesis, because people want to smooth consumption over their lives, the young who are working save, while the old who are retired dissave.

CASE STUDY

The Consumption and Saving of the Elderly

Many economists have studied the consumption and saving of the elderly. Their findings present a problem for the life-cycle model. It appears that the elderly do not dissave as much as the model predicts. In other words, the elderly do not run down their wealth as quickly as one would expect if they were trying to smooth their consumption over their remaining years of life.

There are two chief explanations for why the elderly do not dissave to the extent that the model predicts. Each suggests a direction for further research on consumption.

The first explanation is that the elderly are concerned about unpredictable expenses. Additional saving that arises from uncertainty is called **precautionary saving.** One reason for precautionary saving by the elderly is the possibility of living longer than expected and thus having to provide for a longer than average span of retirement. Another reason is the possibility of illness and large medical bills. The elderly may respond to this uncertainty by saving more in order to be better prepared for these contingencies.

The precautionary-saving explanation is not completely persuasive, because the elderly can largely insure against these risks. To protect against uncertainty regarding life span, they can buy *annuities* from insurance companies. For a fixed fee, annuities offer a stream of income that lasts as long as the recipient lives. Uncertainty about medical expenses should be largely eliminated by both public and private insurance plans.

The second explanation for the failure of the elderly to dissave is that they may want to leave bequests to their children. Economists have proposed various theories of the parent–child relationship and the bequest motive. In Chapter 15 we discussed some of these theories and their implications for consumption and fiscal policy.

Overall, research on the elderly suggests that the simplest life-cycle model cannot fully explain consumer behaviour. There is no doubt that providing for retirement is an important motive for saving, but other motives, such as precautionary saving and bequests, appear important as well.[4]

16-4 | Milton Friedman and the Permanent-Income Hypothesis

In a book published in 1957, Milton Friedman proposed the **permanent-income hypothesis** to explain consumer behaviour. Friedman's permanent-income hypothesis complements Modigliani's life-cycle hypothesis: both use Irving Fisher's theory of the consumer to argue that consumption should not depend on current income alone. But unlike the life-cycle hypothesis, which

[4] To read more about the consumption and saving of the elderly, see Albert Ando and Arthur Kennickell, "How Much (or Little) Life Cycle Saving Is There in Micro Data?" in Rudiger Dornbusch, Stanley Fischer, and John Bossons, eds., *Macroeconomics and Finance: Essays in Honor of Franco Modigliani* (Cambridge, MA: MIT Press, 1986); Michael Hurd, "Research on the Elderly: Economic Status, Retirement, and Consumption and Saving," *Journal of Economic Literature* 28 (June 1990): 565–589; and Xiaofen Lin, "Income, Consumption and Saving Before and After Retirement," in Frank T. Denton, Deb Fretz, and Byron G. Spencer, eds., *Independence and Economic Security in Old Age* (Vancouver: UBC Press, forthcoming).

emphasizes that income follows a regular pattern over a person's lifetime, the permanent-income hypothesis emphasizes that people experience random and temporary changes in their incomes from year to year.[5]

The Hypothesis

Friedman suggested that we view current income Y as the sum of two components, **permanent income** Y^P and **transitory income** Y^T. That is,

$$Y = Y^P + Y^T.$$

Permanent income is the part of income that people expect to persist into the future. Transitory income is the part of income that people do not expect to persist. Put differently, permanent income is average income, and transitory income is the random deviation from that average.

To see how we might separate income into these two parts, consider these examples:

> ➤ Maria, who has a law degree, earned more this year than John, who is a high-school dropout. Maria's higher income resulted from higher permanent income, because her education will continue to provide her a higher salary.

> ➤ Sue, a strawberry grower in the Niagara peninsula area in Ontario, earned less than usual this year because dry weather reduced her crop. Bill, a strawberry grower in British Columbia, earned more than usual because the scarcity of strawberries in Ontario drove up selling prices. Bill's higher income resulted from higher transitory income, because he is no more likely than Sue to have good weather next year.

These examples show that different forms of income have different degrees of persistence. A good education provides a permanently higher income, whereas good weather provides only transitorily higher income. Although one can imagine intermediate cases, it is useful to keep things simple by supposing that there are only two kinds of income: permanent and transitory.

Friedman reasoned that consumption should depend primarily on permanent income, because consumers use saving and borrowing to smooth consumption in response to transitory changes in income. For example, if a person received a permanent raise of $10,000 per year, his consumption would rise by about as much. Yet if a person won $10,000 in a lottery, he would not consume it all in one year. Instead, he would spread the extra consumption over the rest of his life. Assuming an interest rate of zero and a remaining life span of 50 years, consumption would rise by only $200 per year in response to the $10,000 prize. Thus, consumers spend their permanent income, but they save rather than spend most of their transitory income.

Friedman concluded that we should view the consumption function as approximately

---

[5] Milton Friedman, *A Theory of the Consumption Function* (Princeton, NJ: Princeton University Press, 1957).

CHAPTER 16 Consumption | **493**

$$C = \alpha Y^{\mathrm{P}},$$

where α is a constant that measures the fraction of permanent income consumed. The permanent-income hypothesis, as expressed by this equation, states that consumption is proportional to permanent income.

Implications

The permanent-income hypothesis solves the consumption puzzle by suggesting that the standard Keynesian consumption function uses the wrong variable. According to the permanent-income hypothesis, consumption depends on permanent income; yet many studies of the consumption function try to relate consumption to current income. Friedman argued that this *errors-in-variables problem* explains the seemingly contradictory findings.

Let's see what Friedman's hypothesis implies for the average propensity to consume. Divide both sides of his consumption function by Y to obtain

$$APC = C/Y = \alpha Y^{\mathrm{P}}/Y.$$

According to the permanent-income hypothesis, the average propensity to consume depends on the ratio of permanent income to current income. When current income temporarily rises above permanent income, the average propensity to consume temporarily falls; when current income temporarily falls below permanent income, the average propensity to consume temporarily rises.

Now consider the studies of household data. Friedman reasoned that these data reflect a combination of permanent and transitory income. Households with high permanent income have proportionately higher consumption. If all variation in current income came from the permanent component, the average propensity to consume would be the same in all households. But some of the variation in income comes from the transitory component, and households with high transitory income do not have higher consumption. Therefore, researchers find that high-income households have, on average, lower average propensities to consume.

Similarly, consider the studies of time-series data. Friedman reasoned that year-to-year fluctuations in income are dominated by transitory income. Therefore, years of high income should be years of low average propensities to consume. But over long periods of time—say, from decade to decade—the variation in income comes from the permanent component. Hence, in long time-series, one should observe a constant average propensity to consume, as in fact Kuznets found.

CASE STUDY

Income Taxes Versus Sales Taxes as an Instrument for Stabilization Policy

The permanent-income hypothesis can help us to interpret how the economy responds to changes in fiscal policy. According to the *IS–LM* model of Chapters 9 and 10, income-tax cuts stimulate consumption and raise aggregate demand, and income-tax increases depress consumption and reduce aggregate demand. The permanent-income hypothesis, however, states that consumption responds only to changes in permanent income. Therefore, transitory changes in income taxes will have only a negligible effect on consumption and aggregate demand. If a change in personal income taxes is to have a large effect on aggregate demand, it must be permanent.

Several income-tax changes in the United States illustrate the relevance of this reasoning. The first example occurred in 1964 when personal income-tax rates were cut by about 18 percent. At the time, the public was told that the growth in U.S. GDP since World War II had been sufficient to permit the government's revenue needs to be met with lower tax rates. Thus, the tax cut was viewed as permanent, and consumer spending rose markedly. Then, in 1968, the U.S. government wanted to dampen private spending temporarily (while government spending was very high because of the war in Vietnam). The U.S. government introduced a temporary personal income-tax "surcharge" of about 10 percent. Consumption, however, was reduced by only a small amount, just as the permanent-income theory predicts.

The U.S. government tried another temporary tax change in 1975. Because of the recession that followed the Oil Petroleum Exporting Countries (OPEC) crisis, the U.S. government returned to taxpayers some of the taxes already paid in 1974 and reduced income-tax rates for the balance of 1975. Once again, the public realized that this tax break was temporary, and so it had little effect on households' expectations about their long-run average income. Not surprisingly, households saved a large part of their tax rebates instead of spending them.

Finally, President Ronald Reagan introduced a series of tax cuts in the 1981–1984 period, reducing personal income-tax rates by about 23 percent. Households knew that Reagan had campaigned on a promise of smaller government, so the tax cuts were interpreted as likely to be permanent. As a result, these tax cuts did stimulate consumption spending significantly.

How have Canadian authorities responded to these U.S. policy experiments? In the 1978 federal budget, the Canadian government tried to stimulate spending with a sales-tax cut instead of an income-tax cut. A sales tax does not affect consumption only by raising or lowering households' estimates of their permanent income. Instead, a temporary sales-tax cut lowers the price of buying goods now, compared to the price in the future. Indeed, the *more* temporary a sales-tax change is, the more effective it is in changing the timing of people's spending.[6] Thus, sales taxes represent a much more reliable intrument for accomplishing stabilization policy. After all, the whole point of stabilization is to introduce a series of temporary stimuli to aggregate demand.

Unfortunately, until the GST was introduced in 1991, the federal government did not have a retail sales tax with which to implement stabilization pol-

---

[6] Solid evidence is provided in Peter Gusson, "The Role of Provincial Governments in Economic Stabilization: The Case of Ontario's Auto Sales Tax Rebate" (Ottawa: Conference Board of Canada, 1978).

icy. The 1978 budget tried to overcome this problem by having the federal government transfer some of its share of the personal income-tax revenue to the provinces in exchange for the provinces agreeing to lower sales-tax rates for a specified time period. Even though an agreement was reached "behind closed doors," the Quebec government refused to cooperate after the federal budget was made public. Quebec officials claimed that they must resist Ottawa's meddling in provincial affairs. Unfortunately, the political wrangling that ensued left the federal government uninterested in pursuing agreements of this sort again.

By 1991 the federal government had the GST, which gave the government a more predictable and powerful lever to use in attempts to adjust consumer expenditures for stabilization policy purposes. However, the GST has been very unpopular, and the government has tried to avoid drawing any attention to it by not using it as an instrument for short-run stabilization policy.

The fact that personal income-tax changes have significant effects on consumer spending only when those changes are expected to be permanent is a dramatic illustration of the importance of the Lucas critique (which we discussed in Chapter 14). As explained there, the prominent economist Robert Lucas has emphasized that predictions of policy impact are quite inaccurate if economists do not focus on how policy affects expectations. The permanent-income hypothesis is a convenient way of organizing our analysis so that the Lucas critique is respected.

The permanent-income hypothesis has received support from numerous episodes other than government fiscal policies. For example, the dramatic stock market crash of 1987 was widely viewed as transitory, and (as the theory predicts) that event had little effect on consumer spending.

Rational Expectations and Random-Walk Consumption

The permanent-income hypothesis is founded on Fisher's model of intertemporal choice. It builds on the idea that forward-looking consumers base their consumption decisions not only on their current income but also on the income they expect to receive in the future. Thus, the permanent-income hypothesis highlights that consumption depends on people's expectations.

Recent research on consumption has combined this view of the consumer with the assumption of rational expectations. The rational-expectations assumption states that people use all available information to make optimal forecasts about the future. You might recall from Chapter 13 that this assumption has potentially profound implications for the costs of stopping inflation. It can also have profound implications for consumption.

The economist Robert Hall was the first to derive the implications of rational expectations for consumption. He showed that if the permanent-income hypothesis is correct, and if consumers have rational expectations, then changes in consumption over time should be unpredictable. When changes in a variable are unpredictable, the variable is said to follow a *random walk*. According to Hall, the combination of the permanent-income hypothesis and rational expectations implies that consumption follows a random walk.

Hall reasoned as follows. According to the permanent-income hypothesis, consumers face fluctuating income and try their best to smooth their consumption over time. At any moment, consumers choose consumption based on their current expectations of their lifetime incomes. Over time, they change their consumption because they receive news that causes them to revise their expectations. For example, a person getting an unexpected promotion increases consumption, whereas a person getting an unexpected demotion decreases consumption. In other words, changes in consumption reflect "surprises" about lifetime income. If consumers are optimally using all available information, then they should be surprised only by events that were entirely unpredictable. Therefore, changes in their consumption should be unpredictable as well.[7]

The rational-expectations approach to consumption has implications not only for forecasting but also for the analysis of economic policies. *If consumers obey the permanent-income hypothesis and have rational expectations, then only unexpected policy changes influence consumption. These policy changes take effect when they change expectations.* For example, suppose that today the federal government passes a tax increase to be effective next year. In this case, consumers receive the news about their lifetime incomes when the government passes the law (or even earlier if the law's passage was predictable). The arrival of this news causes consumers to revise their expectations and reduce their consumption. The following year, when the tax hike goes into effect, consumption is unchanged because no news has arrived.

Hence, if consumers have rational expectations, policymakers influence the economy not only through their actions but also through the public's expectations of their actions. Expectations, however, cannot be observed directly. Therefore, it is often hard to know how and when changes in fiscal policy alter aggregate demand.

CASE STUDY

Do Predictable Changes in Income Lead to Predictable Changes in Consumption?

Of the many facts about consumer behaviour, one is impossible to dispute: income and consumption fluctuate together over the business cycle. When the economy goes into a recession, both income and consumption fall, and when the economy booms, both income and consumption rise rapidly.

By itself, this fact doesn't say much about the rational-expectations version of the permanent-income hypothesis. Most short-run fluctuations are unpre-

---

[7] Robert E. Hall, "Stochastic Implications of the Life Cycle–Permanent Income Hypothesis: Theory and Evidence," *Journal of Political Economy* 86 (April 1978): 971–987.

dictable. Thus, when the economy goes into a recession, the typical consumer is receiving bad news about his lifetime income, so consumption naturally falls. And when the economy booms, the typical consumer is receiving good news, so consumption rises. This behaviour does not necessarily violate the random-walk theory that changes in consumption are impossible to forecast.

Yet suppose we could identify some *predictable* changes in income. According to the random-walk theory, these changes in income should not cause consumers to revise their spending plans. If consumers had reason to expect income to rise or fall, they should have adjusted their consumption already in response to that information. Thus, predictable changes in income should not lead to predictable changes in consumption.

Data on consumption and income, however, appear not to satisfy this implication of the random-walk theory. When income is expected to fall by $1, consumption will typically fall at the same time by about $0.50. In other words, predictable changes in income lead to predictable changes in consumption that are roughly half as large.

Why is this true? One possible explanation of this behaviour is that some consumers may fail to have rational expectations. Instead, they may base their expectations of future income excessively on current income. Thus, when income rises or falls (even predictably), they act as if they received news about their lifetime resources and change their consumption accordingly. Another possible explanation is that some consumers are borrowing-constrained and, therefore, base their consumption on current income alone. Regardless of which explanation is correct, Keynes's original consumption function starts to look more attractive. That is, current income appears to have a larger role in determining consumer spending than the random-walk theory suggests.[8]

16-5 | Conclusion

In the work of Keynes, Fisher, Modigliani, and Friedman, we have seen a progression of views on consumer behaviour. Keynes proposed that consumption depends largely on current income. Since then, economists have argued that consumers understand that they face an intertemporal decision. Consumers look ahead to their future resources and needs, implying a more complex consumption function than the one that Keynes proposed. Keynes suggested a consumption function of the form

$$\text{Consumption} = f(\text{Current Income}).$$

[8] John Y. Campbell and N. Gregory Mankiw, "Consumption, Income, and Interest Rates: Reinterpreting the Time-Series Evidence," *NBER Macroeconomics Annual* (1989): 185–216; John Shea, "Union Contracts and the Life-Cycle/Permanent-Income Hypothesis," *American Economic Review* 85 (March 1995): 186–200.

Recent work suggests instead that

Consumption

= f(Current Income, Wealth, Expected Future Income, Interest Rates).

In other words, current income is only one determinant of aggregate consumption.

Economists continue to debate the relative importance of these determinants of consumption. There remains disagreement, for example, over whether interest rates have much influence over consumer spending and over whether borrowing constraints are prevalent or rare. Economists sometimes disagree about economic policy because they assume different consumption functions. For instance, as we saw in the previous chapter, the debate over the effects of government debt is partly a debate over the determinants of consumer spending. The key role of consumption in policy evaluation is sure to maintain economists' interest in studying consumer behaviour for many years to come.

Summary

1. Keynes conjectured that the marginal propensity to consume is between zero and one, that the average propensity to consume falls as income rises, and that current income is the primary determinant of consumption. Studies of household data and short time-series confirmed Keynes's conjectures. Yet studies of long time-series found no tendency for the average propensity to consume to fall as income rises over time.

2. Recent work on consumption builds on Irving Fisher's model of the consumer. In this model, the consumer faces an intertemporal budget constraint and chooses consumption for the present and the future to achieve the highest level of lifetime satisfaction. As long as the consumer can save and borrow, consumption depends on the consumer's lifetime resources.

3. Modigliani's life-cycle hypothesis emphasizes that income varies somewhat predictably over a person's life and that consumers use saving and borrowing to smooth their consumption over their lifetimes. According to this hypothesis, consumption depends on both income and wealth.

4. Friedman's permanent-income hypothesis emphasizes that individuals experience both permanent and transitory fluctuations in their income. Because consumers can save and borrow, and because they want to smooth their consumption, consumption does not respond much to transitory income. Consumption depends primarily on permanent income.

KEY CONCEPTS

Marginal propensity to consume	Marginal rate of substitution	Life-cycle hypothesis
Average propensity to consume	Normal good	Precautionary saving
Intertemporal budget constraint	Income effect	Permanent-income hypothesis
Discounting	Substitution effect	Permanent income
Indifference curves	Borrowing constraint	Transitory income

QUESTIONS FOR REVIEW

1. What were Keynes's three conjectures about the consumption function?

2. Describe the evidence that was consistent with Keynes's conjectures and the evidence that was inconsistent with them.

3. How do the life-cycle and permanent-income hypotheses resolve the seemingly contradictory pieces of evidence regarding consumption behaviour?

4. Use Fisher's model of consumption to analyze an increase in second-period income. Compare the case in which the consumer faces a binding borrowing constraint and the case in which he does not.

5. Explain why changes in consumption are unpredictable if consumers obey the permanent-income hypothesis and have rational expectations.

PROBLEMS AND APPLICATIONS

1. The chapter uses the Fisher model to discuss a change in the interest rate for a consumer who saves some of his first-period income. Suppose, instead, that the consumer is a borrower. How does that alter the analysis? Discuss the income and substitution effects on consumption in both periods.

2. Jack and Jill both obey the two-period Fisher model of consumption. Jack earns $100 in the first period and $100 in the second period. Jill earns nothing in the first period and $210 in the second period. Both of them can borrow or lend at the interest rate r.

   a. You observe both Jack and Jill consuming $100 in the first period and $100 in the second period. What is the interest rate r?

   b. Suppose the interest rate increases. What will happen to Jack's consumption in the first period? Is Jack better off or worse off than before the interest-rate rise?

   c. What will happen to Jill's consumption in the first period when the interest rate increases? Is Jill better off or worse off than before the interest-rate increase?

3. The chapter analyzes Fisher's model for the case in which the consumer can save or borrow at an interest rate of r and for the case in which the consumer can save at this rate but cannot borrow at all. Consider now the intermediate case in which the consumer can save at rate r_s and borrow at rate r_b, where $r_s < r_b$.

   a. What is the consumer's budget constraint in the case in which he consumes less than his income in period one?

   b. What is the consumer's budget constraint in the case in which he consumes more than his income in period one?

   c. Graph the two budget constraints and shade the area that represents the combination of first-period and second-period consumption the consumer can choose.

   d. Now add to your graph the consumer's indifference curves. Show three possible outcomes: one in which the consumer saves, one in which he borrows, and one in which he neither saves nor borrows.

   e. What determines first-period consumption in each of the three cases?

4. Explain whether borrowing constraints increase or decrease the potency of fiscal policy to influence aggregate demand in each of the following two cases:

   a. A temporary personal income-tax cut.

   b. An announced future personal income-tax cut.

5. In the discussion of the life-cycle hypothesis in the text, income is assumed to be constant during the period before retirement. For most people, however, income grows over their lifetimes. How does this growth in income influence the lifetime pattern of consumption and wealth accumulation shown in Figure 16-13 under the following conditions?

   a. Consumers can borrow, so their wealth can be negative.

   b. Consumers face borrowing constraints that prevent their wealth from falling below zero.

Do you consider case (a) or case (b) to be more realistic? Why?

6. Demographers predict that the fraction of the population that is elderly will increase over the next 20 years. What does the life-cycle model predict for the influence of this demographic change on the national saving rate?

7. One study found that the elderly who do not have children dissave at about the same rate as the elderly who do have children. What might this finding imply about the reason the elderly do not dissave as much as the life-cycle model predicts?

Investment

Investment is the most volatile component of GDP. When expenditure on goods and services falls during a recession, much of the decline is usually due to a drop in investment spending. In the severe recession of 1982, for example, real GDP fell $14 billion whereas investment spending fell $11 billion, accounting for more than three-quarters of the fall in spending.

Economists study investment to better understand fluctuations in the economy's output of goods and services. The models of GDP we saw in previous chapters, such as the *IS–LM* model in Chapters 10 and 11, were based on a simple investment function relating investment to the real interest rate: $I = I(r)$. That function states that an increase in the real interest rate reduces investment. In this chapter we look more closely at the theory behind this investment function.

There are three types of investment spending. **Business fixed investment** includes the machinery, equipment, and structures that businesses buy to use in production. **Residential investment** includes the new housing that people buy to live in and that landlords buy to rent out. **Inventory investment** includes those goods that businesses put aside in storage, including materials and supplies, work in process, and finished goods. Figure 17-1 plots total investment and its three components in Canada since 1970. You can see that all types of investment fall substantially during recessions, which are shown as shaded areas in the figure.

In this chapter we build models of each type of investment to explain these fluctuations. The models will shed light on the following questions:

➤ Why is investment negatively related to the interest rate?

➤ What causes the investment function to shift?

➤ Why does investment rise during booms and fall during recessions?

At the end of the chapter, we return to these questions and summarize the answers that the models offer.

17-1 | Business Fixed Investment

The largest piece of investment spending, is business fixed capital investment. The term "business" means that these investment goods are bought by firms for use in future production. The term "fixed capital" means that this spending is

figure 17-1

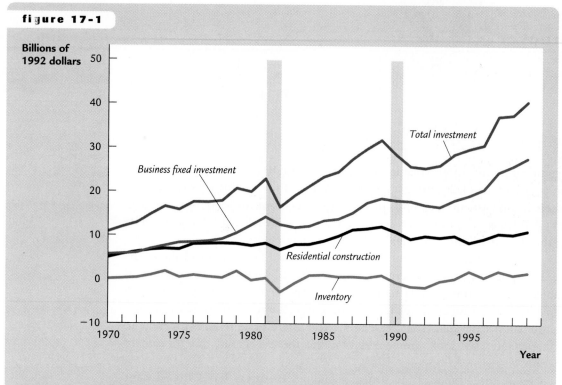

The Three Components of Investment This figure shows total investment, business fixed investment, residential construction, and inventory investment 1970 to 1998. Notice that all types of investment fall substantially during recessions, which are indicated here by the shaded areas.

Source: Statistics Canada, CANSIM series D15702, D15701, D15707.

for capital that will stay put for a while, as opposed to inventory investment, which will be used or sold shortly later. Business fixed investment includes everything from fax machines to factories, computers to company cars.

The standard model of business fixed investment is called the **neoclassical model of investment.** The neoclassical model examines the benefits and costs to firms of owning capital goods. The model shows how the level of investment—the addition to the stock of capital—is related to the marginal product of capital, the interest rate, and the tax rules affecting firms.

To develop the model, imagine that there are two kinds of firms in the economy. *Production firms* produce goods and services using capital that they rent. *Rental firms* make all the investments in the economy; they buy capital and rent it out to the production firms. Of course, most firms in the actual economy perform both functions: they produce goods and services, and they invest in capital for future production. Our analysis is simpler, however, if we separate these two activities by imagining that they take place in different firms.

The Rental Price of Capital

Let's first consider the typical production firm. As we discussed in Chapter 3, this firm decides how much capital to rent by comparing the cost and benefit of each unit of capital. The firm rents capital at a rental rate R and sells its output at a price P; the real cost of a unit of capital to the production firm is R/P. The real benefit of a unit of capital is the marginal product of capital MPK—the extra output produced with one more unit of capital. The marginal product of capital declines as the amount of capital rises: the more capital the firm has, the less an additional unit of capital will add to its output. Chapter 3 concluded that, to maximize profit, the firm rents capital until the marginal product of capital falls to equal the real rental price.

Figure 17-2 shows the equilibrium in the rental market for capital. For the reasons just discussed, the marginal product of capital determines the demand curve. The demand curve slopes downward because the marginal product of capital is low when the level of capital is high. At any point in time, the amount of capital in the economy is fixed, so the supply curve is vertical. The real rental price of capital adjusts to equilibrate supply and demand.

To see what variables influence the equilibrium rental price, let's consider a particular production function. As the appendix to Chapter 3 discusses, many economists consider the Cobb–Douglas production function a good approximation of how the actual economy turns capital and labour into goods and services. The Cobb–Douglas production function is

$$Y = AK^{\alpha}L^{1-\alpha},$$

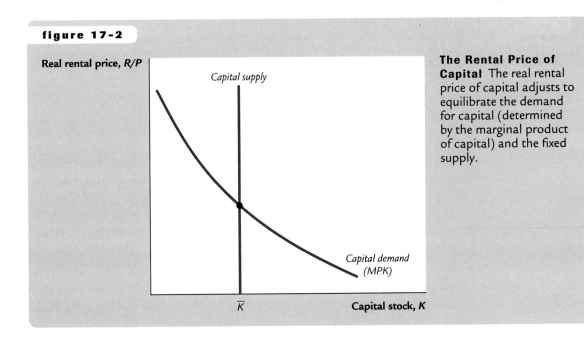

figure 17-2

Real rental price, R/P

Capital supply

Capital demand (MPK)

$\overline{K}$

Capital stock, K

The Rental Price of Capital The real rental price of capital adjusts to equilibrate the demand for capital (determined by the marginal product of capital) and the fixed supply.

where Y is output, K capital, L labour, A a parameter measuring the level of technology, and α a parameter between zero and one that measures capital's share of output. The marginal product of capital for the Cobb–Douglas production function is

$$MPK = \alpha A(L/K)^{1-\alpha}.$$

Because the real rental price equals the marginal product of capital in equilibrium, we can write

$$R/P = \alpha A(L/K)^{1-\alpha}.$$

This expression identifies the variables that determine the real rental price. It shows the following:

> ➤ The lower the stock of capital, the higher the real rental price of capital.

> ➤ The greater the amount of labour employed, the higher the real rental price of capital.

> ➤ The better the technology, the higher the real rental price of capital.

Events that reduce the capital stock (an earthquake), or raise employment (an expansion in aggregate demand), or improve the technology (a scientific discovery) raise the equilibrium real rental price of capital.

The Cost of Capital

Next consider the rental firms. These firms, like car-rental companies, merely buy capital goods and rent them out. Since our goal is to explain the investments made by the rental firms, we begin by considering the benefit and cost of owning capital.

The benefit of owning capital is the revenue from renting it to the production firms. The rental firm receives the real rental price of capital R/P for each unit of capital it owns and rents out.

The cost of owning capital is more complex. For each period of time that it rents out a unit of capital, the rental firm bears three costs:

1. When a rental firm borrows to buy a unit of capital, which it intends to rent out, it must pay interest on the loan. If P_K is the purchase price of a unit of capital and i is the nominal interest rate, then iP_K is the interest cost. Notice that this interest cost would be the same even if the rental firm did not have to borrow: if the rental firm buys a unit of capital using cash on hand, it loses out on the interest it could have earned by depositing this cash in the bank. In either case, the interest cost equals iP_K.

2. While the rental firm is renting out the capital, the price of capital can change. If the price of capital falls, the firm loses, because the firm's asset has fallen in value. If the price of capital rises, the firm gains, because the firm's asset has risen in value. The cost of this loss or gain is $-\Delta P_K$. (The minus sign is here because we are measuring costs, not benefits.)

3. While the capital is rented out, it suffers wear and tear, called **depreciation.** If δ is the rate of depreciation—the fraction of value lost per period because of wear and tear—then the dollar cost of depreciation is δP_K.

The total cost of renting out a unit of capital for one period is therefore

$$\text{Cost of Capital} = iP_K - \Delta P_K + \delta P_K$$
$$= P_K(i - \Delta P_K/P_K + \delta).$$

The cost of capital depends on the price of capital, the interest rate, the rate at which capital prices are changing, and the depreciation rate.

For example, consider the cost of capital to a car-rental company. The company buys cars for $10,000 each and rents them out to other businesses. The company faces an interest rate i of 10 percent per year, so the interest cost iP_K is $1,000 per year for each car the company owns. Car prices are rising at 6 percent per year, so, excluding wear and tear, the firm gets a capital gain ΔP_K of $600 per year. Cars depreciate at 20 percent per year, so the loss due to wear and tear δP_K is $2,000 per year. Therefore, the company's cost of capital is

$$\text{Cost of Capital} = \$1,000 - \$600 + \$2,000$$
$$= \$2,400.$$

The cost to the car-rental company of keeping a car in its capital stock is $2,400 per year.

To make the expression for the cost of capital simpler and easier to interpret, we assume that the price of capital goods rises with the prices of other goods. In this case, $\Delta P_K/P_K$ equals the overall rate of inflation π. Because $i - \pi$ equals the real interest rate r, we can write the cost of capital as

$$\text{Cost of Capital} = P_K(r + \delta).$$

This equation states that the cost of capital depends on the price of capital, the real interest rate, and the depreciation rate.

Finally, we want to express the cost of capital relative to other goods in the economy. The **real cost of capital**—the cost of buying and renting out a unit of capital measured in units of the economy's output—is

$$\text{Real Cost of Capital} = (P_K/P)(r + \delta).$$

This equation states that the real cost of capital depends on the relative price of a capital good P_K/P, the real interest rate r, and the depreciation rate δ.

The Determinants of Investment

Now consider a rental firm's decision about whether to increase or decrease its capital stock. For each unit of capital, the firm earns real revenue R/P and bears the real cost $(P_K/P)(r + \delta)$. The real profit per unit of capital is

$$\text{Profit Rate} = \text{Revenue} - \text{Cost}$$
$$= R/P - (P_K/P)(r + \delta).$$

Because the real rental price in equilibrium equals the marginal product of capital, we can write the profit rate as

$$\text{Profit Rate} = MPK - (P_K/P)(r + \delta).$$

The rental firm makes a profit if the marginal product of capital is greater than the cost of capital. It incurs a loss if the marginal product is less than the cost of capital.

We can now see the economic incentives that lie behind the rental firm's investment decision. The firm's decision regarding its capital stock—that is, whether to add to it or to let it depreciate—depends on whether owning and renting out capital is profitable. The change in the capital stock, called **net investment,** depends on the difference between the marginal product of capital and the cost of capital. *If the marginal product of capital exceeds the cost of capital, firms find it profitable to add to their capital stock. If the marginal product of capital falls short of the cost of capital, they let their capital stock shrink.*

We can also now see that the separation of economic activity between production and rental firms, although useful for clarifying our thinking, is not necessary for our conclusion regarding how firms choose how much to invest. For a firm that both uses and owns capital, the benefit of an extra unit of capital is the marginal product of capital, and the cost is the cost of capital. Like a firm that owns and rents out capital, this firm adds to its capital stock if the marginal product exceeds the cost of capital. Thus, we can write

$$\Delta K = I_n \left[MPK - (P_K/P)(r + \delta) \right],$$

where $I_n(\;)$ is the function showing how much net investment responds to the incentive to invest.

We can now derive the investment function. Total spending on business fixed investment is the sum of net investment and the replacement of depreciated capital. The investment function is

$$I = I_n \left[MPK - (P_K/P)(r + \delta) \right] + \delta K.$$

Business fixed investment depends on the marginal product of capital, the cost of capital, and the amount of depreciation.

This model shows why investment depends on the interest rate. A decrease in the real interest rate lowers the cost of capital. It therefore raises the amount of profit from owning capital and increases the incentive to accumulate more capital. Similarly, an increase in the real interest rate raises the cost of capital and leads firms to reduce their investment. For this reason, the investment schedule relating investment to the interest rate slopes downward, as in panel (a) of Figure 17-3.

The model also shows what causes the investment schedule to shift. Any event that raises the marginal product of capital increases the profitability of investment and causes the investment schedule to shift outward, as in panel (b) of Figure 17-3. For example, a technological innovation that increases the production function parameter A raises the marginal product of capital and, for any given interest rate, increases the amount of capital goods that rental firms wish to buy.

figure 17-3

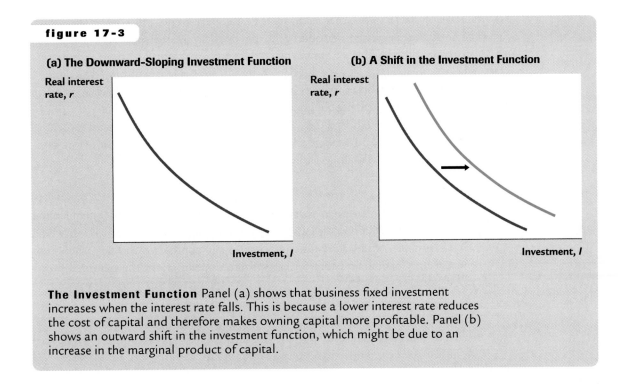

(a) The Downward-Sloping Investment Function

Real interest rate, *r*

Investment, *I*

(b) A Shift in the Investment Function

Real interest rate, *r*

Investment, *I*

The Investment Function Panel (a) shows that business fixed investment increases when the interest rate falls. This is because a lower interest rate reduces the cost of capital and therefore makes owning capital more profitable. Panel (b) shows an outward shift in the investment function, which might be due to an increase in the marginal product of capital.

Finally, consider what happens as this adjustment of the capital stock continues over time. If the marginal product begins above the cost of capital, the capital stock will rise and the marginal product will fall. If the marginal product of capital begins below the cost of capital, the capital stock will fall and the marginal product will rise. Eventually, as the capital stock adjusts, the marginal product of capital approaches the cost of capital. When the capital stock reaches a steady-state level, we can write

$$MPK = (P_K/P)(r + \delta).$$

Thus, in the long run, the marginal product of capital equals the real cost of capital. The speed of adjustment toward the steady state depends on how quickly firms adjust their capital stock, which in turn depends on how costly it is to build, deliver, and install new capital.[1]

CASE STUDY

The Burden of Higher Interest Rates

Journalists frequently refer to high interest rates as a "burden" for Canadians. There are two reasons for this, and we are now in a position to appreciate this

---

[1] Economists often measure capital goods in units such that the price of 1 unit of capital equals the price of 1 unit of other goods and services ($P_K = P$). This was the approach taken implicitly in Chapter 4, for example. In this case, the steady-state condition says that the marginal product of capital net of depreciation, $MPK - \delta$, equals the real interest rate r.

concern. First, in the short run, an increase in interest rates pulls investment down and so lowers aggregate demand. With prices sticky in the short run, a recession can result. But this line of argument cannot explain why a one-time, but permanent, rise in interest rates is a burden. After all, investment will not *keep* falling—long after the one-time increase in borrowing costs—and with flexible prices in the long run, real GDP should gradually return to its natural-rate value.

But that natural rate will be *lower* since it involves a smaller capital stock; as we have learned, firms arrange their affairs so that the marginal product of capital equals the real (rental) cost of capital:

$$MPK = r + \delta.$$

(Units have been chosen so that the purchase price of capital, P_K, equals the purchase price of other goods, P.) In Chapter 3, we learned that the Cobb–Douglas production function is a good approximation of production processes in Canada, and that for this production function, the marginal product of capital is given by

$$MPK = \alpha Y / K = \alpha y / k,$$

where α is capital's share of output. Substituting this expression for MPK into the steady-state capital-demand relationship yields

$$\alpha y = (r + \delta)k.$$

Rewriting this equilibrium condition in change form (holding α and δ constant) results in

$$\alpha \Delta y = (r + \delta)\Delta k + k\Delta r.$$

Since we also know that $\Delta y = MPK \; \Delta k = (r + \delta)\Delta k$, we can use this relationship to eliminate Δk by substitution. The result, after dividing by y, is

$$\Delta y / y = \frac{(-k/y)}{(1 - \alpha)} \Delta r.$$

We can use this equation to illustrate the steady-state "burden" of higher interest rates. Suppose the real interest rate increases permanently by one-half of one percentage point. To see the implications, we substitute $\Delta r = 0.005$ into the equation, along with representative values for the other parameters, $(k/y) = 3$ and $\alpha = 0.33$. The result is

$$\Delta y / y = -1.5 \text{ percent.}$$

This result implies that Canadians lose an amount of material welfare equal to 1.5 percent of GDP *every* year. As this book goes to press, this loss amounts to $15 billion every year. This *annual* loss represents *a lot* of valuable items, such as hospitals and day-care facilities. It appears that standard macroeconomic analysis supports journalists who refer to even "small" increases in interest rates as a major "burden."

function capture these two considerations. The quadratic form is the simplest function that does so, and parameter θ represents the relative importance of the adjustment costs.

With both the long-run desired level of capital and the preexisting level of capital given at each point in time, firms minimize costs by differentiating the cost function with respect to K_t and setting the result equal to zero. The result is

$$(K_t - K_{t-1}) = \gamma(K^* - K_{t-1})$$

where $\gamma = 1/(1 + \theta)$, or more simply,

$$\Delta K = \gamma(K^* - K)$$

or

$$\Delta K/K = \gamma[(K^*/K) - 1].$$

Since γ is a fraction, this investment function involves net investment closing a fraction of the gap between the desired and the actual capital stock each period. And we have just learned that the (K^*/K) ratio exceeds unity whenever the rental price of capital exceeds the cost of capital—that is, when Tobin's q exceeds one.

The advantage of Tobin's q as a measure of the incentive to invest is that it reflects the expected future profitability of capital as well as the current profitability. For example, suppose that the federal government legislates a reduction in the corporate profit tax beginning next year. This expected fall in the corporate tax means greater profits for the owners of capital. These higher expected profits raise the value of stock today, raise Tobin's q, and therefore encourage investment today. Thus, Tobin's q theory of investment emphasizes that investment decisions depend not only on current economic policies, but also on policies expected to prevail in the future.[3]

CASE STUDY

The Stock Market as an Economic Indicator

"The stock market has predicted nine out of the last five recessions." So goes Paul Samuelson's famous quip about the stock market's reliability as an economic indicator. The stock market is in fact quite volatile, and it can give false signals about the future of the economy. Yet one should not ignore the link between the stock market and the economy. Figure 17-4 shows that changes in the stock market often reflect changes in real GDP.

Why do stock prices and economic activity tend to fluctuate together? One reason is given by Tobin's q theory, together with the model of aggregate

---

[3] To read more about the relationship between the neoclassical model of investment and q theory, see Fumio Hayashi, "Tobin's Marginal q and Average q: A Neoclassical Approach," *Econometrica* 50 (January 1982): 213–224; and Lawrence H. Summers, "Taxation and Corporate Investment: A q-theory Approach," *Brookings Papers on Economic Activity* (1981:1): 67–140.

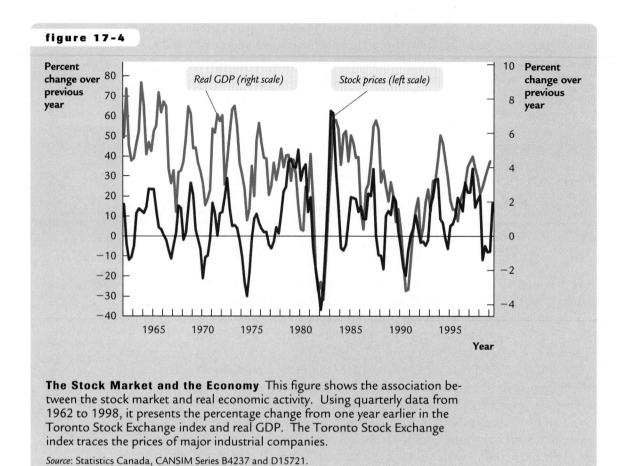

figure 17-4

The Stock Market and the Economy This figure shows the association between the stock market and real economic activity. Using quarterly data from
1962 to 1998, it presents the percentage change from one year earlier in the
Toronto Stock Exchange index and real GDP. The Toronto Stock Exchange
index traces the prices of major industrial companies.

Source: Statistics Canada, CANSIM Series B4237 and D15721.

demand and aggregate supply. Suppose, for instance, that you observe a fall in
stock prices. Because the replacement cost of capital is fairly stable, a fall in the
stock market is usually associated with a fall in Tobin's *q*. A fall in *q* reflects investors' pessimism about the current or future profitability of capital. This
means that the investment function has shifted inward: investment is lower at
any given interest rate. As a result, the aggregate demand for goods and services
contracts, leading to lower output and employment.

There are two additional reasons why stock prices are associated with economic activity. First, because stock is part of household wealth, a fall in stock
prices makes people poorer and thus depresses consumer spending, which also
reduces aggregate demand. Second, a fall in stock prices might reflect bad news
about technological progress and long-run economic growth. If so, this means
that the natural rate of output—and thus aggregate supply—will be expanding
more slowly in the future than was previously expected.

These links between the stock market and the economy are not lost on policymakers, such as those at the Bank of Canada. Indeed, because the stock market often anticipates changes in real GDP, and because data on the stock mar-

ket are available more quickly than data on GDP, the stock market is a closely watched economic indicator.

Financing Constraints

When a firm wants to invest in new capital, say by building a new factory, it often raises the necessary funds in financial markets. This financing may take several forms: obtaining loans from banks, selling bonds to the public, or selling shares in future profits on the stock market. The neoclassical model assumes that if a firm is willing to pay the cost of capital, the financial markets will make the funds available.

Yet sometimes firms face **financing constraints**—limits on the amount they can raise in financial markets. Financing constraints can prevent firms from undertaking profitable investments. When a firm is unable to raise funds in financial markets, the amount it can spend on new capital goods is limited to the amount it is currently earning. Financing constraints influence the investment behaviour of firms just as borrowing constraints influence the consumption behaviour of households. Borrowing constraints cause households to determine their consumption on the basis of current rather than permanent income; financing constraints cause firms to determine their investment on the basis of their current cash flow rather than expected profitability.

To see the impact of financing constraints, consider the effect of a short recession on investment spending. A recession reduces employment, the rental price of capital, and profits. If firms expect the recession to be short-lived, however, they will want to continue investing, knowing that their investments will be profitable in the future. That is, a short recession will have only a small effect on Tobin's q. For firms that can raise funds in financial markets, the recession should have only a small effect on investment.

Quite the opposite is true for firms that face financing constraints. The fall in current profits restricts the amount that these firms can spend on new capital goods and may prevent them from making profitable investments. Thus, financing constraints make investment more sensitive to current economic conditions.[4]

CASE STUDY

Banking Crises and Credit Crunches

Throughout economic history, problems in the banking system have often coincided with downturns in economic activity. This was true, for instance, during the Great Depression of the 1930s (which we discussed in Chapter 11).

---

[4] For empirical work supporting the importance of these financing constraints, see Steven M. Fazzari, R. Glenn Hubbard, and Bruce C. Petersen, "Financing Constraints and Corporate Investment," *Brookings Papers on Economic Activity* (1988:1): 141–195.

Soon after the Depression's onset, many banks in the United States found themselves insolvent, as the value of their assets fell below the value of their liabilities. These banks were, therefore, forced to suspend operations. Many economists believe the widespread bank failures in the United States during this period help explain the Depression's depth and persistence.

Similar patterns, although less severe, can be observed more recently. Problems in the banking system were also part of the recent slump in Japan (discussed in Chapter 11) and the recent financial crisis in Indonesia and other Asian economies (Chapter 12).

Why are banking crises so often at the center of short-run economic fluctuations? Part of the answer lies in the fact that banks have an important role in allocating financial resources. In particular, they serve as *intermediaries* between those people who have income they want to save and those people who have profitable investment projects but need to borrow to invest. When banks become insolvent or nearly so, they are less able to serve this function. Financing constraints become more prevalent, and some investors are forced to forgo some potentially profitable investment projects. Such an increase in financing constraints is sometimes called a *credit crunch*.

The macroeconomic effects of a credit crunch are easily interpreted within the *IS–LM* model. When some would-be investors are denied credit, the demand for investment goods falls at every interest rate. The result is a contractionary shift in the *IS* curve, which in turn leads to a fall in aggregate demand and reduced production and employment. Because of these effects, central bankers are always trying to monitor the health of the nation's banking system. Their goal is to avert banking crises and credit crunches and, when they do occur, to respond as quickly as possible to minimize the resulting disruption to the economy.

17-2| Residential Investment

In this section we consider the determinants of residential investment. We begin by presenting a simple model of the housing market. Residential investment includes the purchase of new housing both by people who plan to live in it themselves and by landlords who plan to rent it to others. To keep things simple, however, it is useful to imagine that all housing is owner-occupied.

The Stock Equilibrium and the Flow Supply

There are two parts to the model. First, the market for the existing stock of houses determines the equilibrium housing price. Second, the housing price determines the flow of residential investment.

Panel (a) of Figure 17-5 shows how the relative price of housing P_H/P is determined by the supply and demand for the existing stock of houses. At any point in time, the supply of houses is fixed. We represent this stock with a vertical supply curve. The demand curve for houses slopes downward, because high prices cause people to live in smaller houses, to share residences, or sometimes even to become homeless. The price of housing adjusts to equilibrate supply and demand.

Panel (b) of Figure 17-5 shows how the relative price of housing determines the supply of new houses. Construction firms buy materials and hire labour to build houses, and then sell the houses at the market price. Their costs depend on the overall price level P (which reflects the cost of wood, bricks, plaster, etc.), and their revenue depends on the price of houses P_H. The higher the relative price of housing, the greater the incentive to build houses, and the more houses are built. The flow of new houses—residential investment—therefore depends on the equilibrium price set in the market for existing houses.

This model of residential investment is similar to the q theory of business fixed investment. According to q theory, business fixed investment depends on the market price of installed capital relative to its replacement cost; this relative price, in turn, depends on the expected profits from owning installed capital. According to this model of the housing market, residential investment depends on the relative price of housing. The relative price of housing, in turn, depends on the demand for housing, which depends on the imputed rent that individuals expect to receive from their housing. Hence, the relative price of housing

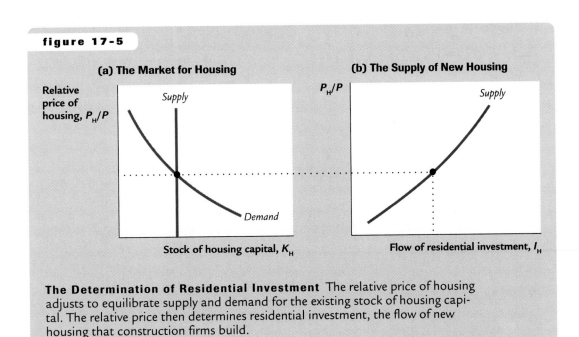

figure 17-5

(a) The Market for Housing   **(b) The Supply of New Housing**

Relative price of housing, P_H/P

Supply

Demand

Stock of housing capital, K_H

P_H/P

Supply

Flow of residential investment, I_H

The Determination of Residential Investment The relative price of housing adjusts to equilibrate supply and demand for the existing stock of housing capital. The relative price then determines residential investment, the flow of new housing that construction firms build.

plays much the same role for residential investment as Tobin's q does for business fixed investment.

Changes in Housing Demand

When the demand for housing shifts, the equilibrium price of housing changes, and this change in turn affects residential investment. The demand curve for housing can shift for various reasons. An economic boom raises national income and therefore the demand for housing. A large increase in the population, perhaps because of immigration, also raises the demand for housing. Panel (a) of Figure 17-6 shows that an expansionary shift in demand raises the equilibrium price. Panel (b) shows that the increase in the housing price increases residential investment.

One important determinant of housing demand is the real interest rate. Many people take out loans—mortgages—to buy their homes; the interest rate is the cost of the loan. Even the few people who do not have to borrow to purchase a home will respond to the interest rate, because the interest rate is the opportunity cost of holding their wealth in housing rather than putting it in a bank. A reduction in the interest rate therefore raises housing demand, housing prices, and residential investment.

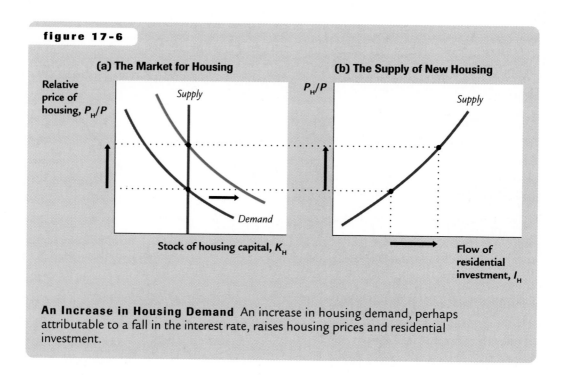

figure 17-6

(a) The Market for Housing

Relative price of housing, P_H/P

Supply

Demand

Stock of housing capital, K_H

(b) The Supply of New Housing

P_H/P

Supply

Flow of residential investment, I_H

An Increase in Housing Demand An increase in housing demand, perhaps attributable to a fall in the interest rate, raises housing prices and residential investment.

WHAT PRICE HOUSE CAN YOU AFFORD?

When someone takes out a mortgage to buy a house, the bank often places a ceiling on the size of the loan. That ceiling depends on the person's income and the market interest rate. A typical bank or trust requirement is that the monthly mortgage payment—including both interest and repayment of principal—not exceed 30 percent of the borrower's monthly income.

Table 17-1 shows how the interest rate affects monthly payments on a $100,000 25-year mortgage, and how the interest rate affects the minimum annual income that is required before banks and trust companies will grant a mortgage.

As you can see, small changes in the interest rate can have a large influence on who can buy a home. For example, an increase in the interest rate from 8 percent to 10 percent raises the monthly payment on a typical mortgage by 17 percent. It also cuts out of the mortgage market all families in the $30,520–$35,760 income range. An increase in the interest rate therefore reduces housing demand, which in turn depresses housing prices and residential investment.

table 17-1

How High Interest Rates Reduce Mortgage Eligibility and Housing Demand for a 25-Year $100,000 Mortgage

Interest Rate	Monthly Payment	Annual Income Required
5%	$582	$23,280
6	640	25,600
7	700	28,000
8	763	30,520
9	828	33,120
10	894	35,760
11	963	38,520
12	1,032	41,280

The Tax Treatment of Housing

Just as the tax laws affect the accumulation of business fixed investment, they also affect the accumulation of residential investment. In this case, however, their effects are nearly the opposite. Rather than discouraging investment, as the corporate profit tax does for businesses, the personal income tax encourages households to invest in housing.

One can view a homeowner as a landlord with himself as a tenant. But he is a landlord with a special tax treatment. The Canadian personal income-tax system does not require him to pay tax on the imputed rent (the rent he "pays" himself). Nor does he have to pay any capital gains tax when the value of his home increases. Many economists have criticized the tax treatment of home-ownership. They believe that, because of this subsidy, Canada invests too much in housing compared to other forms of capital.

17-3 | Inventory Investment

Inventory investment—the goods that businesses put aside in storage—is at the same time negligible and of great significance. It is one of the smallest components of spending, averaging about 1 percent of GDP. Yet its remarkable volatility makes it central to the study of economic fluctuations. In recessions, firms stop replenishing their inventory as goods are sold, and inventory investment becomes negative. In a typical recession, more than half the fall in spending comes from a decline in inventory investment.

Reasons for Holding Inventories

Inventories serve many purposes. Before presenting a model to explain fluctuations in inventory investment, let's discuss some of the motives firms have for holding inventories.

One use of inventories is to smooth the level of production over time. Consider a firm that experiences temporary booms and busts in sales. Rather than adjusting production to match the fluctuations in sales, the firm may find it cheaper to produce goods at a steady rate. When sales are low, the firm produces more than it sells and puts the extra goods into inventory. When sales are high, the firm produces less than it sells and takes goods out of inventory. This motive for holding inventories is called **production smoothing.**

A second reason for holding inventories is that they may allow a firm to operate more efficiently. Retail stores, for example, can sell merchandise more effectively if they have goods on hand to show to customers. Manufacturing firms keep inventories of spare parts to reduce the time that the assembly line is shut down when a machine breaks. In some ways, we can view **inventories as a factor of production:** the larger the stock of inventories a firm holds, the more output it can produce.

A third reason for holding inventories is to avoid running out of goods when sales are unexpectedly high. Firms often have to make production decisions before knowing the level of customer demand. For example, a publisher must decide how many copies of a new book to print before knowing whether the book will be popular. If demand exceeds production and there are no inventories, the good will be out of stock for a period, and the firm will lose sales and profit. Inventories can prevent this from happening. This motive for holding inventories is called **stock-out avoidance.**

A fourth explanation of inventories is dictated by the production process. Many goods require a number of steps in production and, therefore, take time to produce. When a product is only partly completed, its components are counted as part of a firm's inventory. These inventories are called **work in process.**

CASE STUDY

Seasonal Fluctuations and Production Smoothing

Economists have spent much time studying data on production, sales, and inventories to test alternative theories of inventory holding. Much of this research examines whether the production-smoothing theory accurately describes the behaviour of firms. Contrary to what many economists expected, most of the evidence suggests that firms do not use inventories to smooth production over time.

The clearest evidence against production smoothing comes from industries with seasonal fluctuations in demand. In many industries, sales fluctuate regularly over the course of a year. For example, the toy industry sells more of its output in December than in January. One might expect that firms would build up inventories in times of low sales and draw them down in times of high sales.

Yet, in most industries, firms do not use inventories to smooth production over the year. Instead, the seasonal pattern in production closely matches the seasonal pattern in sales. The evidence from seasonal fluctuations suggests that, in most industries, firms see little benefit to smoothing production.[5]

The Accelerator Model of Inventories

Because there are many motives for holding inventories, there are many models of inventory investment. One simple model that explains the data well, without endorsing a particular motive, is the **accelerator model.** This model was developed about half a century ago, and it is sometimes applied to all types of investment. Here we apply it to the type for which it works best—inventory investment.

The accelerator model of inventories assumes that firms hold a stock of inventories that is proportional to the firms' level of output. There are various reasons for this assumption. When output is high, manufacturing firms need more materials and supplies on hand, and they have more goods in the process of being completed. When the economy is booming, retail firms want to have more merchandise on the shelves to show customers. Thus, if N is the economy's stock of inventories and Y is output, then

$$N = \beta Y,$$

where β is a parameter reflecting how much inventory firms wish to hold as a proportion of output.

Inventory investment I is the change in the stock of inventories ΔN. Therefore,

$$I = \Delta N = \beta \, \Delta Y.$$

---

[5] Jeffrey A. Miron and Stephen P. Zeldes, "Seasonality, Cost Shocks, and the Production Smoothing Model of Inventories," *Econometrica* 56 (July 1988): 877–908.

The accelerator model predicts that inventory investment is proportional to the change in output. When output rises, firms want to hold a larger stock of inventory, so inventory investment is high. When output falls, firms want to hold a smaller stock of inventory, so they allow their inventory to run down, and inventory investment is negative.

We can now see how the model earned its name. Because the variable Y is the rate at which firms are producing goods, ΔY is the "acceleration" of production. The model says that inventory investment depends on whether the economy is speeding up or slowing down.

The accelerator mechanism is one of the reasons that business cycles develop momentum and are therefore so difficult to control. We can appreciate this fact by considering the following scenario and applying the accelerator to all components of investment. Suppose that the economy is at its natural rate and that a loss in export sales then reduces GDP and causes a recession. The fact that output has fallen (ΔY is negative) means that investment falls. This makes the recession more severe. Then, when the economy is recovering (ΔY is positive), investment rises. This fact forces the economy to overshoot the natural rate (since ΔY is positive at that point, and that keeps investment high). As time proceeds, the (positive) changes in output get smaller, and this pushes investment lower. The fall-off in investment is what causes the next recession. Thus, it is quite likely that a *onetime* shock like a drop in export sales can set in motion a whole series of overshoots—an *ongoing* business cycle—because of the accelerator mechanism.

Inventories and the Real Interest Rate

Like other components of investment, inventory investment depends on the real interest rate. When a firm holds a good in inventory and sells it tomorrow rather than selling it today, it gives up the interest it could have earned between today and tomorrow. Thus, the real interest rate measures the opportunity cost of holding inventories.

When the real interest rate rises, holding inventories becomes more costly, so rational firms try to reduce their stock. Therefore, an increase in the real interest rate depresses inventory investment. For example, in the 1980s many firms adopted "just-in-time" production plans, which were designed to reduce the amount of inventory by producing goods just before sale. The high real interest rates that prevailed during most of this decade are one possible explanation for this change in business strategy.

17-4| Conclusion

The purpose of this chapter has been to examine the determinants of investment in more detail. Looking back on the various models of investment, we can see three themes.

First, all types of investment spending are inversely related to the real interest rate. A higher interest rate raises the cost of capital to firms that invest in plant and equipment, raises the cost of borrowing to home buyers, and raises the cost of holding inventories. Thus, the models of investment developed here justify the investment function we have used throughout this book.

Second, there are various causes of shifts in the investment function. An improvement in the available technology raises the marginal product of capital and raises business fixed investment. An increase in the population raises the demand for housing and raises residential investment. Finally, various economic policies, such as changes in the investment tax credit and the corporate profit tax, alter the incentives to invest and thus shift the investment function.

Third, it is natural to expect investment to be volatile over the business cycle, because investment spending depends on the output of the economy as well as on the interest rate. In the neoclassical model of business fixed investment, higher employment raises the marginal product of capital and the incentive to invest. Higher output also raises firms' profits and, thereby, relaxes the financing constraints that some firms face. In addition, higher income raises the demand for houses, in turn raising housing prices and residential investment. Higher output raises the stock of inventories firms wish to hold, stimulating inventory investment. Our models predict that an economic boom should stimulate investment and a recession should depress it. This is exactly what we observe.

Summary

1. The marginal product of capital determines the real rental price of capital. The real interest rate, the depreciation rate, and the relative price of capital goods determine the cost of capital. According to the neoclassical model, firms invest if the rental price is greater than the cost of capital, and they disinvest if the rental price is less than the cost of capital.

2. Various parts of the corporate profit tax system influence the incentive to invest. The tax itself discourages investment, while generous depreciation allowances and the investment tax credits encourage it.

3. An alternative way of expressing the neoclassical model is to state that investment depends on Tobin's *q*, the ratio of the market value of installed capital to its replacement cost. This ratio reflects the current and expected future profitability of capital. The higher is *q*, the greater is the market value of installed capital relative to its replacement cost, and the greater is the incentive to invest.

4. In contrast to the assumption of the neoclassical model, firms cannot always raise funds to finance investment. Financing constraints make investment sensitive to firms' current cash flow.

5. Residential investment depends on the relative price of housing. Housing prices in turn depend on the demand for housing and the current fixed

supply. An increase in housing demand, perhaps attributable to a fall in the interest rate, raises housing prices and residential investment.

6. Firms have various motives for holding inventories of goods: smoothing production, using them as a factor of production, avoiding stock-outs, and storing work in process. One model of inventory investment that works well without endorsing a particular motive is the accelerator model. According to this model, the stock of inventories depends on the level of GDP, and inventory investment depends on the change in GDP.

KEY CONCEPTS

Business fixed investment

Residential investment

Inventory investment

Neoclassical model of investment

Depreciation

Real cost of capital

Net investment

Corporate profit tax

Depreciation allowance

Investment tax credit

Stock

Stock market

Tobin's q

Financing constraints

Production smoothing

Inventories as a factor of production

Stock-out avoidance

Work in process

Accelerator model

QUESTIONS FOR REVIEW

1. In the neoclassical model of business fixed investment, under what conditions will firms find it profitable to add to their capital stock?

2. What is Tobin's q, and what does it have to do with investment?

3. Explain why an increase in the interest rate reduces the amount of residential investment.

4. List four reasons firms might hold inventories.

PROBLEMS AND APPLICATIONS

1. Use the neoclassical model of investment to explain the impact of each of the following on the rental price of capital, the cost of capital, and investment:

   a. Anti-inflationary monetary policy raises the real interest rate.

   b. An earthquake destroys part of the capital stock.

   c. Immigration of foreign workers increases the size of the labour force.

2. Suppose that the government levies a tax on oil companies equal to a proportion of the value of the company's oil reserves. (The government assures the firms that the tax is for one time only.) According to the neoclassical model, what effect will the tax have on business fixed investment by

these firms? What if these firms face financing constraints?

3. The *IS–LM* model developed in Chapters 10 and 11 assumes that investment depends only on the interest rate. Yet our theories of investment suggest that investment might also depend on national income: higher income might induce firms to invest more.

   a. Explain why investment might depend on national income.

   b. Suppose that investment is determined by

   $$I = \bar{I} + aY,$$

   where *a* is a constant between zero and one, which measures the influence of national income on investment. With investment set this way, what are the fiscal-policy multipliers in the Keynesian-cross model? Explain.

   c. Suppose that investment depends on both income and the interest rate. That is, the investment function is

   $$I = \bar{I} + aY - br,$$

   where *a* is a constant between zero and one, which measures the influence of national income on investment, and *b* is a constant greater than zero, which measures the influence of the interest rate on investment. Use the *IS–LM* model to consider the short-run impact of an increase in government purchases on national income *Y,* the interest rate *r,* consumption *C,* and investment *I.* How might this investment function alter the conclusions implied by the basic *IS–LM* model?

4. When the stock market crashes, as it did in October 1929 and October 1987, how should the Bank of Canada respond? Why?

5. It is an election year, and the economy is in a recession. The opposition candidate campaigns on a platform of passing an investment tax credit, which would be effective next year after she takes office. What impact does this campaign promise have on economic conditions during the current year?

6. Canada experienced a large increase in the number of births in the 1950s. People in this baby-boom generation reached adulthood and started forming their own households in the 1970s.

   a. Use the model of residential investment to predict the impact of this event on housing prices and residential investment.

   b. For the years 1970 and 1980, compute the real price of housing, measured as the residential investment deflator divided by the GDP deflator. What do you find? Is this finding consistent with the model? (*Hint:* A good source of data is the *Canadian Economic Observer,* published monthly by Statistics Canada and available in the Government Documents section of your university library. Alternatively, you can consult Statistics Canada via the internet, as explained in the preface of this book.)

7. Canadian tax laws encourage investment in housing and discourage investment in business capital. What are the long-run effects of this policy? (*Hint:* Think about the labour market.)

chapter 18

Money Supply and Money Demand

There have been three great inventions since the beginning of time: fire, the wheel, and central banking.

— *Will Rogers*

The supply and demand for money are crucial to many issues in macroeconomics. In Chapter 7, we discussed how economists use the term "money," how the central bank controls the quantity of money, and how monetary policy affects prices and interest rates in the long run when prices are flexible. In Chapters 10 and 11, we saw that the money market is a key element of the *IS–LM* model, which describes the economy in the short run when prices are sticky.

This chapter examines money supply and money demand more closely. In Section 18-1 we see that the banking system plays a key role in determining the money supply, and we discuss various policy instruments that the Bank of Canada can use to alter the money supply. In Section 18-2 we consider the motives behind money demand, and we analyze the household's decision about how much money to hold. In Section 18-3 we discuss how recent changes in the financial system have blurred the distinction between money and other assets and how this development complicates the conduct of monetary policy.

18-1 | Money Supply

Chapter 7 introduced the concept of "money supply" in a highly simplified manner. In that chapter we defined the quantity of money as the number of dollars held by the public, and we assumed that the Bank of Canada controls the supply of money by increasing or decreasing the number of dollars in circulation through open-market operations. Although this explanation is a good first approximation, it is incomplete, for it omits the role of the banking system in determining the money supply. We now present a more complete explanation.

In this section we see that the money supply is determined not only by Bank of Canada policy, but also by the behaviour of households that hold money and of banks in which money is held. We begin by recalling that the money supply includes both currency in the hands of the public and deposits at banks that households can use on demand for transactions. That is, letting M denote the money supply, C currency, and D deposits, we can write

$$\text{Money Supply} = \text{Currency} + \text{Deposits}$$
$$M = C + D.$$

To understand the money supply, we must understand the interaction between currency and deposits and how Bank of Canada policy influences these two components of the money supply.

100-Percent-Reserve Banking

We begin by imagining a world without banks. In such a world, all money takes the form of currency, and the quantity of money is simply the amount of currency that the public holds. For this discussion, suppose that there is $1,000 of currency in the economy.

Now introduce banks. At first, suppose that banks accept deposits but do not make loans. The only purpose of the banks is to provide a safe place for depositors to keep their money.

The deposits that banks have received but have not lent out are called **reserves.** Some reserves are held in the vaults of local banks throughout the country, but most are held at a central bank, such as the Bank of Canada. In our hypothetical economy, all deposits are held as reserves: banks simply accept deposits, place the money in reserve, and leave the money there until the depositor makes a withdrawal or writes a cheque against the balance. This system is called **100-percent-reserve banking.**

Suppose that households deposit the economy's entire $1,000 in Firstbank. Firstbank's **balance sheet**—its accounting statement of assets and liabilities—looks like this:

FIRSTBANK'S BALANCE SHEET	
Assets	**Liabilities**
Reserves $1,000	Deposits $1,000

The bank's assets are the $1,000 it holds as reserves; the bank's liabilities are the $1,000 it owes to depositors. Unlike banks in our economy, this bank is not making loans, so it will not earn profit from its assets. The bank presumably charges depositors a small fee to cover its costs.

What is the money supply in this economy? Before the creation of Firstbank, the money supply was the $1,000 of currency. After the creation of Firstbank, the money supply is the $1,000 of deposits. A dollar deposited in a bank reduces currency by $1 and raises deposits by $1, so the money supply remains the same. *If banks hold 100 percent of deposits in reserve, the banking system does not affect the supply of money.*

Fractional-Reserve Banking

Now imagine that banks start to use some of their deposits to make loans—for example, to families who are buying houses or to firms that are investing in new plants and equipment. The advantage to banks is that they can charge interest on the loans. The banks must keep some reserves on hand so that reserves are available whenever depositors want to make withdrawals. But as long as the amount of new deposits approximately equals the amount of withdrawals, a bank need not keep all its deposits in reserve. Thus, bankers have an incentive to make loans. When they do so, we have **fractional-reserve banking,** a system under which banks keep only a fraction of their deposits in reserve.

Here is Firstbank's balance sheet after it makes a loan:

FIRSTBANK'S BALANCE SHEET			
Assets		**Liabilities**	
Reserves	$200	Deposits	$1,000
Loans	$800		

This balance sheet assumes that the *reserve–deposit ratio*—the fraction of deposits kept in reserve—is 20 percent. Firstbank keeps $200 of the $1,000 in deposits in reserve and lends out the remaining $800.

Notice that Firstbank increases the supply of money by $800 when it makes this loan. Before the loan is made, the money supply is $1,000, equaling the deposits in Firstbank. After the loan is made, the money supply is $1,800: the depositor still has a deposit of $1,000, but now the borrower holds $800 in currency. *Thus, in a system of fractional-reserve banking, banks create money.*

The creation of money does not stop with Firstbank. If the borrower deposits the $800 in another bank (or if the borrower uses the $800 to pay someone who then deposits it), the process of money creation continues. Here is the balance sheet of Secondbank:

SECONDBANK'S BALANCE SHEET			
Assets		**Liabilities**	
Reserves	$160	Deposits	$800
Loans	$640		

Secondbank receives the $800 in deposits, keeps 20 percent, or $160, in reserve, and then loans out $640. Thus, Secondbank creates $640 of money. If this $640 is eventually deposited in Thirdbank, this bank keeps 20 percent, or $128, in reserve and loans out $512, resulting in this balance sheet:

THIRDBANK'S BALANCE SHEET			
Assets		**Liabilities**	
Reserves	$128	Deposits	$640
Loans	$512		

The process goes on and on. With each deposit and loan, more money is created.

Although this process of money creation can continue forever, it does not create an infinite amount of money. Letting rr denote the reserve–deposit ratio, the amount of money that the original $1,000 creates is

$$\text{Original Deposit} = \$1{,}000$$
$$\text{Firstbank Lending} = (1 - rr) \times \$1{,}000$$
$$\text{Secondbank Lending} = (1 - rr)^2 \times \$1{,}000$$
$$\text{Thirdbank Lending} = (1 - rr)^3 \times \$1{,}000$$
$$\vdots$$

$$\overline{\text{Total Money Supply} = [1 + (1 - rr) + (1 - rr)^2}$$
$$+ (1 - rr)^3 + \cdots] \times \$1{,}000$$
$$= (1/rr) \times \$1{,}000$$

Each $1 of reserves generates $(1/rr)$ of money. In our example, $rr = 0.2$, so the original $1,000 generates $5,000 of money.[1]

The banking system's ability to create money is the primary difference between banks and other financial institutions. As we first discussed in Chapter 3, financial markets have the important function of transferring the economy's resources from those households that wish to save some of their income for the future to those households and firms that wish to borrow to buy investment goods to be used in future production. The process of transferring funds from savers to borrowers is called **financial intermediation.** Many institutions in the economy act as financial intermediaries: the most prominent examples are the stock market, the bond market, mortgage loan companies, credit unions, trust companies, and the banking system. For simplicity, we focus in this chapter on just the chartered banks.

Note that although the system of fractional-reserve banking creates money, it does not create wealth. When a bank loans out some of its reserves, it gives borrowers the ability to make transactions and therefore increases the supply of money. The borrowers are also undertaking a debt obligation to the bank, however, so the loan does not make them wealthier. In other words, the creation of money by the banking system increases the economy's liquidity, not its wealth.

A Model of the Money Supply

Now that we have seen how banks create money, let's examine in more detail what determines the money supply. Here we present a model of the money

---

[1] *Mathematical note:* The last step in the derivation of the total money supply uses the algebraic result for the sum of an infinite geometric series (which we used previously in computing the multiplier in Chapter 10). According to this result, if x is a number between -1 and 1, then

$$1 + x + x^2 + x^3 + \cdots = 1/(1 - x).$$

In this application, $x = (1 - rr)$.

supply under fractional-reserve banking. The model has three exogenous variables:

- ➤ The **monetary base** B is the total number of dollars held by the public as currency C and by the banks as reserves R. It is directly controlled by the Bank of Canada.

- ➤ The **reserve–deposit ratio** rr is the fraction of deposits that banks hold in reserve. It is determined by the business policies of banks and, for many years, by the laws regulating banks. By mid-1994 the phasing out of reserve requirement laws was complete, and Canadian banks were no longer subject to any minimum reserve requirement.

- ➤ The **currency–deposit ratio** cr is the amount of currency C people hold as a fraction of their holdings of deposits D. It reflects the preferences of households about the form of money they wish to hold.

Our model shows how the money supply depends on the monetary base, the reserve–deposit ratio, and the currency–deposit ratio. It allows us to examine how Bank of Canada policy and the choices of banks and households influence the money supply.

We begin with the definitions of the money supply and the monetary base:

$$M = C + D,$$
$$B = C + R.$$

The first equation states that the money supply is the sum of currency and deposits. The second equation states that the monetary base is the sum of currency and bank reserves. To solve for the money supply as a function of the three exogenous variables (B, rr, and cr), we begin by dividing the first equation by the second to obtain

$$\frac{M}{B} = \frac{C + D}{C + R}.$$

Then divide both the top and bottom of the expression on the right by D.

$$\frac{M}{B} = \frac{C/D + 1}{C/D + R/D}.$$

Note that C/D is the currency–deposit ratio cr, and that R/D is the reserve–deposit ratio rr. Making these substitutions, and bringing the B from the left to the right side of the equation, we obtain

$$M = \frac{cr + 1}{cr + rr} \times B.$$

This equation shows how the money supply depends on the three exogenous variables.

We can now see that the money supply is proportional to the monetary base. The factor of proportionality, $(cr + 1)/(cr + rr)$, is denoted m and is called the **money multiplier.** We can write

$$M = m \times B.$$

Each dollar of the monetary base produces m dollars of money. Because the monetary base has a multiplied effect on the money supply, the monetary base is sometimes called **high-powered money.**

Here's a numerical example that approximately describes the Canadian economy at the start of the twenty-first century. Suppose that the monetary base B is \$33 billion, the reserve–deposit ratio rr is 0.07, and the currency–deposit ratio cr is 0.5. In this case, the money multiplier is

$$m = \frac{0.5 + 1}{0.5 + 0.07} = 2.6,$$

and the money supply is

$$M = 2.6 \times \$33 \text{ billion} = \$86 \text{ billion}.$$

Each dollar of the monetary base generates 2.6 dollars of money, so the total money supply is \$86 billion.

We can now see how changes in the three exogenous variables—B, rr, and cr—cause the money supply to change.

1. The money supply is proportional to the monetary base. Thus, an increase in the monetary base increases the money supply by the same percentage.

2. The lower the reserve–deposit ratio, the more loans banks make, and the more money banks create from every dollar of reserves. Thus, a decrease in the reserve–deposit ratio raises the money multiplier and the money supply.

3. The lower the currency–deposit ratio, the fewer dollars of the monetary base the public holds as currency, the more base dollars banks hold as reserves, and the more money banks can create. Thus, a decrease in the currency–deposit ratio raises the money multiplier and the money supply.

With this model in mind, we can discuss the ways in which the Bank of Canada influences the money supply.

The Instruments of Monetary Policy

In previous chapters we made the simplifying assumption that the Bank of Canada controls the money supply directly. In fact, the Bank of Canada controls the money supply indirectly by altering the monetary base. To do this, the Bank of Canada has at its disposal two instruments of monetary policy: open-market operations and deposit-switching.

Open-market operations are the purchases and sales of federal government bonds by the Bank of Canada. When the Bank of Canada buys bonds from the public, the dollars it pays for the bonds increase the monetary base and thereby increase the money supply. When the Bank of Canada sells bonds to the public, the dollars it receives reduce the monetary base and thus decrease the money supply.

Open-market operations are also carried out in the foreign exchange market. To fix the exchange rate, and even just to limit what exchange-rate changes are occurring, the Bank of Canada enters the foreign exchange market. To keep the Canadian dollar high when the market pressure is pushing it down, the Bank buys lots of Canadian dollars. This is done by selling some of Canada's foreign exchange reserves, which are held by the Bank of Canada. Since the Canadian dollars bought by the Bank are no longer in private use, the monetary base is reduced. Similarly, to keep the Canadian dollar from rising in value, the Bank sells lots of Canadian dollars. The Bank does this by using the currency to purchase foreign exchange (thus building up the country's foreign exchange reserves). The new currency that is used to pay for the foreign exchange forms part of the domestic monetary base. As a result, buying foreign exchange causes a multiple expansion in the money supply, just like an open-market purchase of bonds does.

Understanding the mechanics behind these open-market operations is fundamental to having an informed opinion about the plausibility of a small country like Canada having a monetary policy that is independent from that of the United States. If a completely floating exchange-rate policy is chosen, the Bank of Canada is under no obligation to make any trades in the foreign exchange market. Thus, open-market operations can be confined to the domestic bond market, and they can be initiated only when domestic monetary policy objectives call for action. If a fixed-exchange-rate policy is chosen, however, the Bank of Canada gets to decide neither the timing nor the magnitude of its open-market operations. These decisions are made by the private participants in the foreign exchange market, and the Bank's role is a residual one—just issuing or withdrawing whatever quantity of domestic monetary base necessary to keep the exchange rate constant.

The moral of the story is this: We *cannot* fix *both* the quantity and the price of our currency. A fixed exchange rate is inconsistent with independent monetary policy. A floating exchange rate is what permits independent monetary policy.

Deposit-switching is the other method used by the Bank of Canada to alter the monetary base. The government of Canada holds large bank deposits because it receives tax payments on a daily basis. These deposits are held both at the Bank of Canada and at the various chartered banks. In terms of the security of its funds, the government does not care where these deposits are held. But from the perspective of monetary policy, the government *does* have a preference. To understand why, consider a switch of government deposits from the Bank of Canada to any one of the chartered banks. (This operation or its reverse is performed daily by the Bank of Canada, on behalf of the government.) The deposit switch increases chartered bank reserves and deposits on a one-for-one basis. With a fractional reserve system, we know that the chartered bank will use a good part of this increase in reserves to extend new loans. Thus, the deposit switch toward chartered banks sets in motion a multiple expansion of the money supply. Similarly, a switch of government deposits away from chartered banks depletes their reserves—inducing a contraction of loans and so a decrease in the money supply.

The **Bank Rate** is the interest rate that the Bank of Canada uses to determine how much it charges if it ever has to lend reserves to chartered banks. Because an increase in the Bank Rate can be interpreted as an increase in chartered bank costs, it is taken as a signal that banks will be cutting back loans and that the money supply is shrinking. Similarly, a decrease in the Bank Rate is a signal that banks can afford to expand loans and that the monetary policy is expansionary.

Although the broad outline of this interpretation is perfectly correct, it is misleading in its detail. Because Canada has only a few major banks, with branch offices all over the country, they rarely have to borrow reserves from the Bank of Canada. If one branch runs a bit short to meet its customers' needs, reserves are just passed on from another branch, or from the "head office." Also, chartered banks can borrow from each other on the "overnight" marked. Given these facts, an increase in the Bank Rate has no direct effect on chartered bank costs.

Individuals and firms write a great many cheques every day to finance their purchases. When these cheques are cleared at the end of the day, they represent instructions for banks to transfer funds to each other (for honouring each other's cheques). Banks make these transfers on a net basis by writing cheques to each other against their own deposit accounts at the Bank of Canada. The total of these accounts is known as the quantity of settlement balances. Banks are not allowed to end the day with a negative balance in their settlement account. The Bank of Canada uses deposit-switching to alter the overall quantity of settlement balances, and so affect the ability of charter banks to make loans.

It is convenient to pay attention to the weekly changes in the Bank Rate because it represents a summary indicator of what the Bank of Canada has been doing. By following the Bank Rate, individuals can be aware of the stance of monetary policy without having to know the details of the fundamental instruments of policy—open-market operations and deposit-switching. To appreciate why, we must understand how the Bank Rate is set and how the overnight loan market operates.

The overnight lending rate is the rate at which chartered banks and other participants in the money market borrow from and lend to each other one-day funds. The Bank of Canada establishes a range—called the *operating band*—in which the overnight lending rate can move up or down. The Bank Rate is set at the upper limit of this band, which is half a percentage point wide. The Bank of Canada commits to lend out reserves at a rate given by the upper limit of the band, and to borrow funds from financial institutions at the lower limit of the band. These commitments ensure that the overnight rate stays within the band.

By changing the operating band and thus the Bank Rate, the Bank of Canada sends a clear signal about the direction in which interest rates will be moving. On the one hand, Bank Rate changes are "trend-setting," since it is the Bank that has announced any change in the operating band. But in another sense, Bank Rate changes follow the market. The Bank only changes the operating band when it has been conducting behind-the-scenes transactions—deposit-switching and open-market operations—and these initiatives are what determine the change in both market yields and Bank Rate.

The other summary indicator that the Bank of Canada publishes in its semiannual *Monetary Policy Report* is the **Monetary Conditions Index** (MCI). It is a weighted average of the interest rate and the exchange rate (the international value of the Canadian dollar). Monetary policy affects aggregate demand through two channels: it affects investment spending through interest rates, and it affects net exports through the exchange rate. Researchers at the Bank have estimated that it takes roughly a 3 percent change in the exchange rate to affect aggregate demand by the same amount as does a 1 percentage-point change in the interest rate. This three-to-one factor is what Bank officials use in calculating the weighted average. Suppose that from one quarter to the next, the Canadian dollar appreciates by 2 percent while the level of Canadian interest rates falls by 1 percentage point. Without the MCI it would be difficult to know whether monetary conditions had become easier or tighter. The more expensive Canadian dollar reduces net exports while the lower borrowing costs stimulate investment. But the MCI provides a unique signal; it falls because its change equals (one times the interest rate change) plus (one-third times the exchange-rate change), or $(1)(-1) + (1/3)(2) = -1/3$. As long as the Bank's target for the MCI has not changed, the lower value for the actual MCI in the short run means that, overall, monetary policy has moved in the expansionary direction.

Although the two instruments—open-market operations and deposit-switching—and the summary indicators of these operations—the Bank Rate and the Monetary Conditions Index—give the Bank of Canada substantial power to influence the money supply, the Bank cannot control the money supply perfectly. Chartered bank discretion in conducting business can cause the money supply to change. For example, banks may decide to hold more reserves than usual, and households may choose to hold more cash. Such increases in *rr* and *cr* reduce the money supply, even though the Bank of Canada might have thought the initial size of the money supply was the appropriate level for maintaining aggregate demand in the economy.

There is a frustrating irony in this sort of development. When banks and their customers get nervous about the future and rearrange their assets to have a higher proportion of cash, they raise the chances that there will actually be a recession. One of the reasons that the Bank of Canada constantly monitors financial market developments is to try to counteract events like this. The Bank tries to use open-market and deposit-switching operations in such a way that the monetary base moves in the opposite direction to the change in the money multiplier (which is caused by the changes in household and banking preferences and practices).

There is a second method of dealing with crises of confidence in financial institutions: the government can insure individuals' deposits in banks and trust companies, a system called **deposit insurance.** Canada has the Canada Deposit Insurance Corporation (CDIC), which insures all deposits up to a maximum of $60,000 per customer. The idea is quite simple. If a bank or trust company extends too many risky loans and goes bankrupt as a result, customers do not lose their deposits. The general taxpayer, through the CDIC, will pay customers up to $60,000 to protect them from the company's failure. Armed with this insurance, depositors do not have to move more into cash when they get nervous, and, as a result, the Bank of Canada has an easier job trying to keep the money supply on course.

CASE STUDY

Bank Failures and Deposit Insurance

As noted earlier, given Canada's branch banking system, banks almost never go bankrupt. Some smaller trust companies, however, have failed. Indeed, there were several such failures in the late 1980s and early 1990s, and since the CDIC went beyond the $60,000 limit and covered *all* deposits, the CDIC has run up quite a bill for taxpayers to cover. This development has sparked some controversy concerning possible reforms to the deposit insurance system. Before evaluating this controversy, however, it is instructive to consider the situation in the United States. U.S. banking is regulated at the state level, which means that there is much less branch banking. Many banks operate in only one state. This unit banking system is far more prone to bank failures. Indeed, whereas Canada had no bank failures during the Great Depression of the 1930s, there were a great many in the United States. And these failures help explain the severity of the Great Depression.

Between August 1929 and March 1933, the U.S. money supply fell 28 percent. As we discussed in Chapter 11, some economists believe that this large decline in the money supply was the primary cause of the Great Depression. But we did not discuss why the money supply fell so dramatically.

The three variables that determine the money supply—the monetary base, the reserve–deposit ratio, and the currency–deposit ratio—are shown in Table 18-1 for 1929 and 1933. You can see that the fall in the money supply cannot be attributed to a fall in the monetary base: in fact, the monetary base rose 18 percent over this period. Instead, the money supply fell because the money multiplier fell 38 percent. The money multiplier fell because the currency–deposit and reserve–deposit ratios both rose substantially.

Most economists attribute the fall in the money multiplier to the large number of bank failures in the early 1930s. From 1930 to 1933, more than 9,000 banks suspended operations, often defaulting on their depositors. The bank failures caused the money supply to fall by altering the behaviour of both depositors and bankers.

Bank failures raised the currency–deposit ratio by reducing public confidence in the banking system. People feared that bank failures would continue, and they began to view currency as a more desirable form of money than deposits. When they withdrew their deposits, they drained the banks of reserves.

table 18-1

The Money Supply and Its Determinants: 1929 and 1933

	August 1929	March 1933
Money Supply	**26.5**	**19.0**
Currency	3.9	5.5
Deposits	22.6	13.5
Monetary Base	**7.1**	**8.4**
Currency	3.9	5.5
Reserves	3.2	2.9
Money Multiplier	**3.7**	**2.3**
Reserve—deposit ratio	0.14	0.21
Currency—deposit ratio	0.17	0.41

Source: Adapted from Milton Friedman and Anna Schwartz, *A Monetary History of the United States, 1867–1960* (Princeton, NJ: Princeton University Press, 1963), Appendix A.

The process of money creation reversed itself, as banks responded to lower reserves by reducing their outstanding balance of loans.

In addition, the bank failures raised the reserve–deposit ratio by making bankers more cautious. Having just observed many bank runs, bankers became apprehensive about operating with a small amount of reserves. They therefore increased their holdings of reserves to well above the legal minimum. Just as households responded to the banking crisis by holding more currency relative to deposits, bankers responded by holding more reserves relative to loans. Together these changes caused a large fall in the money multiplier.

Although it is easy to explain why the money supply fell, it is more difficult to decide whether to blame the U.S. central bank, the Federal Reserve. One might argue that the monetary base did not fall, so the Fed should not be blamed. Critics of Fed policy during this period make two arguments. First, they claim that the Fed should have taken a more vigorous role in preventing bank failures by acting as a *lender of last resort* when banks needed cash during bank runs. This would have helped maintain confidence in the banking system and prevented the large fall in the money multiplier. Second, they point out that the Fed could have responded to the fall in the money multiplier by increasing the monetary base even more than it did. Either of these actions would likely have prevented such a large fall in the money supply, which in turn might have reduced the severity of the Great Depression.

Like Canada, the United States now has deposit insurance, so a sudden fall in the money multiplier is much less likely today. But also like Canada, U.S. taxpayers are frustrated with how the deposit insurance system requires the general taxpayer to subsidize depositors that do not exercise care concerning where they deposit their funds. This is a classic problem that is involved with any form of insurance. In this case, insurance lowers the cost to depositors of failures, but it also raises the probability that those very failures will occur. This is because the insurance eliminates the need for depositors to assess and monitor the riskiness of financial institutions. Current discussions in Canada have raised suggestions like following the "co-insurance" system of Great Britain. The essential feature of this reform is that there is a deductible, so that individuals lose 2 percent or 3 percent of their deposits when the institution fails. With this feature, depositors remain well protected, but they still have some incentive to avoid institutions that are obviously shaky.

18-2 | Money Demand

We now turn to the other side of the money market and examine what determines money demand. In previous chapters, we used simple money demand functions. We started with the quantity theory, which assumes that the demand for real balances is proportional to income. That is, the quantity theory assumes

$$(M/P)^{\mathrm{d}} = kY,$$

where k is a constant measuring how much money people want to hold for every dollar of income. We then considered a more general and realistic money demand function that assumes the demand for real money balances depends on both the interest rate and income:

$$(M/P)^{\mathrm{d}} = L(i, Y).$$

We used this money demand function when we discussed the link between money and prices in Chapter 7 and when we developed the *IS–LM* model in Chapters 10 and 11.

There is, of course, much more to say about what determines how much money people choose to hold. Just as studies of the consumption function rely on microeconomic models of the consumption decision, studies of the money demand function rely on microeconomic models of the money demand decision. In this section we first discuss in broad terms the different ways to model money demand. We then develop one prominent model.

Recall that money serves three functions: it is a unit of account, a store of value, and a medium of exchange. The first function—money as a unit of account—does not by itself generate any demand for money, because one can quote prices in dollars without holding any. By contrast, money can serve its other two functions only if people hold it. Theories of money demand emphasize the role of money either as a store of value or as a medium of exchange.

Portfolio Theories of Money Demand

Theories of money demand that emphasize the role of money as a store of value are called **portfolio theories.** According to these theories, people hold money as part of their portfolio of assets. The key insight is that money offers a different combination of risk and return than other assets. In particular, money offers a safe (nominal) return, whereas the prices of stocks and bonds may rise or fall. Thus, some economists have suggested that households choose to hold money as part of their optimal portfolio.[2]

Portfolio theories predict that the demand for money should depend on the risk and return offered by money and by the various assets households can hold instead of money. In addition, money demand should depend on total wealth, because wealth measures the size of the portfolio to be allocated among money and the alternative assets. For example, we might write the money demand function as

$$(M/P)^d = L(r_s, r_b, \pi^e, W),$$

where r_s is the expected real return on stock, r_b is the expected real return on bonds, π^e is the expected inflation rate, and W is real wealth. An increase in r_s or r_b reduces money demand, because other assets become more attractive. An increase in π^e also reduces money demand, because money becomes less attractive. (Recall that $-\pi^e$ is the expected real return to holding money.) An increase in W raises money demand, because higher wealth means a larger portfolio.

From the standpoint of portfolio theories, we can view our money demand function, $L(i, Y)$, as a useful simplification. First, it uses real income Y as a proxy for real wealth W. If we think of wealth very broadly defined to include human capital, income is the yield on wealth. Second, the only return variable it includes is the nominal interest rate, which is the sum of the real return on bonds and expected inflation (that is, $i = r_b + \pi^e$). According to portfolio theories, however, the money demand function should include the expected returns on other assets as well.

Are portfolio theories useful for studying money demand? The answer depends on which measure of money we are considering. The most narrow measures of money, such as $M1$, include only currency and deposits in chequing accounts. These forms of money earn zero or very low rates of interest. There are other assets—such as savings accounts, treasury bills, and guaranteed investment certificates—that earn higher rates of interest and have the same risk characteristics as currency and chequing accounts. Economists say that money ($M1$) is a **dominated asset:** as a store of value, it exists alongside other assets that are always better. Thus, it is not optimal for people to hold money as part of their portfolio, and portfolio theories cannot explain the demand for these dominated forms of money.

Portfolio theories are more plausible as theories of money demand if we adopt a broad measure of money. The broad measures include many of those assets that dominate currency and chequing accounts. $M2$, for example, includes savings and other notice accounts. When we examine why people hold assets in the form of $M2$, rather than bonds or stock, the portfolio considerations of risk and return may be paramount. Hence, although the portfolio approach to money demand may not be plausible when applied to $M1$, it may be a good theory to explain the demand for $M2$ or $M3$.

---

[2] James Tobin, "Liquidity Preference as Behavior Toward Risk," *Review of Economic Studies* 25 (February 1958): 65–86.

CASE STUDY

Currency and the Underground Economy

How much currency are you holding right now in your wallet? How many $100 bills?

In Canada today, the amount of currency per person is about $1,000 and about half of that is in large-denomination notes. Most people find this fact surprising, because they hold much smaller amounts and in smaller denominations.

Some of this currency is used by people in the underground economy—that is, by those engaged in illegal activity such as the drug trade and by those trying to hide income to evade taxes. People whose wealth was earned illegally may have fewer options for investing their portfolio, because by holding wealth in banks, bonds, or stock, they assume a greater risk of detection. For criminals, currency may not be a dominated asset: it may be the best store of value available.

Some economists point to the large amount of currency in the underground economy as one reason that some inflation may be desirable. Recall that inflation is a tax on the holders of money, because inflation erodes the real value of money. A drug dealer holding $20,000 in cash pays an inflation tax of $2,000 per year when the inflation rate is 10 percent. The inflation tax is one of the few taxes those in the underground economy cannot evade. Government estimates of the underground economy put it at 4.5 percent of GDP in 1994.

Transactions Theories of Money Demand

Theories of money demand that emphasize the role of money as a medium of exchange are called **transactions theories.** These theories acknowledge that money is a dominated asset and stress that people hold money, unlike other assets, to make purchases. These theories best explain why people hold narrow measures of money, such as currency and chequing accounts, as opposed to holding assets that dominate them, such as savings accounts or treasury bills.

Transactions theories of money demand take many forms, depending on how one models the process of obtaining money and making transactions. All these theories assume that money has the cost of earning a low rate of return and the benefit of making transactions more convenient. People decide how much money to hold by trading off these costs and benefits.

To see how transactions theories explain the money demand function, let's develop one prominent model of this type. The **Baumol–Tobin model** was developed in the 1950s by economists William Baumol and James Tobin, and it remains a leading theory of money demand.[3]

---

[3] William Baumol, "The Transactions Demand for Cash: An Inventory Theoretic Approach," *Quarterly Journal of Economics* 66 (November 1952): 545–556; James Tobin, "The Interest Elasticity of the Transactions Demand for Cash," *Review of Economics and Statistics* (August 1956): 241–247.

The Baumol–Tobin Model of Cash Management

The Baumol–Tobin model analyzes the costs and benefits of holding money. The benefit of holding money is convenience: people hold money to avoid making a trip to the bank every time they wish to buy something. The cost of this convenience is the forgone interest they would have received had they left the money deposited in a savings account that paid interest.

To see how people trade off these benefits and costs, consider a person who plans to spend Y dollars gradually over the course of a year. (For simplicity, assume that the price level is constant, so real spending is constant over the year.) How much money should he hold in the process of spending this amount? That is, what is the optimal size of average cash balances?

Consider the possibilities. He could withdraw the Y dollars at the beginning of the year and gradually spend the money. Panel (a) of Figure 18-1 shows his money holdings over the course of the year under this plan. His money holdings begin the year at Y and end the year at zero, averaging $Y/2$ over the year.

A second possible plan is to make two trips to the bank. In this case, he withdraws $Y/2$ dollars at the beginning of the year, gradually spends this amount over the first half of the year, and then makes another trip to withdraw $Y/2$ for the second half of the year. Panel (b) of Figure 18-1 shows that money holdings over the year vary between $Y/2$ and zero, averaging $Y/4$. This plan has the advantage that less money is held on average, so the individual forgoes

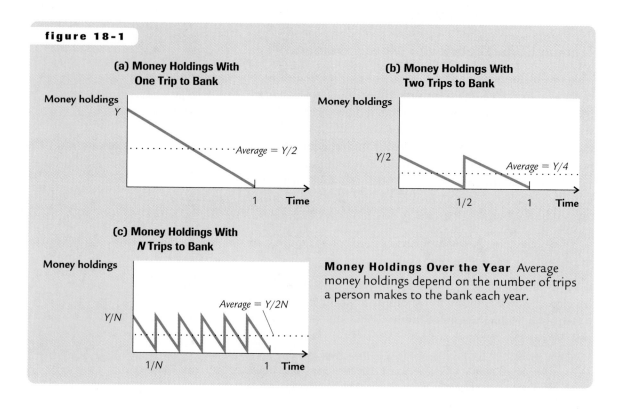

figure 18-1

(a) Money Holdings With One Trip to Bank

Money holdings

Y

$\cdots\cdots$Average = $Y/2$

1   Time

(b) Money Holdings With Two Trips to Bank

Money holdings

$Y/2$

Average = $Y/4$

1/2   1   Time

(c) Money Holdings With *N* Trips to Bank

Money holdings

Average = $Y/2N$

Y/N

1/N   1   Time

Money Holdings Over the Year Average money holdings depend on the number of trips a person makes to the bank each year.

less interest, but it has the disadvantage of requiring two trips to the bank rather than one.

More generally, suppose the individual makes N trips to the bank over the course of the year. On each trip, he withdraws Y/N dollars; he then spends the money gradually over the following $1/N$th of the year. Panel (c) of Figure 18-1 shows that money holdings vary between Y/N and zero, averaging $Y/(2N)$.

The question is, what is the optimal choice of N? The greater N is, the less money the individual holds on average and the less interest he forgoes. But as N increases, so does the inconvenience of making frequent trips to the bank.

Suppose that the cost of going to the bank is some fixed amount F. We can view F as representing the value of the time spent traveling to and from the bank and waiting in line to make the withdrawal. For example, if a trip to the bank takes 15 minutes and a person's wage is $12 per hour, then F is $3. Also, let i denote the interest rate; because money does not bear interest, i measures the opportunity cost of holding money.

Now we can analyze the optimal choice of N, which determines money demand. For any N, the average amount of money held is $Y/(2N)$, so the forgone interest is $iY/(2N)$. Because F is the cost per trip to the bank, the total cost of making trips to the bank is FN. The total cost the individual bears is the sum of the forgone interest and the cost of trips to the bank:

$$\text{Total Cost} = \text{Forgone Interest} + \text{Cost of Trips}$$
$$= iY/(2N) + FN.$$

The larger the number of trips N, the smaller the forgone interest, and the larger the cost of going to the bank.

Figure 18-2 shows how total cost depends on N. There is one value of N that minimizes total cost. The optimal value of N, denoted N^*, is[4]

$$N^* = \sqrt{iY/2F}.$$

Average money holding is

$$\text{Average Money Holding} = Y/(2N^*)$$
$$= \sqrt{YF/2i}.$$

This expression shows that the individual holds more money if the fixed cost of going to the bank F is higher, if expenditure Y is higher, or if the interest rate i is lower.

So far, we have been interpreting the Baumol–Tobin model as a model of the demand for currency. That is, we have used it to explain the amount of money held outside of banks. Yet one can interpret the model more broadly.

---

[4] *Mathematical note:* Deriving this expression for the optimal choice of N requires simple calculus. Differentiate total cost C with respect to N to obtain

$$dC/dN = -iYN^{-2}/2 + F.$$

At the optimum, $dC/dN = 0$, which yields the formula for N^*.

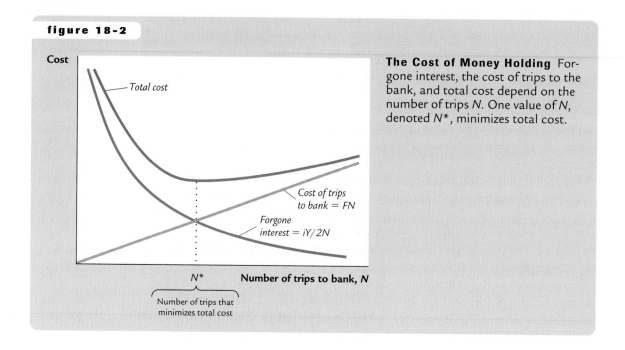

figure 18-2

Cost

Total cost

Cost of trips to bank = FN

Forgone interest = iY/2N

N*

Number of trips to bank, N

Number of trips that minimizes total cost

The Cost of Money Holding Forgone interest, the cost of trips to the bank, and total cost depend on the number of trips N. One value of N, denoted N*, minimizes total cost.

Imagine a person who holds a portfolio of monetary assets (currency and chequing accounts) and nonmonetary assets (stocks and bonds). Monetary assets are used for transactions but offer a low rate of return. Let i be the difference in the return between monetary and nonmonetary assets, and let F be the cost of transferring nonmonetary assets into monetary assets, such as a brokerage fee. The decision about how often to pay the brokerage fee is analogous to the decision about how often to make a trip to the bank. Therefore, the Baumol–Tobin model describes this person's demand for monetary assets. By showing that money demand depends positively on expenditure Y and negatively on the interest rate i, the model provides a microeconomic justification for the money demand function, $L(i, Y)$, that we have used throughout this book.

One implication of the Baumol–Tobin model is that any change in the fixed cost of going to the bank F alters the money demand function—that is, it changes the quantity of money demanded for any given interest rate and income. It is easy to imagine events that might influence this fixed cost. The spread of automatic teller machines, for instance, reduces F by reducing the time it takes to withdraw money. Similarly, the introduction of internet banking reduces F by makes it easier to transfer funds among accounts. On the other hand, an increase in real wages increases F by increasing the value of time. And an increase in banking fees increases F directly. Thus, although the Baumol–Tobin model gives us a very specific money demand function, it does not give us reason to believe that this function will necessarily be stable over time.

CASE STUDY

Empirical Studies of Money Demand

Many economists have studied the data on money, income, and interest rates to learn more about the money demand function. One purpose of these studies is to estimate how money demand responds to changes in income and the interest rate. The sensitivity of money demand to these two variables determines the slope of the *LM* curve; it thus influences how monetary and fiscal policy affect the economy.

Another purpose of the empirical studies is to test the theories of money demand. The Baumol–Tobin model, for example, makes precise predictions for how income and interest rates influence money demand. The model's square-root formula implies that the income elasticity of money demand is 1/2: a 10-percent increase in income should lead to a 5-percent increase in the demand for real balances. It also says that the interest elasticity of money demand is 1/2: a 10-percent increase in the interest rate (say, from 10 percent to 11 percent) should lead to a 5-percent decrease in the demand for real balances.

Most empirical studies of money demand do not confirm these predictions. They find that the income elasticity of money demand is larger than 1/2 and that the interest elasticity is smaller than 1/2. Thus, although the Baumol–Tobin model may capture part of the story behind the money demand function, it is not completely correct.

One possible explanation for the failure of the Baumol–Tobin model is that some people may have less discretion over their money holdings than the model assumes. For example, consider a person who must go to the bank once a week to deposit her paycheque; while at the bank, she takes advantage of her visit to withdraw the currency needed for the coming week. For this person, the number of trips to the bank, N, does not respond to changes in expenditure or the interest rate. Because N is fixed, average money holdings ($Y/2N$) are proportional to expenditure and insensitive to the interest rate.

Now imagine that the world is populated with two sorts of people. Some obey the Baumol–Tobin model, so they have income and interest elasticities of 1/2. The others have a fixed N, so they have an income elasticity of 1 and an interest elasticity of zero. In this case, the overall demand for money looks like a weighted average of the demands of the two groups. The income elasticity will be between 1/2 and 1, and the interest elasticity will be between 1/2 and zero, as the empirical studies find.[5]

---

[5] To learn more about the empirical studies of money demand, see Stephen M. Goldfeld and Daniel E. Sichel, "The Demand for Money," *Handbook of Monetary Economics,* volume 1 (Amsterdam: North-Holland, 1990): 299–356; and David Laidler, *The Demand for Money: Theories and Evidence,* 3d ed. (New York: Harper & Row, 1985).

18-3 | Financial Innovation and the Rise of Near Money

Traditional macroeconomic analysis groups assets into two categories: those used as a medium of exchange as well as a store of value (currency, chequing accounts) and those used only as a store of value (stocks, bonds, savings accounts). The first category of assets is called "money." In this chapter we discussed its supply and demand.

Although the distinction between monetary and nonmonetary assets remains a useful theoretical tool, in recent years it has become more difficult to use in practice. In part because of deregulation of banks and other financial institutions, and in part because of improved computer technology, the past decade has seen rapid financial innovation. Monetary assets such as chequing accounts once paid no interest; today they can earn market interest rates and are comparable to nonmonetary assets as stores of value. Nonmonetary assets such as stocks and bonds were once inconvenient to buy and sell; today mutual funds allow depositors to hold stocks and bonds and to make withdrawals simply by writing cheques from their accounts. These nonmonetary assets that have acquired some of the liquidity of money are called **near money.**

The existence of near money complicates monetary policy by making the demand for money unstable. Since money and near money are close substitutes, households can easily switch their assets from one form to the other. Such changes can occur for minor reasons and do not necessarily reflect changes in spending. Thus, the velocity of money becomes less predictable, and the quantity of money gives faulty signals about aggregate demand.

One response to this problem is to use a broad definition of money that includes near money. Yet, since there is a continuum of assets in the world with varying characteristics, it is not clear how to choose a subset to label "money." Moreover, if we adopt a broad definition of money, the Bank of Canada's ability to control this quantity may be limited.

The potential instability in money demand caused by near money has been an important practical problem for the Bank of Canada. In recent years, different measures of the money supply have given rather conflicting signals. For example, in 1990, $M2$ grew by almost 11 percent while $M1$ shrank by 1 percent. Then, in 1993, $M2$ growth had fallen to 3.2 percent while $M1$ growth had shot up to 10.4 percent. It is partly because of these problems that the Bank of Canada shifted away from attempting to target any particular monetary aggregate in the 1980s. Since then, the Bank has been adjusting the monetary base by whatever it takes to target the inflation rate directly.

18-4 | Conclusion

Money is at the heart of much macroeconomic analysis. Models of money supply and money demand can help shed light on the long-run determinants of the price level and the short-run causes of economic fluctuations. The rise of near money in recent years has shown that there is still much to be learned. Building reliable microeconomic models of money and near money remains a central challenge for macroeconomists.

Summary

1. The system of fractional-reserve banking creates money, because each dollar of reserves generates many dollars of deposits.

2. The supply of money depends on the monetary base, the reserve–deposit ratio, and the currency–deposit ratio. An increase in the monetary base leads to a proportionate increase in the money supply. A decrease in the reserve–deposit ratio or in the currency–deposit ratio increases the money multiplier and thus the money supply.

3. The Bank of Canada changes the money supply using two policy instruments. It can increase the monetary base by making an open-market purchase of bonds or foreign exchange, or by switching government deposits out of the Bank of Canada and into the chartered banks. Both of these operations cause a reduction of interest rates, and so they can be monitored by observing a drop in the Bank Rate.

4. Portfolio theories of money demand stress the role of money as a store of value. They predict that the demand for money depends on the risk and return on money and alternative assets.

5. Transactions theories of money demand, such as the Baumol–Tobin model, stress the role of money as a medium of exchange. They predict that the demand for money depends positively on expenditure and negatively on the interest rate.

6. Financial innovation has led to the creation of assets with many of the attributes of money. These near monies make the demand for money less stable, which complicates the conduct of monetary policy.

KEY CONCEPTS

Reserves	Currency–deposit ratio	Deposit insurance
100-percent-reserve banking	Money multiplier	Portfolio theories
Balance sheet	High-powered money	Dominated asset
Fractional-reserve banking	Open-market operations	Transactions theories
Financial intermediation	Deposit-switching	Baumol–Tobin model
Monetary base	Bank Rate	Near money
Reserve–deposit ratio	Monetary Conditions Index	

QUESTIONS FOR REVIEW

1. Explain how banks create money.

2. What are the two ways in which the Bank of Canada can influence the money supply?

3. Why might a banking crisis lead to a fall in the money supply?

4. Explain the difference between portfolio and transactions theories of money demand.

5. According to the Baumol–Tobin model, what determines how often people go to the bank? What does this decision have to do with money demand?

6. In what way does the existence of near money complicate the conduct of monetary policy?

PROBLEMS AND APPLICATIONS

1. The U.S. money supply fell during the years 1929 to 1933 because both the currency–deposit ratio and the reserve–deposit ratio increased. Use the model of the money supply and the data in Table 18-1 to answer the following hypothetical questions about this episode.

   a. What would have happened to the money supply if the currency–deposit ratio had risen but the reserve–deposit ratio had remained the same?

   b. What would have happened to the money supply if the reserve–deposit ratio had risen but the currency–deposit ratio had remained the same?

   c. Which of the two changes was more responsible for the fall in the money supply?

2. To increase tax revenue, the U.S. government in 1932 imposed a 2-cent tax on cheques written on deposits in bank accounts. (In today's dollars, this tax was about 25 cents per cheque.)

   a. How do you think the cheque tax affected the currency–deposit ratio? Explain.

   b. Use the model of the money supply under fractional-reserve banking to discuss how this tax affected the money supply.

   c. Now use the *IS–LM* model to discuss the impact of this tax on the economy. Was the cheque tax a good policy to implement in the middle of the Great Depression?

3. Suppose that an epidemic of street crime sweeps the country, making it more likely that your wallet will be stolen. Using the Baumol–Tobin model, explain (in words, not equations) how this crime wave will affect the optimal frequency of trips to the bank and the demand for money.

4. Let's see what the Baumol–Tobin model says about how often you should go to the bank to withdraw cash.

   a. How much do you buy per year with currency (as opposed to cheques or credit cards)? This is your value of *Y*.

   b. How long does it take you to go to the bank? What is your hourly wage? Use these two figures to compute your value of *F*.

   c. What interest rate do you earn on the money you leave in your bank account? This is your value of *i*. (Be sure to write *i* in decimal form—that is, 6 percent should be expressed 0.06.)

   d. According to the Baumol–Tobin model, how many times should you go to the bank each year, and how much should you withdraw each time?

   e. In practice, how often do you go to the bank, and how much do you withdraw?

   f. Compare the predictions of the Baumol–Tobin model to your behaviour. Does the model describe how you actually behave? If not, why not? How would you change the model to make it a better description of your behaviour?

5. In Chapter 6, we defined the velocity of money as the ratio of nominal expenditure to the quantity of money. Let's now use the Baumol–Tobin model to examine what determines velocity.

   a. Recalling that average money holdings equal $Y/(2N)$, write velocity as a function of the number of trips to the bank N. Explain your result.

   b. Use the formula for the optimal number of trips to express velocity as a function of expenditure Y, the interest rate i, and the cost of a trip to the bank F.

   c. What happens to velocity when the interest rate rises? Explain.

   d. What happens to velocity when the price level rises? Explain.

   e. As the economy grows, what should happen to the velocity of money? (*Hint:* Think about how economic growth will influence Y and F.)

   f. Suppose now that the number of trips to the bank is fixed rather than discretionary. What does this assumption imply about velocity?

chapter 19

Advances in the Theory of Economic Fluctuations

What is the best way to explain short-run fluctuations in output and employment? How should monetary and fiscal policy respond to these fluctuations? Most economists believe that these questions are best answered using the model of aggregate demand and aggregate supply. This book has, therefore, developed and applied this model thoroughly. Yet as we approach the end of the book, let's take a step closer to the frontier of modern economic research and examine the continuing debate over the theory of short-run economic fluctuations. This chapter discusses two recent strands of research—**real business cycle theory** and **new Keynesian economics**.

As a matter of logic, the output of the economy can fluctuate either because the natural rate of output fluctuates or because the output of the economy has deviated from its natural rate. Throughout most of this book, we have presumed that the natural rate of output grows smoothly over time (as explained by the Solow growth model) and that most short-run fluctuations are deviations from the natural rate (as explained by the model of aggregate demand and aggregate supply). New Keynesian theory accepts these presumptions. By contrast, real business cycle theory—a viewpoint held by a small but significant minority of economists—suggests that deviations from the natural rate are not significant and that most fluctuations should be viewed as changes in the natural, or equilibrium, level of output.

We begin this chapter by examining the theory of real business cycles. According to this theory, short-run economic fluctuations should be explained while maintaining the assumptions of the classical model, which we have used to study the long run. Most important, real business cycle theory assumes that prices are fully flexible, even in the short run. Almost all microeconomic analysis is based on the premise that prices adjust to clear markets. Advocates of real business cycle theory argue that macroeconomic analysis should be based on the same assumption.

Because real business cycle theory assumes complete price flexibility, it is consistent with the classical dichotomy: in this theory, nominal variables, such as the money supply and the price level, do not influence real variables, such as output and employment. To explain fluctuations in real variables, real business cycle theory emphasizes real changes in the economy, such as changes in production technologies, that can alter the economy's natural rate. The "real" in real business cycle theory refers to the theory's exclusion of nominal variables in explaining short-run economic fluctuations.

figure 19-1

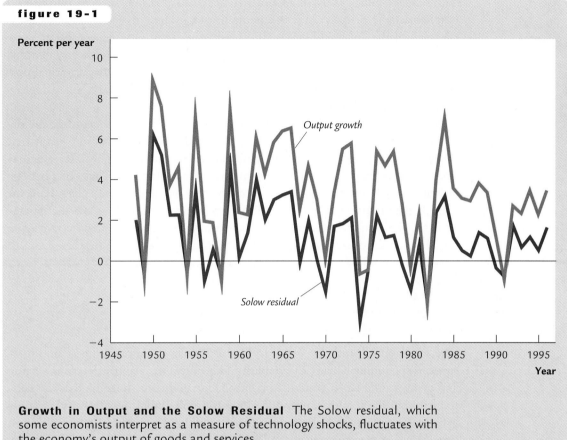

Growth in Output and the Solow Residual The Solow residual, which some economists interpret as a measure of technology shocks, fluctuates with the economy's output of goods and services.

Source: U.S. Department of Commerce, U. S. Department of Labor, and authors' calculations.

that measured productivity is low in recessions because workers are not working as hard as usual and because more of their output is not measured. Unfortunately, there is no clear evidence on the importance of labour hoarding and the cyclical mismeasurement of output. Therefore, different interpretations of Figure 19-1 persist. This disagreement is one part of the debate between advocates and critics of real business cycle theory.[4]

The Neutrality of Money

Just as money has no role in the Crusoe economy, real business cycle theory assumes that money in our economy is neutral, even in the short run. That

[4] For the two sides of this debate, see Edward C. Prescott, "Theory Ahead of Business Cycle Measurement," and Lawrence H. Summers, "Some Skeptical Observations on Real Business Cycle Theory." Both are in *Quarterly Review,* Federal Reserve Bank of Minneapolis (Fall 1986).

is, monetary policy is assumed not to affect real variables such as output and employment. Not only does the neutrality of money give real business cycle theory its name, but neutrality is also the theory's most radical assumption.

Critics argue that the evidence does not support short-run monetary neutrality. They point out that reductions in money growth and inflation are almost always associated with periods of high unemployment. Monetary policy appears to have a strong influence on the real economy.

Advocates of real business cycle theory argue that their critics confuse the direction of causation between money and output. These advocates claim that the money supply is endogenous: fluctuations in output might cause fluctuations in the money supply. For example, when output rises because of a beneficial technology shock, the quantity of money demanded rises. The Bank of Canada may respond by raising the money supply to accommodate the greater demand. This endogenous response of money to economic activity may give the illusion of monetary non-neutrality.[5]

CASE STUDY

Testing for Monetary Neutrality

The direction of causation between fluctuations in the money supply and fluctuations in output is hard to establish. The only sure way to determine cause and effect would be to conduct a controlled experiment. Imagine that the central bank set the money supply according to some random process. Every January, the Governor of the Bank of Canada would flip a coin. Heads would mean an expansionary monetary policy for the coming year; tails a contractionary one. After a number of years we would know with confidence the effects of monetary policy. If output and employment usually rose after the coin came up heads and usually fell after it came up tails, then we would conclude that monetary policy has real effects. Yet if the flip of the coin were unrelated to subsequent economic performance, then we would conclude that real business cycle theorists are right about the neutrality of money.

Unfortunately for scientific progress, but fortunately for the economy, economists are not allowed to conduct such experiments. Instead, we must glean what we can from the data that history gives us.

One classic study in the history of monetary policy is the 1963 book by Milton Friedman and Anna Schwartz, *A Monetary History of the United States, 1867–1960.* This book describes the historical events that shaped decisions over monetary policy and the economic events that resulted from those decisions. Friedman and Schwartz claim, for instance, that the death in 1928 of Benjamin Strong, the president of the New York Federal Reserve Bank, was one cause of the Great Depression of the 1930s: Strong's death left a power

---

[5] Robert G. King and Charles I. Plosser, "Money, Credit, and Prices in a Real Business Cycle," *American Economic Review* 74 (June 1984): 363–380.

vacuum at the Fed, which prevented the Fed from responding vigorously as economic conditions deteriorated. In other words, Strong's death, like the Fed's coin coming up tails, was a random event leading to more contractionary monetary policy.[6]

A more recent study by Christina Romer and David Romer follows in the footsteps of Friedman and Schwartz. The Romers carefully read through the minutes of the meetings of the Federal Reserve's Open Market Committee, which sets monetary policy in the United States. From these minutes, they identified dates when the Fed appears to have shifted its policy toward reducing the rate of inflation. The Romers argue that these dates are, in essence, the equivalent of the Fed's coin coming up tails. They then show that the economy experienced a decline in output and employment after each of these dates. Thus, the Romers' evidence appears to establish the short-run non-neutrality of money.[7]

Interpretations of history, however, are always open to dispute. No one can be sure what would have happened during the 1930s had Benjamin Strong lived. Similarly, not everyone is convinced that the Romers' dates are as exogenous as a coin's flip: perhaps the Fed was actually responding to events that would have caused declining output and employment even without Fed action. Thus, while most economists are convinced that monetary policy has an important role in the business cycle, this judgment is based on the accumulation of evidence from many studies. There is no "smoking gun" that convinces absolutely everyone.

The Flexibility of Wages and Prices

Real business cycle theory assumes that wages and prices adjust quickly to clear markets, just as Crusoe always achieves his optimal level of GDP without any impediment from a market imperfection. Advocates of this theory believe that the market imperfection of sticky wages and prices is not important for understanding economic fluctuations. They also believe that the assumption of flexible prices is superior methodologically to the assumption of sticky prices, because it ties macroeconomic theory more closely to microeconomic theory.

Critics point out that many wages and prices are not flexible. They believe that this inflexibility explains both the existence of unemployment and the non-neutrality of money. To explain why prices are sticky, they rely on the various new Keynesian theories that we discuss in the next section.

---

[6] Milton Friedman and Anna J. Schwartz, *A Monetary History of the United States, 1867–1960* (Princeton, NJ: Princeton University Press, 1960).

[7] Christina Romer and David Romer, "Does Monetary Policy Matter? A New Test in the Spirit of Friedman and Schwartz," *NBER Macroeconomics Annual* (1989): 121–170.

WHAT IS NEW CLASSICAL ECONOMICS?

Real business cycle theory is called **new classical economics** because it uses the assumptions of the classical model—especially flexible prices and monetary neutrality—to study short-run economic fluctuations. Yet real business cycle theory is not the only part of macroeconomics that bears the label "new classical." Most economists use the term broadly to describe the many challenges to the Keynesian orthodoxy that prevailed in the 1960s.

According to this broad definition, one can apply the label "new classical" to some of the ideas we discussed in earlier chapters, including rational expectations (Chapter 13), the Lucas critique (Chapter 14), the problem of time inconsistency (Chapter 14), and the Ricardian view of government debt (Chapter 15). Some economists apply the label "new classical" to any model in which prices are fully flexible in the short run. By this definition, the worker-misperception and imperfect-information models of aggregate supply (Chapter 13) are new classical, even though they violate the classical dichotomy.

Although real business cycle theory is widely called "new classical," in some ways the term is a misnomer, for the classical economists themselves never suggested that money was neutral in the short run. For example, David Hume, in his 1752 essay "Of Money," stressed that money was neutral only in the long run:

> In my opinion, it is only in the interval or intermediate situation, between the acquisition of money and the rise in prices, that the increasing quantity of gold or silver is favourable to industry. . . . The farmer or gardener, finding that their commodities are taken off, apply themselves with alacrity to the raising of more. . . . It is easy to trace the money in its progress through the whole commonwealth; where we shall find that it must first quicken the diligence of every individual, before it increases the price of labour.

In suggesting the hypothesis that money is neutral in the short run, real business cycle theory pushes the assumptions of classical economics further than did the classical economists themselves.[8]

19-2 | New Keynesian Economics

Most economists are skeptical of the basic version of the theory of real business cycles and believe that short-run fluctuations in output and employment involve deviations from the economy's natural rate. They think these deviations occur because wages and prices are slow to adjust to changing economic conditions. As we have discussed in Chapters 9 and 13, this stickiness makes the

---

[8] For a textbook that emphasizes the new classical approach, see Robert J. Barro and Robert F. Lucas, *Macroeconomics,* 1st Canadian ed. (Burr Ridge, IL: Irwin, 1994). To read more about real business cycle theory, see N. Gregory Mankiw, "Real Business Cycles: A New Keynesian Perspective," *Journal of Economic Perspectives* 3 (Summer 1989): 79–90; Bennett T. McCallum, "Real Business Cycle Models," in R. Barro, ed., *Modern Business Cycle Theory* (Cambridge, MA: Harvard University Press, 1989), 16–50; and Charles I. Plosser, "Understanding Real Business Cycles," *Journal of Economic Perspectives* 3 (Summer 1989): 51–77.

Staggering also affects wage determination. Consider, for example, how a fall in the money supply works its way through the economy. A smaller money supply reduces aggregate demand, which in turn requires a proportionate fall in nominal wages to maintain full employment. Each worker might be willing to take a lower nominal wage if all other wages were to fall proportionately. The worker could then reasonably expect a reduction in the overall level of goods prices. But each worker is reluctant to be the first to take a pay cut, knowing that this means, at least temporarily, a fall in his or her relative wage. Since the setting of wages is staggered, the reluctance of each worker to reduce his or her wage first makes the overall level of wages slow to respond to changes in aggregate demand. In other words, the staggered setting of individual wages makes the overall level of wages sticky.[13]

CASE STUDY

If You Want to Know Why Firms Have Sticky Prices, Ask Them

How sticky are prices, and why are they sticky? As we have seen, these questions are at the heart of new Keynesian theories of short-run economic fluctuations (as well as of the traditional model of aggregate demand and aggregate

---

table 19-1

The Frequency of Price Adjustment

This table is based on answers to the question: How often do the prices of your most important products change in a typical year?

Frequency	Percentage of Firms
Less than once	10.2
Once	39.3
1.01 to 2	15.6
2.01 to 4	12.9
4.01 to 12	7.5
12.01 to 52	4.3
52.01 to 365	8.6
More than 365	1.6

Source: Table 4.1, Alan S. Blinder, "On Sticky Prices: Academic Theories Meet the Real World," in N. G. Mankiw, ed., *Monetary Policy* (Chicago: University of Chicago Press, 1994): 117–154.

---

[13] For more on the effects of staggering, see John Taylor, "Staggered Price Setting in a Macro Model," *American Economic Review* 69 (May 1979): 108–113; and Olivier J. Blanchard, "Price Asynchronization and Price Level Inertia," in R. Dornbusch and Mario Henrique Simonsen, eds., *Inflation, Debt, and Indexation* (Cambridge, MA: MIT Press, 1983), 3–24.

supply). In an intriguing study, economist Alan Blinder attacked these questions directly by surveying firms about their price-adjustment decisions.

Blinder began by asking firm managers how often they change prices. The answers, summarized in Table 19-1, yielded two conclusions. First, sticky prices are quite common. The typical firm in the economy adjusts its prices once or twice a year. Second, there are large differences among firms in the

table 19-2

Theories of Price Stickiness

Theory and Brief Description	Percentage of Firms That Accepted Theory
Coordination failure: Firms hold back on price changes, waiting for others to go first	60.6
Cost-based pricing with lags: Price rises are delayed until costs rise	55.5
Delivery lags, service, etc.: Firms prefer to vary other product attributes, such as delivery lags, service, or product quality	54.8
Implicit contracts: Firms tacitly agree to stabilize prices, perhaps out of "fairness" to customers	50.4
Nominal contracts: Prices are fixed by explicit contracts	35.7
Costs of price adjustment: Firms incur costs of changing prices	30.0
Procyclical elasticity: Demand curves become less elastic as they shift in	29.7
Pricing points: Certain prices (like $9.99) have special psychological significance	24.0
Inventories: Firms vary inventory stocks instead of prices	20.9
Constant marginal cost: Marginal cost is flat and markups are constant	19.7
Hierarchical delays: Bureaucratic delays slow down decisions	13.6
Judging quality by price: Firms fear customers will mistake price cuts for reductions in quality	10.0

Source: Tables 4.3 and 4.4, Alan S. Blinder, "On Sticky Prices: Academic Theories Meet the Real World," in N. G. Mankiw, ed., *Monetary Policy* (Chicago: University of Chicago Press, 1994): 117–154.

frequency of price adjustment. About 10 percent of firms change prices more often than once a week, and about the same number change prices less often than once a year.

Blinder then asked the firm managers why they don't change prices more often. In particular, he explained to the managers 12 economic theories of sticky prices and asked them to judge how well each of these theories describe their firms. Table 19-2 summarizes the theories and ranks them by the percentage of managers who accepted the theory. Notice that each of the theories was endorsed by some of the managers, and each was rejected by a large number as well. One interpretation is that different theories apply to different firms, depending on industry characteristics, and that price stickiness is a macroeconomic phenomenon without a single microeconomic explanation.

Among the 12 theories, coordination failure tops the list. According to Blinder, this is an important finding, for it suggests that the theory of coordination failure explains price stickiness, which in turn explains why the economy experiences short-run fluctuations around its natural rate. He writes, "the most obvious policy implication of the model is that more coordinated wage and price setting—somehow achieved—could improve welfare. But if this proves difficult or impossible, the door is opened to activist monetary policy to cure recessions."[14]

19-3| Conclusion

Recent developments in the theory of short-run economic fluctuations remind us that we do not understand economic fluctuations as well as we would like. Fundamental questions about the economy remain open to dispute. Is the stickiness of wages and prices a key to understanding economic fluctuations? Does monetary policy have real effects?

The way economists answer these questions affects how they view the role of economic policy. Economists who believe that wages and prices are sticky, such as those pursuing new Keynesian theories, often believe that monetary and fiscal policy should be used to try to stabilize the economy. Price stickiness is a type of market imperfection, and it leaves open the possibility that government policies can raise economic well-being for society as a whole.

By contrast, real business cycle theory suggests that the government's influence on the economy is limited and that even if the government could stabilize the economy, it should not try. According to this theory, the ups and downs of the business cycle are the natural and efficient response of the economy to

---

[14] To read more about this study, see Alan S. Blinder, "On Sticky Prices: Academic Theories Meet the Real World," in *Monetary Policy,* N. G. Mankiw, ed. (Chicago: University of Chicago Press, 1994): 117–154; or Alan S. Blinder, Elie R.D. Canetti, David E. Lebow, and Jeremy E. Rudd, *Asking About Prices: A New Approach to Understanding Price Stickiness* (New York: Russell Sage Foundation, 1998).

changing technological possibilities. The standard real business cycle model does not include any type of market imperfection. In this model, the "invisible hand" of the marketplace guides the economy to an optimal allocation of resources.

To evaluate alternative views of the economy, research economists bring to bear a wide variety of evidence, as we have seen in this chapter's five case studies. They have used micro data to study intertemporal substitution, macro data to examine the cyclical behaviour of technology, the minutes of central bank meetings to test monetary neutrality, experiments to gauge the likelihood of coordination failure, and surveys to judge theories of price stickiness. Economists differ in which pieces of evidence they find most convincing, and so the theory of economic fluctuations remains a source of frequent and heated debate.

Although this chapter has divided recent research into two distinct camps, not all economists fall entirely into one camp or the other. Over time, more economists have been trying to incorporate the strengths of both approaches into their research. Real business cycle theory places a heavy emphasis on intertemporal optimization and forward-looking behaviour, while new Keynesian theory stresses the importance of sticky prices and other market imperfections. Increasingly, theories at the research frontier meld many of these elements to advance our understanding of economic fluctuations. It is this kind of work that makes macroeconomics an exciting field of study.

Summary

1. The theory of real business cycles is an explanation of short-run economic fluctuations built on the assumptions of the classical model, including the classical dichotomy and the flexibility of wages and prices. According to this theory, economic fluctuations are the natural and efficient response of the economy to changing economic circumstances, especially changes in technology.

2. Advocates and critics of real business cycle theory disagree about whether employment fluctuations represent intertemporal substitution of labour, whether technology shocks cause most economic fluctuations, whether monetary policy affects real variables, and whether the short-run stickiness of wages and prices is important for understanding economic fluctuations.

3. New Keynesian research on short-run economic fluctuations builds on the traditional model of aggregate demand and aggregate supply and tries to provide a better explanation of why wages and prices are sticky in the short run. One new Keynesian theory suggests that even small costs of price adjustment can have large macroeconomic effects because of aggregate-demand externalities. Another theory suggests that recessions occur as a type of coordination failure. A third theory suggests that staggering in price adjustment makes the overall price level sluggish in response to changing economic conditions.

The long-run analysis of Chapter 7 stresses that growth in the money supply is the ultimate determinant of inflation. That is, in the long run, a currency loses real value over time if and only if the central bank prints more and more of it. This lesson can explain the decade-to-decade variation in the inflation rate that we have observed in Canada, as well as the far more dramatic hyperinflations that various countries have experienced from time to time.

We have also seen many of the long-run effects of high money growth and high inflation. In Chapter 7 we saw that, according to the Fisher effect, high inflation raises the nominal interest rate (so that the real interest rate would remain unaffected if it were not for the fact that the Canadian income-tax system taxes *nominal* interest income and capital gains). In Chapter 8 we saw that high inflation leads to a depreciation of the currency in the market for foreign exchange.

The long-run determinants of unemployment are very different. According to the classical dichotomy—the irrelevance of nominal variables in the determination of real variables—growth in the money supply does not affect unemployment in the long run. As we saw in Chapter 6, the natural rate of unemployment is determined by the rates of job separation and job finding, which in turn are determined by the process of job search and by the rigidity of the real wage.

Thus, we concluded that persistent inflation and persistent unemployment are unrelated problems. To combat inflation in the long run, policymakers must reduce the growth in the money supply. To combat unemployment, they must alter the structure of labour markets. In the long run, there is no tradeoff between inflation and unemployment.

Lesson No. 4: In the short run, policymakers who control monetary and fiscal policy face a tradeoff between inflation and unemployment.

Although inflation and unemployment are not related in the long run, in the short run there is a tradeoff between these two variables, which is illustrated by the short-run Phillips curve. As we discussed in Chapter 13, policymakers can use monetary and fiscal policies to expand aggregate demand, which lowers unemployment and raises inflation. Or they can use these policies to contract aggregate demand, which raises unemployment and lowers inflation.

Policymakers face a fixed tradeoff between inflation and unemployment only in the short

"And please let Alan Greenspan accept the things he cannot change, give him the courage to change the things he can and the wisdom to know the difference."

run. Over time, the short-run Phillips curve shifts for two reasons. First, supply shocks, such as changes in the price of oil, change the short-run tradeoff; an adverse supply shock offers policymakers the difficult choice between higher inflation or higher unemployment. Second, when people change their expectations of inflation, the short-run tradeoff between inflation and unemployment changes. The adjustment of expectations ensures that the tradeoff exists only in the short run. That is, only in the short run does unemployment deviate from its natural rate, and only in the short run does monetary policy have real effects. In the long run, the classical model of Chapters 3 through 8 describes the world.

The Four Most Important Unresolved Questions of Macroeconomics

So far, we have been discussing some of the broad lessons about which most economists would agree. We now turn to four questions about which there is continuing debate. Some of the disagreements concern the validity of alternative economic theories; others concern how economic theory should be applied to economic policy.

Question No. 1: How should policymakers try to raise the economy's natural rate of output?

The economy's natural rate of output depends on the amount of capital, the amount of labour, and the level of technology. Any policy designed to raise output in the long run must aim to increase the amount of capital, improve the use of labour, or enhance the available technology. There is, however, no simple and costless way to achieve these goals.

The Solow growth model of Chapters 4 and 5 shows that increasing the amount of capital requires raising the economy's rate of saving and investment. Therefore, many economists advocate policies to raise national saving. Yet the Solow model also shows that raising the capital stock requires a period of reduced consumption for current generations. Some argue that policymakers should not encourage current generations to make this sacrifice, because technological progress will ensure that future generations are better off than current generations. Moreover, even those who advocate increased saving and investment disagree about how to encourage additional saving and whether the investment should be in privately owned plants and equipment or in public infrastructure, such as roads and schools.

To improve the economy's use of its labour force, most policymakers would like to lower the natural rate of unemployment. Yet, as we discussed in Chapter 6, this is not an easy task. The natural rate of unemployment could likely be reduced by decreasing employment-insurance benefits (and thus increasing the

Budget surplus: An excess of receipts over expenditure.

Business cycle: Economy-wide fluctuations in output, incomes, and employment.

Business fixed investment: Equipment and structures that businesses buy for use in future production.

Capital: 1. The stock of equipment and structures used in production. 2. The funds to finance the accumulation of equipment and structures.

Capital budgeting: An accounting procedure that measures both assets and liabilities.

Central bank: The institution responsible for the conduct of monetary policy, such as the Bank of Canada in Canada.

Classical dichotomy: The theoretical separation of real and nominal variables in the classical model, which implies that nominal variables do not influence real variables. (Cf. neutrality of money.)

Classical model: A model of the economy derived from the ideas of the classical, or pre-Keynesian, economists; a model based on the assumptions that wages and prices adjust to clear markets and that monetary policy does not influence real variables. (Cf. Keynesian model.)

Closed economy: An economy that does not engage in international trade. (Cf. open economy.)

Cobb–Douglas production function: A production function of the form $F(K, L) = AK^{\alpha}L^{1-\alpha}$, where K is capital, L is labour, and A and α are parameters.

Commodity money: Money that is intrinsically useful and would be valued even if it did not serve as money. (Cf. fiat money, money.)

Competition: A situation in which there are many individuals or firms so that the actions of any one of them do not influence market prices.

Constant returns to scale: A property of a production function whereby a proportionate increase in all factors of production leads to an increase in output of the same proportion.

Consumer price index (CPI): A measure of the overall level of prices that shows the cost of a fixed basket of consumer goods relative to the cost of the same basket in a base year.

Consumption: Goods and services purchased by consumers.

Consumption function: A relationship showing the determinants of consumption; for example, a relationship between consumption and disposable income, $C = C(Y - T)$.

Contractionary policy: Policy that reduces aggregate demand, real income, and employment. (Cf. expansionary policy.)

Coordination failure: A situation in which decisionmakers reach an outcome that is inferior for all of them because of their inability to jointly choose strategies that would result in a preferred outcome.

Corporate profit tax: The tax levied on the accounting profit of corporations.

Cost of capital: The amount forgone by holding a unit of capital for one period, including interest, depreciation, and the gain or loss from the change in the price of capital.

Cost-push inflation: Inflation resulting from shocks to aggregate supply. (Cf. demand-pull inflation.)

Countercyclical: Moving in the opposite direction from output, incomes, and employment over the business cycle; rising during recessions and falling during recoveries. (Cf. acyclical, procyclical.)

CPI: *See* consumer price index.

Crowding out: The reduction in investment that results when expansionary fiscal policy raises the interest rate.

Currency: The sum of outstanding paper money and coins.

Cyclical unemployment: The unemployment associated with short-run economic fluctuations; the deviation of the unemployment rate from the natural rate.

Cyclically adjusted budget deficit: The budget deficit adjusted for the influence of the business cycle on government spending and tax revenue; the budget deficit that would occur if the economy's production and employment were at their natural rates.

Debt-deflation theory: A theory according to which an unexpected fall in the price level redistributes real wealth from debtors to creditors and, therefore, reduces total spending in the economy.

Deflation: A decrease in the overall level of prices. (Cf. disinflation, inflation.)

Deflator: *See* GDP deflator.

Demand deposits: Assets that are held in banks and can be used on demand to make transactions, such as chequing accounts.

Demand-pull inflation: Inflation resulting from shocks to aggregate demand. (Cf. cost-push inflation.)

Demand shocks: Exogenous events that shift the aggregate demand curve.

Deposit insurance: Insurance provided by the Canada Deposit Insurance Corporation (CDIC) to individuals and firms that deposited funds in a bank or trust company that has gone bankrupt.

Deposit switching: The switching of federal government deposits between the Bank of Canada and the chartered banks for the purposes of regulating the money supply.

Depreciation: 1. The reduction in the capital stock that occurs over time because of aging and use. 2. A fall in the value of a currency relative to other currencies in the market for foreign exchange. (Cf. appreciation.)

Depreciation allowances: Deductions permitted in the calculation of corporate taxes to allow for the wearing out of capital equipment.

Depression: A very severe recession.

Devaluation: An action by the central bank to decrease the value of a currency under a system of fixed exchange rates. (Cf. revaluation.)

Diminishing marginal product: A characteristic of a production function whereby the marginal product of a factor falls as the amount of the factor increases while all other factors are held constant.

Discounting: The reduction in value of future expenditure and receipts, compared to current expenditure and receipts, resulting from the presence of a positive interest rate.

Discouraged workers: Individuals who have left the labour force because they believe that there is little hope of finding a job.

Disinflation: A reduction in the rate at which prices are rising. (Cf. deflation, inflation.)

Disposable income: Income remaining after the payment of taxes.

Dominated asset: An asset that offers an inferior return compared to another asset in all possible realizations of future uncertainty.

Double coincidence of wants: A situation in which each of two individuals has precisely the good that the other wants.

Economic profit: The amount of revenue remaining for the owners of a firm after all the factors of production have been compensated. (Cf. accounting profit, profit.)

Efficiency of labour: A variable in the Solow growth model that measures the health, education, skills, and knowledge of the labour force.

Efficiency units of labour: A measure of the labour force that incorporates both the number of workers and the efficiency of each worker.

Efficiency-wage theories: Theories of real-wage rigidity and unemployment according to which firms raise labour productivity and profits by keeping real wages above the equilibrium level.

Elasticity: The percentage change in a variable caused by a 1 percent change in another variable.

Employment insurance (EI): A government program under which unemployed workers can collect benefits for a certain period after losing their jobs.

Endogenous growth theory: Models of economic growth that try to explain the rate of technological change.

Endogenous variable: A variable that is explained by a particular model; a variable whose value is determined by the model's solution. (Cf. exogenous variable.)

Equilibrium: A state of balance between opposing forces, such as the balance of supply and demand in a market.

Euler's theorem: The mathematical result economists use to show that economic profit must be zero if the production function has constant returns to scale and if factors are paid their marginal products.

***Ex ante* real interest rate:** The real interest rate anticipated when a loan is made; the nominal interest rate minus expected inflation. (Cf. *ex post* real interest rate.)

***Ex post* real interest rate:** The real interest rate actually realized; the nominal interest rate minus actual inflation. (Cf. *ex ante* real interest rate.)

Exchange rate: The rate at which a country makes exchanges in world markets. (Cf. nominal exchange rate, real exchange rate.)

Exogenous variable: A variable that a particular model takes as given; a variable whose value is independent of the model's solution. (Cf. endogenous variable.)

Expansionary policy: Policy that raises aggregate demand, real income, and employment. (Cf. contractionary policy.)

Exports: Goods and services sold to other countries.

Factor of production: An input used to produce goods and services; for example, capital or labour.

Factor price: The amount paid for one unit of a factor of production.

Factor share: The proportion of total income being paid to a factor of production.

Federal Reserve (the Fed): The central bank of the United States.

Fiat money: Money that is not intrinsically useful and is valued only because it is used as money. (Cf. commodity money, money.)

Financial intermediation: The process by which resources are allocated from those individuals who wish to save some of their income for future consumption to those individuals and firms who wish to borrow to buy investment goods for future production.

Fiscal dividend: The new room in the budget that is created by decreased interest payment obligations on the national debt.

Financing constraint: A limit on the quantity of funds a firm can raise—such as through borrowing—in order to buy capital.

Fiscal policy: The government's choice regarding levels of spending and taxation.

Fisher effect: The one-for-one influence of expected inflation on the nominal interest rate.

Fisher equation: The equation stating that the nominal interest rate is the sum of the real interest rate and expected inflation ($i = r + \pi^e$).

Fixed exchange rate: An exchange rate that is set by the central bank's willingness to buy and sell the domestic currency for foreign currencies at a predetermined price. (Cf. floating exchange rate.)

Flexible prices: Prices that adjust quickly to equilibrate supply and demand. (Cf. sticky prices.)

Floating exchange rate: An exchange rate that the central bank allows to change in response to changing economic conditions and economic policies. (Cf. fixed exchange rate.)

Flow: A variable measured as a quantity per unit of time. (Cf. stock.)

Foreign debt: The debt accumulated by domestic households, firms, and governments that must be financed by sending interest payments to foreigners each year.

Fractional-reserve banking: A system in which banks keep only some of their deposits on reserve. (Cf. 100-percent-reserve banking.)

Frictional unemployment: The unemployment that results because it takes time for workers to search for the jobs that best suit their skills and tastes. (Cf. wait unemployment.)

Full-employment budget deficit: *See* cyclically adjusted budget deficit.

GDP: *See* gross domestic product.

GDP deflator: The ratio of nominal GDP to real GDP; a measure of the overall level of prices that shows the cost of the currently produced basket of goods relative to the cost of that basket in a base year.

General equilibrium: The simultaneous equilibrium of all the markets in the economy.

GNP: *See* gross national product.

Gold standard: A monetary system in which gold serves as money or in which all money is convertible into gold.

Golden Rule level of capital: The saving rate in the Solow growth model that leads to the steady state in which consumption per worker (or consumption per efficiency unit of labour) is maximized.

Government purchases: Goods and services bought by the government. (Cf. transfer payments.)

Government-purchases multiplier: The change in aggregate income resulting from a one-dollar change in government purchases.

Gross domestic product (GDP): The total income earned domestically, including the income earned by foreign-owned factors of production; the total expenditure on domestically produced goods and services.

Gross national product (GNP): The total income of all residents of a nation, including the income from factors of production used abroad; the total expenditure on the nation's output of goods and services.

High-powered money: The sum of currency and bank reserves; also called the monetary base.

Hyperinflation: Extremely high inflation.

Hysteresis: The long-lasting influence of history, such as on the natural rate of unemployment.

Identification problem: The difficulty of isolating a particular relationship in data when two or more variables are related in more than one way.

Imperfect-information model: The model of aggregate supply emphasizing that individuals do not always know the overall price level because they cannot observe the prices of all goods and services in the economy.

Import quota: A legal limit on the amount of a good that can be imported.

Imports: Goods and services bought from other countries.

Imputed value: An estimate of the value of a good or service that is not sold in the marketplace and therefore does not have a market price.

Income effect: The change in consumption of a good resulting from a movement to a higher or lower indifference curve, holding the relative price constant. (Cf. substitution effect.)

Index of leading indicators: *See* leading indicators.

Indexed bonds and taxes: Bonds with interest each year equal to a specified real return plus whatever the previous year's inflation had been; a tax system in which all exemptions and tax-bracket boundaries are adjusted each year by the rate of inflation.

Indifference curves: A graphical representation of preferences that shows different combinations of goods producing the same level of satisfaction.

Inflation: An increase in the overall level of prices. (Cf. deflation, disinflation.)

Inflation tax: The revenue raised by the government through the creation of money; also called seigniorage.

Inside lag: The time between a shock hitting the economy and the policy action taken to respond to the shock. (Cf. outside lag.)

Insiders: Workers who are already employed and therefore have an influence on wage bargaining. (Cf. outsiders.)

Interest rate: The market price at which resources are transferred between the present and the future; the return to saving and the cost of borrowing.

Intermediation: *See* financial intermediation.

Intertemporal budget constraint: The budget constraint applying to expenditure and income in

**Federal
Government
Deficit–GDP Ratio**

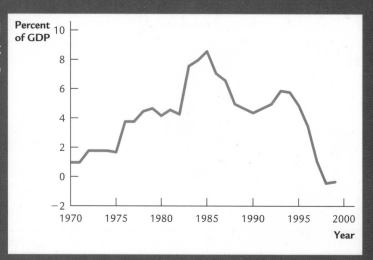

**Money Growth
(*M*1)**

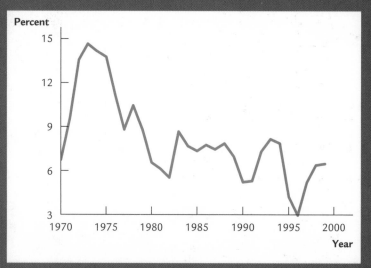